ANTHROPOLOGY 97/98

Twentieth Edition

Editor

Elvio Angeloni
Pasadena City College

Elvio Angeloni received his B.A. from UCLA in 1963, his M.A. in anthropology from UCLA in 1965, and his M.A. in communication arts from Loyola Marymount University in 1976. He has produced several films, including *Little Warrior,* winner of the Cinemedia VI Best Bicentennial Theme, and *Broken Bottles,* shown on PBS. He most recently served as an academic adviser on the instructional television series *Faces of Culture.*

Annual Editions
A Library of Information from the Public Press
Dushkin Publishing Group/Brown & Benchmark Publishers
Sluice Dock, Guilford, Connecticut 06437

*Visit us on the Internet—*http://www.dushkin.com

The Annual Editions Series

ANNUAL EDITIONS is a series of over 65 volumes designed to provide the reader with convenient, low-cost access to a wide range of current, carefully selected articles from some of the most important magazines, newspapers, and journals published today. ANNUAL EDITIONS are updated on an annual basis through a continuous monitoring of over 300 periodical sources. All ANNUAL EDITIONS have a number of features that are designed to make them particularly useful, including topic guides, annotated tables of contents, unit overviews, and indexes. For the teacher using ANNUAL EDITIONS in the classroom, an Instructor's Resource Guide with test questions is available for each volume.

VOLUMES AVAILABLE

Abnormal Psychology
Adolescent Psychology
Africa
Aging
American Foreign Policy
American Government
American History, Pre-Civil War
American History, Post-Civil War
American Public Policy
Anthropology
Archaeology
Biopsychology
Business Ethics
Child Growth and Development
China
Comparative Politics
Computers in Education
Computers in Society
Criminal Justice
Criminology
Developing World
Deviant Behavior
Drugs, Society, and Behavior
Dying, Death, and Bereavement

Early Childhood Education
Economics
Educating Exceptional Children
Education
Educational Psychology
Environment
Geography
Global Issues
Health
Human Development
Human Resources
Human Sexuality
India and South Asia
International Business
Japan and the Pacific Rim
Latin America
Life Management
Macroeconomics
Management
Marketing
Marriage and Family
Mass Media
Microeconomics

Middle East and the
    Islamic World
Multicultural Education
Nutrition
Personal Growth and Behavior
Physical Anthropology
Psychology
Public Administration
Race and Ethnic Relations
Russia, the Eurasian Republics,
    and Central/Eastern Europe
Social Problems
Social Psychology
Sociology
State and Local Government
Urban Society
Western Civilization,
    Pre-Reformation
Western Civilization,
    Post-Reformation
Western Europe
World History, Pre-Modern
World History, Modern
World Politics

Cataloging in Publication Data
Main entry under title: Annual Editions: Anthropology. 1997/98.
    1. Anthropology—Periodicals. I. Angeloni, Elvio, *comp.* II. Title: Anthropology.
301.2   74–84595   ISBN 0–697–37201–4   ISSN 1091–613X

Twentieth Edition

Cover: Tibetan Buddhists conduct classic infant burial ceremony in the Himalayas.
Photo by: Martin Etter/Anthro-Photo.

Printed on Recycled Paper

Printed in the United States of America

Editors/Advisory Board

PEOPLES DISCUSSED IN ANNUAL EDITIONS:
ANTHROPOLOGY 97/98

Map Location Number	People	Article Number
1.	Yąnomamö	1, 13, 23
2.	Punjabi	2
3.	!Kung–Kalahari Desert	3, 17, 23
4.	Nigerian	19
5.	Tiv	9
6.	Eskimo (Inupiaq)	10
	Koyukon Indians	10
7.	Eskimo (Inuit)	23
8.	Masai	28
9.	Kaliai	15
10.	Simbu	16
11.	Semai–Central Malaysia	17
	Mehinacu–Brazil	17
	Siuai–Solomon Islands	17
	Kaoka–Solomon Islands	17
	Trobrianders–South Pacific	17
12.	Tibetans	18
13.	Hausa	19
14.	Dobe San–Kalahari Desert	23
	Hadza–Tanzania	23
	Tiwi–Northeast coast of Australia	23
15.	Laguna Pueblo	24
16.	Mandingo	26
17.	Mbuti Pygmies	11, 31
18.	Fore–Papua New Guinea	42

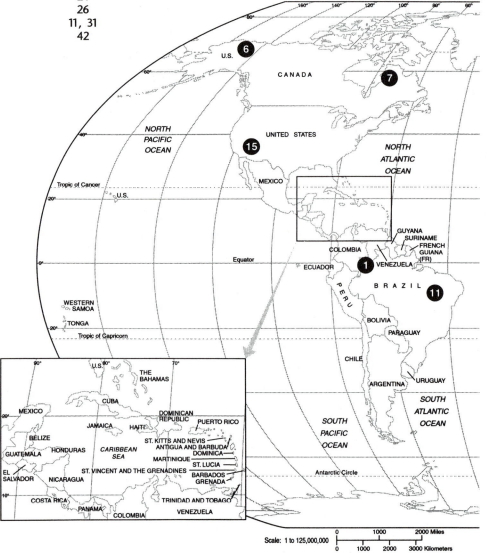

Scale: 1 to 125,000,000

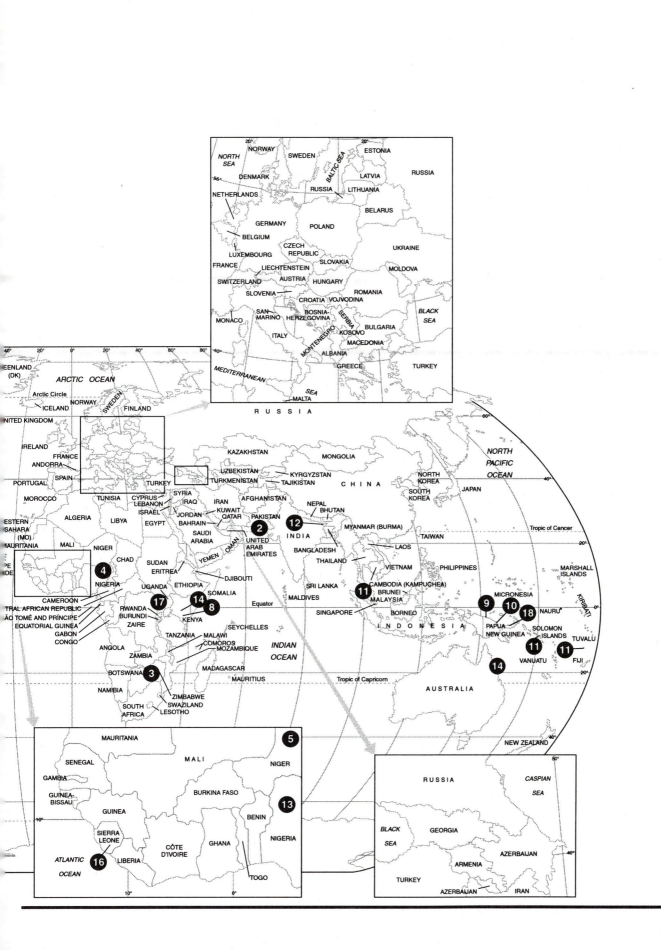

To the Reader

In publishing ANNUAL EDITIONS we recognize the enormous role played by the magazines, newspapers, and journals of the *public press* in providing current, first-rate educational information in a broad spectrum of interest areas. Many of these articles are appropriate for students, researchers, and professionals seeking accurate, current material to help bridge the gap between principles and theories and the real world. These articles, however, become more useful for study when those of lasting value are carefully *collected, organized, indexed,* and *reproduced* in a *low-cost format,* which provides easy and permanent access when the material is needed. That is the role played by ANNUAL EDITIONS. Under the direction of each volume's *academic editor,* who is an expert in the subject area, and with the guidance of an *Advisory Board,* each year we seek to provide in each ANNUAL EDITION a current, well-balanced, carefully selected collection of the best of the public press for your study and enjoyment. We think that you will find this volume useful, and we hope that you will take a moment to let us know what you think.

The twentieth edition of *Annual Editions: Anthropology* contains a variety of articles on contemporary issues in social and cultural anthropology. In contrast to the broad range of topics and minimum depth typical of standard textbooks, this anthology provides an opportunity to read firsthand accounts by anthropologists of their own research. In allowing scholars to speak for themselves about the issues on which they are expert, we are better able to understand the kind of questions anthropologists ask, the ways in which they ask them, and how they go about searching for answers. Indeed, where there is disagreement among anthropologists, this format allows the readers to draw their own conclusions.

Given the very broad scope of anthropology—in time, space, and subject matter—the present collection of highly readable articles has been selected according to certain criteria. The articles have been chosen from both professional and nonprofessional publications for the purpose of supplementing the standard textbook in cultural anthropology that is used in introductory courses. Some of the articles are considered classics in the field, while others have been selected for their timely relevance.

Included in this volume are a number of features designed to make it useful for students, re-

searchers, and professionals in the field of anthropology. While the articles are arranged along the lines of broadly unifying themes, the *topic guide* can be used to establish specific reading assignments tailored to the needs of a particular course of study. Other useful features include the *table of contents* abstracts, which summarize each article and present key concepts in italics, and a comprehensive *index*. In addition, each unit is preceded by an overview, which provides a background for informed reading of the articles, emphasizes critical issues, and presents *challenge questions*.

Annual Editions: Anthropology 97/98 will continue to be updated annually. Those involved in producing the volume wish to make the next one as useful and effective as possible. Your criticism and advice are welcomed. Please fill out the article rating form on the last page of the book and let us know your opinions. Any anthology can be improved. This continues to be—annually.

Elvio Angeloni
Editor

(Internet address: evangeloni@paccd.cc.ca.us)

Contents

UNIT 1

Anthropological Perspectives

Five selections examine the role of anthropologists in studying different cultures. The innate problems in developing productive relationships between anthropologists and exotic cultures are considered by reviewing a number of fieldwork experiences.

UNIT 2

Culture and Communication

Four selections discuss communication as an element of culture. Ingrained social and cultural values have a tremendous effect on an individual's perception or interpretation of both verbal and nonverbal communication.

The concepts in bold italics are developed in the article. For further expansion please refer to the Topic Guide and the Index.

UNIT 3

The Organization of Society and Culture

Eight selections discuss the influence of the environment and culture on the organization of the social structure of groups.

The concepts in bold italics are developed in the article. For further expansion please refer to the Topic Guide and the Index.

UNIT 4

Other Families, Other Ways

Five selections examine some
of the influences on the family
structure of different cultures.
The strength of the family unit
is affected by both economic
and social pressures.

The concepts in bold italics are developed in the article. For further expansion please refer to the Topic Guide and the Index.

UNIT 5

Gender and Status

Seven selections discuss some of the sex roles prescribed by the social, economic, and political forces of a culture.

The concepts in bold italics are developed in the article. For further expansion please refer to the Topic Guide and the Index.

UNIT 6

Religion, Belief, and Ritual

Six selections examine the role of ritual, religion, and belief in a culture. The need to develop a religion is universal among societies.

The concepts in bold italics are developed in the article. For further expansion please refer to the Topic Guide and the Index.

UNIT 7

Sociocultural Change: The Impact of the West

Nine articles examine the influence that the developed world has had on primitive culture. Exposure to the industrial West often has disastrous effects on the delicate balance of a primitive society.

The concepts in bold italics are developed in the article. For further expansion please refer to the Topic Guide and the Index.

The concepts in bold italics are developed in the article. For further expansion please refer to the Topic Guide and the Index.

Topic Guide

This topic guide suggests how the selections in this book relate to topics of traditional concern to students and professionals involved with the study of anthropology. It is useful for locating articles that relate to each other for reading and research. The guide is arranged alphabetically according to topic. Articles may, of course, treat topics that do not appear in the topic guide. In turn, entries in the topic guide do not necessarily constitute a comprehensive listing of all the contents of each selection.

TOPIC AREA	TREATED IN	TOPIC AREA	TREATED IN
Acculturation	4. Cross-Cultural Experience 14. Keepers of the Oaks 16. From Shells to Money 22. Who Needs Love! 24. Yellow Woman 38. Arrow of Disease 39. Pastoralism and the Demise of Communal Property in Tanzania 40. Paavahu and Paanaqawu 41. Pacific Haze 42. Growing Up as a Fore 43. Last Chance for First Peoples 44. From Hammocks to Health	Cultural Identity	4. Cross-Cultural Experience 5. Cultural Relativism and Universal Rights 8. Empire of Uniformity 24. Yellow Woman 26. Bundu Trap 39. Pastoralism and the Demise of Communal Property in Tanzania 40. Paavahu and Paanaqawu 43. Last Chance for First Peoples 44. From Hammocks to Health
Aggression and Violence	5. Cultural Relativism and Universal Rights 27. War against Women 33. Rituals of Death 36. Heart of Darkness, Heart of Light 38. Arrow of Disease	Cultural Relativity and Ethnocentrism	1. Doing Fieldwork among the Yąnomamö 3. Eating Christmas in the Kalahari 4. Cross-Cultural Experience 5. Cultural Relativism and Universal Rights 7. Why Don't You Say What You Mean? 21. Arranging a Marriage in India 26. Bundu Trap 34. Body Ritual among the Nacirema
Children and Child Care	12. Why Women Change 19. Young Traders of Northern Nigeria 20. Death without Weeping 24. Yellow Woman 26. Bundu Trap 29. Little Emperors 31. Mbuti Pygmies 44. From Hammocks to Health	Ecology and Society	8. Empire of Uniformity 10. Understanding Eskimo Science 11. Hunting, Gathering, and the Molimo 12. Why Women Change 13. Yąnomami Keep on Trekking 14. Keepers of the Oaks 16. From Shells to Money 17. Life without Chiefs 18. When Brothers Share a Wife 23. Society and Sex Roles 37. Why Can't People Feed Themselves? 38. Arrow of Disease 39. Pastoralism and the Demise of Communal Property in Tanzania 40. Paavahu and Paanaqawu 43. Last Chance for First Peoples
Cross-Cultural Experience	1. Doing Fieldwork among the Yąnamamö 2. Doctor, Lawyer, Indian Chief 3. Eating Christmas in the Kalahari 4. Cross-Cultural Experience 5. Cultural Relativism and Universal Rights 7. Why Don't You Say What You Mean? 9. Shakespeare in the Bush 10. Understanding Eskimo Science 15. Too Many Bananas 20. Death without Weeping 21. Arranging a Marriage in India 36. Heart of Darkness, Heart of Light 43. Last Chance for First Peoples		
Cultural Diversity	4. Cross-Cultural Experience 5. Cultural Relativism and Universal Rights 7. Why Don't You Say What You Mean? 8. Empire of Uniformity 21. Arranging a Marriage in India 24. Yellow Woman 25. Status, Property, and the Value on Virginity 39. Pastoralism and the Demise of Communal Property in Tanzania 43. Last Chance for First Peoples	Economic and Political Systems	2. Doctor, Lawyer, Indian Chief 8. Empire of Uniformity 11. Hunting, Gathering, and the Molimo 13. Yąnomami Keep on Trekking 14. Keepers of the Oaks 15. Too Many Bananas 16. From Shells to Money 17. Life without Chiefs 18. When Brothers Share a Wife 19. Young Traders of Northern Nigeria 20. Death without Weeping 23. Society and Sex Roles 24. Yellow Woman 25. Status, Property, and the Value on Virginity 29. Little Emperors 37. Why Can't People Feed Themselves? 38. Arrow of Disease

TOPIC AREA	TREATED IN	TOPIC AREA	TREATED IN
Economic and Political Systems (continued)	39. Pastoralism and the Demise of Communal Property in Tanzania 40. Paavahu and Paanaqawu 43. Last Chance for First Peoples 44. From Hammocks to Health	Medicine and Healing	30. Psychotherapy in Africa 34. Body Ritual among the Nacirema 36. Heart of Darkness, Heart of Light 43. Last Chance for First Peoples
Gender/Sexuality	5. Cultural Relativism and Universal Rights 12. Why Women Change 18. When Brothers Share a Wife 22. Who Needs Love! 23. Society and Sex Roles 24. Yellow Woman 25. Status, Property, and the Value of Virginity 26. Bundu Trap 27. War against Women 29. Little Emperors	Poverty	20. Death without Weeping 27. War against Women 37. Why Can't People Feed Themselves? 39. Pastoraliam and the Demise of Communal Property in Tanzania
		Rituals	5. Cultural Relativism and Universal Rights 16. From Shells to Money 26. Bundu Trap 28. Initiation of a Maasai Warrior 30. Psychotherapy in Africa 31. Mbuti Pygmies 32. Secrets of Haiti's Living Dead 33. Rituals of Death 34. Body Ritual among the Nacirema 35. Superstition and Ritual in American Baseball 40. Paavahu and Paanaqawu
Health and Welfare	5. Cultural Relativism and Universal Rights 20. Death without Weeping 26. Bundu Trap 27. War against Women 29. Little Emperors 30. Psychotherapy in Africa 34. Body Ritual among the Nacirema 37. Why Can't People Feed Themselves? 38. Arrow of Disease 41. Pacific Haze 43. Last Chance for First Peoples 44. From Hammocks to Health		
		Social Equality	7. Why Don't You Say What You Mean? 16. From Shells to Money 17. Life without Chiefs 22. Who Needs Love! 24. Yellow Woman 25. Status, Property, and the Value on Virginity 27. War against Women 31. Mbuti Pygmies
Hunter-Collectors	10. Understanding Eskimo Science 11. Hunting, Gathering, and the Molimo 12. Why Women Change 14. Keepers of the Oaks 17. Life without Chiefs 31. Mbuti Pygmies	Social Relationships	1. Doing Fieldwork among the Yąnomamö 2. Doctor, Lawyer, Indian Chief 3. Eating Christmas in the Kalahari 4. Cross-Cultural Experience 11. Hunting, Gathering, and the Molimo 12. Why Women Change 15. Too Many Bananas 16. From Shells to Money 21. Arranging a Marriage in India 22. Who Needs Love! 24. Yellow Woman 25. Status, Property, and the Value on Virginity 26. Bundu Trap 27. War against Women 29. Little Emperors 31. Mbuti Pygmies 32. Secrets of Haiti's Living Dead 36. Heart of Darkness, Heart of Light
Language	4. Cross-Cultural Experience 6. Language, Appearance, and Reality 7. Why Don't You Say What You Mean? 8. Empire of Uniformity 9. Shakespeare in the Bush		
Marriage, Kinship, and Family Systems	4. Cross-Cultural Experience 12. Why Women Change 16. From Shells to Money 18. When Brothers Share a Wife 19. Young Traders of Northern Nigeria 20. Death without Weeping 21. Arranging a Marriage in India 22. Who Needs Love! 23. Society and Sex Roles 24. Yellow Woman 25. Status, Property, and the Value on Virginity 26. Bundu Trap 27. War against Women 29. Little Emperors		

Anthropological Perspectives

For at least a century, the goals of anthropology have been to describe societies and cultures throughout the world and to compare the differences and similarities among them. Anthropologists study in a variety of settings and situations, ranging from small hamlets and villages to neighborhoods and corporate offices of major urban centers throughout the world. They study hunters and gatherers, peasants, farmers, labor leaders, politicians, and bureaucrats. They examine religious life in Latin America as well as revolutionary movements.

Wherever practicable, anthropologists take on the role of "participant observer." Through active involvement in the lifeways of people, they hope to gain an insider's perspective without sacrificing the objectivity of the trained scientist. Sometimes the conditions for achieving such a goal seem to form an almost insurmountable barrier, but anthropologists call on persistence, adaptability, and imagination to overcome the odds against them.

The diversity of focus in anthropology means that it is earmarked less by its particular subject matter than by its perspective. Although the discipline relates to both the biological and social sciences, anthropologists know that the boundaries drawn between disciplines are highly artificial. For example, while in theory it is possible to examine only the social organization of a family unit or the organization of political power in a nation-state, in reality it is impossible to separate the biological from the social, from the economic, from the political. The explanatory perspective of anthropology, as the articles in this unit demonstrate, is to seek out interrelationships among all these factors. The first four articles in this section illustrate varying degrees of difficulty an anthropologist may encounter in taking on the role of the participant observer. Napoleon Chagnon's essay, "Doing Fieldwork among the Yąnomamö," for instance, shows the hardships imposed by certain physical conditions, the unwillingness of the people to provide needed information, and the vast differences in values and attitudes to be bridged by the anthropologist just in order to get along.

Richard Kurin, in "Doctor, Lawyer, Indian Chief," and Richard Lee, in "Eating Christmas in the Kalahari," apparently had few problems with the physical conditions and the personalities of the people they were studying. However, they were not completely accepted by the communities until they modified their behavior to conform to the expectations of their hosts and found ways to participate as equals in the socioeconomic exchange systems.

Huang Shu-min, in "A Cross-Cultural Experience: A Chinese Anthropologist in the United States," shows how "culture shock" can work both ways, as he learns the importance of personal hygiene in the expression of American middle-class values.

The final article in this unit, "Cultural Relativism and Universal Rights," goes to the heart of one of the key issues in anthropology: How does one maintain the objectivity of cultural relativism while not becoming a party to the violation of human rights? Taking the matter one step further, the author argues that anthropologists are in a unique position to actively promote human rights and are ethically bound to do so.

Much is at stake in these discussions, since the purpose of anthropology is not only to describe and explain, but also to develop a special vision of the world in which cultural alternatives (past, present, and future) can be measured against one another and used as guides for human action.

Looking Ahead: Challenge Questions

What is culture shock?

How can anthropologists who become personally involved with a community through participant observation maintain their objectivity as scientists?

In what ways do the results of fieldwork depend on the kinds of questions asked?

How does cross-cultural experience help us to understand ourselves?

In what sense is sharing intrinsic to egalitarianism?

How can we avoid the pitfalls of cultural relativity and ethnocentrism in dealing with what we think of as harmful practices in other cultures?

Doing Fieldwork among the Yąnomamö[1]

Napoleon A. Chagnon

VIGNETTE

The Yąnomamö are thinly scattered over a vast and verdant tropical forest, living in small villages that are separated by many miles of unoccupied land. They have no writing, but they have a rich and complex language. Their clothing is more decorative than protective. Well-dressed men sport nothing more than a few cotton strings around their wrists, ankles, and waists. They tie the foreskins of their penises to the waiststring. Women dress about the same. Much of their daily life revolves around gardening, hunting, collecting wild foods, collecting firewood, fetching water, visiting with each other, gossiping, and making the few material possessions they own: baskets, hammocks, bows, arrows, and colorful pigments with which they paint their bodies. Life is relatively easy in the sense that they can 'earn a living' with about three hours' work per day. Most of what they eat they cultivate in their gardens, and most of that is plantains—a kind of cooking banana that is usually eaten green, either roasted on the coals or boiled in pots. Their meat comes from a large variety of game animals, hunted daily by the men. It is usually roasted on coals or smoked, and is always well done. Their villages are round and open—and very public. One can hear, see, and smell almost everything that goes on anywhere in the village. Privacy is rare, but sexual discreetness is possible in the garden or at night while others sleep. The villages can be as small as 40 to 50 people or as large as 300 people, but in all cases there are many more children and babies than there are adults. This is true of most primitive populations and of our own demographic past. Life expectancy is short.

The Yąnomamö fall into the category of Tropical Forest Indians called 'foot people'. They avoid large rivers and live in interfluvial plains of the major rivers. They have neighbors to the north, Carib-speaking Ye'kwana, who are true 'river people': They make elegant, large dugout canoes and travel extensively along the major waterways. For the Yąnomamö, a large stream is an obstacle and can be crossed only in the dry season. Thus, they have traditionally avoided larger rivers and, because of this, contact with outsiders who usually come by river.

They enjoy taking trips when the jungle abounds with seasonally ripe wild fruits and vegetables. Then, the large village—the *shabono*—is abandoned for a few weeks and everyone camps out for from one to several days away from the village and garden. On these trips, they make temporary huts from poles, vines, and leaves, each family making a separate hut.

Two major seasons dominate their annual cycle: the wet season, which inundates the low-lying jungle, making travel difficult, and the dry season—the time of visiting other villages to feast, trade, and politic with allies. The dry season is also the time when raiders can travel and strike silently at their unsuspecting enemies. The Yąnomamö are still conducting intervillage warfare, a phenomenon that affects all aspects of their social organization, settlement pattern, and daily routines. It is not simply 'ritualistic' war: At least one-fourth of all adult males die violently in the area I lived in.

Social life is organized around those same principles utilized by all tribesmen: kinship relationships, descent from ancestors, marriage exchanges between kinship/descent groups, and the transient charisma of distinguished headmen who attempt to keep order in the village and whose responsibility it is to determine the village's relationships with those in other villages. Their positions are largely the result of kinship and marriage patterns; they come from the largest kinship groups within the village. They can, by their personal wit, wisdom, and charisma, become autocrats, but most of them are largely 'greaters' among equals. They, too, must clear gardens, plant crops, collect wild foods, and hunt. They are simultaneously peacemakers and valiant warriors. Peacemaking often requires the threat or actual use of force, and most headmen have an acquired reputation for being *waiteri*: fierce.

The social dynamics within villages are involved with giving and receiving marriageable girls. Marriages are arranged by older kin, usually men, who are brothers, uncles, and the father. It is a political process, for girls are promised in marriage while they are young, and the men who do this attempt to create alliances with other men via marriage exchanges. There is a shortage of women due in part to a sex-ratio imbalance in the younger age categories, but also complicated by the fact that some men have multiple wives. Most fighting within the village stems from sexual affairs or failure to deliver a promised woman—or out-and-out seizure of a married woman by some other man. This can lead to internal fighting and conflict of such an intensity that villages split up and fission, each group then becoming a new village and, often, enemies to each other.

But their conflicts are not blind, uncontrolled violence. They have a series of graded forms of violence that ranges from chest-pounding and club-fighting duels to out-and-out shooting to kill. This gives them a good deal of flexibility in settling disputes without immediate resort to lethal violence. In addition, they have developed patterns of alliance and friendship that serve to limit violence—trading and feasting with others in order to become friends. These alliances can, and often do, result in intervillage exchanges of marriageable women, which leads to additional amity between villages. No good thing lasts forever, and most alliances crumble. Old friends become hostile and, occasionally, treacherous. Each village must therefore be keenly aware that its neighbors are fickle and must behave accordingly. The thin line between friendship and animosity must be traversed by the village leaders, whose political acumen and strategies are both admirable and complex.

Each village, then, is a replica of all others in a broad sense. But each village is part of a larger political, demographic, and ecological process, and it is difficult to attempt to understand the village without knowing something of the larger forces that affect it and it's particular history with all its neighbors.

COLLECTING THE DATA IN THE FIELD

I have now spent over 60 months with Yąnomamö, during which time I gradually learned their language and, up to a point, submerged myself in their culture and way of life.[2] As my research progressed, the thing that impressed me most was the importance that aggression played in shaping their culture. I had the opportunity to witness a good many incidents that expressed individual vindictiveness on the one hand and collective bellicosity on the other hand. These ranged in seriousness from the ordinary incidents of wife beating and chest pounding to dueling and organized raids by parties that set out with the intention of ambushing and killing men from enemy villages. One of the villages . . . was raided approximately twenty-five times during my first 15 months of fieldwork—six times by the group among whom I was living. And, the history of every village I investigated, from 1964 to 1991, was intimately bound up in patterns of warfare with neighbors that shaped its politics and determined where it was found at any point in time and how it dealt with it's current neighbors.

The fact that the Yąnomamö have lived in a chronic state of warfare is reflected in their mythology, ceremonies, settlement pattern, political behavior, and marriage practices. Accordingly, I have organized this case study in such a way that students can appreciate the effects of warfare on Yąnomamö culture in general and on their social organization and political relationships in particular.

I collected the data under somewhat trying circumstances, some of which I

will describe to give a rough idea of what is generally meant when anthropologists speak of 'culture shock' and 'fieldwork.' It should be borne in mind, however, that each field situation is in many respects unique, so that the problems I encountered do not necessarily exhaust the range of possible problems other anthropologists have confronted in other areas. There are a few problems, however, that seem to be nearly universal among anthropological fieldworkers, particularly those having to do with eating, bathing, sleeping, lack of privacy, loneliness, or discovering that the people you are living with have a lower opinion of you than you have of them—or you yourself are not as culturally or emotionally 'flexible' as you assumed.

The Yąnomamö can be difficult people to live with at times, but I have spoken to colleagues who have had difficulties living in the communities they studied. These things vary from society to society, and probably from one anthropologist to the next. I have also done limited fieldwork among the Yąnomamö's northern neighbors, the Carib-speaking Ye'kwana Indians. By contrast to many experiences I had among the Yanomamö, the Ye'kwana were very pleasant and charming, all of them anxious to help me and honor bound to show any visitor the numerous courtesies of their system of etiquette. In short, they approached the image of 'primitive man' that I had conjured up in my mind before doing fieldwork, a kind of 'Rousseauian' view, and it was sheer pleasure to work with them. Other anthropologists have also noted sharp contrasts in the people they study from one field situation to another. One of the most startling examples of this is in the work of Colin Turnbull, who first studied the Ituri Pygmies (1965, 1983) and found them delightful to live with, but then studied the Ik (1972) of the desolate outcroppings of the Kenya/Uganda/Sudan border region, a people he had difficulty coping with intellectually, emotionally, and physically. While it is possible that the anthropologist's reactions to a particular people are personal and idiosyncratic, it nevertheless remains true that there are enormous differences between whole peoples, differences that affect the anthropologist in often dramatic ways.

Hence, what I say about some of my experiences is probably equally true of the experiences of many other field-workers. I describe some of them here for the benefit of future anthropologists—because I think I could have profited by reading about the pitfalls and field problems of my own teachers. At the very least I might have been able to avoid some of my more stupid errors. In this regard there is a growing body of excellent descriptive work on field research. Students who plan to make a career in anthropology should consult these works, which cover a wide range of field situations in the ethnographic present.[3]

The Longest Day: The First One
My first day in the field illustrated to me what my teachers meant when they spoke of 'culture shock.' I had traveled in a small, aluminum rowboat propelled by a large outboard motor for two and a half days. This took me from the territorial capital, a small town on the Orinoco River, deep into Yąnomamö country. On the morning of the third day we reached a small mission settlement, the field 'headquarters' of a group of Americans who were working in two Yąnomamö villages. The missionaries had come out of these villages to hold their annual conference on the progress of their mission work and were conducting their meetings when I arrived. We picked up a passenger at the mission station, James P. Barker, the first non-Yąnomamö to make a sustained, permanent contact with the tribe (in 1950). He had just returned from a year's furlough in the United States, where I had earlier visited him before leaving for Venezuela. He agreed to accompany me to the village I had selected for my base of operations to introduce me to the Indians. This village was also his own home base, but he had not been there for over a year and did not plan to join me for another three months. Mr. Barker had been living with this particular group about five years.

We arrived at the village, Bisaasi-teri, about 2:00 P.M. and docked the boat along the muddy bank at the terminus of the path used by Yąnomamö to fetch their drinking water. It was hot and muggy, and my clothing was soaked with perspiration. It clung uncomfortably to my body, as it did thereafter for the remainder of the work. The small biting gnats, *bareto,* were out in astronomical numbers, for it was the beginning of the dry season. My face and hands were swollen from the venom of their numerous stings. In just a few moments I was to meet my first Yąnomamö, my first primitive man. What would he be like? I had visions of entering the village and seeing 125 social facts running about altruistically calling each other kinship terms and sharing food, each waiting and anxious to have me collect his genealogy. I would wear them out in turn. Would they like me? This was important to me; I wanted them to be so fond of me that they would adopt me into their kinship system and way of life. I had heard that successful anthropologists always get adopted by their people. I had learned during my seven years of anthropological training at the University of Michigan that kinship was equivalent to society in primitive tribes and that it was a moral way of life, 'moral' being something 'good' and 'desirable.' I was determined to work my way into their moral system of kinship and become a member of their society—to be 'accepted' by them.

How Did They Accept You?
My heart began to pound as we approached the village and heard the buzz of activity within the circular compound. Mr. Barker commented that he was anxious to see if any changes had taken place while he was away and wondered how many of them had died during his absence. I nervously felt my back pocket to make sure that my notebook was still there and felt personally more secure when I touched it.

The entrance to the village was covered over with brush and dry palm leaves. We pushed them aside to expose the low opening to the village. The excitement of meeting my first Yąnomamö was almost unbearable as I duck-waddled through the low passage into the village clearing.

I looked up and gasped when I saw a dozen burly, naked, sweaty, hideous men staring at us down the shafts of their drawn arrows! Immense wads of green tobacco were stuck between their lower teeth and lips making them look even more hideous, and strands of dark-green slime dripped or hung from their nostrils—strands so long that they clung to their pectoral muscles or drizzled down their chins. We arrived at the village while the men were blowing a hallucinogenic drug up their noses. One of the side effects of the drug is a runny nose. The mucus is always saturated with the green powder and they usually let it run freely from their nostrils. My next discovery was that there were a dozen or so vicious, underfed dogs snapping at my legs, circling me as if I were to be their next meal. I just stood there holding my notebook, helpless and pathetic. Then the stench of the decaying vegetation and filth hit me and I almost got sick. I was horrified. What kind of welcome was this for the person who came here to live with you and learn your way of life, to become friends with you? They put their weapons down when they recognized Barker and returned to their chanting, keeping a nervous eye on the village entrances.

We had arrived just after a serious fight. Seven women had been abducted the day before by a neighboring group, and the local men and their guests had just that morning recovered five of them in a brutal club fight that nearly ended in a shooting war. The abductors, angry because they had lost five of their seven new captives, vowed to raid the Bisaasi-teri. When we arrived and entered the village unexpectedly, the Indians feared that we were the raiders. On several occasions during the next two hours the men in the village jumped to their feet, armed themselves, nocked their arrows and waited nervously for the noise outside the village to be identified. My enthusiasm for collecting ethnographic facts diminished in proportion to the number of times such an alarm was raised. In fact, I was relieved when Barker suggested that we sleep across the river for the evening. It would be safer over there.

As we walked down the path to the boat, I pondered the wisdom of having decided to spend a year and a half with these people before I had even seen what they were like. I am not ashamed to admit that had there been a diplomatic way out, I would have ended my fieldwork then and there. I did not look forward to the next day—and months—when I would be left alone with the Yąnomanö; I did not speak a word of their language, and they were decidedly different from what I had imagined them to be. The whole situation was depressing, and I wondered why I ever decided to switch from physics and engineering in the first place. I had not eaten all day, I was soaking wet from perspiration, the *bareto* were biting me, and I was covered with red pigment, the result of a dozen or so complete examinations I had been given by as many very pushy Yąnomamö men. These examinations capped an otherwise grim day. The men would blow their noses into their hands, flick as much of the mucus off that would separate in a snap of the wrist, wipe the residue into their hair, and then carefully examine my face, arms, legs, hair, and the contents of my pockets. I asked Barker how to say, 'Your hands are dirty'; my comments were met by the Yąnomamö in the following way: They would 'clean' their hands by spitting a quantity of slimy tobacco juice into them, rub them together, grin, and then proceed with the examination.

Mr. Barker and I crossed the river and slung our hammocks. When he pulled his hammock out of a rubber bag, a heavy, disagreeable odor of mildewed cotton and stale wood smoke came with it. 'Even the missionaries are filthy,' I thought to myself. Within two weeks, everything I owned smelled the same way, and I lived with that odor for the remainder of the fieldwork. My own habits of personal cleanliness declined to such levels that I didn't even mind being examined by the Yąnomamö, as I was not much cleaner than they were after I had adjusted to the circumstances. it is difficult to blow your nose gracefully when you are stark naked and the invention of hankerchiefs is millenia away.

Life in the Jungle: Oatmeal, Peanut Butter, and Bugs

It isn't easy to plop down in the Amazon Basin for a year and get immediately into the anthropological swing of things. You have been told about horrible diseases, snakes, jaguars, electric eels, little spiny fish that will swim up your urine into your penis, quicksand, and getting lost. Some of the dangers are real, but your imagination makes them more real and threatening than many of them really are. What my teachers never bothered to advise me about, however, was the mundane, nonexciting, and trivial stuff—like eating, defecating, sleeping, or keeping clean. These turned out to be the bane of my existence during the first several months of field research. I set up my household in Barker's abandoned mud hut, a few yards from the village of Bisaasi-teri, and immediately set to work building my own mud/thatch hut with the help of the Yąnomamö. Meanwhile, I had to eat and try to do my 'field research.' I soon discovered that it was an enormously time-consuming task to maintain my own body in the manner to which it had grown accustomed in the relatively antiseptic environment of the northern United States. Either I could be relatively well fed and relatively comfortable in a fresh change of clothes and do very little fieldwork, or I could do considerably more fieldwork and be less well fed and less comfortable.

It is appalling how complicated it can be to make oatmeal in the jungle. First, I had to make two trips to the river to haul the water. Next, I had to prime my kerosene stove with alcohol to get it burning, a tricky procedure when you are trying to mix powdered milk and fill a coffee pot at the same time. The alcohol prime always burned out before I could turn the kerosene on, and I would have to start all over. Or, I would turn the kerosene on, optimistically hoping that the Coleman element was still hot enough to vaporize the fuel, and start a small fire in my palm-thatched hut as the liquid kerosene squirted all over the table and walls and then ignited. Many amused Yąnomanö onlookers quickly learned the English phrase 'Oh, Shit!', and, once they discovered that the phrase offended and irritated the missionaries, they used it as often as they could in their presence. I usually had to start over with the alcohol. Then I had to boil the oatmeal and pick the bugs out of it. All my supplies, of course, were carefully stored in rat-proof, moisture-proof, and insect-proof containers, not one of which ever served its purpose adequately. Just taking things out of the multiplicity of containers and repacking them afterward was a minor project in itself. By the time I had hauled the water to cook with, unpacked my food, prepared the oatmeal, milk, and coffee, heated water for dishes, washed and dried the dishes, repacked the food in the containers, stored the containers in locked trunks, and cleaned up my mess, the ceremony of preparing breakfast had brought me almost up to lunch time!

Eating three meals a day was simply out of the question. I solved the problem by eating a single meal that could be prepared in a single container, or, at most, in two containers, washed my dishes only when there were no clean ones left, using cold river water, and wore each change of clothing at least a week to cut down on my laundry problem—a courageous undertaking in the tropics. I reeked like a jockstrap that had been left to mildew in the bottom of some dark gym locker. I also became less concerned about sharing my provisions with the rats, insects, Yąnomamö, and the elements, thereby eliminating the need for my complicated storage process. I was able to last most of the day on *café con leche,* heavily sugared espresso coffee diluted about five to one with hot milk. I would prepare this in the evening and store it in a large thermos. Frequently, my single meal was no more complicated than a can of sardines and a package of soggy crackers. But at least two or three times a week I would do something 'special' and sophisticated, like make a batch of oatmeal or boil rice and add a can of tuna fish or tomato paste to it. I even saved time by devising a water system that obviated the trips to the river. I had a few sheets of tin roofing brought in and made a rain water trap; I caught the water on the tin surface, funneled it into an empty gasoline drum, and then ran a plastic hose from the drum to my hut. When the drum was exhausted in the dry season, I would get a few Yąnomamö boys to fill it with buckets of water from the river, 'paying' them with crackers, of which they grew all too fond all too soon.

I ate much less when I traveled with the Yąnomamö to visit other villages. Most of the time my travel diet consisted of roasted or boiled green plantains (cooking bananas) that I obtained from the Yąnomamö, but I always carried a few cans of sardines with me in case I got lost or stayed away longer than I had planned. I found peanut butter and crackers a very nourishing 'trail' meal, and a simple one to prepare. It was nutritious and portable, and only one tool was required to make the meal: a hunting knife that could be cleaned by wiping the blade on a convenient leaf. More importantly, it was one of the few foods the Yąnomamö would let me eat in relative peace. It looked suspiciously like animal feces to them, an impression I encouraged. I referred to the peanut butter as the feces of babies or 'cattle'. They found this disgusting and repugnant. They did not know what 'cattle' were, but were increasingly aware that I ate several canned products of such an animal. Tin cans were thought of as containers made of 'machete skins', but how the cows got inside was always a mystery to them. I went out of my way to describe my foods in such a way as to make them sound unpalatable to them, for it gave me some peace of mind while I ate: They wouldn't beg for a share of something that was too horrible to contem-

plate. Fieldworkers develop strange defense mechanisms and strategies, and this was one of my own forms of adaptation to the fieldwork. On another occasion I was eating a can of frankfurters and growing very weary of the demands from one of the onlookers for a share in my meal. When he finally asked what I was eating, I replied: 'Beef.' He then asked: 'Shąki![4] What part of the animal are you eating?' To which I replied, 'Guess.' He muttered a contemptuous epithet, but stopped asking for a share. He got back at me later, as we shall see.

Meals were a problem in a way that had nothing to do with the inconvenience of preparing them. Food sharing is important to the Yąnomamö in the context of displaying friendship. 'I am hungry!' is almost a form of greeting with them. I could not possibly have brought enough food with me to feed the entire village, yet they seemed to overlook this logistic fact as they begged for my food. What became fixed in their minds was the fact that I did not share my food with whomsoever was present—usually a small crowd—at each and every meal. Nor could I easily enter their system of reciprocity with respect to food. Every time one of them 'gave' me something 'freely', he would dog me for months to 'pay him back', not necessarily with food but with knives, fishhooks, axes, and so on. Thus, if I accepted a plantain from someone in a different village while I was on a visit, he would most likely visit me in the future and demand a machete as payment for the time that he 'fed' me. I usually reacted to these kinds of demands by giving a banana, the customary reciprocity in their culture—food for food—but this would be a disappointment for the individual who had nursed visions of that single plantain growing into a machete over time. Many years after beginning my fieldwork I was approached by one of the prominent men who demanded a machete for a piece of meat he claimed he had given me five or six years earlier.

Despite the fact that most of them knew I would not share my food with them at their request, some of them

always showed up at my hut during mealtime. I gradually resigned myself to this and learned to ignore their persistent demands while I ate. Some of them would get angry because I failed to give in, but most of them accepted it as just a peculiarity of the subhuman foreigner who had come to live among them. If or when I did accede to a request for a share of my food, my hut quickly filled with Yąnomamö, each demanding their share of the food that I had just given to one of them. Their begging for food was not provoked by hunger, but by a desire to try something new and to attempt to establish a coercive relationship in which I would accede to a demand. If one received something, all others would immediately have to test the system to see if they, too, could coerce me.

A few of them went out of their way to make my meals downright unpleasant—to spite me for not sharing, especially if it was a food that they had tried before and liked, or a food that was part of their own cuisine. For example, I was eating a cracker with peanut butter and honey one day. The Yąnomamö will do almost anything for honey, one of the most prized delicacies in their own diet. One of my cynical onlookers—the fellow who had earlier watched me eating frankfurters—immediately recognized the honey and knew that I would not share the tiny precious bottle. It would be futile to even ask. Instead, he glared at me and queried icily, 'Shąki! What kind of animal semen are you pouring onto your food and eating?' His question had the desired effect and my meal ended.

Finally, there was the problem of being lonely and separated from your own kind, especially your family. I tried to overcome this by seeking personal friendships among the Yąnomamö. This usually complicated the matter because all my 'friends' simply used my confidence to gain privileged access to my hut and my cache of steel tools and trade goods—and looted me when I wasn't looking. I would be bitterly disappointed that my erstwhile friend thought no more of me than to finesse our personal relationship exclusively with the intention of getting at my locked up possessions, and my depression would hit new lows every time I discovered this. The loss of the possessions bothered me much less than the shock that I was, as far as most of them were concerned, nothing more than a source of desirable items. No holds were barred in relieving me of these, since I was considered something subhuman, a non-Yąnomamö.

The hardest thing to learn to live with was the incessant, passioned, and often aggressive demands they would make. It would become so unbearable at times that I would have to lock myself in my hut periodically just to escape from it. Privacy is one of our culture's most satisfying achievements, one you never think about until you suddenly have none. It is like not appreciating how good your left thumb feels until someone hits it with a hammer. But I did not want privacy for its own sake; rather, I simply had to get away from the begging. Day and night for almost the entire time I lived with the Yąnomamö I was plagued by such demands as: 'Give me a knife, I am poor!'; 'If you don't take me with you on your next trip to Widokaiyateri, I'll chop a hole in your canoe!'; 'Take us hunting up the Mavaca River with your shotgun or we won't help you!'; 'Give me some matches so I can trade with the Reyaboböwei-teri, and be quick about it or I'll hit you!'; 'Share your food with me, or I'll burn your hut!'; 'Give me a flashlight so I can hunt at night!'; 'Give me all your medicine, I itch all over!'; 'Give me an ax or I'll break into your hut when you are away and steal all of them!' And so I was bombarded by such demands day after day, month after month, until I could not bear to see a Yąnomamö at times.

It was not as difficult to become calloused to the incessant begging as it was to ignore the sense of urgency, the impassioned tone of voice and whining, or the intimidation and aggression with which many of the demands were made. It was likewise difficult to adjust to the fact that the Yąnomamö refused to accept 'No' for an answer until or unless it seethed with passion and intimidation—which it did after a few

months. So persistent and characteristic is the begging that the early 'semi-official' maps made by the Venezuelan Malaria Control Service (*Malarialogía*) designated the site of their first permanent field station, next to the village of Bisaasi-teri, as *Yababuhii:* 'Gimme.'I had to become like the Yąnomamö to be able to get along with them on their terms: somewhat sly, aggressive, intimidating, and pushy.

It became indelibly clear to me shortly after I arrived there that had I failed to adjust in this fashion I would have lost six months of supplies to them in a single day or would have spent most of my time ferrying them around in my canoe or taking them on long hunting trips. As it was, I did spend a considerable amount of time doing these things and did succumb often to their outrageous demands for axes and machetes, at least at first, for things changed as I became more fluent in their language and learned how to defend myself socially as well as verbally. More importantly, had I failed to demonstrate that I could not be pushed around beyond a certain point, I would have been the subject of far more ridicule, theft, and practical jokes than was the actual case. In short, I had to acquire a certain proficiency in their style of interpersonal politics and to learn how to imply subtly that certain potentially undesirable, but unspecified, consequences might follow if they did such and such to me. They do this to each other incessantly in order to establish precisely the point at which they cannot goad or intimidate an individual any further without precipitating some kind of retaliation. As soon as I realized this and gradually acquired the self-confidence to adopt this strategy, it became clear that much of the intimidation was calculated to determine my flash point or my 'last ditch' position—and I got along much better with them. Indeed, I even regained some lost ground. It was sort of like a political, interpersonal game that everyone had to play, but one in which each individual sooner or later had to give evidence that his bluffs and implied threats could be backed up with a sanction. I suspect

that the frequency of wife beating is a component in this syndrome, since men can display their *waiteri* (ferocity) and 'show' others that they are capable of great violence. Beating a wife with a club is one way of displaying ferocity, one that does not expose the man to much danger—unless the wife has concerned, aggressive brothers in the village who will come to her aid. Apparently an important thing in wife beating is that the man has displayed his presumed potential for violence and the intended message is that other men ought to treat him with circumspection, caution, and even deference.

After six months, the level of Yąnomamö demand was tolerable in Bisaasi-teri, the village I used for my base of operations. We had adjusted somewhat to each other and knew what to expect with regard to demands for food, trade goods, and favors. Had I elected to remain in just one Yąnomamö village for the entire duration of my first 15 months of fieldwork, the experience would have been far more enjoyable than it actually was. However, as I began to understand the social and political dynamics of this village, it became patently obvious that I would have to travel to many other villages to determine the demographic bases and political histories that lay behind what I could understand in the village of Bisaasi-teri. I began making regular trips to some dozen neighboring Yąnomamö villages as my language fluency improved. I collected local genealogies there, or rechecked and cross-checked those I had collected elsewhere. Hence, the intensity of begging was relatively constant and relatively high for the duration of my fieldwork, for I had to establish my personal position in each village I visited and revisited.

For the most part, my own 'fierceness' took the form of shouting back at the Yąnomamö as loudly and as passionately as they shouted at me, especially at first, when I did not know much of the language. As I became more fluent and learned more about their political tactics, I became more sophisticated in the art of bluffing and brinksmanship. For example, I paid one young man a machete (then worth about $2.50) to cut a palm tree and help me make boards from the wood. I used these to fashion a flooring in the bottom of my dugout canoe to keep my possession out of the water that always seeped into the canoe and sloshed around. That afternoon I was working with one of my informants in the village. The long-awaited mission supply boat arrived and most of the Yąnomamö ran out of the village to see the supplies and try to beg items from the crew. I continued to work in the village for another hour or so and then went down to the river to visit with the men on the supply boat. When I reached the river I noticed, with anger and frustration, that the Yąnomamö had chopped up all my new floor boards to use as crude paddles to get their own canoes across the river to the supply boat.[5] I knew that if I ignored this abuse I would have invited the Yąnomamö to take even greater liberties with my possessions in the future. I got into my canoe, crossed the river, and docked amidst their flimsy, leaky craft. I shouted loudly to them, attracting their attention. They were somewhat sheepish, but all had mischievous grins on their impish faces. A few of them came down to the canoe, where I proceeded with a spirited lecture that revealed my anger at their audacity and license. I explained that I had just that morning paid one of them a machete for bringing me the palmwood, how hard I had worked to shape each board and place it in the canoe, how carefully and painstakingly I had tied each one in with vines, how much I had perspired, how many *bareto* bites I had suffered, and so on. Then, with exaggerated drama and finality, I withdrew my hunting knife as their grins disappeared and cut each one of their canoes loose and set it into the strong current of the Orinoco River where it was immediately swept up and carried downstream. I left without looking back and huffed over to the other side of the river to resume my work.

They managed to borrow another canoe and, after some effort, recovered their dugouts. Later, the headman of the village told me, with an approving chuckle, that I had done the correct thing. Everyone in the village, except, of course, the culprits, supported and defended my actions—and my status increased as a consequence.

Whenever I defended myself in such ways I got along much better with the Yąnomamö and gradually acquired the respect of many of them. A good deal of their demeanor toward me was directed with the forethought of establishing the point at which I would draw the line and react defensively. Many of them, years later, reminisced about the early days of my fieldwork when I was timid and *mohode* ("stupid") and a little afraid of them, those golden days when it was easy to bully me into giving my goods away for almost nothing.

Theft was the most persistent situation that required some sort of defensive action. I simply could not keep everything I owned locked in trunks, and the Yąnomamö came into my hut and left at will. I eventually developed a very effective strategy for recovering almost all the stolen items: I would simply ask a child who took the item and then I would confiscate that person's hammock when he was not around, giving a spirited lecture to all who could hear on the antisociality of thievery as I stalked off in a faked rage with the thief's hammock slung over my shoulder. Nobody ever attempted to stop me from doing this, and almost all of them told me that my technique for recovering my possessions was ingenious. By nightfall the thief would appear at my hut with the stolen item or send it over with someone else to make an exchange to recover his hammock. He would be heckled by his covillagers for having got caught and for being embarrassed into returning my item for his hammock. The explanation was usually, 'I just borrowed your ax! I wouldn't think of stealing it!'

Collecting Yąnomamö Genealogies and Reproductive Histories
My purpose for living among Yąnomamö was to systematically collect certain kinds of information on genealogy, reproduction, marriage practices, kinship, settlement patterns, migrations, and politics. Much of the fundamental data was genealogical—who was the parent of whom, tracing these connections as far back in time as Yąnomamö knowledge and memory permitted. Since 'primitive' society is organized largely by kinship relationships, figuring out the social organization of the Yąnomamö essentially meant collecting extensive data on genealogies, marriage, and reproduction. This turned out to be a staggering and very frustrating problem. I could not have deliberately picked a more difficult people to work with in this regard. They have very stringent name taboos and eschew mentioning the names of prominent living people was well as all deceased friends and relatives. They attempt to name people in such a way that when the person dies and they can no longer use his or her name, the loss of the word in their language is not inconvenient. Hence, they name people for specific and minute parts of things, such as 'toenail of sloth,' 'whisker of howler monkey,' and so on, thereby being able to retain the words 'toenail' or 'whisker' but somewhat handicapped in referring to these anatomical parts of sloths and monkeys respectively. The taboo is maintained even for the living, for one mark of prestige is the courtesy others show you by not using your name publicly. This is particularly true for men, who are much more competitive for status than women in this culture, and it is fascinating to watch boys grow into young men, demanding to be called either by a kinship term in public, or by a teknonymous reference such as 'brother of Himotoma'. The more effective they are at getting others to avoid using their names, the more public acknowledgment there is that they are of high esteem and social standing. Helena Valero, a Brazilian woman who was captured as a child by a Yąnomamö raiding party, was married for many years to a Yąnomamö headman before she discovered what his name was (Biocca, 1970; Valero, 1984). The sanctions behind the taboo are more complex than just this, for they involve

a combination of fear, respect, admiration, political deference, and honor.

At first I tried to use kinship terms alone to collect genealogies, but Yąnomamö kinship terms, like the kinship terms in all systems, are ambiguous at some point because they include so many possible relatives (as the term 'uncle' does in our own kinship system). Again, their system of kin classification merges many relatives that we 'separate' by using different terms: They call both their actual father and their father's brother by a single term, whereas we call one 'father' and the other 'uncle.' I was forced, therefore, to resort to personal names to collect unambiguous genealogies or 'pedigrees'. They quickly grasped what I was up to and that I was determined to learn everyone's 'true name', which amounted to an invasion of their system of prestige and etiquette, if not a flagrant violation of it. They reacted to this in a brilliant but devastating manner: They invented false names for everybody in the village and systematically learned them, freely revealing to me the 'true' identities of everyone. I smugly thought I had cracked the system and enthusiastically constructed elaborate genealogies over a period of some five months. They enjoyed watching me learn their names and kinship relationships. I naively assumed that I would get the 'truth' to each question and the best information by working in public. This set the stage for converting my serious project into an amusing hoax of the grandest proportions. Each 'informant' would try to outdo his peers by inventing a name even more preposterous or ridiculous than what I had been given by someone earlier, the explanations for discrepancies being 'Well, he has two names and this is the other one.' They even fabricated devilishly improbable genealogical relationships, such as someone being married to his grandmother, or worse yet, to his mother-in-law, a grotesque and horrifying prospect to the Yanomamö. I would collect the desired names and relationships by having my informant whisper the name of the person softly into my ear, noting that he or she was the parent of such and

such or the child of such and such, and so on. Everyone who was observing my work would then insist that I repeat the name aloud, roaring in hysterical laughter as I clumsily pronounced the name, sometimes laughing until tears streamed down their faces. The 'named' person would usually react with annoyance and hiss some untranslatable epithet at me, which served to reassure me that I had the 'true' name. I conscientiously checked and rechecked the names and relationships with multiple informants, pleased to see the inconsistencies disappear as my genealogy sheets filled with those desirable little triangles and circles, thousands of them.

My anthropological bubble was burst when I visited a village about 10 hours' walk to the southwest of Bisaasi-teri some five months after I had begun collecting genealogies on the Bisaasi-teri. I was chatting with the local headman of this village and happened to casually drop the name of the wife of the Bisaasi-teri headman. A stunned silence followed, and then a villagewide roar of uncontrollable laughter, choking, gasping, and howling followed. It seems that I thought the Bisaasi-teri headman was married to a woman named "hairy cunt." It also seems that the Bisaasi-teri headman was called 'long dong' and his brother 'eagle shit.' The Bisaasi-teri headman had a son called "asshole" and a daughter called 'fart breath.' And so on. Blood welled up my temples as I realized that I had nothing but nonsense to show for my five months' of dedicated genealogical effort, and I had to throw away almost all the information I had collected on this the most basic set of data I had come there to get. I understood at that point why the Bisaasi-teri laughed so hard when they made me repeat the names of their covillagers, and why the 'named' person would react with anger and annoyance as I pronounced his 'name' aloud.

I was forced to change research strategy—to make an understatement to describe this serious situation. The first thing I did was to begin working in private with my informants to eliminate the horseplay and distraction that

attended public sessions. Once I did this, my informants, who did not know what others were telling me, began to agree with each other and I managed to begin learning the 'real' names, starting first with children and gradually moving to adult women and then, cautiously, adult men, a sequence that reflected the relative degree of intransigence at revealing names of people. As I built up a core of accurate genealogies and relationships—a core that all independent informants had verified repetitiously—I could 'test' any new informant by soliciting his or her opinion and knowledge about these 'core' people whose names and relationships I was confident were accurate. I was, in this fashion, able to immediately weed out the mischievous informants who persisted in trying to deceive me. Still, I had great difficulty getting the names of dead kinsmen, the only accurate way to extend genealogies back in time. Even my best informants continued to falsify names of the deceased, especially closely related deceased. The falsifications at this point were not serious and turned out to be readily corrected as my interviewing methods improved (see below). Most of the deceptions were of the sort where the informant would give me the name of a living man as the father of some child whose actual father was dead, a response that enabled the informant to avoid using the name of a deceased kinsman or friend.

The quality of a genealogy depends in part on the number of generations it embraces, and the name taboo prevented me from making any substantial progress in learning about the deceased ancestors of the present population. Without this information, I could not, for example, document marriage patterns and interfamilial alliances through time. I had to rely on older informants for this information, but these were the most reluctant informants of all for this data. As I became more proficient in the language and more skilled at detecting fabrications, my informants became better at deception. One old man was particularly cunning and persuasive, following a sort of Mark Twain policy that the most effective lie is a sincere lie. He specialized in making a ceremony out of false names for dead ancestors. He would look around nervously to make sure nobody was listening outside my hut, enjoin me never to mention the name again, become very anxious and spooky, and grab me by the head to whisper a secret name into my ear. I was always elated after a session with him, because I managed to add several generations of ancestors for particular members of the village. Others steadfastly refused to give me such information. To show my gratitude, I paid him quadruple the rate that I had been paying the others. When word got around that I had increased the pay for genealogical and demographic information, volunteers began pouring into my hut to 'work' for me, assuring me of their changed ways and keen desire to divest themselves of the 'truth'.

Enter Rerebawä: Inmarried Tough Guy

I discovered that the old man was lying quite by accident. A club fight broke out in the village one day, the result of a dispute over the possession of a woman. She had been promised to a young man in the village, a man named Rerebawä, who was particularly aggressive. He had married into Bisaasi-teri and was doing his 'bride service'— a period of several years during which he had to provide game for his wife's father and mother, provide them with wild foods he might collect, and help them in certain gardening and other tasks. Rerebawä had already been given one of the daughters in marriage and was promised her younger sister as his second wife. He was enraged when the younger sister, then about 16 years old, began having an affair with another young man in the village, Bäkotawä, making no attempt to conceal it. Rerebawä challenged Bäkotawä to a club fight. He swaggered boisterously out to the duel with his 10-foot-long club, a roof-pole he had cut from the house on the spur of the moment, as is the usual procedure. He hurled insult after insult at both Bäkotawä and his father, trying to goad them into a fight.

His insults were bitter and nasty. They tolerated them for a few moments, but Rerebawä's biting insults provoked them to rage. Finally, they stormed angrily out of their hammocks and ripped out roof-poles, now returning the insults verbally, and rushed to the village clearing. Rerebawä continued to insult them, goading them into striking him on the head with their equally long clubs. Had either of them struck his head—which he held out conspicuously for them to swing at—he would then have the right to take his turn on their heads with his club. His opponents were intimidated by his fury, and simply backed down, refusing to strike him, and the argument ended. He had intimidated them into submission. All three retired pompously to their respective hammocks, exchanging nasty insults as they departed. But Rerebawä had won the showdown and thereafter swaggered around the village, insulting the two men behind their backs at every opportunity. He was genuinely angry with them, to the point of calling the older man by the name of his long-deceased father. I quickly seized on this incident as an opportunity to collect an accurate genealogy and confidentially asked Rerebawä about his adversary's ancestors. Rerebawä had been particularly 'pushy' with me up to this point, but we soon became warm friends and staunch allies: We were both 'outsiders' in Bisaasi-teri and, although he was a Yąnomamö, he nevertheless had to put up with some considerable amount of pointed teasing and scorn from the locals, as all inmarried 'sons-in-law' must. He gave me the information I requested of his adversary's deceased ancestors, almost with devilish glee. I asked about dead ancestors of other people in the village and got prompt, unequivocal answers: He was angry with everyone in the village. When I compared his answers to those of the old man, it was obvious that one of them was lying. I then challenged his answers. He explained, in a sort of 'you damned fool, don't you know better?' tone of voice that everyone in the village knew the old man was lying to me and gloating over it when I was out of earshot. The

names the old man had given to me were names of dead ancestors of the members of a village so far away that he thought I would never have occasion to check them out authoritatively. As it turned out, Rerebawä knew most of the people in that distant village and recognized the names given by the old man.

I then went over all my Bisaasi-teri genealogies with Rerebawä, genealogies I had presumed to be close to their final form. I had to revise them all because of the numerous lies and falsifications they contained, much of it provided by the sly old man. Once again, after months of work, I had to recheck everything with Rerebawä's aid. Only the living members of the nuclear families turned out to be accurate; the deceased ancestors were mostly fabrications.

Discouraging as it was to have to recheck everything all over again, it was a major turning point in my fieldwork. Thereafter, I began taking advantage of local arguments and animosities in selecting my informants, and used more extensively informants who had married into the village in the recent past. I also began traveling more regularly to other villages at this time to check on genealogies, seeking out villages whose members were on strained terms with the people about whom I wanted information. I would then return to my base in the village of Bisaasi-teri and check with local informants the accuracy of the new information. I had to be careful in this work and scrupulously select my local informants in such a way that I would not be inquiring about *their* closely related kin. Thus, for each of my local informants, I had to make lists of names of certain deceased people that I dared not mention in their presence. But despite this precaution, I would occasionally hit a new name that would put some informants into a rage, or into a surly mood, such as that of a dead 'brother' or 'sister'[6] whose existence had not been indicted to me by other informants. This usually terminated my day's work with that informant, for he or she would be too touchy or upset to continue any further, and I would be reluctant to take a chance on accidentally discovering another dead close kinsman soon after discovering the first.

These were unpleasant experiences, and occasionally dangerous as well, depending on the temperament of my informant. On one occasion I was planning to visit a village that had been raided recently by one of their enemies. A woman, whose name I had on my census list for that village, had been killed by the raiders. Killing women is considered to be bad form in Yąnomamö warfare, but this woman was deliberately killed for revenge. The raiders were unable to bushwhack some man who stepped out of the village at dawn to urinate, so they shot a volley of arrows over the roof into the village and beat a hasty retreat. Unfortunately, one of the arrows struck and killed a woman, an accident. For that reason, her village's raiders *deliberately* sought out and killed a woman in retaliation—whose name was on my list. My reason for going to the village was to update my census data on a name-by-name basis and estimate the ages of all the residents. I knew I had the name of the dead woman in my list, but nobody would dare to utter her name so I could remove it. I knew that I would be in very serious trouble if I got to the village and said her name aloud, and I desperately wanted to remove it from my list. I called on one of my regular and usually cooperative informants and asked him to tell me the woman's name. He refused adamantly, explaining that she was a close relative—and was angry that I even raised the topic with him. I then asked him if he would let me whisper the names of *all* the women of that village in his ear, and he would simply have to nod when I hit the right name. We had been 'friends' for some time, and I thought I was able to predict his reaction, and thought that our friendship was good enough to use this procedure. He agreed to the procedure, and I began whispering the names of the women, one by one. We were alone in my hut so that nobody would know what we were doing and nobody could hear us. I read the names softly, continuing to

the next when his response was a negative. When I ultimately hit the dead woman's name, he flew out of his chair, enraged and trembling violently, his arm raised to strike me: 'You son-of-a-bitch!' he screamed. 'If you say her name in my presence again, I'll kill you in an instant!' I sat there, bewildered, shocked, and confused. And frightened, as much because of his reaction, but also because I could imagine what might happen to me should I unknowingly visit a village to check genealogy accuracy without knowing that someone had just died there or had been shot by raiders since my last visit. I reflected on the several articles I had read as a graduate student that explained the 'genealogical method,' but could not recall anything about its being a potentially lethal undertaking. My furious informant left my hut, never again to be invited back to be an informant. I had other similar experiences in different villages, but I was always fortunate in that the dead person had been dead for some time, or was not very closely related to the individual into whose ear I whispered the forbidden name. I was usually cautioned by one of the men to desist from saying any more names lest I get people 'angry'.[7]

Kąobawä: The Bisaasi-teri Headman Volunteers to Help Me

I had been working on the genealogies for nearly a year when another individual came to my aid. It was Kąobawä, the headman of Upper Bisaasi-teri. The village of Bisaasi-teri was split into two components, each with its own garden and own circular house. Both were in sight of each other. However, the intensity and frequency of internal bickering and argumentation was so high that they decided to split into two separate groups but remain close to each other for protection in case they were raided. One group was downstream from the other; I refer to that group as the 'Lower' Bisaasi-teri and call Kąobawä's group 'Upper' (upstream) Bisaasi-teri, a convenience they themselves adopted after separating from each other. I spent most

of my time with the members of Kąobawä's group, some 200 people when I first arrived there. I did not have much contact with Kąobawä during the early months of my work. He was a somewhat retiring, quiet man, and among the Yąomamö, the outsider has little time to notice the rare quiet ones when most everyone else is in the front row, pushing and demanding attention. He showed up at my hut one day after all the others had left. He had come to volunteer to help me with the genealogies. He was 'poor,' he explained, and needed a machete. He would work only on the condition that I did not ask him about his own parents and other very close kinsmen who had died. He also added that he would not lie to me as the others had done in the past.

This was perhaps the single most important event in my first 15 months of field research, for out of this fortuitous circumstance evolved a very warm friendship, and among the many things following from it was a wealth of accurate information on the political history of Kąobawä's village and related villages, highly detailed genealogical information, sincere and useful advice to me, and hundreds of valuable insights into the Yąnomamö way of life. Kąobawä's familiarity with his group's history and his candidness were remarkable. His knowledge of details was almost encyclopedic, his memory almost photographic. More than that, he was enthusiastic about making sure I learned the truth, and he encouraged me, indeed, *demanded* that I learn all details I might otherwise have ignored. If there were subtle details he could not recite on the spot, he would advise me to wait until he could check things out with someone else in the village. He would often do this clandestinely, giving me a report the next day, telling me who revealed the new information and whether or not he thought they were in a position to know it. With the information provided by Kąobawä and Rerebawä, I made enormous gains in understanding village interrelationships based on common ancestors and political histories and became lifelong friends with both. And both men knew that I had to learn about his recently deceased kin from the other one. It was one of those quiet understandings we all had but none of us could mention.

Once again I went over the genealogies with Kaobawä to recheck them, a considerable task by this time. They included about two thousand names, representing several generations of individuals from four different villages. Rerebawä's information was very accurate, and Kaobawä's contribution enabled me to trace the genealogies further back in time. Thus, after nearly a year of intensive effort on genealogies, Yanomamö demographic patterns and social organization began to make a good deal of sense to me. Only at this point did the patterns through time begin to emerge in the data, and I could begin to understand how kinship groups took form, exchanged women in marriage over several generations, and only then did the fissioning of larger villages into smaller ones emerge as a chronic and important feature of Yanomamö social, political, demographic, economic, and ecological adaptation. At this point I was able to begin formulating more sophisticated questions, for there was now a pattern to work from and one to flesh out. Without the help of Rerebawä and Kaobawä it would have taken much longer to make sense of the plethora of details I had collected from not only them, but dozens of other informants as well.

I spent a good deal of time with these two men and their families, and got to know them much better than I knew most Yanomamö. They frequently gave their information in a way which related themselves to the topic under discussion. We became warm friends as time passed, and the formal 'informant/anthropologist' relationship faded into the background. Eventually, we simply stopped 'keeping track' of work and pay. They would both spend hours talking with me, leaving without asking for anything. When they wanted something, they would ask for it no matter what the relative balance of reciprocity between us might have been at that point. . . .

For many of the customary things that anthropologists try to communicate about another culture, these two men and their families might be considered to be 'exemplary' or 'typical'. For other things, they are exceptional in many regards, but the reader will, even knowing some of the exceptions, understand Yanomamö culture more intimately by being familiar with a few examples.

Kaobawä was about 40 years old when I first came to his village in 1964. I say "about 40" because the Yanomamö numeration system has only three numbers: one, two, and more-than-two. It is hard to give accurate ages or dates for events when the informants have no means in their language to reveal such detail. Kaobawä is the headman of his village, meaning that he has somewhat more responsibility in political dealings with other Yanomamö groups, and very little control over those who live in his group except when the village is being raided by enemies. We will learn more about political leadership and warfare in a later chapter, but most of the time men like Kaobawä are like the North American Indian 'chief' whose authority was characterized in the following fashion: "One word from the chief, and each man does as he pleases." There are different 'styles' of political leadership among the Yanomamö. Some leaders are mild, quiet, inconspicuous most of the time, but intensely competent. They act parsimoniously, but when they do, people listen and conform. Other men are more tyrannical, despotic, pushy, flamboyant, and unpleasant to all around them. They shout orders frequently, are prone to beat their wives, or pick on weaker men. Some are very violent. I have met headmen who run the entire spectrum between these polar types, for I have visited some 60 Yanomamö villages. Kaobawä stands at the mild, quietly competent end of the spectrum. He has had six wives thus far—and temporary affairs with as many more, at least one of which resulted in a child that is publicly acknowledged as his child. When I first met him he had just two wives: Bahimi

and Koamashima. Bahimi had two living children when I first met her; many others had died. She was the older and enduring wife, as much a friend to him as a mate. Their relationship was as close to what we think of as 'love' in our culture as I have seen among the Yanomamö. His second wife was a girl of about 20 years, Koamashima. She had a new baby boy when I first met her, her first child. There was speculation that Kaobawä was planning to give Koamashima to one of his younger brothers who had no wife; he occasionally allows his younger brother to have sex with Koamashima, but only if he asks in advance. Kaobawä gave another wife to one of his other brothers because she was *beshi* ("horny"). In fact, this earlier wife had been married to two other men, both of whom discarded her because of her infidelity. Kaobawä had one daughter by her. However, the girl is being raised by Kaobawä's brother, though acknowledged to be Kaobawä's child.

Bahimi, his oldest wife, is about five years younger than he. She is his cross-cousin—his mother's brother's daughter. Ideally, all Yanomamö men should marry a cross-cousin. . . . Bahimi was pregnant when I began my fieldwork, but she destroyed the infant when it was born—a boy in this case—explaining tearfully that she had no choice. The new baby would have competed for milk with Ariwari, her youngest child, who was still nursing. Rather than expose Ariwari to the dangers and uncertainty of an early weaning, she chose to terminate the newborn instead. By Yanomamö standards, this has been a very warm, enduring marriage. Kaobawä claims he beats Bahimi only 'once in a while, and only lightly' and she, for her part, never has affairs with other men.

Kaobawä is a quiet, intense, wise, and unobtrusive man. It came as something of a surprise to me when I learned that he was the headman of his village, for he stayed at the sidelines while others would surround me and press their demands on me. He leads more by example than by coercion. He can afford to be this way at his age, for he established his reputation for being forthright and as fierce as the situation required when he was younger, and the other men respect him. He also has five mature brothers or half-brothers in his village, men he can count on for support. He also has several other mature 'brothers' (parallel cousins, whom he must refer to as 'brothers' in his kinship system) in the village who frequently come to his aid, but not as often as his 'real' brothers do. Kąobawä has also given a number of his sisters to other men in the village and has promised his young (8-year-old) daughter in marriage to a young man who, for that reason, is obliged to help him. In short, his 'natural' or 'kinship' following is large, and partially because of this support, he does not have to display his aggressiveness to remind his peers of his position.

Rerebawä is a very different kind of person. He is much younger—perhaps in his early twenties. He has just one wife, but they have already had three children. He is from a village called Karohi-teri, located about five hours' walk up the Orinoco, slightly inland off to the east of the river itself. Kąobawä's village enjoys amicable relationships with Rerebawä's, and it is for this reason that marriage alliances of the kind represented by Rerebawä's marriage into Kąobawä's village occur between the two groups. Rerebawä told me that he came to Bisaasi-teri because there were no eligible women from him to marry in his own village, a fact that I later was able to document when I did a census of his village and a preliminary analysis of its social organization. Rerebawä is perhaps more typical than Kąobawä in the sense that he is chronically concerned about his personal reputation for aggressiveness and goes out of his way to be noticed, even if he has to act tough. He gave me a hard time during my early months of fieldwork, intimidating, teasing, and insulting me frequently. He is, however, much braver than the other men his age and is quite prepared to back up his threats with immediate action—as in the club fight incident just described above. Moreover, he is fascinated with political relationships and knows the details of intervillage relationships

over a large area of the tribe. In this respect he shows all the attributes of being a headman, although he has too many competent brothers in his own village to expect to move easily into the leadership position there.

He does not intend to stay in Kąobawä's group and refuses to make his own garden—a commitment that would reveal something of an intended long-term residence. He feels that he has adequately discharged his obligations to his wife's parents by providing them with fresh game, which he has done for several years. They should let him take his wife and return to his own village with her, but they refuse and try to entice him to remain permanently in Bisaasi-teri to continue to provide them with game when they are old. It is for this reason that they promised to give him their second daughter, their only other child, in marriage. Unfortunately, the girl was opposed to the marriage and ultimately married another man, a rare instance where the woman in the marriage had this much influence on the choice of her husband.

Although Rerebawä has displayed his ferocity in many ways, one incident in particular illustrates what his character can be like. Before he left his own village to take his new wife in Bisaasi-teri, he had an affair with the wife of an older brother. When it was discovered, his brother attacked him with a club. Rerebawä responded furiously: He grabbed an ax and drove his brother out of the village after soundly beating him with the blunt side of the single-bit ax. His brother was so intimidated by the thrashing and promise of more to come that he did not return to the village for several days. I visited this village with Koabawä shortly after this event had taken place; Rerebawä was with me as my guide. He made it a point to introduce me to this man. He approached his hammock, grabbed him by the wrist, and dragged him out on the ground: 'This is the brother whose wife I screwed when he wasn't around!' A deadly insult, one that would usually provoke a bloody club fight among more valiant Yąnomamö. The man did nothing. He slunk sheepishly back into his hammock, shamed,

but relieved to have Rerebawä release his grip.

Even though Rerebawä is fierce and capable of considerable nastiness, he has a charming, witty side as well. He has a biting sense of humor and can entertain the group for hours with jokes and clever manipulations of language. And, he is one of few Yąnomamö that I feel I can trust. I recall indelibly my return to Bisaasi-teri after being away a year—the occasion of my second field trip to the Yąnomamö. When I reached Bisaasi-teri, Rerebawä was in his own village visiting his kinsmen. Word reached him that I had returned, and he paddled downstream immediately to see me. He greeted me with an immense bear hug and exclaimed, with tears welling up in his eyes, 'Shaki! Why did you stay away so long? Did you not know that my will was so cold while you were gone that I could not at times eat for want of seeing you again?' I, too, felt the same way about him—then, and now.

Of all the Yąnomamö I know, he is the most genuine and the most devoted to his culture's ways and values. I admire him for that, although I cannot say that I subscribe to or endorse some of these values. By contrast, Kąobawä is older and wiser, a polished diplomat. He sees his own culture in a slightly different light and seems even to question aspects of it. Thus, while many of his peers enthusiastically accept the 'explanations' of things given in myths, he occasionally reflects on them—even laughing at some of the most preposterous of them. . . . Probably more of the Yąnomamö are like Rerebawä than like Kąobawä, or at least try to be. . . .

NOTES

1. The word Yąnomamö is nasalized through its entire length, indicated by the diacritical mark ' ̨ '. When this mark appears on any Yąnomamö word, the whole word is nasalized. The vowel 'ö' represents a sound that does not occur in the English language. It is similar to the umlaut 'ö' in the German language or the 'oe' equivalent, as in the poet Goethe's name. Unfortunately, many presses and typesetters simply eliminate diacritical marks, and this has led to multiple spellings of the word Yąnomamö—and

multiple mispronunciations. Some anthropologists have chosen to introduce a slightly different spelling of the word Yąnomamö since I began writing about them, such as Yąnomami, leading to additional misspellings as their diacritics are characteristically eliminated by presses, and to the *incorrect* pronunciation 'Yanomameee.' Vowels indicated as 'ä' are pronounced as the 'uh' sound in the word 'duck'. Thus, the name Kąobawä would be pronounced 'cow-ba-wuh,' but entirely nasalized.

2. I spent a total of 60 months among the Yąnomamö between 1964 and 1991. The first edition of this case study was based on the first 15 months I spent among them in Venezuela. I have, at the time of this writing, made 20 field trips to the Yąnomamö and this edition reflects the new information and understandings I have acquired over the years. I plan to return regularly to continue what has now turned into a life-long study.

3. See Spindler (1970) for a general discussion of field research by anthropologists who have worked in other cultures. Nancy Howell has recently written a very useful book (1990) on some of the medical, personal, and environmental hazards of doing field research, which includes a selected bibliography on other field-work problems.

4. They could not pronounce "Chagnon." It sounded to them like their name for a pesky bee, shaki, and that is what they called me: pesky, noisome bee.

5. The Yąnomamö in this region acquired canoes very recently. The missionaries would purchase them from the Ye'kwana Indians to the north for money, and then trade them to the Yąnomamö in exchange for labor, produce, or 'informant' work in translating. It should be emphasized that those Yąnomamö who lived on navigable portions of the Upper Orinoco River moved there recently from the deep forest in order to have contact with the missionaries and acquire the trade goods the missionaries (and their supply system) brought.

6. Rarely were there actual brothers or sisters. In Yąnomamö kinship classifications, certain kinds of cousins are classified as siblings. See Chapter 4.

7. Over time, as I became more and more 'accepted' by the Yąnomamö, they became less and less concerned about my genealogical inquiries and, now, provide me with this information quite willingly because I have been very discrete with it. Now, when I revisit familiar villages I am called aside by someone who whispers to me things like, "Don't ask about so-and-so's father."

Doctor, Lawyer, Indian Chief

*As Punjabi villagers say, "You never really know who a man is
until you know who his grandfather and his ancestors were"*

Richard Kurin

*Richard Kurin is the Deputy Director
of Folklife Programs at the Smithsonian Institution.*

I was full of confidence when—
equipped with a scholarly proposal,
blessings from my advisers, and
generous research grants—I set out
to study village social structure in the
Punjab province of Pakistan. But
after looking for an appropriate
fieldwork site for several weeks without success, I began to think that my
research project would never get off
the ground. Daily I would seek out
villages aboard my puttering motor
scooter, traversing the dusty dirt
roads, footpaths, and irrigation
ditches that crisscross the Punjab.
But I couldn't seem to find a village
amenable to study. The major problem was that the villagers I did approach were baffled by my presence.
They could not understand why anyone would travel ten thousand miles
from home to a foreign country in
order to live in a poor village, interview illiterate peasants, and then
write a book about it. Life, they were
sure, was to be lived, not written
about. Besides, they thought, what of
any importance could they possibly

tell me? Committed as I was to ethnographic research, I readily understood their viewpoint. I was a *babu
log*—literally, a noble; figuratively, a
clerk; and simply, a person of the city.
I rode a motor scooter, wore tight-
fitting clothing, and spoke Urdu, a
language associated with the urban
literary elite. Obviously, I did not
belong; and the villagers simply did
not see me fitting into their society.

The Punjab, a region about the size
of Colorado, straddles the northern
border of India and Pakistan. Partitioned between the two countries in
1947, the Punjab now consists of a
western province, inhabited by Muslims, and an eastern one, populated in
the main by Sikhs and Hindus. As its
name implies—*punj* meaning "five"
and *ab* meaning "rivers"—the region
is endowed with plentiful resources to
support widespread agriculture and a
large rural population. The Punjab
has traditionally supplied grains,
produce, and dairy products to the
peoples of neighboring and considerably more arid states, earning it a
reputation as the breadbasket of
southern Asia.

Given this predilection for agriculture, Punjabis like to emphasize that
they are earthy people, having values
they see as consonant with rural life.
These values include an appreciation
of, and trust in, nature; simplicity and

directness of expression; an awareness of the basic drives and desires
that motivate men (namely, *zan, zar,
zamin*—"women, wealth, land"); a
concern with honor and shame as
abiding principles of social organization; and for Muslims, a deep faith in
Allah and the teachings of his prophet
Mohammad.

Besides being known for its fertile
soils, life-giving rivers, and superla-
tive agriculturists, the Punjab is also
perceived as a zone of transitional
culture, a region that has experienced
repeated invasions of peoples from
western and central Asia into the
Indian subcontinent. Over the last
four thousand years, numerous
groups, among them Scythians, Par-
thians, Huns, Greeks, Moguls, Per-
sians, Afghans, and Turks, have
entered the subcontinent through the
Punjab in search of bountiful land,
riches, or power. Although Punjabis—notably Rajputs, Sikhs, and
Jats—have a reputation for courage
and fortitude on the battlefield, their
primary, self-professed strength has
been their ability to incorporate new,
exogenous elements into their society
with a minimum of conflict. Punjabis
are proud that theirs is a multiethnic
society in which diverse groups have
been largely unified by a common
language and by common customs
and traditions.

Given this background, I had not expected much difficulty in locating a village in which to settle and conduct my research. As an anthropologist, I viewed myself as an "earthy" social scientist who, being concerned with basics, would have a good deal in common with rural Punjabis. True, I might be looked on as an invader of a sort; but I was benevolent, and sensing this, villagers were sure to incorporate me into their society with even greater ease than was the case for the would-be conquering armies that had preceded me. Indeed, they would welcome me with open arms.

I was wrong. The villagers whom I approached attributed my desire to live with them either to neurotic delusions or nefarious ulterior motives. Perhaps, so the arguments went, I was really after women, land, or wealth.

On the day I had decided would be my last in search of a village, I was driving along a road when I saw a farmer running through a rice field and waving me down. I stopped and he climbed on the scooter. Figuring I had nothing to lose, I began to explain why I wanted to live in a village. To my surprise and delight, he was very receptive, and after sharing a pomegranate milkshake at a roadside shop, he invited me to his home. His name was Allah Ditta, which means "God given," and I took this as a sign that I had indeed found my village.

"My" village turned out to be a settlement of about fifteen hundred people, mostly of the Nunari *qaum,* or "tribe." The Nunaris engage primarily in agriculture (wheat, rice, sugar cane, and cotton), and most families own small plots of land. Members of the Bhatti tribe constitute the largest minority in the village. Although traditionally a warrior tribe, the Bhattis serve in the main as the village artisans and craftsmen.

On my first day in the village I tried explaining in great detail the purposes of my study to the village elders and clan leaders. Despite my efforts, most of the elders were perplexed about why I wanted to live in their village. As a guest, I was entitled to the hospitality traditionally be-stowed by Muslim peoples of Asia, and during the first evening I was assigned a place to stay. But I was an enigma, for guests leave, and I wanted to remain. I was also perceived as being strange, for I was both a non-Muslim and a non-Punjabi, a type of person not heretofore encountered by most of the villagers. Although I tried to temper my behavior, there was little I could say or do to dissuade my hosts from the view that I embodied the antithesis of Punjabi values. While I was able to converse in their language, Jatki, a dialect of western Punjabi, I was only able to do so with the ability of a four-year-old. This achievement fell far short of speaking the *t'et',* or "genuine form," of the villagers. Their idiom is rich with the terminology of agricultural operations and rural life. It is unpretentious, uninflected, and direct, and villagers hold high opinions of those who are good with words, who can speak to a point and be convincing. Needless to say, my infantile babble realized none of these characteristics and evoked no such respect.

Similarly, even though I wore indigenous dress, I was inept at tying my *lungi,* or pant cloth. The fact that my *lungi* occasionally fell off and revealed what was underneath gave my neighbors reason to believe that I indeed had no shame and could not control the passions of my *nafs,* or "libidinous nature."

This image of a doltish, shameless infidel barely capable of caring for himself lasted for the first week of my residence in the village. My inability to distinguish among the five varieties of rice and four varieties of lentil grown in the village illustrated that I knew or cared little about nature and agricultural enterprise. This display of ignorance only served to confirm the general consensus that the mysterious morsels I ate from tin cans labeled "Chef Boy-ar-Dee" were not really food at all. Additionally, I did not oil and henna my hair, shave my armpits, or perform ablutions, thereby convincing some commentators that I was a member of a species of subhuman beings, possessing little in the form of either common or moral sense. That the villagers did not quite grant me the status of a person was reflected by their not according me a proper name. In the Punjab, a person's name is equated with honor and respect and is symbolized by his turban. A man who does not have a name, or whose name is not recognized by his neighbors, is unworthy of respect. For such a man, his turban is said to be either nonexistent or to lie in the dust at the feet of others. To be given a name is to have one's head crowned by a turban, an acknowledgment that one leads a responsible and respectable life. Although I repeatedly introduced myself as "Rashid Karim," a fairly decent Pakistani rendering of Richard Kurin, just about all the villagers insisted on calling me *Angrez* ("Englishman"), thus denying me full personhood and implicitly refusing to grant me the right to wear a turban.

As I began to pick up the vernacular, to question villagers about their clan and kinship structure and trace out relationships between different families, my image began to change. My drawings of kinship diagrams and preliminary census mappings were looked upon not only with wonder but also suspicion. My neighbors now began to think there might be a method to my madness. And so there was. Now I had become a spy. Of course it took a week for people to figure out whom I was supposedly spying for. Located as they were at a cross-roads of Asia, at a nexus of conflicting geopolitical interests, they had many possibilities to consider. There was a good deal of disagreement on the issue, with the vast majority maintaining that I was either an American, Russian, or Indian spy. A small, but nonetheless vocal, minority held steadfastly to the belief that I was a Chinese spy. I thought it all rather humorous until one day a group confronted me in the main square in front of the nine-by-nine-foot mud hut that I had rented. The leader spoke up and accused me of spying. The remainder of the group grumbled *jahsus! jahsus!* ("spy! spy!"), and I realized that this ad hoc committee of inquiry had the potential of becoming a mob.

To be sure, the villagers had good reason to be suspicious. For one, the times were tense in Pakistan—a national political crisis gripped the country and the populace had been anxious for months over the uncertainty of elections and effective governmental functions. Second, keenly aware of their history, some of the villagers did not have to go too far to imagine that I was at the vanguard of some invading group that had designs upon their land. Such intrigues, with far greater sophistication, had been played out before by nations seeking to expand their power into the Punjab. That I possessed a gold seal letter (which no one save myself could read) from the University of Chicago to the effect that I was pursuing legitimate studies was not enough to convince the crowd that I was indeed an innocent scholar.

I repeatedly denied the charge, but to no avail. The shouts of *jahsus! jahsus!* prevailed. Confronted with this I had no choice.

"Okay," I said. "I admit it. I am a spy!"

The crowd quieted for my long-awaited confession.

"I am a spy and am here to study this village, so that when my country attacks you we will be prepared. You see, we will not bomb Lahore or Karachi or Islamabad. Why should we waste our bombs on millions of people, on factories, dams, airports, and harbors? No, it is far more advantageous to bomb this strategic small village replete with its mud huts, livestock, Persian wheels, and one light bulb. And when we bomb this village, it is imperative that we know how Allah Ditta is related to Abdullah, and who owns the land near the well, and what your marriage customs are."

Silence hung over the crowd, and then one by one the assemblage began to disperse. My sarcasm had worked. The spy charges were defused. But I was no hero in light of my performance, and so I was once again relegated to the status of a nonperson without an identity in the village.

I remained in limbo for the next week, and although I continued my attempts to collect information about village life, I had my doubts as to whether I would ever be accepted by the villagers. And then, through no effort of my own, there was a breakthrough, this time due to another Allah Ditta, a relative of the village headman and one of my leading accusers during my spying days.

I was sitting on my woven string bed on my porch when Allah Ditta approached, leading his son by the neck. "Oh, *Angrez!*" he yelled, "this worthless son of mine is doing poorly in school. He is supposed to be learning English, but he is failing. He has a good mind, but he's lazy. And his teacher is no help, being more intent upon drinking tea and singing film songs than upon teaching English. Oh son of an Englishman, do you know English?"

"Yes, I know English," I replied, "after all, I am an *Angrez.*"

"Teach him," Allah Ditta blurted out, without any sense of making a tactful request.

And so, I spent the next hour with the boy, reviewing his lessons and correcting his pronunciation and grammar. As I did so, villagers stopped to watch and listen, and by the end of the hour, nearly one hundred people had gathered around, engrossed by this tutoring session. They were stupefied. I was an effective teacher, and I actually seemed to know English. The boy responded well, and the crowd reached a new consensus. I had a brain. And in recognition of this achievement I was given a name—"Ustad Rashid," or Richard the Teacher.

Achieving the status of a teacher was only the beginning of my success. The next morning I awoke to find the village sugar vendor at my door. He had a headache and wanted to know if I could cure him.

"Why do you think I can help you?" I asked.

Bhai Khan answered, "Because you are a *ustad,* you have a great deal of knowledge."

The logic was certainly compelling. If I could teach English, I should be

able to cure a headache. I gave him two aspirins.

An hour later, my fame had spread. Bhai Khan had been cured, and he did not hesitate to let others know that it was the *ustad* who had been responsible. By the next day, and in fact for the remainder of my stay, I was to see an average of twenty-five to thirty patients a day. I was asked to cure everything from coughs and colds to typhoid, elephantiasis, and impotency. Upon establishing a flourishing and free medical practice, I received another title, *hakim,* or "physician." I was not yet an anthropologist, but I was on my way.

A few days later I took on yet another role. One of my research interests involved tracing out patterns of land ownership and inheritance. While working on the problem of figuring out who owned what, I was approached by the village watchman. He claimed he had been swindled in a land deal and requested my help. As the accused was not another villager, I agreed to present the watchman's case to the local authorities.

Somehow, my efforts managed to achieve results. The plaintiff's grievance was redressed, and I was given yet another title in the village—*wakil,* or "lawyer." And in the weeks that followed, I was steadily called upon to read, translate, and advise upon various court orders that affected the lives of the villagers.

My roles as teacher, doctor, and lawyer not only provided me with an identity but also facilitated my integration into the economic structure of the community. As my imputed skills offered my neighbors services not readily available in the village, I was drawn into exchange relationships known as *seipi. Seipi* refers to the barter system of goods and services among village farmers, craftsmen, artisans, and other specialists. Every morning Roshan the milkman would deliver fresh milk to my hut. Every other day Hajam Ali the barber would stop by and give me a shave. My next-door neighbor, Nura the cobbler, would repair my sandals when required. Ghulam the horse-cart driver would transport me to town when my motor scooter was in disrepair. The parents of my students would send me sweets and sometimes delicious meals. In return, none of my neighbors asked for direct payment for the specific actions performed. Rather, as they told me, they would call upon me when they had need of my services. And they did. Nura needed cough syrup for his children, the milkman's brother needed a job contact in the city, students wanted to continue their lessons, and so on. Through *seipi* relations, various neighbors gave goods and services to me, and I to them.

Even so, I knew that by Punjabi standards I could never be truly accepted into village life because I was not a member of either the Nunari or Bhatti tribe. As the villagers would say, "You never really know who a man is until you know who his grandfather and his ancestors were." And to know a person's grandfather or ancestors properly, you had to be a member of the same or a closely allied tribe.

The Nunari tribe is composed of a number of groups. The nucleus consists of four clans—Naul, Vadel, Sadan, and More—each named for one of four brothers thought to have originally founded the tribe. Clan members are said to be related to blood ties, also called *pag da sak,* or "ties of the turban." In sharing the turban, members of each clan share the same name. Other clans, unrelated by ties of blood to these four, have become attached to this nucleus through a history of marital relations or of continuous political and economic interdependence. Marital relations, called *gag da sak,* or "ties of the skirt," are conceived of as relations in which alienable turbans (skirts) in the form of women are exchanged with other, non-turban-sharing groups. Similarly, ties of political and economic domination and subordination are thought of as relations in which the turban of the client is given to that of the patron. A major part of my research work was concerned with reconstructing how the four brothers formed the Nunari tribe, how additional clans became associated with

it, and how clan and tribal identity were defined by nomenclature, codes of honor, and the symbols of sharing and exchanging turbans.

To approach these issues I set out to reconstruct the genealogical relationships within the tribe and between the various clans. I elicited genealogies from many of the villagers and questioned older informants about the history of the Nunari tribe. Most knew only bits and pieces of this history, and after several months of interviews and research, I was directed to the tribal genealogists. These people, usually not Nunaris themselves, perform the service of memorizing and then orally relating the history of the tribe and the relationships among its members. The genealogist in the village was an aged and arthritic man named Hedayat, who in his later years was engaged in teaching the Nunari genealogy to his son, who would then carry out the traditional and hereditary duties of his position.

The villagers claimed that Hedayat knew every generation of the Nunari from the present to the founding brothers and even beyond. So I invited Hedayat to my hut and explained my purpose.

"Do you know Allah Ditta son of Rohm?" I asked.

"Yes, of course," he replied.

"Who was Rohm's father?" I continued.

"Shahadat Mohammad," he answered.

"And his father?"

"Hamid."

"And his?"

"Chigatah," he snapped without hesitation.

I was now quite excited, for no one else in the village had been able to recall an ancestor of this generation. My estimate was that Chigatah had been born sometime between 1850 and 1870. But Hedayat went on.

"Chigatah's father was Kamal. And Kamal's father was Nanak. And Nanak's father was Sikhu. And before him was Dargai, and before him Maiy. And before him was Siddiq. And Siddiq's father was Nur. And Nur's Asmat. And Asmat was of Channa.

And Channa of Nau. And Nau of Bhatta. And Bhatta was the son of Koduk."

Hedayat had now recounted sixteen generations of lineal ascendants related through the turban. Koduk was probably born in the sixteenth century. But still Hedayat continued.

"Sigun was the father of Koduk. And Man the father of Sigun. And before Man was his father Maneswar. And Maneswar's father was the founder of the clan, Naul."

This then was a line of the Naul clan of the Nunari tribe, ascending twenty-one generations from the present descendants (Allah Ditta's sons) to the founder, one of four brothers who lived perhaps in the fifteenth century. I asked Hedayat to recite genealogies of the other Nunari clans, and he did, with some blanks here and there, ending with Vadel, More, and Saddan, the other three brothers who formed the tribal nucleus. I then asked the obvious question, "Hedayat, who was the father of these four brothers? Who is the founding ancestor of the Nunari tribe?"

"The father of these brothers was not a Muslim. He was an Indian rajput [chief]. The tribe actually begins with the conversion of the four brothers," Hedayat explained.

"Well then," I replied, "who was this Indian chief?"

He was a famous and noble chief who fought against the Moguls. His name was Raja Kurin, who lived in a massive fort in Kurinnagar, about twenty-seven miles from Delhi."

"What!" I asked, both startled and unsure of what I had heard.

"Raja Kurin is the father of the brothers who make up—"

"But his name! It's the same as mine," I stammered. "Hedayat, my name is Richard Kurin. What a coincidence! Here I am living with your tribe thousands of miles from my home and it turns out that I have the same name as the founder of the tribe! Do you think I might be related to Raja Kurin and the Nunaris?"

Hedayat looked at me, but only for an instant. Redoing his turban, he tilted his head skyward, smiled, and asked, "What is the name of your father?"

I had come a long way. I now had a name that could be recognized and respected, and as I answered Hedayat, I knew that I had finally and irrevocably fit into "my" village. Whether by fortuitous circumstances or by careful manipulation, my neighbors had found a way to take an invading city person intent on studying their life and transform him into one of their own, a full person entitled to wear a turban for participating in, and being identified with, that life. As has gone on for centuries in the region, once again the new and exogenous had been recast into something Punjabi.

Epilogue: There is no positive evidence linking the Nunaris to a historical Raja Kurin, although there are several famous personages identified by that name (also transcribed as Karan and Kurran). Estimated from the genealogy recited by Hedayat, the founding of the tribe by the four brothers appears to have occurred sometime between 440 and 640 years ago, depending on the interval assumed for each generation. On that basis, the most likely candidate for Nunari progenitor (actual or imputed) is Raja Karan, ruler of Anhilvara (Gujerat), who was defeated by the Khilji Ala-ud-Din in 1297 and again in 1307. Although this is slightly earlier than suggested by the genealogical data, such genealogies are often telescoped or otherwise unreliable.

Nevertheless, several aspects of Hedayat's account make this association doubtful. Hedayat clearly identifies Raja Kurin's conquerors as Moguls, whereas the Gujerati Raja Karan was defeated by the Khiljis. Second, Hedayat places the Nunari ancestor's kingdom only twenty-seven miles from Delhi. The Gujerati Raja Karan ruled several kingdoms, none closer than several hundred miles to Delhi.

Other circumstances, however, offer support for this identification of the Nunari ancestor. According to Hedayat, Raja Kurin's father was named Kam Deo. Although the historical figure was the son of Serung Deo, the use of "Deo," a popular title for the rajas of the Vaghela and Solonki dynasties, does seem to place the Nunari founder in the context of medieval Gujerat. Furthermore, Hedayat clearly identifies the saint (*pir*) said to have initiated the conversion of the Nunaris to Islam. This saint, Mukhdum-i-Jehaniyan, was a contemporary of the historical Raja Karan.

Also of interest, but as yet unexplained, is that several other groups living in Nunari settlement areas specifically claim to be descended from Raja Karan of Gujerat, who is said to have migrated northward into the Punjab after his defeat. Controverting this theory, the available evidence indicates that Raja Karan fled, not toward the Punjab, but rather southward to the Deccan, and that his patriline ended with him. It is his daughter Deval Devi who is remembered: she is the celebrated heroine of "Ashiqa," a famous Urdu poem written by Amir Khusrau in 1316. She was married to Khizr Khan, the son of Karan's conqueror; nothing is known of her progeny.

Eating Christmas in the Kalahari

Richard Borshay Lee

Richard Borshay Lee is a full professor of anthropology at the University of Toronto. He has done extensive fieldwork in southern Africa, is coeditor of Man the Hunter *(1968) and* Kalahari Hunter-Gatherers *(1976), and author of* The !Kung San: Men, Women, and Work in a Foraging Society.

The !Kung Bushmen's knowledge of Christmas is thirdhand. The London Missionary Society brought the holiday to the southern Tswana tribes in the early nineteenth century. Later, native catechists spread the idea far and wide among the Bantu-speaking pastoralists, even in the remotest corners of the Kalahari Desert. The Bushmen's idea of the Christmas story, stripped to its essentials, is "praise the birth of white man's god-chief"; what keeps their interest in the holiday high is the Tswana-Herero custom of slaughtering an ox for his Bushmen neighbors as an annual goodwill gesture. Since the 1930's, part of the Bushmen's annual round of activities has included a December congregation at the cattle posts for trading, marriage brokering, and several days of trance-dance feasting at which the local Tswana headman is host.

As a social anthropologist working with !Kung Bushmen, I found that the Christmas ox custom suited my purposes. I had come to the Kalahari to study the hunting and gathering subsistence economy of the !Kung, and to accomplish this it was essential not to provide them with food, share my own food, or interfere in any way with their food-gathering activities. While liberal handouts of tobacco and medical supplies were appreciated, they were scarcely adequate to erase the glaring disparity in wealth between the anthropologist, who maintained a two-month inventory of canned goods, and the Bushmen, who rarely had a day's supply of food on hand. My approach, while paying off in terms of data, left me open to frequent accusations of stinginess and hard-heartedness. By their lights, I was a miser.

The Christmas ox was to be my way of saying thank you for the cooperation of the past year; and since it was to be our last Christmas in the field, I determined to slaughter the largest, meatiest ox that money could buy, insuring that the feast and trance-dance would be a success.

Through December I kept my eyes open at the wells as the cattle were brought down for watering. Several animals were offered, but none had quite the grossness that I had in mind. Then, ten days before the holiday, a Herero friend led an ox of astonishing size and mass up to our camp. It was solid black, stood five feet high at the shoulder, had a five-foot span of horns, and must have weighed 1,200 pounds on the hoof. Food consumption calculations are my specialty, and I quickly figured that bones and viscera aside, there was enough meat—at least four pounds—for every man, woman, and child of the 150 Bushmen in the vicinity of /ai/ai who were expected at the feast.

Having found the right animal at last, I paid the Herero £20 ($56) and asked him to keep the beast with his herd until Christmas day. The next morning word spread among the people that the big solid black one was the ox chosen by /ontah (my Bushman name; it means, roughly, "whitey") for the Christmas feast. That afternoon I received the first delegation. Ben!a, an outspoken sixty-year-old mother of five, came to the point slowly.

"Where were you planning to eat Christmas?"

"Right here at /ai/ai," I replied.

"Alone or with others?"

"I expect to invite all the people to eat Christmas with me."

"Eat what?"

"I have purchased Yehave's black ox, and I am going to slaughter and cook it."

"That's what we were told at the well but refused to believe it until we heard it from yourself."

"Well, it's the black one," I replied expansively, although wondering what she was driving at.

"Oh, no!" Ben!a groaned, turning to her group. "They were right." Turning back to me she asked, "Do you expect us to eat that bag of bones?"

"Bag of bones! It's the biggest ox at /ai/ai."

"Big, yes, but old. And thin. Everybody knows there's no meat on that old ox. What did you expect us to eat off it, the horns?"

Everybody chuckled at Ben!a's one-liner as they walked away, but all I could manage was a weak grin.

That evening it was the turn of the young men. They came to sit at our evening fire. /gaugo, about my age, spoke to me man-to-man.

"/ontah, you have always been square with us," he lied. "What has happened to change your heart? That sack of guts and bones of Yehave's will hardly feed one camp, let alone all the Bushmen around /ai/ai." And he proceeded to enumerate the seven camps in the /ai/ai vicinity, family by family. "Perhaps you have forgotten that we are not few, but many. Or are you too blind to tell the difference between a proper cow and an old wreck? That ox is thin to the point of death."

"Look, you guys," I retorted, "that is a beautiful animal, and I'm sure you will eat it with pleasure at Christmas."

"Of course we will eat it; it's food. But it won't fill us up to the point where we will have enough strength to dance. We will eat and go home to bed with stomachs rumbling."

That night as we turned in, I asked my wife, Nancy: "What did you think of the black ox?"

"It looked enormous to me. Why?"

"Well, about eight different people have told me I got gypped; that the ox is nothing but bones."

"What's the angle?" Nancy asked. "Did they have a better one to sell?"

"No, they just said that it was going to be a grim Christmas because there won't be enough meat to go around. Maybe I'll get an independent judge to look at the beast in the morning."

Bright and early, Halingisi, a Tswana cattle owner, appeared at our camp. But before I could ask him to give me his opinion on Yehave's black ox, he gave me the eye signal that indicated a confidential chat. We left the camp and sat down.

"/ontah, I'm surprised at you: you've lived here for three years and still haven't learned anything about cattle."

"But what else can a person do but choose the biggest, strongest animal one can find?" I retorted.

"Look, just because an animal is big doesn't mean that it has plenty of meat on it. The black one was a

beauty when it was younger, but now it is thin to the point of death."

"Well I've already bought it. What can I do at this stage?"

"Bought it already? I thought you were just considering it. Well, you'll have to kill it and serve it, I suppose. But don't expect much of a dance to follow."

My spirits dropped rapidly. I could believe that Ben!a and /gaugo just might be putting me on about the black ox, but Halingisi seemed to be an impartial critic. I went around that day feeling as though I had bought a lemon of a used car.

In the afternoon it was Tomazo's turn. Tomazo is a fine hunter, a top trance performer . . . and one of my most reliable informants. He approached the subject of the Christmas cow as part of my continuing Bushman education.

"My friend, the way it is with us Bushmen," he began, "is that we love meat. And even more than that, we love fat. When we hunt we always search for the fat ones, the ones dripping with layers of white fat: fat that turns into a clear, thick oil in the cooking pot, fat that slides down your gullet, fills your stomach and gives you a roaring diarrhea," he rhapsodized.

"So, feeling as we do," he continued, "it gives us pain to be served such a scrawny thing as Yehave's black ox. It is big, yes, and no doubt its giant bones are good for soup, but fat is what we really crave and so we will eat Christmas this year with a heavy heart."

The prospect of a gloomy Christmas now had me worried, so I asked Tomazo what I could do about it.

"Look for a fat one, a young one . . . smaller, but fat. Fat enough to make us //gom ('evacuate the bowels'), then we will be happy."

My suspicions were aroused when Tomazo said that he happened to know of a young, fat, barren cow that the owner was willing to part with. Was Tomazo working on commission, I wondered? But I dispelled this unworthy thought when we approached the Herero owner of the

cow in question and found that he had decided not to sell.

The scrawny wreck of a Christmas ox now became the talk of the /ai/ai water hole and was the first news told to the outlying groups as they began to come in from the bush for the feast. What finally convinced me that real trouble might be brewing was the visit from u!au, an old conservative with a reputation for fierceness. His nickname meant spear and referred to an incident thirty years ago in which he had speared a man to death. He had an intense manner; fixing me with his eyes, he said in clipped tones:

"I have only just heard about the black ox today, or else I would have come here earlier. /ontah, do you honestly think you can serve meat like that to people and avoid a fight?" He paused, letting the implications sink in. "I don't mean fight you, /ontah; you are a white man. I mean a fight between Bushmen. There are many fierce ones here, and with such a small quantity of meat to distribute, how can you give everybody a fair share? Someone is sure to accuse another of taking too much or hogging all the choice pieces. Then you will see what happens when some go hungry while others eat."

The possibility of at least a serious argument struck me as all too real. I had witnessed the tension that surrounds the distribution of meat from a kudu or gemsbok kill, and had documented many arguments that sprang up from a real or imagined slight in meat distribution. The owners of a kill may spend up to two hours arranging and rearranging the piles of meat under the gaze of a circle of recipients before handing them out. And I also knew that the Christmas feast at /ai/ai would be bringing together groups that had feuded in the past.

Convinced now of the gravity of the situation, I went in earnest to search for a second cow; but all my inquiries failed to turn one up.

The Christmas feast was evidently going to be a disaster, and the incessant complaints about the meagerness of the ox had already taken the fun out of it for me. Moreover, I was getting bored with the wisecracks, and after losing my temper a few times, I resolved to serve the beast anyway. If the meat fell short, the hell with it. In the Bushmen idiom, I announced to all who would listen:

"I am a poor man and blind. If I have chosen one that is too old and too thin, we will eat it anyway and see if there is enough meat there to quiet the rumbling of our stomachs."

On hearing this speech, Ben!a offered me a rare word of comfort. "It's thin," she said philosophically, "but the bones will make a good soup."

At dawn Christmas morning, instinct told me to turn over the butchering and cooking to a friend and take off with Nancy to spend Christmas alone in the bush. But curiosity kept me from retreating. I wanted to see what such a scrawny ox looked like on butchering, and if there *was* going to be a fight, I wanted to catch every word of it. Anthropologists are incurable that way.

The great beast was driven up to our dancing ground, and a shot in the forehead dropped it in its tracks. Then, freshly cut branches were heaped around the fallen carcass to receive the meat. Ten men volunteered to help with the cutting. I asked /gaugo to make the breast bone cut. This cut, which begins the butchering process for most large game, offers easy access for removal of the viscera. But it also allows the hunter to spot-check the amount of fat on the animal. A fat game animal carries a white layer up to an inch thick on the chest, while in a thin one, the knife will quickly cut to bone. All eyes fixed on his hand as /gaugo, dwarfed by the great carcass, knelt to the breast. The first cut opened a pool of solid white in the black skin. The second and third cut widened and deepened the creamy white. Still no bone. It was pure fat; it must have been two inches thick.

"Hey /gau," I burst out, "that ox is loaded with fat. What's this about the ox being too thin to bother eating? Are you out of your mind?"

"Fat?" /gau shot back, "You call that fat? This wreck is thin, sick,

dead!" And he broke out laughing. So did everyone else. They rolled on the ground, paralyzed with laughter. Everybody laughed except me; I was thinking.

I ran back to the tent and burst in just as Nancy was getting up. "Hey, the black ox. It's fat as hell! They were kidding about it being too thin to eat. It was a joke or something. A put-on. Everyone is really delighted with it!"

"Some joke," my wife replied. "It was so funny that you were ready to pack up and leave /ai/ai."

If it had indeed been a joke, it had been an extraordinarily convincing one, and tinged, I thought, with more than a touch of malice as many jokes are. Nevertheless, that it was a joke lifted my spirits considerably, and I returned to the butchering site where the shape of the ox was rapidly disappearing under the axes and knives of the butchers. The atmosphere had become festive. Grinning broadly, their arms covered with blood well past the elbow, men packed chunks of meat into the big cast-iron cooking pots, fifty pounds to the load, and muttered and chuckled all the while about the thinness and worthlessness of the animal and /ontah's poor judgment.

We danced and ate that ox two days and two nights; we cooked and distributed fourteen potfuls of meat and no one went home hungry and no fights broke out.

But the "joke" stayed in my mind. I had a growing feeling that something important had happened in my relationship with the Bushmen and that the clue lay in the meaning of the joke. Several days later, when most of the people had dispersed back to the bush camps, I raised the question with Hakekgose, a Tswana man who had grown up among the !Kung, married a !Kung girl, and who probably knew their culture better than any other non-Bushman.

"With us whites," I began, "Christmas is supposed to be the day of friendship and brotherly love. What I can't figure out is why the Bushmen went to such lengths to criticize and belittle the ox I had bought for the feast. The animal was

perfectly good and their jokes and wisecracks practically ruined the holiday for me."

"So it really did bother you," said Hakekgose. "Well, that's the way they always talk. When I take my rifle and go hunting with them, if I miss, they laugh at me for the rest of the day. But even if I hit and bring one down, it's no better. To them, the kill is always too small or too old or too thin; and as we sit down on the kill site to cook and eat the liver, they keep grumbling, even with their mouths full of meat. They say things like, 'Oh this is awful! What a worthless animal! Whatever made me think that this Tswana rascal could hunt!' "

"Is this the way outsiders are treated?" I asked.

"No, it is their custom; they talk that way to each other too. Go and ask them."

/gaugo had been one of the most enthusiastic in making me feel bad about the merit of the Christmas ox. I sought him out first.

"Why did you tell me the black ox was worthless, when you could see that it was loaded with fat and meat?"

"It is our way," he said smiling. "We always like to fool people about that. Say there is a Bushman who has been hunting. He must not come home and announce like a braggard, 'I have killed a big one in the bush!' He must first sit down in silence until I or someone else comes up to his fire and asks, 'What did you see today?' He replies quietly, 'Ah, I'm no good for hunting. I saw nothing at all [pause] just a little tiny one.' Then I smile to myself," /gaugo continued, "because I know he has killed something big.

"In the morning we make up a party of four or five people to cut up and carry the meat back to the camp. When we arrive at the kill we examine it and cry out, 'You mean to say you have dragged us all the way out here in order to make us cart home your pile of bones? Oh, if I had known it was this thin I wouldn't have come.' Another one pipes up, 'People, to think I gave up a nice day in the shade for this. At home we may be hungry but at least we have nice cool water to drink.' If the horns are big, someone says, 'Did you think that somehow you were going to boil down the horns for soup?'

"To all this you must respond in kind. 'I agree,' you say, 'this one is not worth the effort; let's just cook the liver for strength and leave the rest for the hyenas. It is not too late to hunt today and even a duiker or a steenbok would be better than this mess.'

"Then you set to work nevertheless; butcher the animal, carry the meat back to the camp and everyone eats," /gaugo concluded.

Things were beginning to make sense. Next, I went to Tomazo. He corroborated /gaugo's story of the obligatory insults over a kill and added a few details of his own.

"But," I asked, "why insult a man after he has gone to all that trouble to track and kill an animal and when he is going to share the meat with you so that your children will have something to eat?"

"Arrogance," was his cryptic answer.

"Arrogance?"

"Yes, when a young man kills much meat he comes to think of himself as a chief or a big man, and he thinks of the rest of us as his servants or inferiors. We can't accept this. We refuse one

who boasts, for someday his pride will make him kill somebody. So we always speak of his meat as worthless. This way we cool his heart and make him gentle."

"But why didn't you tell me this before?" I asked Tomazo with some heat.

"Because you never asked me," said Tomazo, echoing the refrain that has come to haunt every field ethnographer.

The pieces now fell into place. I had known for a long time that in situations of social conflict with Bushmen I held all the cards. I was the only source of tobacco in a thousand square miles, and I was not incapable of cutting an individual off for non-cooperation. Though my boycott never lasted longer than a few days, it was an indication of my strength. People resented my presence at the water hole, yet simultaneously dreaded my leaving. In short I was a perfect target for the charge of arrogance and for the Bushmen tactic of enforcing humility.

I had been taught an object lesson by the Bushmen; it had come from an unexpected corner and had hurt me in a vulnerable area. For the big black ox was to be the one totally generous, unstinting act of my year at /ai/ai,

and I was quite unprepared for the reaction I received.

As I read it, their message was this: There are no totally generous acts. All "acts" have an element of calculation. One black ox slaughtered at Christmas does not wipe out a year of careful manipulation of gifts given to serve your own ends. After all, to kill an animal and share the meat with people is really no more than Bushmen do for each other every day and with far less fanfare.

In the end, I had to admire how the Bushmen had played out the farce—collectively straight-faced to the end. Curiously, the episode reminded me of the *Good Soldier Schweik* and his marvelous encounters with authority. Like Schweik, the Bushmen had retained a thorough-going skepticism of good intentions. Was it this independence of spirit, I wondered, that had kept them culturally viable in the face of generations of contact with more powerful societies, both black and white? The thought that the Bushmen were alive and well in the Kalahari was strangely comforting. Perhaps, armed with that independence and with their superb knowledge of their environment, they might yet survive the future.

A Cross-Cultural Experience: A Chinese Anthropologist in the United States

Huang Shu-min

Huang Shu-min is a professor of Anthropology at Iowa State University, where he has been teaching since 1975. Born and raised in China and Taiwan, Huang spent much of his research periods in these two regions. He received his B.A. in Anthropology from National Taiwan University (1967) and his M.A. and Ph.D. in Anthropology from Michigan State University (1973, 1977).

Using a variety of interesting and sometimes humorous encounters with Americans, Professor Huang Shu-min describes how these experiences can lead to a better understanding of one's own culture. He emphasizes that although these experiences can lead to greater awareness, it is difficult even for anthropologists to free themselves of the assumptions about their own culture.

Born and raised in many areas of China, including the Mainland, Hong Kong, and Taiwan, I have developed a deep appreciation for the enormous cultural variations in China. Ever since I can remember, I seemed to have been surrounded by people—including my own family members—who speak many languages and entertain various tastes in food and clothing that characterize regional differences in China.

However, despite my exposure to such a diverse way of life, I was probably brought up as a normal, average Chinese, taught to believe in the traditional Chinese values, manners, and beliefs characteristic of Confucian literati. A reverence for age and custom, a high motivation toward scholarly achievement, and a strong sense of responsibility toward society had all been incorporated into my thinking throughout the process of growth.

Contact with anthropology in my college years in Taiwan, however, brought about basic changes in my life. Anthropology claims that much of our behavior, customs, and even ways of thinking are molded by our culture, which is essentially a set of artificially designed symbols accumulated throughout human history. Accepting such a premise, I began to question the validity and rationale of all the values, beliefs, and even ways of thinking that I once had stood for and cherished. As a consequence, I was, to borrow a phrase from Muriel Dimen-Schein (1977), "drawn to its (anthropology's) moral emphasis that our culture was not the best or only way to live, and alternatives existed." My soul-searching along this line has not led to a total rejection of my culture; rather, I began to develop a habit of looking at my own behavior from an objective point of view and to be critical of things that I had taken for granted.

My career in anthropology has eventually brought me to study and to teach in the United States. Situated in an entirely different culture, I have been able not only to look at my own culture from this objective point of view but also to make a constant comparison between my own cultural practices and those of Americans. To bring my professional training into everyday situations, which involves explaining ordinary events against both the Chinese and American frames of thought, I have tried to explore the extent to which human beings are influenced by their specific cultures. The following incidents have occurred during my residence in the United States and form the foundation for some of my reflections.

INTRODUCTION TO AMERICA

My initiation into American culture was through my older sister, who had lived in San Francisco for some time before I arrived in 1970. Apparently aghast at my appearance when we met at the airport, especially my dandruff-ridden hair and unshaved face, she warned me that Americans are extremely sensitive about physical appearances. I should from then on use dandruff-proof shampoo and shave my face every day—even though there is not much to work on.

I was puzzled by her notions, for I had heard about the counterculture movement in the United States, especially on campuses across the country. My limited knowledge about the counterculture seemed to indicate the development of an alternative way of life, which also implied, to some extent, the rejection of American middle-class values. If that was the case, why bother with this physical appearance–laden life-style? I kept this question to myself, for I thought my sister was just old-fashioned and conservative, and so there was no point in arguing with her.

I stayed in San Francisco for a month, and during that period I made many sightseeing tours around the city. My specific interest was in the hippie ghettoes. As a novice in anthropology, I believed that the counterculture movement presented a unique opportunity to study how culture can be changed in a well-intentioned manner. Based on my superficial observations, these people appeared to be sincere about developing an alternative way of life in direct opposition to that of middle-class values: long and uncombed hair, bare feet, patched blue jeans and free-floating along the sidewalks, for example.

I was very much impressed by what I saw. But then I suddenly noticed that I had not seen anyone with dandruff. I brought up this question to an acquaintance who was very much involved in this particular way of life. "Oh, yes," he replied in a typically nonchalant manner, "dandruff is indeed a problem to many of us. But we use dandruff-proof shampoo."

Disappointed? No. It only confirmed an idea that I had but could not prove with evidence: While we may claim to reject our culture's values and moral standards en masse, in the deeper layer of the heart and mind, our thinking and behavior may still operate, even though unconsciously, under the same set of beliefs.

CULTURE AND HAIR COLOR

My graduate years at Michigan State University were some of the most interesting experiences during my time at school. We had a large student body—thirty-odd in my first-year class. A great number of my classmates were from different nations, and many of the other American students also had had personal experiences in other parts of the world. We formed a very close group, often having parties, picnics, and other activities together.

One day after class, we stayed in the classroom chatting about recent events. Suddenly, someone in the group mentioned the long absence of a female classmate: "Strange, I have not seen the little redhead for the past few days!"

Little redhead? The notion did not ring a bell at all. How could he refer to someone in such a strange way? Did this person really have red hair? Why had I never noticed this? I took a hard look around the classroom and realized that there were indeed different hair styles and colors among my classmates, something that I had never paid attention to!

The discovery that Americans frequently divide their hair into categories and use this taxonomical difference as a point of reference was something entirely new to me. Chinese would never refer to another person by describing his or her hair, for every Chinese has dark, straight hair, except the aged and bald. Because hair is an insignificant difference, Chinese probably do not have an acute conceptual system to categorize people on the basis of hair traits and, as a consequence, tend to neglect this physical characteristic entirely.

PRIMARY AND SECONDARY LANGUAGES

One incident that happened before I came to the States puzzled me for some time. In 1969, I was working with Professor and Mrs. Gallin in Taipei, studying rural migrants in the city. One day my father came to see me and also had a chat with Professor Gallin. Because my father does not speak English and his Mandarin has an accent that Professor Gallin could not quite follow, I had to serve as translator in the conversation. When my father spoke to me for the translation, I noticed that he used Taiwanese (or Min-nan), the native language in Taiwan, instead of the Mandarin or Cantonese that we normally use. Even though my father and I speak flawless Taiwanese, we never use it in our direct, personal conversation.

So, I mildly reminded my father that because Professor Gallin is not a Taiwanese, and because he was talking to him through me, there was no need to use this particular language. My suggestion was to no avail, and my father kept speaking to me in Taiwanese. After a few more protests, I decided to ignore it, thinking that my father was probably too excited by speaking to a "foreign barbarian."

When studying in Michigan, a similar incident occurred, which rekindled my old puzzlement. One day I was in the Gallins' house when another professor came for a visit and brought with him an Austrian friend. It was late in the afternoon, and we all decided to stay for dinner at the Gallins' invitation. Over the dinner table, Professor Gallin talked to this Austrian visitor about some general things, and suddenly he spoke in Chinese to this Austrian. He said, *"Ch'ing-lai, puke-ch'i,"* which literally means, "Please help yourself; don't be polite." Unaware of this slip of the tongue, Professor Gallin continued the conversation in English.

These two incidents led me to theorize that cognition probably operates on several planes. The first and probably the most "instinctive" cognitive plane involves a person's primary language and the intimate way of life and cultural values in which one is brought up. Beyond this are the secondary and tertiary planes, which involve bodies of knowledge of foreign cultures. So when people encounter another person who does not belong to their primary cognitive community, they would probably immediately project their secondary or tertiary cognitive systems to this person, thinking that would fit the circumstance. If my hypothesis is correct, then there would be nothing unusual if we see a student majoring in Spanish who tries to communicate with a Japanese tourist in Spanish!

1. ANTHROPOLOGICAL PERSPECTIVES

WHAT NOT TO SAY

It is a custom for Chinese to say something auspicious when two newly met friends part. Phrases like "Wish you make a fortune," or "Wish you success in your business" (or study, voyage, and so on) are appropriate on such occasions. Because in traditional China marriage was often arranged by parents, it was quite common for one to greet a couple in love with a phrase like "Wish you marry soon"—meaning that this couple would convince their parents to accept their own choice. This kind of greeting is still commonly used in Taiwan, and I suspect it is also true in Hong Kong, although to a lesser extent. But, used in a different cultural context, this kind of expression may cause some problems.

Once I was invited to a party in which the American host and hostess entertained a couple of their friends and some Chinese students. We were introduced to the host's younger sister and her boyfriend—both were college students and had lived together for some time. They professed their emotional attachment toward each other and also indicated their suspicion concerning the meaning of a formal marriage: "We prefer our current arrangement," said the young man. "If two persons really love each other, there is no need to bind them together with some kind of socially sanctioned contract."

It was a pleasant evening, and about the time we were to leave, a Chinese student approached the young lovers and inadvertently said, "Wish to see you marry soon!"

He probably did not literally mean what he had said nor even realize what he had said. But the reaction from this young couple was obvious. The young man was stunned and stood there with a stiffened mouth. Blushing, the young woman protested, "But we don't believe in marriage!"

FOOD

One aspect of American culture that I have not been able to develop full appreciation of is food. Brought up in a culture whose menu contains a wide range of food varieties and flavors, I consider American food rather plain. And, worst of all, when I have American meals, I often feel full rather quickly, sometimes after just the salad. But then in a short while, I will feel hungry.

Originally, I thought that this was a phenomenon peculiar to me, mainly because I do not have a taste for American food and hence cannot eat too much of it. Believing that Chinese dishes have a better taste than anything else, I never had the slightest idea that Americans could have the same problem when eating Chinese food.

One day, my wife and I invited a few colleagues of mine over for supper. Our conversation somehow had focused on food preparation in different cultures. I jokingly remarked that even though I am an anthropologist by training, my appetite does not really match my intellectual capacity. I told them of the peculiar problem I had in eating American meals and indicated the possible reason as I saw it. On hearing that, one of our guests burst into laughter. "This is exactly the same problem I have when I come to your house for dinner," he said. "Even though I am quite full now, I will be very hungry by the time I arrive home. And I used to think this was so because of the strange taste of Chinese food!" I was surprised to find that the same opinion was shared by others.

I was puzzled by this cross-cultural eating problem. Perhaps the differences in taste are not the cause of the problem. Comparing dietary differences between American and Chinese food from another angle, I began to realize that food variety and content is the main difference between them. Chinese food contains many starchy items, such as rice, bean products, and vegetables, while American food has more meat tissue. When eating meals, the human digestive system probably has certain expectations on the quantity of specific items habitually established in the culture. People may feel full when the quota for certain food items has been met but still feel hungry for the unmet ones. For that reason, we may all have problems eating a cross-cultural meal.

A COMPLEX PHENOMENON

Human culture is a complex phenomenon: It provides a way of life, cues for actions, and logic for reasoning for the members of a cultural community. Because we frequently all too strongly adhere to our own culture, we fail to understand or appreciate the alternative ways of life. It is not an easy task to eliminate the cultural bias that hinders a mutual understanding across cultural boundaries. Even among anthropologists, who claim to study human cultures objectively, the same kind of prejudices persist, for we are products of our unique cultures as are any other human beings. Anthropologists may be credited for providing a large amount of literature describing the "other cultures." But perhaps more is needed. Other cultures may serve as a mirror for us to look at our own practices as culture-bound human beings. We need to be as critical of our own ways of thinking, value standards, and behavior patterns as we are of the cultures that we study. It is hoped that, by such a consistent practice of self-examination, we may come to understand the deeper meaning of culture on a first-hand basis.

ACKNOWLEDGEMENT

I am grateful to Professor and Mrs. Bernard Gallin, both at Michigan State University, for introducing me to anthropology and American culture. Appreciations are also due to my colleagues and associates at Iowa State University, especially those who were involved in the course, "Cross-Cultural Exploration: Introduction to the Third World." Most of my ideas and reflections were discussed and developed in that class.

REFERENCE

Dimen-Schein, Muriel. 1977. The Anthropological Imagination. New York: McGraw-Hill.

Cultural Relativism and Universal Rights

Carolyn Fluehr-Lobban

Carolyn Fluehr-Lobban is a professor of anthropology and director of the Study Abroad/International Studies program at Rhode Island College.

Cultural relativism, long a key concept in anthropology, asserts that since each culture has its own values and practices, anthropologists should not make value judgments about cultural differences. As a result, Anthropological pedagogy has stressed that the study of customs and norms should be value-free, and that the appropriate role of the anthropologist is that of observer and recorder.

Today, however, this view is being challenged by critics inside and outside the discipline, especially those who want anthropologists to take a stand on key human-rights issues. I agree that the time has come for anthropologists to become more actively engaged in safeguarding the rights of people whose lives and cultures they study.

Historically, anthropology as a discipline has declined to participate in the dialogue that produced international conventions regarding human rights. For example, in 1947, when the executive board of the American Anthropological Association withdrew from discussions that led to the "Universal Declaration of Human Rights," it did so in the belief that no such

declaration would be applicable to all human beings. But the world and anthropology have changed. Because their research involved extended interaction with people at the grassroots, anthropologists are in a unique position to lend knowledge and expertise to the international debate regarding human rights.

Doing so does not represent a complete break with the traditions of our field. After all, in the past, anthropologists did not hesitate to speak out against such reprehensible practices as Nazi genocide and South African apartheid. And they have testified in U.S. courts against government rules that impinge on the religious traditions or sacred lands of Native Americans, decrying government policies that treat groups of people unjustly.

> *"The exchange of ideas across cultures is already fostering a growing acceptance of the universal nature of some human rights, regardless of cultural differences."*

However, other practices that violate individual rights or oppress particular groups have not been denounced.

Anthropologists generally have not spoken out, for example, against the practice in many cultures of female circumcision, which critics call a mutilation of women. They have been unwilling to pass judgment on such forms of culturally based homicide as the killing of infants or the aged. Some have withheld judgment on acts of communal violence, such as clashes between Hindus and Muslims in India or Tutsis and Hutus in Rwanda, perhaps because the animosities between those groups are of long standing.

Moreover, as a practical matter, organized anthropology's refusal to participate in drafting the 1947 human-rights declaration has meant that anthropologists have not had much of a role in drafting later human-rights statements, such as the United Nations' "Convention on the Elimination of All Forms of Discrimination Against Women," approved in 1979. In many international forums discussing women's rights, participants have specifically rejected using cultural relativism as a barrier to improving women's lives.

The issue of violence against women throws the perils of cultural relativism into stark relief. Following the lead of human-rights advocates, a growing number of anthropologists and others are coming to recognize that violence against women should be acknowledged as a violation of a basic human right to be free from harm. They believe that such violence cannot be excused or justified on cultural grounds.

Let me refer to my own experience. For nearly 25 years, I have conducted research in the Sudan, one of the African countries where the practice of female circumcision is widespread, affecting the vast majority of females in the northern Sudan. Chronic infections are a common result, and sexual intercourse and childbirth are rendered difficult and painful. However, cultural ideology in the Sudan holds that an uncircumcised woman is not respectable, and few families would risk their daughter's chances of marrying by not having her circumcised. British colonial officials outlawed the practice in 1946, but this served only to make it surreptitious and thus more dangerous. Women found it harder to get treatment for mistakes or for side effects of the illegal surgery.

"The issue of violence against women throws the perils of cultural relativism into stark relief."

For a long time I felt trapped between, on one side, my anthropologist's understanding of the custom and of the sensitivities about it among the people with whom I was working, and, on the other, the largely feminist campaign in the West to eradicate what critics see as a "barbaric" custom. To ally myself with Western feminists and condemn female circumcision seemed to me to be a betrayal of the value system and culture of the Sudan, which I had come to understand. But as I was asked over the years to comment on female circumcision because of my expertise in the Sudan, I came to realize how deeply I felt that the practice was harmful and wrong.

In 1993, female circumcision was one of the practices deemed harmful by delegates at the international Human Rights Conference in Vienna. During their discussions, they came to view circumcision as a violation of the rights of children as well as of the women who suffer its consequences throughout life. Those discussions made me realize that there was a moral agenda larger than myself, larger than Western culture or the culture of the northern Sudan or my discipline. I decided to join colleagues from other disciplines and cultures in speaking out against the practice.

Some cultures are beginning to change, although cause and effect are difficult to determine. Women's associations in the Ivory Coast are calling for an end to female circumcision. In Egypt, the Cairo Institute of Human Rights has reported the first publicly acknowledged marriage of an uncircumcised woman. In the United States, a Nigerian woman recently was granted asylum on the ground that her returning to her country would result in the forcible circumcision of her daughter, which was deemed a violation of the girl's human rights.

To be sure, it is not easy to achieve consensus concerning the point at which cultural practices cross the line and become violations of human rights. But it is important that scholars and human-rights activists discuss the issue. Some examples of when the line is crossed may be clearer than others. The action of a Japanese wife who feels honor-bound to commit suicide because of the shame of her husband's infidelity can be explained and perhaps justified by the traditional code of honor in Japanese society. However, when she decides to take the lives of her children as well, she is committing murder, which may be easier to condemn than suicide.

What about "honor" killings of sisters and daughters accused of sexual misconduct in some Middle Eastern and Mediterranean societies? Some anthropologists have explained this practice in culturally relativist terms, saying that severe disruptions of the moral order occur when sexual impropriety is alleged or takes place. To restore the social equilibrium and avoid feuds, the local culture required the shedding of blood to wash away the shame of sexual dishonor. The practice of honor killings, which victimizes mainly women, has been defended in some local courts as less serious than premeditated murder, because it stems from long-standing cultural traditions. While some judges have agreed, anthropologists should see a different picture: a pattern of cultural discrimination against women.

As the issue of domestic violence shows, we need to explore the ways that we balance individual and cultural rights. The "right" of a man to discipline, slap, hit, or beat his wife (and often, by extension, his children) is widely recognized across many cultures in which male dominance is an accepted fact of life. Indeed, the issue of domestic violence has only recently been added to the international human-rights agenda, with the addition of women's rights to the list of basic human rights at the Vienna conference.

The fact that domestic violence is being openly discussed and challenged in some societies (the United States is among the leaders) helps to encourage dialogue in societies in which domestic violence has been a taboo subject. This dialogue is relatively new, and no clear principles have emerged. But anthropologists could inform and enrich the discussion, using their knowledge of family and community life in different cultures.

Cases of genocide may allow the clearest insight into where the line between local culture and universal morality lies. Many anthropologists have urged the Brazilian and Venezuelan governments to stop gold miners from slaughtering the Yanomami people, who are battling the encroachment of miners on their rain forests. Other practices that harm individuals or categories of people (such as the elderly, women, and enslaved or formerly enslaved people) may not represent genocide *per se,* and thus may present somewhat harder questions about the morality of traditional practices. We need to focus on the harm done, however, and not on the scale of the abuse. We need to be sensitive to cultural differences but not allow them to override widely recognized human rights.

The exchange of ideas across cultures is already fostering a growing acceptance of the universal nature of some human rights, regardless of cultural differences. The right of individuals to be free from harm or the threat of harm, and the right of cultural minorities to exist freely within states, are just two examples of rights that are beginning to be universally recognized—although not universally applied.

Fortunately, organized anthropology is beginning to change its attitude toward cultural relativism and human rights. The theme of the 1994 convention of the American Anthropological Association was human rights. At the sessions organized around the topic, many anthropologists said they no longer were absolutely committed to cultural relativism. The association has responded to the changing attitude among its members by forming a Commission for Human Rights, charged with developing a specifically anthropological perspective on those rights, and with challenging violations and promoting education about them.

Nevertheless, many anthropologists continue to express strong support for cultural relativism. One of the most contentious issues arises from the fundamental question: What authority do we Westerners have to impose our own concept of universal rights on the rest of humanity? It is true that Western ideas of human rights have so far dominated international discourse. On the other hand, the cultural relativists' argument is often used by repressive governments to deflect international criticism of their abuse of their citizens. At the very least, anthropologists need to condemn such misuse of cultural relativism, even if it means that they may be denied permission to do research in the country in question.

Personally, I would go further: I believe that we should not let the concept of relativism stop us from using national and international forums to examine ways to protect the lives and dignity of people in every culture. Because of our involvement in local societies, anthropologists could provide early warnings of abuses—for example, by reporting data to international human-rights organizations, and by joining the dialogue at international conferences. When there is a choice between defending human rights and defending cultural relativism, anthropologists should choose to protect and promote human rights. We cannot just be bystanders.

Culture and Communication

Anthropologists are interested in all aspects of human behavior and how they interrelate with each other. Language is a form of such behavior (albeit primarily verbal behavior) and, therefore, worthy of study. It is patterned and passed down from one generation to the next through learning, not instinct. In keeping with the idea that language is integral to human social interaction, it has long been recognized that human communication through language is by its nature different from the kind of communication found among other animals. Central to this difference is the fact that humans communicate abstractly, with symbols that have meaning independent of the immediate sensory experiences of either the sender or receiver of messages. Thus, for instance, humans are able to refer to the future and the past instead of just the here and now.

Recent experiments have shown that anthropoid apes can be taught a small portion of Ameslan (American Sign Language). It must be remembered, however, that their very rudimentary ability has to be tapped by painstaking human effort, and that the degree of difference between apes and humans serves only to emphasize the peculiarly human need for and development of language.

Just as the abstract quality of symbols lifts our thoughts beyond immediate sense perception, it also inhibits our ability to think about and convey the full meaning of our personal experience. No categorical term can do justice to its referents—the variety of forms to which the term refers. The degree to which this is an obstacle to clarity of thought and communication relates to the degree of abstraction in the symbols involved. The word "chair," for instance, would not present much difficulty, since it has objective referents. However, consider the trouble we have in thinking and communicating with words whose referents are not tied to immediate sense perception—words such as "freedom," "democracy," and "justice." At best, the likely result is symbolic confusion: an inability to think or communicate in objectively definable symbols. At worst, language may be used to purposefully obfuscate, as William Lutz shows in "Language, Appearance, and Reality: Doublespeak in 1984."

A related issue has to do with the fact that languages differ as to what is relatively easy to express within the restrictions of their particular vocabularies. Thus, although a given language may not have enough words to cope with a new situation or a new field of activity, the typical solution is to invent words or to borrow them. In this way, it may be said that any language can be used to teach anything. This point is illustrated by Laura Bohannan's attempt to convey the "true" meaning of Shakespeare's *Hamlet* to the West African Tiv (see "Shakespeare in the Bush"). Much of her task was devoted to finding the most appropriate words in the Tiv language to convey her Western thoughts. At least part of her failure was due to the fact that some of the words are just not there, and her inventions were unacceptable to the Tiv.

Given the potential diversity of linguistic expression, it is surprising to find a case of a single language displacing hundreds, a phenomenon that is explained by Jared Diamond in "Empire of Diversity."

Finally, as Deborah Tannen, in "Why Don't You Say What You Mean?" points out, there are subtleties to language that cannot be found in a dictionary and whose meaning can only be interpreted in the context of the social situation.

Taken collectively, the articles in this unit show how symbolic confusion may occur between individuals or groups as well as demonstrate the tremendous potential of recent research to enhance effective communication among all of us.

Looking Ahead: Challenge Questions

What common strategies are used throughout the world to overcome linguistic barriers?

How can language restrict our thought processes?

Under what circumstances may indirectness convey more security and power than directness?

In what ways is communication difficult in a cross-cultural situation?

Under what circumstances does one language displace another?

What kinds of messages are transmitted through nonverbal communication?

How has this section enhanced your ability to communicate more effectively?

UNIT 2

Language, Appearance, and Reality: Doublespeak in 1984

William D. Lutz

William D. Lutz, chair of the Department of English at Rutgers University, is also chair of the National Council of Teachers of English (NCTE) Committee on Public Doublespeak and editor of the Quarterly Review of Doublespeak.

There are at least four kinds of doublespeak. The first kind is the euphemism, a word or phrase that is designed to avoid a harsh or distasteful reality. When a euphemism is used out of sensitivity for the feelings of someone or out of concern for a social or cultural taboo, it is not doublespeak. For example, we express grief that someone has *passed away* because we do not want to say to a grieving person, "I'm sorry your father is dead." The euphemism *passed away* functions here not just to protect the feelings of another person but also to communicate our concern over that person's feelings during a period of mourning.

However, when a euphemism is used to mislead or deceive, it becomes doublespeak. For example, the U.S. State Department decided in 1984 that in its annual reports on the status of human rights in countries around the world it would no longer use the word *killing*. Instead, it uses the phrase *unlawful or arbitrary deprivation of life*. Thus the State Department avoids discussing the embarrassing situation of the government-sanctioned killings in countries that are supported by the United States. This use of language constitutes doublespeak because it is designed to mislead, to cover up the unpleasant. Its real intent is at variance with its apparent intent. It is language designed to alter our perception of reality.

A second kind of doublespeak is jargon, the specialized language of a trade, profession, or similar group. It is the specialized language of doctors, lawyers, engineers, educators, or car mechanics. Jargon can serve an important and useful function. Within a group, jargon allows members of the group to communicate with each other clearly, efficiently, and quickly. Indeed, it is a mark of membership in the group to be able to use and understand the group's jargon. For example, lawyers speak of an *involuntary conversion* of property when discussing the loss or destruction of property through theft, accident, or condemnation. When used by lawyers in a legal situation, such jargon is a legitimate use of language, since all members of the group can be expected to understand the term.

However, when a member of the group uses jargon to communicate with a person outside the group, and uses it knowing that the nonmember does not understand such language, then there is doublespeak. For example, a number of years ago a commercial airliner crashed on takeoff, killing three passengers, injuring twenty-one others, and destroying the airplane, a 727. The insured value of the airplane was greater than its book value, so the airline made a profit of three million dollars on the destroyed airplane. But the airline had two problems: it did not want to talk about one of its airplanes crashing and it had to account for the three million dollars when it issued its annual report to its stockholders. The airline solved these problems by inserting a footnote in its annual report explaining that this three million dollars was due to "the involuntary conversion of a 727." Note that airline officials could thus claim to have explained the crash of the airplane and the subsequent three million dollars in profit. However, since most stockholders in the company, and indeed most of the general public, are not familiar with legal jargon, the use of such jargon constitutes doublespeak.

A third kind of doublespeak is gobbledygook or bureaucratese. Basically, such doublespeak is simply a matter of piling on words, of overwhelming the audience with words, the bigger the better. For example, when Alan Greenspan was chairman of the President's Council of Economic Advisors, he made this statement when testifying before a Senate committee:

It is a tricky problem to find the particular calibration in timing that would be appropriate to stem the acceleration in risk premiums created by falling incomes without prematurely aborting the decline in the inflation-generated risk premiums.

Did Alan Greenspan's audience really understand what he was saying? Did he believe his statement really explained anything? Perhaps there is some meaning beneath all those words, but it would take some time to search it out. This seems to be language that pretends to communicate but does not.

The fourth kind of doublespeak is inflated language. Inflated language designed to make the ordinary seem extraordinary, the common, uncommon; to make everyday things seem impressive; to give an air of importance to people, situations, or things that would not normally be considered important; to make the simple seem complex. With this kind of language, car mechanics become *automotive internists,* elevator operators become members of the *vertical transportation corps,* used cars become not just *preowned* but *experienced cars.* When the Pentagon uses the phrase *pre-emptive counterattack* to mean that American forces attacked first, or when it uses the phrase *engage the enemy on all sides* to describe an ambush of American troops, or when it uses the phrase *tactical redeployment* to describe a retreat by American troops, it is using doublespeak. The electronics company that sells the television set with *non-multicolor capability* is also using the doublespeak of inflated language.

Doublespeak is not a new use of language peculiar to the politics or economics of the twentieth century. Thucydides in *The Peloponnesian War* wrote that

revolution thus ran its course from city to city. . . . Words had to change their ordinary meanings and to take those which were now given them. Reckless audacity came to be considered the courage of a loyal ally; prudent hesitation, specious cowardice; moderation was held to be a cloak for unmanliness; ability to see all sides of a question, inaptness to act on any. Frantic violence become the attribute of manliness; cautious plotting, a justifiable means of self-defense. The advocate of extreme measures was always trustworthy; his opponent, a man to be suspected.[1]

Caesar in his account of the Gallic Wars described his brutal conquest as "pacifying" Gaul. Doublespeak has a long history.

Military doublespeak seems always to have been with us. In 1947 the name of the War Department was changed to the more pleasing if misleading *Defense Department.* During the Vietnam War the American public learned that it was an *incursion,* not an invasion; a *protective reaction strike* or a *limited duration protective reaction strike* or *air support,* not bombing; and *incontinent ordinance,* not bombs and artillery shells, fell on civilians. This use of language continued with the invasion of Grenada, which was conducted not by the United States Army, Navy, or Air Force, but by the Caribbean Peace Keeping Forces. Indeed, according to the Pentagon, it was not an invasion of Grenada, but a *predawn, vertical insertion.* And it wasn't that the armed forces lacked intelligence data on Grenada before the invasion, it was just that "we were not micromanaging Grenada intelligencewise until about that time frame." In today's army forces, it's not a shovel but a *combat emplacement evacuator,* not a toothpick but a *wood interdental stimulator,* not a pencil but a portable, handheld communications inscriber, not a bullet hole but a *ballistically induced aperture in the subcutaneous environment.*

Members of the military and politicians are not the only ones who use doublespeak. People in all parts of society use it. Take educators, for example. On some college campuses what was once the Department of Physical Education is now the *Department of Human Kinetics* or the *College of Applied Life Studies.* Home Economics is now the *School of Human Resources and Family Studies.* College campuses no longer have libraries but *learning resource centers.* Those are not desks in the classroom, they are *pupil stations.* Teachers—*classroom managers* who apply an *action plan* to a *knowledge base*—are concerned with the *basic fundamentals,* which are *inexorably linked* to the *education user's* (not student's) *time-on-task.* Students don't take tests; now it is *criterion referencing testing* which measures whether a student has achieved the *operational curricular objectives.* A school system in Pennsylvania uses the following grading system on report cards: "no effort, less than minimal effort, minimal effort, more than minimal effort, less than full effort, full effort, better than full effort, effort increasing, effort decreasing." Some college students in New York come from *economically nonaffluent* families, while the coach at a Southern university wasn't fired, "he just won't be asked to continue in that job." An article in a scholarly journal suggests teaching students three approaches to writing to help them become better writers: "concretization of goals, procedural facilitation, and modeling planning." An article on family relationships entitled "Familial Love and Intertemporal Optimality" observes that "an altruistic utility function promotes intertemporal efficiency. However, altruism creates an externality that implies that satisfying the condition for efficiency, does not insure intertemporal optimality." A research report issued by the U.S. Office of Education contains this sentence: "In other words, feediness is the shared information between toputness, where toputness is at a time just prior to the inputness." Educations contributes more than its share to current doublespeak.

The world of business has produced large amounts of doublespeak. If an airplane crash is one of the worst things that can happen to an airline company, a recall of automobiles because of a safety defect is one of the worst things that can happen to an automobile company. So a few years ago, when one of the three largest car companies in America had to recall two of its models to correct mechanical defects, the company sent a letter to all those who had bought those models. In its letter, the company said that the rear axle bearings of the cars "can deteriorate" and that "continued driving with a failed bearing could result in disengagement of the axle shaft and adversely affect vehicle control." This is the language of nonresponsibility. What are "mechanical deficiencies"—poor design, bad workmanship? If they do, what causes the deterioration? Note that "continued driving" is the subject of the sentence and suggests that it is not the company's poor manufacturing which is at fault but the driver who persists in driving. Note, too, "failed bearing," which implies that the bearing failed, not the company. Finally, "adversely affect vehicle control" means nothing more than that the driver could lose control of the car and get killed.

If we apply Hugh Rank's criteria for examining such language, we quickly discover the doublespeak here. What the car company should be saying to its customers is that the car the company sold them has a serious defect which should be corrected immediately—otherwise the customer runs the risk of being killed. But the reader of the letter must find this message beneath the doublespeak the company has used to disguise the harshness of its message. We will probably never know how many of the customers never brought their cars in for the necessary repairs because they did not think the problem serious enough to warrant the inconvenience involved.

When it come time to fire employees, business has produced more than enough doublespeak to deal with the unpleasant situation. Employees are, of course, never fired. They are *selected out, placed out, non-retained, released, dehired, non-renewed.* A corporation will *eliminate the redundancies in the human resources area,* assign *candidates for derecruitment* to a *mobility pool, revitalize the department* by placing executives on *special assignment, enhance the efficiency of operations, streamline the field sales organization,* or *further rationalize marketing efforts.* The reality behind all this doublespeak is that companies are firing employees, but no one wants the stockholders, public, or competition to know that times are tough and people have to go.

Recently the oil industry has been hard hit by declining sales and a surplus of oil. Because of *reduced demand for product,* which results in *spare refining capacity* and problems in *down-stream operations,* oil companies have been forced to *re-evaluate and consolidate their operations* and take *appropriate cost reduction actions,* in order to *enhance the efficiency of operations,* which has meant the *elimination of marginal outlets, accelerating the divestment program,* and the *disposition of low throughput marketing units.* What this doublespeak really means is that oil companies have fired employees, cut back on expenses, and closed gas stations and oil refineries because there's surplus of oil and people are not buying as much gas and oil as in the past.

One corporation faced with declining business sent a memorandum to its employees advising them that the company's "business plans are under revi-

sion and now reflect a more moderate approach toward our operating and capital programs." The result of this "more moderate approach" is a "surplus of professional/technical employees." To "assist in alleviating the surplus, selected professional and technical employees" have been "selected to participate" in a "Voluntary Program." Note that individuals were selected to "resign voluntarily." What this memorandum means, of course, is that expenses must be cut because of declining business, so employees will have to be fired.

It is rare to read that the stock market *fell.* Members of the financial community prefer to say that the stock market *retreated, eased, made a technical adjustment* or a *technical correction,* or perhaps that *prices were off due to profit taking,* or *off in light trading,* or *lost ground.* But the stock market never falls, not if stockbrokers have their say. As a side note, it is interesting to observe that the stock market never rises because of a *technical adjustment* or *correction,* nor does it ever *ease* upwards.

The business sections of newspapers, business magazines, corporate reports, and executive speeches are filled with words and phrases such as *marginal rates of substitution, equilibrium price, getting off margin, distribution coalition, non-performing assets,* and *encompassing organizations.* Much of this is jargon or inflated language designed to make the simple seem complex, but there are other examples of business doublespeak that mislead, that are designed to avoid a harsh reality. What should we make of such expressions as *negative deficit* or *revenue excesses* for profit, *invest in* for buy, *price enhancement* or *price adjustment* for price increase, *shortfall* for a mistake in planning or *period of accelerated negative growth* or *negative economic growth* for recession?

Business doublespeak often attempts to give substance to wind, to make ordinary actions seem complex. Executives *operate* in *timeframes* within the *context* of which a *task force* will serve as the proper *conduit* for all the necessary *input* to *program a scenario* that,

within acceptable *parameters,* and with the proper *throughput,* will *generate* the *maximum output* for a *print out* of *zero defect terminal objectives* that will *enhance the bottom line.*

There are instances, however, where doublespeak becomes more than amusing, more than a cause for a weary shake of the head. When the anesthetist turned the wrong knob during a Caesarean delivery and killed the mother and unborn child, the hospital called it a *therapeutic misadventure.* The Pentagon calls the neutron bomb "an efficient nuclear weapon that eliminates an enemy with a minimum degree of damage to friendly territory." The Pentagon also calls expected civilian casualties in a nuclear war *collateral damage.* And it was the Central Intelligence Agency which during the Vietnam War created the phrase *eliminate with extreme prejudice* to replace the more direct verb *kill.*

Identifying doublespeak can at times be difficult. For example, on July 27, 1981, President Ronald Reagan said in a speech televised to the American public: "I will not stand by and see those of you who are dependent on Social Security deprived of the benefits you've worked so hard to earn. You will continue to receive your checks in the full amount due you." This speech had been billed as President Reagan's position on Social Security, a subject of much debate at the time. After the speech, public opinion polls revealed that the great majority of the public believed that President Reagan had affirmed his support for Social Security and that he would not support cuts in benefits. However, five days after the speech, on July 31, 1981, an article in the *Philadelphia Inquirer* quoted White House spokesman David Gergen as saying that President Reagan's words had been "carefully chosen." What President Reagan did mean, according to Gergen, was that he was reserving the right to decide who was "dependent" on those benefits, who had "earned" them, and who, therefore, was "due" them.[2]

The subsequent remarks of David Gergen reveal the real intent of President Reagan as opposed to his apparent intent. Thus Hugh Rank's criteria for analyzing language to determine whether it is doublespeak, when applied in light of David Gergen's remarks, reveal the doublespeak of President Reagan. Here indeed is the insincerity of which Orwell wrote. Here, too, is the gap between the speaker's real and declared aim.

In 1982 the Republican National Committee sponsored a television advertisement which pictured an elderly, folksy postman delivering Social Security checks "with the 7.4% cost-of-living raise that President Reagan promised." The postman then added that "he promised that raise and he kept his promise, in spite of those sticks-in-the-mud who tried to keep him from doing what we elected him to do." The commercial was, in fact, deliberately misleading. The cost-of-living increases had been provided automatically by law since 1975, and President Reagan tried three times to roll them back or delay them but was overruled by congressional opposition. When these discrepancies were pointed out to an official of the Republican National Committee, he called the commercial "inoffensive" and added, "Since when is a commercial supposed to be accurate? Do women really smile when they clean their ovens?"

Again, applying Hugh Rank's criteria to this advertisement reveals the doublespeak in it once we know the facts of past actions by President Reagan. Moreover, the official for the Republican National Committee assumes that all advertisements, whether for political candidates or commercial products, are lies, or in his doublespeak term, *inaccurate*. Thus, the real intent of the advertisement was to mislead while the apparent purpose was to inform the public of President Reagan's position on possible cuts in Social Security benefits. Again there is insincerity, and again there is a gap between the speaker's real and declared aims.

In 1981 Secretary of State Alexander Haig testified before congressional committees about the murder of three American nuns and a Catholic lay worker in El Salvador. The four women had been raped and shot at close range, and there was clear evidence that the crime had been committed by soldiers of the Salvadoran government. Before the House Foreign Affairs Committee, Secretary Haig said,

I'd like to suggest to you that some of the investigations would lead one to believe that perhaps the vehicle the nuns were riding in may have tried to run a roadblock, or may accidentally have been perceived to have been doing so, and there'd been an exchange of fire and then perhaps those who inflicted the casualties sought to cover it up. And this could have been at a very low level of both competence and motivation in the context of the issue itself. But the facts on this are not clear enough for anyone to draw a definitive conclusion.

The next day, before the Senate Foreign Relations Committee, Secretary Haig claimed that press reports on his previous testimony were inaccurate. When Senator Claiborne Pell asked whether Secretary Haig was suggesting the possibility that "the nuns may have run through a roadblock." Secretary Haig replied, "You mean that they tried to violate . . .? Not at all, no, not at all. My heavens! The dear nuns who raised me in my parochial schooling would forever isolate me from their affections and respect." When Senator Pell asked Secretary Haig, "Did you mean that the nuns were firing at the people, or what did 'exchange of fire' mean?" Secretary Haig replied, "I haven't met any pistol-packing nuns in my day, Senator. What I meant was that if one fellow starts shooting, then the next thing you know they all panic." Thus did the secretary of state of the United States explain official government policy on the murder of four American citizens in a foreign land.

Secretary Haig's testimony implies that the women were in some way responsible for their own fate. By using such vague wording as "would lead one to believe" and "may accidentally have been perceived to have been," he avoids any direct assertion. The use of "inflicted the casualties" not only avoids using the word *kill* but also implies that at the worst the kill-ings were accidental or justifiable. The result of this testimony is that the secretary of state has become an apologist for murder. This is indeed language in defense of the indefensible; language designed to make lies sound truthful and murder respectable; language designed to give an appearance of solidity to pure wind.

These last three examples of doublespeak should make it clear that doublespeak is not the product of careless language or sloppy thinking. Indeed, most doublespeak is the product of clear thinking and is language carefully designed and constructed to appear to communicate when in fact it does not. It is language designed not to lead but to mislead. It is language designed to distort reality and corrupt the mind. It is not a tax increase but *revenue enhancement* or *tax base broadening,* so how can you complain about higher taxes? It is not acid rain, but *poorly buffered precipitation,* so don't worry about all those dead trees. That is not the Mafia in Atlantic City, New Jersey, those are *members of a career offender cartel,* so don't worry about the influence of organized crime in the city. The judge was not addicted to the pain-killing drug he was taking, it was just that the drug had "established an inter-relationship with the body, such that if the drug is removed precipitously, there is a reaction," so don't worry that his decisions might have been influenced by his drug addiction. It's not a Titan II nuclear-armed, intercontinental ballistic missile with a warhead 630 times more powerful than the atomic bomb dropped on Hiroshima, it is just a *very large, potentially disruptive re-entry system,* so don't worry about the threat of nuclear destruction. It is not a neutron bomb but a *radiation enhancement device,* so don't worry about escalating the arms race. It is not an invasion but a *rescue mission,* or a *predawn vertical insertion,* so don't worry about any violations of United States or international law.

Doublespeak has become so common in our everyday lives that we fail to notice it. We do not protest when we are asked to check our packages at the desk "for our convenience" when it is not for our convenience at all but for someone else's convenience. We see advertisements for *genuine imitation leather, virgin vinyl,* or *real counterfeit diamonds* and do not question the language or the supposed quality of the product. We do not speak of slums or ghettos but of the *inner city* or *substandard housing where the disadvantaged* live and thus avoid talking about the poor who have to live in filthy, poorly heated, ramshackle apartments or houses. Patients do not die in the hospital; it is just *negative patient care outcome.*

Doublespeak which calls cab drivers *urban transportation specialists,* elevator operators *members of the vertical transportation corps,* and automobile mechanics *automotive internists* can be considered humorous and relatively harmless. However, doublespeak which calls a fire in a nuclear reactor building *rapid oxidation,* an explosion in a nuclear power plant an *energetic disassembly,* the illegal overthrow of a legitimate administration *destablizing a government,* and lies *inoperative statements* is language which attempts to avoid responsibility, which attempts to make the bad seem good, the negative appear positive, something unpleasant appear attractive, and which seems to communicate but does not. It is language designed to alter our perception of reality and corrupt our minds. Such language does not provide us with the tools needed to develop and preserve civilization. Such language breeds suspicion, cynicism, distrust, and, ultimately, hostility.

Doublespeak is insidious because it can infect and ultimately destroy the function of language, which is communication between people and social groups. If this corrupting process does occur, it can have serious conse-

quences in a country that depends upon an informed electorate to make decisions in selecting candidates for office and deciding issues of public policy. After a while we may really believe that politicians don't lie but only *misspeak,* that illegal acts are merely *inappropriate actions,* that fraud and criminal conspiracy are just *miscertification.* And if we really believe that we understand such language, then the world of *Nineteen Eighty-four* with its control of reality through language is not far away.

The consistent use of doublespeak can have serious and far-reaching consequences beyond the obvious ones. The pervasive use of doublespeak can spread so that doublespeak becomes the coin of the political realm with speakers and listeners convinced that they really understand such language. President Jimmy Carter could call the aborted raid to free the hostages in Tehran in 1980 an "incomplete success" and really believe that he had made a statement that clearly communicated with the American public. So, too, President Ronald Reagan could say in 1985 that "ultimately our security and our hopes for success at the arms reduction talks hinge on the determination that we show here to continue our program to rebuild and refortify our defenses" and really believe that greatly increasing the amount of money spent building new weapons will lead to a reduction in the number of weapons in the world.

The task of English teachers is to teach not just the effective use of language but respect for language as well. Those who use language to conceal or prevent or corrupt thought must be called to account. Only by teaching respect for and love of language can teachers of English instill in students

the sense of outrage they should experience when they encounter doublespeak. But before students can experience that outrage, they must first learn to use language effectively, to understand its beauty and power. Only then will we begin to make headway in the fight against doublespeak, for only by using language well will we come to appreciate the perversion inherent in doublespeak.

In his book *The Miracle of Language,* Charlton Laird notes that

language is . . . the most important tool man ever devised. . . . Language is [man's] basic tool. It is the tool more than any other with which he makes his living, makes his home, makes his life. As man becomes more and more a social being, as the world becomes more and more a social community, communication grows ever more imperative. And language is the basis of communication. Language is also the instrument with which we think, and thinking is the rarest and most needed commodity in the world.[3]

In this opinion Laird echoes Orwell's comment that "if thought corrupts language, language can also corrupt thought."[4] Both men have given us a legacy of respect for language, a respect that should prompt us to cry "Enough!" when we encounter doublespeak. The greatest honor we can do Charlton Laird is to continue to have the greatest respect of language in all its manifestations, for, as Laird taught us, language is a miracle.

NOTES AND REFERENCES

1. Thucydides, *The Peloponnesian Way,* 3.82.
2. David Hess, "Reagan's Language on Benefits Confused, Angered Many," *Philadelphia Inquirer,* July 31, 1981, p. 6-A.
3. Charlton Laird, *The Miracle of Language* (New York: Fawcett, Premier Books, 1953), p. 224.
4. Orwell, *The Collected Essays,* 4:137.

Why Don't You Say What You Mean?

Directness is not necessarily logical or effective. Indirectness is not necessarily manipulative or insecure.

Deborah Tannen

Deborah Tannen is University Professor of Linguistics at Georgetown University.

A university president was expecting a visit from a member of the board of trustees. When her secretary buzzed to tell her that the board member had arrived, she left her office and entered the reception area to greet him. Before ushering him into her office, she handed her secretary a sheet of paper and said: "I've just finished drafting this letter. Do you think you could type it right away? I'd like to get it out before lunch. And would you please do me a favor and hold all calls while I'm meeting with Mr. Smith?"

When they sat down behind the closed door of her office, Mr. Smith began by telling her that he thought she had spoken inappropriately to her secretary. "Don't forget," he said. "*You're* the president!"

Putting aside the question of the appropriateness of his admonishing the president on her way of speaking, it is revealing—and representative of many Americans' assumptions—that the indirect way in which the university president told her secretary what to do struck him as self-deprecating. He took it as evidence that she didn't think she had the right to make demands of her secretary. He probably thought he was giving her a needed pep talk, bolstering her self-confidence.

I challenge the assumption that talking in an indirect way necessarily reveals powerlessness, lack of self-confidence or anything else about the character of the speaker. Indirectness is a fundamental element in human communication. It is also one of the elements that varies most from one culture to another, and one that can cause confusion and misunderstanding when speakers have different habits with regard to using it. I also want to dispel the assumption that American women tend to be more indirect than American men. Women and men are both indirect, but in addition to differences associated with their backgrounds—regional, ethnic and class—they tend to be indirect in different situations and in different ways.

At work, we need to get others to do things, and we all have different ways of accomplishing this. Any individual's ways will vary depending on who is being addressed—a boss, a peer or a subordinate. At one extreme are bald commands. At the other are requests so indirect that they don't sound like requests at all, but are just a statement of need or a description of a situation. People with direct styles of asking others to do things perceive indirect requests—if they perceive them as requests at all—as manipulative. But this is often just a way of blaming others for our discomfort with their styles.

The indirect style is no more manipulative than making a telephone call, asking "Is Rachel there?" and expecting whoever answers the phone to put Rachel on. Only a child is likely to answer "Yes" and continue holding the phone—not out of orneriness but because of inexperience with the conventional meaning of the questions. (A mischievous adult might do it to tease.) Those who feel that indirect orders are illogical or manipulative do not recognize the conventional nature of indirect requests.

Issuing orders indirectly can be the prerogative of those in power. Imagine, for example, a master who says "It's cold in here" and expects a servant to make a move to close a window, while a servant who says the same thing is not likely to see his employer rise to correct the situation and make him more comfortable. Indeed, a Frenchman raised in Brittany tells me that his family never gave bald commands to their servants but always communicated orders in indirect and highly polite ways. This pattern renders less surprising the finding of David Bellinger and Jean Berko Gleason that fathers' speech to their young children had a higher incidence than mothers' of both direct imperatives like "Turn the bolt with the wrench" *and* indirect orders like "The wheel is going to fall off."

The use of indirectness can hardly be understood without the cross-cul-

From *The New York Times Magazine*, August 28, 1994, pp. 46-49. Adapted from *Talking 9 to 5: How Women's and Men's Conversational Styles Affect Who Gets Heard, Who Gets Credit, and What Gets Done at Work* by Deborah Tannen, Ph.D. © 1994 by Deborah Tannen, Ph.D. Reprinted by permission of William Morrow & Company, Inc.

tural perspective. Many Americans find it self-evident that directness is logical and aligned with power while indirectness is akin to dishonesty and reflects subservience. But for speakers raised in most of the world's cultures, varieties of indirectness are the norm in communication. This is the pattern found by a Japanese sociolinguist, Kunihiko Harada, in his analysis of a conversation he recorded between a Japanese boss and a subordinate.

The markers of superior status were clear. One speaker was a Japanese man in his late 40's who managed the local branch of a Japanese private school in the United States. His conversational partner was Japanese-American woman in her early 20's who worked at the school. By virtue of his job, his age and his native fluency in the language being taught, the man was in the superior position. Yet when he addressed the woman, he frequently used polite language and almost always used indirectness. For example, he had tried and failed to find a photography store that would make a black-and-white print from a color negative for a brochure they were producing. He let her know that he wanted her to take over the task by stating the situation and allowed her to volunteer to do it: (This is a translation of the Japanese conversation.)

On this matter, that, that, on the leaflet? This photo, I'm thinking of changing it to black-and-white and making it clearer. . . . I went to a photo shop and asked them. They said they didn't do black-and-white. I asked if they knew any place that did. They said they didn't know. They weren't very helpful, but anyway, a place must be found, the negative brought to it, the picture developed.

Harada observes, "Given the fact that there are some duties to be performed and that there are two parties present, the subordinate is supposed to assume that those are his or her obligation." It was precisely because of his higher status that the boss was free to choose whether to speak formally or informally, to assert his power or to play it down and build rapport—an option not available to the subordinate,

who would have seemed cheeky if she had chosen a style that enhanced friendliness and closeness.

The same pattern was found by a Chinese sociolinguist, Yuling Pan, in a meeting of officials involved in a neighborhood youth program. All spoke in ways that reflected their place in the hierarchy. A subordinate addressing a superior always spoke in a deferential way, but a superior addressing a subordinate could either be authoritarian, demonstrating his power, or friendly, establishing rapport. The ones in power had the option of choosing which style to use. In this spirit, I have been told by people who prefer their bosses to give orders indirectly that those who issue bald commands must be pretty insecure; otherwise why would they have to bolster their egos by throwing their weight around?

I am not inclined to accept that those who give orders directly are really insecure and powerless, any more than I want to accept that judgment of those who give indirect orders. The conclusion to be drawn is that ways of talking should not be taken as obvious evidence of inner psychological states like insecurity or lack of confidence. Considering the many influences on conversational style, individuals have a wide range of ways of getting things done and expressing their emotional states. Personality characteristics like insecurity cannot be linked to ways of speaking in an automatic, self-evident way.

Those who expect orders to be given indirectly are offended when they come unadorned. One woman said that when her boss gives her instructions, she feels she should click her heels, salute, and say "Yes, Boss!" His directions strike her as so imperious as to border on the militaristic. Yet I received a letter from a man telling me that indirect orders were a fundamental part of his military training: He wrote:

Many years ago, when I was in the Navy, I was training to be a radio technician. One class I was in was taught by a chief radioman, a regular Navy man who had been to sea, and who was then in his third hitch. The

students, about 20 of us, were fresh out of boot camp, with no sea duty and little knowledge of real Navy life. One day in class the chief said it was hot in the room. The students didn't react, except to nod in agreement. The chief repeated himself: "It's hot in this room." Again there was no reaction from the students.

Then the chief explained. He wasn't looking for agreement or discussion from us. When he said that the room was hot, he expected us to do something about it—like opening the window. He tried it one more time, and this time all of us left our workbenches and headed for the windows. We had learned. And we had many opportunities to apply what we had learned.

This letter especially intrigued me because "It's cold in here" is the standard sentence used by linguists to illustrate an indirect way of getting someone to do something—as I used it earlier. In this example, it is the very obviousness and rigidity of the military hierarchy that makes the statement of a problem sufficient to trigger corrective action on the part of subordinates.

A man who had worked at the Pentagon reinforced the view that the burden of interpretation is on subordinates in the military—and he noticed the difference when he moved to a position in the private sector. He was frustrated when he'd say to his new secretary, for example, "Do we have a list of invitees?" and be told, "I don't know; we probably do" rather than "I'll get it for you." Indeed, he explained, at the Pentagon, such a question would likely be heard as a reproach that the list was not already on his desk.

The suggestion that indirectness is associated with the military must come as a surprise to many. But everyone is indirect, meaning more than is put into words and deriving meaning from words that are never actually said. It's a matter of where, when and how we each tend to be indirect and look for hidden meanings. But indirectness has a built-in liability. There is a risk that the other will either miss or choose to ignore your meaning.

On Jan. 13, 1982, a freezing cold, snowy day in Washington, Air Florida Flight 90 took off from National Airport, but could not get the lift it needed to keep climbing. It crashed into a bridge linking Washington to the state of Virginia and plunged into the Potomac. Of the 79 people on board all but 5 perished, many floundering and drowning in the icy water while horror-stricken bystanders watched helplessly from the river's edge and millions more watched, aghast, on their television screens. Experts later concluded that the plane had waited too long after de-icing to take off. Fresh buildup of ice on the wings and engine brought the plane down. How could the pilot and co-pilot have made such a blunder? Didn't at least one of them realize it was dangerous to take off under these conditions?

Charlotte Linde, a linguist at the Institute for Research on Learning in Palo Alto, Calif., has studied the "black box" recordings of cockpit conversations that preceded crashes as well as tape recordings of conversations that took place among crews during flight simulations in which problems were presented. Among the black box conversations she studied was the one between the pilot and co-pilot just before the Air Florida crash. The pilot, it turned out, had little experience flying in icy weather. The co-pilot had a bit more, and it became heartbreakingly clear on analysis that he had tried to warn the pilot, but he did so indirectly.

The co-pilot repeatedly called attention to the bad weather and to ice building up on other planes:

Co-pilot: Look how the ice is just hanging on his, ah, back, back there, see that? . . .
Co-pilot: See all those icicles on the back there and everything?
Captain: Yeah.

He expressed concern early on about the long waiting time between de-icing:

Co-pilot: Boy, this is a, this is a losing battle here on trying to de-ice those things, it [gives] you a false feeling of security, that's all that does.

Shortly after they were given clearance to take off, he again expressed concern:

Co-pilot: Let's check these tops again since we been setting here awhile.
Captain: I think we get to go here in a minute.

When they were about to take off, the co-pilot called attention to the engine instrument readings, which were not normal:

Co-pilot: That don't seem right, does it? [three-second pause] Ah, that's not right. . . .
Captain: Yes, it is, there's 80.
Co-pilot: Naw, I don't think that's right. [seven-second pause] Ah, maybe it is.
Captain: Hundred and twenty.
Co-pilot: I don't know.

The takeoff proceeded, and 37 seconds later the pilot and co-pilot exchanged their last words.

The co-pilot repeatedly called attention to dangerous conditions, but the captain didn't get the message.

The co-pilot had repeatedly called the pilot's attention to dangerous conditions but did not directly suggest they abort the takeoff. In Linde's judgment, he was expressing his concern indirectly, and the captain didn't pick up on it—with tragic results.

That the co-pilot was trying to warn the captain indirectly is supported by evidence from another airline accident—a relatively minor one—investigated by Linde that also involved the unsuccessful use of indirectness.

On July 9, 1978, Allegheny Airlines Flight 453 was landing at Monroe County Airport in Rochester, when it overran the runway by 728 feet. Everyone survived. This meant that the captain and co-pilot could be interviewed. It turned out that the plane had

been flying too fast for a safe landing. The captain should have realized this and flown around a second time, decreasing his speed before trying to land. The captain said he simply had not been aware that he was going too fast. But the co-pilot told interviewers that he "tried to warn the captain in subtle ways, like mentioning the possibility of a tail wind and the flowness of flap extension." His exact words were recorded in the black box. The crosshatches indicate words deleted by the National Transportation Safety Board and were probably expletives:

Co-pilot: Yeah, it looks like you got a tail wind here.
Yeah.
[?]: Yeah [it] moves awfully # slow.
Co-pilot: Yeah the # flaps are slower than a #.
Captain: We'll make it, gonna have to add power.
Co-pilot: I know.

The co-pilot thought the captain would understand that if there was a tail wind, it would result in the plane going too fast, and if the flaps were slow, they would be inadequate to break the speed sufficiently for a safe landing. He thought the captain would then correct for the error by not trying to land. But the captain said he didn't interpret the co-pilot's remarks to mean they were going too fast.

Linde believes it is not a coincidence that the people being indirect in these conversations were the co-pilots. In her analyses of flight-crew conversations she found it was typical for the speech of subordinates to be more mitigated—polite, tentative or indirect. She also found that topics broached in a mitigated way were more likely to fail, and that captains were more likely to ignore hints from their crew members than the other way around. These findings are evidence that not only can indirectness and other forms of mitigation be misunderstood, but they are also easier to ignore.

In the Air Florida case, it is doubtful that the captain did not realize what the co-pilot was suggesting when he said, "Let's check these tops again since we been setting here awhile" (though it seems safe to assume he did not realize the gravity of the co-pilot's concern). But the indirectness of the co-pilot's phrasing certainly made it easier for the pilot to ignore it. In this sense, the captain's response, "I think we get to go here in a minute," was an indirect way of saying, "I'd rather not." In view of these patterns, the flight crews of some airlines are now given training to express their concerns, even to superiors, in more direct ways.

The conclusion that people should learn to express themselves more directly has a ring of truth to it—especially for Americans. But direct communication is not necessarily always preferable. If more direct expression is better communication, then the most direct-speaking crews should be the best ones. Linde was surprised to find in her research that crews that used the most mitigated speech were often judged the best crews. As part of the study of talk among cockpit crews in flight simulations, the trainers observed and rated the performances of the simulation crews. The crews they rated top in performance had a higher rate of mitigation than crews they judged to be poor.

This finding seems at odds with the role played by indirectness in the examples of crashes that we just saw. Linde concluded that since every utterance functions on two levels—the referential (what it says) and the relational (what it implies about the speaker's relationships), crews that attend to the relational level will be better crews. A similar explanation was suggested by

Kunihiko Harada. He believes that the secret of successful communication lies not in teaching subordinates to be more direct, but in teaching higher-ups to be more sensitive to indirect meaning. In other words, the crashes resulted not only because the co-pilots tried to alert the captains to danger indirectly but also because the captains were not attuned to the co-pilots' hints. What made for successful performance among the best crews might have been the ability—or willingness—of listeners to pick up on hints, just as members of families or longstanding couples come to understand each other's meaning without anyone being particularly explicit.

It is not surprising that a Japanese sociolinguist came up with this explanation; what he described is the Japanese system, by which good communication is believed to take place when meaning is gleaned without being stated directly—or at all.

While Americans believe that "the squeaky wheel gets the grease" (so it's best to speak up), the Japanese say, "The nail that sticks out gets hammered back in" (so it's best to remain silent if you don't want to be hit on the head). Many Japanese scholars writing in English have tried to explain to bewildered Americans the ethics of a culture in which silence is often given greater value than speech, and ideas are believed to be best communicated without being explicitly stated. Key concepts in Japanese give a flavor of the attitudes toward language that they reveal—and

set in relief the strategies that Americans encounter at work when talking to other Americans.

Takie Sugiyama Lebra, a Japanese-born anthropologist, explains that one of the most basic values in Japanese culture is *omoiyari,* which she translates as "empathy." Because of *omoiyari,* it should not be necessary to state one's meaning explicitly; people should be able to sense each other's meaning intuitively. Lebra explains that it is typical for a Japanese speaker to let sentences trail off rather than complete them because expressing ideas before knowing how they will be received seems intrusive. "Only an insensitive, uncouth person needs a direct, verbal, complete message," Lebra says.

Sasshi, the anticipation of another's message through insightful guesswork, is considered an indication of maturity.

Considering the value placed on direct communication by Americans in general, and especially by American business people, it is easy to imagine that many American readers may scoff at such conversational habits. But the success of Japanese businesses makes it impossible to continue to maintain that there is anything inherently inefficient about such conversational conventions. With indirectness, as with all aspects of conversational style, our own habitual style seems to make sense—seems polite, right and good. The light cast by the habits and assumptions of another culture can help us see our way to the flexibility and respect for other styles that is the only best way of speaking.

Empire of Uniformity

With its vast area and long history of settlement, China ought to have hundreds of distinct languages and cultures. In fact, all the evidence indicates that it once did. So what happened to them all?

JARED DIAMOND

Jared Diamond is a contributing editor of Discover, *a professor of physiology at the* UCLA *School of Medicine, a recipient of a MacArthur genius award, and a research associate in ornithology at the American Museum of Natural History. Expanded versions of many of his* Discover *articles appear in his book* The Third Chimpanzee: The Evolution and Future of the Human Animal, *which won Britain's 1992* copus *prize for best science book and the* Los Angeles Times *science book prize.*

Immigration, affirmative action, multilingualism, ethnic diversity—my state of California pioneered these controversial policies, and it is now pioneering a backlash against them. A glance into the classrooms of the Los Angeles public schools, where my sons are being educated, fleshes out the abstract debates with the faces of children. Those pupils speak more than 80 languages in their homes; English-speaking whites are in the minority. Every single one of my sons' playmates has at least one parent or grandparent who was born outside the United States. That's true of my sons also—three of their four grandparents were immigrants to this country. But the diversity that results from such immigration isn't new to America. In fact, immigration is simply restoring the diversity that existed here for thousands of years and that diminished only recently; the area that now makes up the mainland United States, once home to hundreds of Native American tribes and languages, did not come under the control of a single government until the late nineteenth century.

In these respects, ours is a thoroughly "normal" country. Like the United States, all but one of the world's six most populous nations are melting pots that achieved political unification recently and that still support hundreds of languages and ethnic groups. Russia, for example, once a small Slavic state centered on Moscow, did not even begin its expansion beyond the Ural Mountains until 1582. From then until the late nineteenth century, Russia swallowed up dozens of non-Slavic peoples, many of whom, like the people of Chechnya today, retain their original language and cultural identity. India, Indonesia, and Brazil are also recently political creations (or re-creations, in the case of India) and are home to about 850, 703, and 209 languages, respectively.

The great exception to this rule of the recent melting pot is the world's most populous nation, China. Today China appears politically, culturally, and linguistically monolithic. (For the purposes of this article, I exclude the linguistically and culturally distinct Tibet, which was also politically separate until recently.) China was already unified politically in 221 B.C. and has remained so for most of the centuries since then. From the beginnings of literacy in China over 3,000 years ago, it has had only a single writing system, unlike the dozens in use in modern Europe. Of China's billion-plus people, over 700 million speak Mandarin, the language with by far the largest number of native speakers in the world. Some 250 million other Chinese speak seven languages as similar to Mandarin and to each other as Spanish is to Italian. Thus, while modern American history is the story of how our continent's expanse became American, and Russia's history is the story of how Russia became Russian, China's history appears to be entirely different. It seems absurd to ask how China became Chinese. China has *been* Chinese almost from the beginning of its recorded history.

We take this unity of China so much for granted that we forget how astonishing it is. Certainly we should not have expected such unity on the basis of genetics. While a coarse racial classification of world peoples lumps all Chinese people together as Mongoloids, that category conceals much more variation than is found among such (equally ill-termed) Caucasian peoples as Swedes, Italians, and Irish. Northern and southern Chinese, in particular, are genetically and physically rather different from each other: northerners are most similar to Tibetans and Nepali, southerners to Vietnamese and Filipinos. My northern and southern Chinese friends can often distinguish each other at a glance: northerners tend to be taller, heavier, paler, with more pointed noses and smaller eyes.

The existence of such differences is hardly surprising: northern and southern China differ in environment and climate, with the north drier and colder. That such genetic differences arose between the peoples of these two regions simply

2. CULTURE AND COMMUNICATION

implies a long history of their moderate isolation from each other. But if such isolation existed, then how did these peoples end up with such similar languages and cultures?

China's linguistic near-unity is also puzzling in comparison with the linguistic *dis*unity of other parts of the world. For instance, New Guinea, although it was first settled by humans only about 40,000 years ago, evolved roughly 1,000 languages. Western Europe has by now about 40 native languages acquired just in the past 6,000 to 8,000

years, including languages as different as English, Finnish, and Russian. Yet New Guinea's peoples are spread over an area less than one-tenth that of China's. And fossils attest to human presence in China for hundreds of thousands of years. By rights, tens of thousands of distinct languages should have arisen in China's large area over that long time span; what has happened to them? China too must once have been a melting pot of diversity, as all other populous nations still are. It differs from them only in having been unified much

earlier: in that huge pot, the melting happened long ago.

A glance at a linguistic map is an eye-opener to all of us accustomed to thinking of China as monolithic. In addition to its eight "big" languages—Mandarin and its seven close relatives (often referred to collectively as Chinese), with between 11 million and 700 million speakers each—China also has some 160 smaller languages, many of them with just a few thousand speakers. All these languages fall into four families, which differ greatly in their distributions.

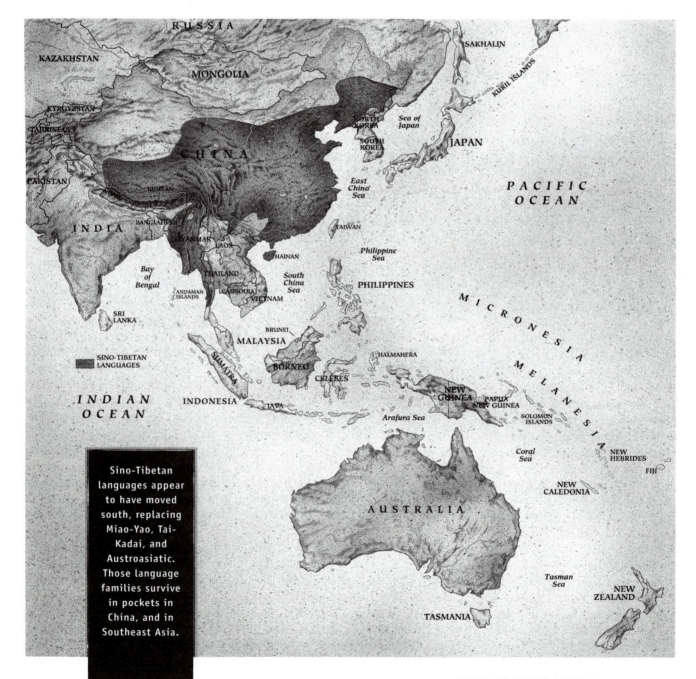

Sino-Tibetan languages appear to have moved south, replacing Miao-Yao, Tai-Kadai, and Austroasiatic. Those language families survive in pockets in China, and in Southeast Asia.

MAPS BY SUSAN JOHNSTON CARLSON

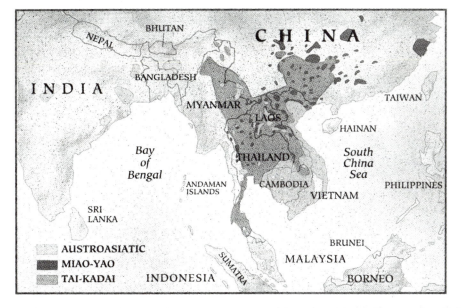

AUSTROASIATIC
MIAO-YAO
TAI-KADAI

At one extreme, Mandarin and its relatives, which constitute the Chinese subfamily of the Sino-Tibetan language family, are distributed continuously from the top of the country to the bottom. One distinctive feature of all Sino-Tibetan languages is that most words consist of a single syllable, like English it or *book;* long, polysyllabic words are unthinkable. One could walk through China, from Manchuria in the north to the Gulf of Tonkin in the south, without ever stepping off land occupied by native speakers of Chinese.

The other three families have broken distributions, being spoken by islands of people surrounded by a sea of speakers of Chinese and other languages. The 6 million speakers of the Miao-Yao family are divided among five languages, bearing colorful names derived from the characteristic colors of the speakers' clothing: Red Miao, White Miao (alias Striped Miao), Black Miao, Green Miao (alias Blue Miao), and Yao. Miao-Yao speakers live in dozens of small enclaves scattered over half a million square miles from southern China to Thailand.

The 60 million speakers of languages in the Austroasiatic family, such as Vietnamese and Cambodian, are also scattered across the map, from Vietnam in the east to the Malay Peninsula in the south to northeastern India in the west. Austroasiatic languages are characterized by an enormous proliferation of vowels, which can be nasal or nonnasal, long or extra-short, creaky, breathy, or normal,

produced with the tongue high, medium high, medium low, or low, and with the front, center, or back of the tongue. All these choices combine to yield up to 41 distinctive vowel sounds per language, in contrast to the mere dozen or so of English.

The 50 million speakers of China's fourth language family, Tai-Kadai, are scattered from southern China southward into peninsular Thailand and west to Myanmar (Burma). In Tai-Kadai languages, as in most Sino-Tibetan languages, a single word may have different meanings depending on its tone, or pitch. For example, in Thai itself the syllable *maa* means "horse" when pronounced at a high pitch, "come" at a medium pitch, and "dog" at a rising pitch.

Seen on a map, the current fragmented distribution of these language groups suggests a series of ancient helicopter flights that dropped speakers here and there over the Asian landscape. But of course nothing like that could have happened, and the actual process was subtractive rather than additive. Speakers of the now dominant language expanded their territory and displaced original residents or induced them to abandon their native tongues. The ancestors of modern speakers of Thai and Laotian, and possibly Cambodian and Burmese as well, all moved south from southern China and adjacent areas to their present locations within historical times, successively inundating the settled descendants of previous migra-

tions. Chinese speakers were especially vigorous in replacing and linguistically converting other ethnic groups, whom they looked down on as primitive and inferior. The recorded history of China's Chou Dynasty, from 1111 B.C. to 256 B.C., describes the conquest and absorption of most of China's non-Chinese-speaking population by Chinese-speaking states.

Before those relatively recent migrations, who spoke what where? To reconstruct the linguistic map of the East Asia of several thousand years ago, we can reverse the historically known linguistic expansions of recent millennia. We can also look for large, continuous areas currently occupied by a single language or related language group; these areas testify to a geographic expansion of that group so recent that there has not been enough time for it to differentiate into many languages. Finally, we can reason conversely that modern areas with a high diversity of languages within a given language family lie closer to the early center of distribution of that language family. Using those three types of reasoning to turn back the linguistic clock, we conclude that speakers of Chinese and other Sino-Tibetan languages originally occupied northern China. The southern parts of the country were variously inhabited by speakers of Miao-Yao, Austroasiatic, and Tai-Kadai languages—until they were largely replaced by their Sino-Tibetan speaking neighbors.

An even more drastic linguistic upheaval appears to have swept over tropical Southeast Asia to the south of China, in Thailand, Myanmar, Laos, Cambodia, Vietnam, and peninsular Malaysia. It's likely that whatever languages were originally spoken there have now become extinct—most of the modern languages of those countries appear to be recent invaders, mainly from southern China. We might also guess that if Miao-Yao languages could be so nearly overwhelmed, there must have been still other language families in southern China that left no modern descendants whatsoever. As we shall see, the Austronesian family (to which all Philippine and Polynesian languages belong) was probably once spoken on the Chinese mainland. We know about it only because it spread to Pacific islands and survived there.

The language replacements in East Asia are reminiscent of the way European languages, especially English and Spanish, spread into the New World. English, of course, came to replace the hundreds of Native American languages not because it sounded musical to indigenous ears but because English-speaking invaders killed most Native Americans by war, murder, and disease and then pressured the survivors into adopting the new majority language. The immediate cause of the Europeans' success was their relative technological superiority. That superiority, however, was ultimately the result of a geographic accident that allowed agriculture and herding to develop in Eurasia 10,000 years earlier. The consequent explosion in population allowed the Europeans to develop complex technologies and social organization, giving their descendants great political and technological advantages over the people they conquered. Essentially the same processes account for why English replaced aboriginal Australian languages and why Bantu languages replaced subequatorial Africa's original Pygmy and Khoisan languages.

East Asia's linguistic upheavals thus hint that some Asians enjoyed similar advantages over other Asians. But to flesh out the details of that story, we must turn from linguistics to archeology.

As everywhere else in the world, the eastern Asian archeological record for most of human history reveals only the debris of hunter-gatherers using unpolished stone tools. The first eastern Asian evidence for something different comes from China, where crop remains, bones of domestic animals, pottery, and polished stone tools appear by around 7500 B.C. That's no more than a thousand years after the beginnings of agriculture in the Fertile Crescent, the area with the oldest established food production in the world.

In China plant and animal domestication may even have started independently in two or more places. Besides differences in climate between north and south, there are also ecological differences between the interior uplands (which are characterized by mountains like our Appalachians) and the coastal lowlands (which are flat and threaded with rivers, like the Carolinas). Incipient farmers in each area would have had different wild plants and animals to draw on. In fact, the earliest identified crops were two drought-resistant species of millet in northern China, but rice in the south.

The same sites that provided us with the earliest evidence of crops also contained bones of domestic pigs, dogs, and chickens—a livestock trinity that later spread as far as Polynesia. These animals and crops were gradually joined by China's many other domesticates. Among the animals were water buffalo (the most important, since they were used for pulling plows), as well as silkworms, ducks, and geese. Familiar later Chinese crops include soybeans, hemp, tea, apricots, pears, peaches, and citrus fruits. Many of these domesticated animals and crops spread westward in ancient times from China to the Fertile Crescent and Europe; at the same time, Fertile Crescent domesticates spread eastward to China. Especially significant western contributions to ancient China's economy were wheat and barley, cows and horses, and to a lesser extent, sheep and goats.

As elsewhere in the world, food production in China gradually led to the other hallmarks of "civilization." A superb Chinese tradition of bronze metallurgy arose around 3000 B.C., allowing China to develop by far the earliest cast iron production in the world by 500 B.C. The following 1,500 years saw the outpouring of a long list of Chinese inventions: canal lock gates, deep drilling, efficient animal harnesses, gunpowder, kites, magnetic compasses, paper, porcelain, printing, sternpost rudders, and wheelbarrows, to name just a few.

China's size and ecological diversity initially spawned many separate local cultures. In the fourth millennium B.C. those local cultures expanded geographically and began to interact, compete with each other, and coalesce. Fortified towns appeared in China in the third millennium B.C., with cemeteries containing luxuriously decorated graves juxtaposed with simpler ones—a clear sign of emerging class differences. China became home to stratified societies with rulers who could mobilize a large labor force of commoners, as we can infer from the remains of huge urban defensive walls, palaces, and the Grand Canal—the longest canal in the world—linking northern and southern China. Writing unmistakably ancestral to that of modern China is preserved from the second millennium B.C., though it probably arose earlier. The first of China's dynasties, the Hsia Dynasty, arose around 2000 B.C. Thereafter, our archeological knowledge of China's emerging cities and states becomes supplemented by written accounts.

Along with rice cultivation and writing, a distinctively Chinese method for reading the future also begins to appear persistently in the archeological record, and it too attests to China's cultural coalescence. In place of crystal balls and Delphic oracles, China turned to scapulimancy—burning the scapula (shoulder bone) or other large bone of an animal, such as a cow, then prophesying from the pattern of cracks in the burned bone. From the earliest known appearance of oracle bones in northern China, archeologists have traced scapulimancy's spread throughout China's cultural sphere.

Just as exchanges of domesticates between ecologically diverse regions enriched Chinese food production, exchanges between culturally diverse regions enriched Chinese culture and technology, and fierce competition between warring chiefdoms drove the formation of ever larger and more centralized states. China's long west-east rivers (the Yellow River in the north, the Yangtze in the south) allowed crops and technology to spread quickly between inland and coast, while their diffusion north and south was made easy by the broad, relatively gentle terrain north of the Yangtze, which eventually permitted the two river systems to be joined by canals. All those geographic factors contributed to the early cultural and political unification of China. In contrast, western Europe, with an area comparable to China's but fragmented by mountains such as the Alps, and with a highly indented coastline and no such rivers, has never been unified politically.

Some developments spread from south to north in China, especially iron smelting and rice cultivation. But the predominant direction of spread seems to have been the other way. From northern China came bronze technology, Sino-Tibetan languages, and state formation. The country's first three dynasties (the Hsia, Shang, and Chou) all arose in the north in the second millennium B.C. The northern dominance is clearest, however, for writing. Unlike western Eurasia, with its plethora of early methods for recording language, including Sumerian cuneiform, Egyptian hieroglyphics, Hittite, Minoan, and the Semitic alphabet, China developed just one writing system. It arose in the north, preempted or replaced any other nascent system, and evolved into the writing used today.

Preserved documents show that already in the first millennium B.C. ethnic Chinese tended to feel culturally superior to non-Chinese "barbarians," and northern Chinese considered even southern Chinese barbarians. For example, a late Chou Dynasty writer described China's other peoples as follows: "The people of those five regions—the Middle states and the Jung, Yi, and other wild tribes around them—had all their several natures, which they could not be made to alter. The tribes on the east were called Yi. They had their hair unbound, and tattooed their bodies. Some of them ate their food without its being cooked by fire." The author went on to describe wild tribes to the south, west, and north indulging in equally barbaric practices, such as turning their feet inward, tattooing their foreheads, wearing skins, living in caves, not eating cereals, and, again, eating their food raw.

States modeled on the Chou Dynasty were organized in southern China during the first millennium B.C., culminating in China's political unification under the Chin Dynasty in 221 B.C. China's cultural unification accelerated during that same period, as literate "civilized" Chinese states absorbed or were copied by the preliterate "barbarians." Some of

that cultural unification was ferocious: for instance, the first Chin emperor condemned all previously written historical books as worthless and ordered them burned, much to the detriment of our understanding of early Chinese history. That and other draconian measures must have helped spread northern China's Sino-Tibetan languages over most of China.

So overwhelming was the Chinese steamroller that the former peoples of the region have left behind few traces.

Chinese innovations contributed heavily to developments in neighboring regions as well. For instance, until roughly 4000 B.C. most of tropical Southeast Asia was still occupied by hunter-gatherers making pebble and flake stone tools. Thereafter, Chinese-derived crops, polished stone tools, village living, and pottery spread into the area, probably accompanied by southern Chinese language families. The southward expansions from southern China of Laotians, Thai, and Vietnamese, and probably Burmese and Cambodians also, completed the "Sinification" of tropical Southeast Asia. All those modern peoples appear to be recent offshoots of their southern Chinese cousins.

So overwhelming was this Chinese steamroller that the former peoples of the region have left behind few traces in the modern populations. Just three relict groups of hunter-gatherers—the Semang Negritos of the Malay Peninsula, the Andaman Islanders, and the Veddoid Negritos of Sri Lanka—remain to give us any clue as to what those peoples were like. They suggest that tropical Southeast Asia's former inhabitants may have had dark skin and curly hair, like modern New Guineans and unlike southern Chinese and modern tropical

Southeast Asians. Those people may also be the last survivors of the source population from which New Guinea and aboriginal Australia were colonized. As to their speech, only on the remote Andaman Islands do languages unrelated to the southern Chinese language families persist—perhaps the last linguistic survivors of what may have been hundreds of now extinct aboriginal Southeast Asian languages.

While one prong of the Chinese expansion thus headed southwest into Indochina and Myanmar, another headed southeast into the Pacific Ocean. Part of the evidence suggesting this scenario comes from genetics and linguistics: the modern inhabitants of Indonesia and the Philippines are fairly homogeneous in their genes and appearance and resemble southern Chinese. Their languages are also homogeneous, almost all belonging to a closely knit family called Austronesian, possibly related to Tai-Kadai.

But just as in tropical Southeast Asia, the archeological record in the Pacific shows more direct evidence of the Chinese steamroller. Until 6,000 years ago, Indonesia and the Philippines were sparsely occupied by hunter-gatherers. Beginning in the fourth or fifth millennium B.C., pottery and stone tools of unmistakably southern Chinese origins appear on the island of Taiwan, which is in the straits between the southern Chinese coast and the Philippines. Around 3000 B.C. that same combination of technological advances spread as a wave to the Philippines, then throughout the islands of Indonesia, accompanied by gardening and by China's livestock trinity (pigs, chickens, and dogs). Around 1600 B.C. the wave reached the islands north of New Guinea, then spread eastward through the previously uninhabited islands of Polynesia. By 500 A.D. the Polynesians, an Austronesian speaking people of ultimately Chinese origin, had reached Easter Island, 10,000 miles from the Chinese coast. With Polynesian settlement of Hawaii and New Zealand around the same time or soon thereafter, ancient China's occupation of the Pacific was complete.

Throughout most of Indonesia and the Philippines, the Austronesian expansion obliterated the region's former inhabitants. Scattered bands of hunter-gatherers were no match for the tools, weapons, numbers, subsistence methods, and probably also germs carried by the invading Austronesian farmers. Only the Negrito Pygmies in the mountains of Luzon and some other Philippine islands appear to represent survivors of those former hunter-gatherers, but they too lost their original tongues and adopted Austronesian languages from their new neighbors. However, on New Guinea and adjacent islands, indigenous people had already developed agriculture and built up numbers sufficient to keep out the Austronesian invaders. Their languages, genes, and faces live on in modern New Guineans and Melanesians.

Even Korea and Japan were heavily influenced by China, although their geographic isolation from the mainland saved them from losing their languages or physical and genetic distinctness. Korea and Japan adopted rice from China in the second millennium B.C., bronze metallurgy in the first millennium B.C., and writing in the first or early second millennium A.D.

Not all cultural advances in East Asia stemmed from China, of course, nor were Koreans, Japanese, and tropical Southeast Asians noninventive "barbarians" who contributed nothing. The ancient Japanese developed pottery at least as early as the Chinese did, and they settled in villages subsisting on Japan's rich seafood resources long before the arrival of agriculture. Some crops were probably domesticated initially or independently in Japan, Korea, and tropical Southeast Asia. But China's role was still disproportionately large. Indeed, the influence of Chinese culture is still so great that Japan has no thought of discarding its Chinese-derived writing system despite its disadvantages for representing Japanese speech, while Korea is only now replacing its clumsy Chinese-derived writing with its wonderful indigenous Hangul alphabet. The persistence of Chinese writing in Japan and Korea is a vivid twentieth-century legacy of plant and animal domestication that began in China 10,000 years ago. From those achievements of East Asia's first farmers, China became Chinese, and peoples from Thailand to Easter Island became their cousins.

Shakespeare in the Bush

Laura Bohannan

Laura Bohannan is a former professor of anthropology at the University of Illinois, at Chicago.

Just before I left Oxford for the Tiv in West Africa, conversation turned to the season at Stratford. "You Americans," said a friend, "often have difficulty with Shakespeare. He was, after all, a very English poet, and one can easily misinterpret the universal by misunderstanding the particular."

I protested that human nature is pretty much the same the whole world over; at least the general plot and motivation of the greater tragedies would always be clear—everywhere—although some details of custom might have to be explained and difficulties of translation might produce other slight changes. To end an argument we could not conclude, my friend gave me a copy of *Hamlet* to study in the African bush: it would, he hoped, lift my mind above its primitive surroundings, and possibly I might, by prolonged meditation, achieve the grace of correct interpretation.

It was my second field trip to that African tribe, and I thought myself ready to live in one of its remote sections—an area difficult to cross even on foot. I eventually settled on the hillock of a very knowledgeable old man, the head of a homestead of some hundred and forty people, all of whom were either his close relatives or their wives and children. Like the other elders of the vicinity, the old man spent most of his time performing ceremonies seldom seen these days in the more accessible parts of the tribe. I was delighted. Soon there would be three months of enforced isolation and leisure, between the harvest that takes place just before the rising of the swamps and the clearing of new farms when the water goes down. Then, I thought, they would have even more time to perform ceremonies and explain them to me.

I was quite mistaken. Most of the ceremonies demanded the presence of elders from several homesteads. As the swamps rose, the old men found it too difficult to walk from one homestead to the next, and the ceremonies gradually ceased. As the swamps rose even higher, all activities but one came to an end. The women brewed beer from maize and millet. Men, women, and children sat on their hillocks and drank it.

People began to drink at dawn. By midmorning the whole homestead was singing, dancing, and drumming. When it rained, people had to sit inside their huts: there they drank and sang or they drank and told stories. In any case, by noon or before, I either had to join the party or retire to my own hut and my books. "One does not discuss serious matters when there is beer. Come, drink with us." Since I lacked their capacity for the thick native beer, I spent more and more time with *Hamlet*. Before the end of the second month, grace descended on me. I was quite sure that *Hamlet* had only one possible interpretation, and that one universally obvious.

Early every morning, in the hope of having some serious talk before the beer party, I used to call on the old man at his reception hut—a circle of posts supporting a thatched roof above a low mud wall to keep out wind and rain. One day I crawled through the low doorway and found most of the men of the homestead sitting huddled in their ragged cloths on stools, low plank beds, and reclining chairs, warming themselves against the chill of the rain around a smoky fire. In the center were three pots of beer. The party had started.

The old man greeted me cordially. "Sit down and drink." I accepted a large calabash full of beer, poured some into a small drinking gourd, and tossed it down. Then I poured some more into the same gourd for the man second in seniority to my host before I handed my calabash over to a young man for further distribution. Important people shouldn't ladle beer themselves.

From *Natural History*, August/September 1966. © 1966 by Laura Bohannan. Reprinted by permission of the author.

2. CULTURE AND COMMUNICATION

"It is better like this," the old man said, looking at me approvingly and plucking at the thatch that had caught in my hair. "You should sit and drink with us more often. Your servants tell me that when you are not with us, you sit inside your hut looking at a paper."

The old man was acquainted with four kinds of "papers": tax receipts, bride price receipts, court fee receipts, and letters. The messenger who brought him letters from the chief used them mainly as a badge of office, for he always knew what was in them and told the old man. Personal letters for the few who had relatives in the government or mission stations were kept until someone went to a large market where there was a letter writer and reader. Since my arrival, letters were brought to me to be read. A few men also brought me bride price receipts, privately, with requests to change the figures to a higher sum. I found moral arguments were of no avail, since in-laws are fair game, and the technical hazards of forgery difficult to explain to an illiterate people. I did not wish them to think me silly enough to look at any such papers for days on end, and I hastily explained that my "paper" was one of the "things of long ago" of my country.

"Ah," said the old man. "Tell us."

I protested that I was not a storyteller. Story telling is a skilled art among them; their standards are high, and the audiences critical—and vocal in their criticism. I protested in vain. This morning they wanted to hear a story while they drank. They threatened to tell me no more stories until I told them one of mine. Finally, the old man promised that no one would criticize my style "for we know you are struggling with our language." "But," put in one of the elders, "you must explain what we do not understand, as we do when we tell you our stories." Realizing that here was my chance to prove *Hamlet* universally intelligible, I agreed.

The old man handed me some more beer to help me on with my storytelling. Men filled their long wooden pipes and knocked coals from the fire to place in the pipe bowls; then, puffing contentedly, they sat back to listen. I began in the proper style, "Not yesterday, not yesterday, but long ago, a thing occurred. One night three men were keeping watch outside the homestead of the great chief, when suddenly they saw the former chief approach them."

"Why was he no longer their chief?"

"He was dead," I explained. "That is why they were troubled and afraid when they saw him."

"Impossible," began one of the elders, handing his pipe on to his neighbor, who interrupted, "Of course it wasn't the dead chief. It was an omen sent by a witch. Go on."

Slightly shaken, I continued. "One of these three was a man who knew things"—the closest translation for scholar, but unfortunately it also meant witch. The second elder looked triumphantly at the first. "So he spoke to the dead chief saying, 'Tell us what we must do so you may rest in your grave,' but the dead chief did not answer. He vanished, and they could see him no more. Then the man who knew things—his name was Horatio—said this event was the affair of the dead chief's son, Hamlet."

There was a general shaking of heads round the circle. "Had the dead chief no living brothers? Or was this son the chief?"

"No," I replied. "That is, he had one living brother who became the chief when the elder brother died."

The old men muttered: such omens were matters for chiefs and elders, not for youngsters; no good could come of going behind a chief's back; clearly Horatio was not a man who knew things.

"Yes, he was," I insisted, shooing a chicken away from my beer. "In our country the son is next to the father. The dead chief's younger brother had become the great chief. He had also married his elder brother's widow only about a month after the funeral."

"He did well," the old man beamed and announced to the others, "I told you that if we knew more about Europeans, we would find they really were very like us. In our country also," he added to me, "the younger brother marries the elder brother's widow and becomes the father of his children. Now, if your uncle, who married your widowed mother, is your father's full brother, then he will be a real father to you. Did Hamlet's father and uncle have one mother?"

His question barely penetrated my mind; I was too upset and thrown too far off balance by having one of the most important elements of *Hamlet* knocked straight out of the picture. Rather uncertainly I said that I thought they had the same mother, but I wasn't sure—the story didn't say. The old man told me severely that these genealogical details made all the difference and that when I got home I must ask the elders about it. He shouted out the door to one of his younger wives to bring his goatskin bag.

Determined to save what I could of the mother motif, I took a deep breath and began again. "The son Hamlet was very sad because his mother had married again so quickly. There was no need for her to do so, and it is our custom for a widow not to go to her next husband until she has mourned for two years."

"Two years is too long," objected the wife, who had appeared with the old man's battered goatskin bag. "Who will hoe your farms for you while you have no husband?"

"Hamlet," I retorted without thinking, "was old enough to hoe his mother's farms himself. There was no need for her to remarry." No one looked convinced. I gave up. "His mother and the great chief told Hamlet not to be sad, for the great chief himself would be a father to Hamlet. Furthermore, Hamlet would be the next chief: therefore he must stay to learn the things of a chief. Hamlet agreed to remain, and all the rest went off to drink beer."

While I paused, perplexed at how to render Hamlet's disgusted soliloquy to an audience convinced that Claudius and Gertrude had behaved in the best possible manner, one of the younger men asked me who had married the other wives of the dead chief.

"He had no other wives," I told him.

"But a chief must have many wives! How else can he brew beer and prepare food for all his guests?"

I said firmly that in our country even chiefs had only one wife, that they had servants to do their work, and that they paid them from tax money.

It was better, they returned, for a chief to have many wives and sons who would help him hoe his farms and feed his people; then everyone loved the chief who gave much and took nothing—taxes were a bad thing.

I agreed with the last comment, but for the rest fell back on their favorite way of fobbing off my questions: "That is the way it is done, so that is how we do it."

I decided to skip the soliloquy. Even if Claudius was here thought quite right to marry his brother's widow, there remained the poison motif, and I knew they would disapprove of fratricide. More hopefully I resumed, "That night Hamlet kept watch with the three who had seen his dead father. The dead chief again appeared, and although the others were afraid, Hamlet followed his dead father off to one side. When they were alone, Hamlet's dead father spoke."

"Omens can't talk!" The old man was emphatic.

"Hamlet's dead father wasn't an omen. Seeing him might have been an omen, but he was not." My audience looked as confused as I sounded. "It *was* Hamlet's dead father. It was a thing we call a 'ghost.' " I had to use the English word, for unlike many of the neighboring tribes, these people didn't believe in the survival after death of any individuating part of the personality.

"What is a 'ghost?' An omen?"

"No, a 'ghost' is someone who is dead but who walks around and can talk, and people can hear him and see him but not touch him."

They objected. "One can touch zombis."

"No, no! It was not a dead body the witches had animated to sacrifice and eat. No one else made Hamlet's dead father walk. He did it himself."

"Dead men can't walk," protested my audience as one man.

I was quite willing to compromise. "A 'ghost' is the dead man's shadow."

But again they objected. "Dead men cast no shadows."

"They do in my country," I snapped.

The old man quelled the babble of disbelief that arose immediately and told me with that insincere, but courteous, agreement one extends to the fancies of the young, ignorant, and superstitious, "No doubt in your country the dead can also walk without being zombis." From the depths of his bag he produced a withered fragment of kola nut, bit off one end to show it wasn't poisoned, and handed me the rest as a peace offering.

"Anyhow," I resumed, "Hamlet's dead father said that his own brother, the one who became chief, had poisoned him. He wanted Hamlet to avenge him. Hamlet believed this in his heart, for he did not like his father's brother." I took another swallow of beer. "In the country of the great chief, living in the same homestead, for it was a very large one, was an important elder who was often with the chief to advise and help him. His name was Polonius. Hamlet was courting his daughter, but her father and her brother . . .[I cast hastily about for some tribal analogy] warned her not to let Hamlet visit her when she was alone on her farm, for he would be a great chief and so could not marry her."

"Why not?" asked the wife, who had settled down on the edge of the old man's chair. He frowned at her for asking stupid questions and growled, "They lived in the same homestead."

"That was not the reason," I informed them. "Polonius was a stranger who lived in the homestead because he helped the chief, not because he was a relative."

"Then why couldn't Hamlet marry her?"

"He could have," I explained, "but Polonius didn't think he would. After all, Hamlet was a man of great importance who ought to marry a chief's daughter, for in his country a man could have only one wife. Polonius was afraid that if Hamlet made love to his daughter, then no one else would give a high price for her."

"That might be true," remarked one of the shrewder elders, "but a chief's son would give his mistress's father enough presents and patronage to more than make up the difference. Polonius sounds like a fool to me."

"Many people think he was," I agreed. "Meanwhile Polonius sent his son Laertes off to Paris to learn the things of that country, for it was the homestead of a very great chief indeed. Because he was afraid that Laertes might waste a lot of money on beer and women and gambling, or get into trouble by fighting, he sent one of his servants to Paris secretly, to spy out what Laertes was doing. One day Hamlet came upon Polonius's daughter Ophelia. He behaved so oddly he frightened her. Indeed"—I was fumbling for words to express the dubious quality of Hamlet's madness—"the chief and many others had also noticed that when Hamlet talked one could understand the words but not what they meant. Many people thought that he had become mad." My audience suddenly became much more attentive. "The great chief wanted to know what was wrong with Hamlet, so he sent for two of Hamlet's age mates [school friends would have taken long explanation] to talk to Hamlet and find out what troubled his heart. Hamlet, seeing that they had been bribed by the chief to betray him, told them nothing. Polonius, however, insisted that Hamlet was mad because he had been forbidden to see Ophelia, whom he loved."

"Why," inquired a bewildered voice, "should anyone bewitch Hamlet on that account?"

"Bewitch him?"

"Yes, only witchcraft can make anyone mad, unless, of course, one sees the beings that lurk in the forest."

2. CULTURE AND COMMUNICATION

I stopped being a storyteller, took out my notebook and demanded to be told more about these two causes of madness. Even while they spoke and I jotted notes, I tried to calculate the effect of this new factor on the plot. Hamlet had not been exposed to the beings that lurk in the forests. Only his relatives in the male line could bewitch him. Barring relatives not mentioned by Shakespeare, it had to be Claudius who was attempting to harm him. And, of course, it was.

For the moment I staved off questions by saying that the great chief also refused to believe that Hamlet was mad for the love of Ophelia and nothing else. "He was sure that something much more important was troubling Hamlet's heart."

"Now Hamlet's age mates," I continued, "had brought with them a famous storyteller. Hamlet decided to have this man tell the chief and all his homestead a story about a man who had poisoned his brother because he desired his brother's wife and wished to be chief himself. Hamlet was sure the great chief could not hear the story without making a sign if he was indeed guilty, and then he would discover whether his dead father had told him the truth."

The old man interrupted, with deep cunning, "Why should a father lie to his son?" he asked.

I hedged: "Hamlet wasn't sure that it really was his dead father." It was impossible to say anything, in that language, about devil-inspired visions.

"You mean," he said, "it actually was an omen, and he knew witches sometimes send false ones. Hamlet was a fool not to go to one skilled in reading omens and divining the truth in the first place. A man-who-sees-the-truth could have told him how his father died, if he really had been poisoned, and if there was witchcraft in it; then Hamlet could have called the elders to settle the matter."

The shrewd elder ventured to disagree. "Because his father's brother was a great chief, one-who-sees-the-truth might therefore have been afraid to tell it. I think it was for that reason that a friend of Hamlet's father—a witch and an elder—sent an omen so his friend's son would know. Was the omen true?"

"Yes," I said, abandoning ghosts and the devil; a witch-sent omen it would have to be. "It was true, for when the storyteller was telling his tale before all the homestead, the great chief rose in fear. Afraid that Hamlet knew his secret he planned to have him killed."

The stage set of the next bit presented some difficulties of translation. I began cautiously. "The great chief told Hamlet's mother to find out from her son what he knew. But because a woman's children are always first in her heart, he had the important elder Polonius hide behind a cloth that hung against the wall of Hamlet's mother's sleeping hut. Hamlet started to scold his mother for what she had done."

There was a shocked murmur from everyone. A man should never scold his mother.

"She called out in fear, and Polonius moved behind the cloth. Shouting, 'A rat!' Hamlet took his machete and slashed through the cloth." I paused for dramatic effect. "He had killed Polonius!"

The old men looked at each other in supreme disgust. "That Polonius truly was a fool and a man who knew nothing! What child would not know enough to shout, 'It's me!' " With a pang, I remembered that these people are ardent hunters, always armed with bow, arrow, and machete; at the first rustle in the grass an arrow is aimed and ready, and the hunter shouts "Game!" If no human voice answers immediately, the arrow speeds on its way. Like a good hunter Hamlet had shouted, "A rat!"

I rushed in to save Polonius's reputation. "Polonius did speak. Hamlet heard him. But he thought it was the chief and wished to kill him earlier that evening. . . ." I broke down, unable to describe to these pagans, who had no belief in individual afterlife, the difference between dying at one's prayers and dying "unhousel'd, disappointed, unaneled."

This time I had shocked my audience seriously. "For a man to raise his hand against his father's brother and and the one who has become his father—that is a terrible thing. The elders ought to let such a man be bewitched."

I nibbled at my kola nut in some perplexity, then pointed out that after all the man had killed Hamlet's father.

"No," pronounced the old man, speaking less to me than to the young men sitting behind the elders. "If your father's brother has killed your father, you must appeal to your father's age mates; *they* may avenge him. No man may use violence against his senior relatives." Another thought struck him. "But if his father's brother had indeed been wicked enough to bewitch Hamlet and make him mad that would be a good story indeed, for it would be his fault that Hamlet, being mad, no longer had any sense and thus was ready to kill his father's brother."

There was a murmur of applause. *Hamlet* was again a good story to them, but it no longer seemed quite the same story to me. As I thought over the coming complications of plot and motive, I lost courage and decided to skim over dangerous ground quickly.

"The great chief," I went on, "was not sorry that Hamlet had killed Polonius. It gave him a reason to send Hamlet away, with his two treacherous mates, with letters to a chief of a far country, saying that Hamlet should be killed. But Hamlet changed the writing on their papers, so that the chief killed his age mates instead." I encountered a reproachful glare from one of the men whom I had told undetectable forgery was not merely immoral but beyond human skill. I looked the other way.

"Before Hamlet could return, Laertes came back for his father's funeral. The great chief told him Hamlet had killed Polonius. Laertes swore to kill Hamlet because of this, and because his sister Ophelia, hearing her father had been killed by the man she loved, went mad and drowned in the river."

"Have you already forgotten what we told you?" The old man was reproachful. "One cannot take vengeance on a madman; Hamlet killed Polonius in his madness. As for the girl, she not only went mad, she was drowned. Only witches can make people drown. Water itself can't hurt anything. It is merely something one drinks and bathes in."

I began to get cross. "If you don't like the story, I'll stop."

The old man made soothing noises and himself poured me some more beer. "You tell the story well, and we are listening. But it is clear that the elders of your country have never told you what the story really means. No, don't interrupt! We believe you when you say your marriage customs are different, or your clothes and weapons. But people are the same everywhere; therefore, there are always witches and it is we, the elders, who know how witches work. We told you it was the great chief who wished to kill Hamlet, and now your own words have proved us right. Who were Ophelia's male relatives?"

"There were only her father and her brother." *Hamlet* was clearly out of my hands.

"There must have been many more; this also you must ask of your elders when you get back to your country. From what you tell us, since Polonius was dead, it must have been Laertes who killed Ophelia, although I do not see the reason for it."

We had emptied one pot of beer, and the old men argued the point with slightly tipsy interest. Finally one of them demanded of me, "What did the servant of Polonius say on his return?"

With difficulty I recollected Reynaldo and his mission. "I don't think he did return before Polonius was killed."

"Listen," said the elder, "and I will tell you how it was and how your story will go, then you may tell me if I am right. Polonius knew his son would get into trouble, and so he did. He had many fines to pay for fighting, and debts from gambling. But he had only two ways of getting money quickly. One was to marry off his sister at once, but it is difficult to find a man who will marry a woman desired by the son of a chief. For if the chief's heir commits adultery with your wife, what can you do? Only a fool calls a case against a man who will someday be his judge. Therefore Laertes had to take the second way: he killed his sister by witchcraft, drowning her so he could secretly sell her body to the witches."

I raised an objection. "They found her body and buried it. Indeed Laertes jumped into the grave to see his sister once more—so, you see, the body was truly there. Hamlet, who had just come back, jumped in after him."

"What did I tell you?" The elder appealed to the others. "Laertes was up to no good with his sister's body. Hamlet prevented him, because the chief's heir, like a chief, does not wish any other man to grow rich and powerful. Laertes would be angry, because he would have killed his sister without benefit to himself. In our country he would try to kill Hamlet for that reason. Is this not what happened?"

"More or less," I admitted. "When the great chief found Hamlet was still alive, he encouraged Laertes to try to kill Hamlet and arranged a fight with machetes between them. In the fight both the young men were wounded to death. Hamlet's mother drank the poisoned beer that the chief meant for Hamlet in case he won the fight. When he saw his mother die of poison, Hamlet, dying, managed to kill his father's brother with his machete."

"You see, I was right!" exclaimed the elder.

"That was a very good story," added the old man, "and you told it with very few mistakes. There was just one more error, at the very end. The poison Hamlet's mother drank was obviously meant for the survivor of the fight, whichever it was. If Laertes had won, the great chief would have poisoned him, for no one would know that he arranged Hamlet's death. Then, too, he need not fear Laertes' witchcraft; it takes a strong heart to kill one's only sister by witchcraft.

"Sometime," concluded the old man, gathering his ragged toga about him, "you must tell us some more stories of your country. We, who are elders, will instruct you in their true meaning, so that when you return to your own land your elders will see that you have not been sitting in the bush, but among those who know things and who have taught you wisdom."

The Organization of Society and Culture

Human beings do not interact with one another or think about their world in random fashion. Instead, they engage in both structured and recurrent physical and mental activities. In this section, such patterns of behavior and thought—referred to here as the organization of society and culture—may be seen in a number of different contexts. A good example is the Yanomami of Amazonia (see "The Yanomami Keep on Trekking").

Of special importance are the ways in which people make a living—in other words, the production, distribution, and consumption of goods and services. It is only by knowing the basic subsistence systems that we can hope to gain insight into the other levels of social and cultural phenomena, for, as anthropologists have found, they are all inextricably bound together, as related in the essay by Glen Martin, "Keepers of the Oaks."

Noting the various aspects of a sociocultural system in harmonious balance, however, does not imply an anthropological seal of approval. To understand infanticide (killing of the newborn) in the manner that it is practiced among some peoples is neither to condone nor condemn it. The adaptive patterns that have been in existence for a great length of time, such as many of the patterns of hunters and gatherers, probably owe their existence to their contributions to long-term human survival.

The articles in this unit demonstrate that anthropologists are far more interested in problems than they are in place. The article "Hunting, Gathering, and the Molimo" is from Kevin Duffy's book *Children of the Forest* and conveys the skillful contributions of women in hunting as well as gathering, which contradicts the standard stereotypes about gender and role in subsistence societies. In fact, without firsthand descriptions like Richard Nelson's in "Understanding Eskimo Science," the very notion that such people (whether men or women) could have a profound understanding of their environment would be beyond belief.

Anthropologists, however, are not content with the data derived from individual experience. On the contrary, personal descriptions must become the basis for sound anthropological theory. Otherwise, they remain meaning-less, isolated relics of culture in the manner of museum pieces. Thus, in "Why Women Change," Jared Diamond sets forth a plausible explanation (in the context of hunting and gathering societies) as to why women experience menopause. Then, in "Too Many Bananas, Not Enough Pineapples, and No Watermelon at All: Three Object Lessons in Living with Reciprocity," David Counts provides us with ground rules for reciprocity that were derived from his own particular field experience and yet are cross-culturally applicable. Karl Rambo, in "From Shells to Money," shows that the adoption of money as a medium of exchange does not in itself create in a market mentality, especially if a people's basic subsistence system remains intact. Finally, "Life without Chiefs" by Marvin Harris expresses that constant striving in anthropology to develop a general perspective from particular events by showing how shifts in technology may result in centralization of political power and marked changes in lifestyle.

While the articles in this unit are to some extent descriptive, they also serve to challenge both academic and commonsense notions about why people behave and think as they do. They remind us that assumptions are never really safe. Any time anthropologists can be kept on their toes, their field as a whole is the better for it.

Looking Ahead: Challenge Questions

What traditional Inuit (Eskimo) practices do you find contrary to values professed in your society, but important to Eskimo survival under certain circumstances?

What can contemporary hunter-collector societies tell us about the quality of life in the prehistoric past?

Why do women experience menopause?

In what sense was agriculture practiced in prehistoric California?

Why do the Simbu value money as a medium of ceremonial exchange rather than as a means to accumulate personal wealth?

Under what circumstances do social stratification and centralization of power appear in human societies?

What are the rules of reciprocity?

UNIT 3

Understanding Eskimo Science

Traditional hunters' insights into the natural world are worth rediscovering.

Richard Nelson

Just below the Arctic Circle in the boreal forest of interior Alaska; an amber afternoon in mid-November; the temperature -20°; the air adrift with frost crystals, presaging the onset of deeper cold.

Five men—Koyukon Indians—lean over the carcass of an exceptionally large black bear. For two days they've traversed the Koyukuk River valley, searching for bears that have recently entered hibernation dens. The animals are in prime condition at this season but extremely hard to find. Den entrances, hidden beneath 18 inches of powdery snow, are betrayed only by the subtlest of clues—patches where no grass protrudes from the surface because it's been clawed away for insulation, faint concavities hinting of footprint depressions in the moss below.

Earlier this morning the hunters took a yearling bear. In accordance with Koyukon tradition, they followed elaborate rules for the proper treatment of killed animals. For example, the bear's feet were removed first, to keep its spirit from wandering. Also, certain parts were to be eaten away from the village, at a kind of funeral feast. All the rest would be eaten either at home or at community events, as people here have done for countless generations.

Koyukon hunters know that an animal's life ebbs slowly, that it remains aware and sensitive to how people treat its body. This is especially true for the potent and demanding spirit of the bear.

The leader of the hunting group is Moses Sam, a man in his 60s who has trapped in this territory since childhood. He is known for his detailed knowledge of the land and for his extraordinary success as a bear hunter. "No one else has that kind of luck with bears," I've been told. "Some people are born with it. He always takes good care of his animals—respects them. That's how he keeps his luck."

Moses pulls a small knife from his pocket, kneels beside the bear's head, and carefully slits the clear domes of its eyes. "Now," he explains softly, "the bear won't see if one of us makes a mistake or does something wrong."

Contemporary Americans are likely to find this story exotic, but over the course of time episodes like this have been utterly commonplace, the essence of people's relationship to the natural world. After all, for 99 percent of human history we lived exclusively as hunter-gatherers; by comparison, agriculture has existed only for a moment and urban societies scarcely more than a blink.

From this perspective, much of human experience over the past several million years lies beyond our grasp. Probably no society has been so deeply alienated as ours from the community of nature, has viewed the natural world from a greater distance of mind, has lapsed into a murkier comprehension of its connections with the sustaining environment. Because of this, we have great difficulty understanding our rootedness to earth, our affinities with non-human life.

I believe it's essential that we learn from traditional societies, especially those whose livelihood depends on the harvest of a wild environment—hunters, fishers, trappers, and gatherers. These people have accumulated bodies of knowledge much like our own sciences. And they can give us vital insights about responsible membership in the community of life, insights founded on a wisdom we'd long forgotten and now are beginning to rediscover.

Since the mid-1960s I have worked as an ethnographer in Alaska, living intermittently in remote northern communities and recording native traditions centered around the natural world. I spent about two years in Koyukon Indian villages and just over a year with Inupiaq Eskimos on the Arctic coast—traveling by dog team and snowmobile, recording traditional knowledge, and learning the hunter's way.

Eskimos have long inhabited some of the harshest environments on earth, and they are among the most exquisitely adapted of all human groups. Because plant life is so scarce in their northern terrain, Eskimos depend more than any other people on hunting.

Eskimos are famous for the cleverness of their technology—kayaks, harpoons, skin clothing, snow houses, dog teams. But I believe their greatest genius, and the basis of their success, lies in the less tangible realm of the intellect—the nexus of mind and nature. For what repeatedly struck me above all else was their profound knowledge of the environment.

Several times, when my Inupiaq hunting companion did something especially clever, he'd point to his head and declare: "You see—Eskimo scientist!" At first I took it as hyperbole, but as time went by I realized he was speaking the truth. Scientists had often come to his village, and he saw in them a familiar commitment to the empirical method.

Traditional Inupiaq hunters spend a lifetime acquiring knowledge—from others in the community and from their own observations. If they are to survive, they must have absolutely reliable information. When I first went to live with Inupiaq people, I doubted many things they told me. But the longer I stayed, the more I trusted their teachings.

The Inupiaq hunter possesses as much knowledge as a highly trained scientist in our own society.

For example, hunters say that ringed seals surfacing in open leads—wide cracks in the sea ice—can reliably forecast the weather. Because an unexpected gale might set people adrift on the pack ice, accurate prediction is a matter of life and death. When seals rise chest-high in the water, snout pointed skyward, not going anywhere in particular, it indicates stable weather, the Inupiaq say. But if they surface briefly, head low, snout parallel to the water, and show themselves only once or twice, watch for a sudden storm. And take special heed if you've also noticed the sled dogs howling incessantly, stars twinkling erratically, or the current running strong from the south. As time passed, my own experiences with seals and winter storms affirmed what the Eskimos said.

Like a young Inupiaq in training, I gradually grew less skeptical and started to apply what I was told. For example, had I ever been rushed by a polar bear, I would have jumped away to the animal's *right* side. Inupiaq elders say polar bears are left-handed, so you have a slightly better chance to

avoid their right paw, which is slower and less accurate. I'm pleased to say I never had the chance for a field test. But in judging assertions like this, remember that Eskimos have had close contact with polar bears for several thousand years.

During winter, ringed and bearded seals maintain tunnel-like breathing holes in ice that is many feet thick. These holes are often capped with an igloo-shaped dome created by water sloshing onto the surface when the animal enters from below. Inupiaq elders told me that polar bears are clever enough to excavate around the base of this dome, leaving it perfectly intact but weak enough that a hard swat will shatter the ice and smash the seal's skull. I couldn't help wondering if this were really true; but then a younger man told me he'd recently followed the tracks of a bear that had excavated one seal hole after another, exactly as the elders had described.

In the village where I lived, the most respected hunter was Igruk, a man in his 70s. He had an extraordinary sense of animals—a gift for understanding and predicting their behavior. Although he was no longer quick and strong, he joined a crew hunting bowhead whales during the spring migration, his main role being that of adviser. Each time Igruk spotted a whale coming from the south, he counted the number of blows, timed how long it stayed down, and noted the distance it traveled along the open lead, until it vanished toward the north. This way he learned to predict, with uncanny accuracy, where hunters could expect the whale to resurface.

I believe the expert Inupiaq hunter possesses as much knowledge as a highly trained scientist in our own society, although the information may be of a different sort. Volumes could be written on the behavior, ecology, and utilization of Arctic animals—polar bear, walrus, bowhead whale, beluga, bearded seal, ringed seal, caribou, musk ox, and others—based entirely on Eskimo knowledge.

Comparable bodies of knowledge existed in every Native American cul-

ture before the time of Columbus. Since then, even in the far north, Western education and cultural change have steadily eroded these traditions. Reflecting on a time before Europeans arrived, we can imagine the whole array of North American animal species—deer, elk, black bear, wolf, mountain lion, beaver, coyote, Canada goose, ruffed grouse, passenger pigeon, northern pike—each known in hundreds of different ways by tribal communities; the entire continent, sheathed in intricate webs of knowledge. Taken as a whole, this composed a vast intellectual legacy, born of intimacy with the natural world. Sadly, not more than a hint of it has ever been recorded.

Like other Native Americans, the Inupiaq acquired their knowledge through gradual accretion of naturalistic observations—year after year, lifetime after lifetime, generation after generation, century after century. Modern science often relies on other techniques—specialized full-time observation, controlled experiments, captive-animal studies, technological devises like radio collars—which can provide similar information much more quickly.

Yet Eskimo people have learned not only *about* animals but also *from* them. Polar bears hunt seals not only by waiting at their winter breathing holes, but also by stalking seals that crawl up on the ice to bask in the spring warmth. Both methods depend on being silent, staying downwind, keeping out of sight, and moving only when the seal is asleep or distracted. According to the elders, a stalking bear will even use one paw to cover its conspicuous black nose.

Inupiaq methods for hunting seals, both at breathing holes and atop the spring ice, are nearly identical to those of the polar bear. Is this a case of independent invention? Or did ancestral Eskimos learn the techniques by watching polar bears, who had perfected an adaptation to the sea-ice environment long before humans arrived in the Arctic?

The hunter's genius centers on knowing an animal's behavior so well he can turn it to his advantage. For instance, Igruk once saw a polar bear far off across flat ice, where he couldn't stalk it without being seen. But he knew an old technique of mimicking a seal. He lay down in plain sight, conspicuous in his dark parka and pants, then lifted and dropped his head like a seal, scratched the ice, and imitated flippers with his hands. The bear mistook his pursuer for prey. Each time Igruk lifted his head the animal kept still; whenever Igruk "slept" the bear crept closer. When it came near enough, a gunshot pierced the snowy silence. That night, polar bear meat was shared among the villagers.

"Each animal knows way more than you do," a Koyukon Indian elder was fond of telling me.

A traditional hunter like Igruk plumbs the depths of his intellect—his capacity to manipulate complex knowledge. But he also delves into his animal nature, drawing from intuitions of sense and body and heart: feeling the wind's touch, listening for the tick of moving ice, peering from crannies, hiding as if he himself were the hunted. He moves in a world of eyes, where everything watches—the bear, the seal, the wind, the moon and stars, the drifting ice, the silent waters below. He is beholden to powers we have long forgotten or ignored.

In Western society we rest comfortably on our own accepted truths about the nature of nature. We treat the environment as if it were numb to our presence and blind to our behavior. Yet despite our certainty on this matter, accounts of traditional people throughout the world reveal that most of humankind has concluded otherwise. Perhaps our scientific method really does follow the path to a single, absolute truth. But there may be wisdom in accepting other possibilities and opening ourselves to different views of the world.

I remember asking a Koyukon man about the behavior and temperament of the Canada goose. He described it as a gentle and good-natured animal, then added: "Even if [a goose] had the power to knock you over, I don't think it would do it."

For me, his words carried a deep metaphorical wisdom. They exemplified the Koyukon people's own restraint toward the world around them. And they offered a contrast to our culture, in which possessing the power to overwhelm the environment has long been sufficient justification for its use.

We often think of this continent as having been a pristine wilderness when the first Europeans arrived. Yet for at least 12,000 years, and possibly twice that long, Native American people had inhabited and intensively utilized the land; had gathered, hunted, fished, settled, and cultivated; had learned the terrain in all its details, infusing it with meaning and memory; and had shaped every aspect of their life around it. That humans could sustain membership in a natural community for such an enormous span of time without profoundly degrading it fairly staggers the imagination. And it gives strong testimony to the adaptation of mind—the braiding together of knowledge and ideology—that linked North America's indigenous people with their environment.

A Koyukon elder, who took it upon himself to be my teacher, was fond of telling me: "Each animal knows way more than you do." He spoke as if it summarized all that he understood and believed.

This statement epitomizes relationships to the natural world among many Native American people. And it goes far in explaining the diversity and fecundity of life on our continent when the first sailing ship approached these shores.

There's been much discussion in recent years about what biologist E. O. Wilson has termed "biophilia"—a deep, pervasive, ubiquitous, all-embracing affinity for nonhuman life. Evidence for this "instinct" may be elusive in Western cultures, but not among tradi-

tional societies. People like the Koyukon manifest biophilia in virtually all dimensions of their existence. Connectedness with nonhuman life infuses the whole spectrum of their thought, behavior, and belief.

It's often said that a fish might have no concept of water, never having left it. In the same way, traditional peoples might never stand far enough outside themselves to imagine a generalized concept of biophilia. Perhaps it would be impossible for people so intimately bound with the natural world, people who recognize that all nature is our own embracing community. Perhaps, to bring a word like *biophilia* into their language, they would first need to separate themselves from nature.

In April 1971 I was in a whaling camp several miles off the Arctic coast with a group of Inupiaq hunters, including Igruk, who understood animals so well he almost seemed to enter their minds.

Onshore winds had closed the lead that migrating whales usually follow, but one large opening remained, and here the Inupiaq men placed their camp. For a couple of days there had been no whales, so everyone stayed inside the warm tent, talking and relaxing. The old man rested on a soft bed of caribou skins with his eyes closed. Then, suddenly, he interrupted the conversation: "I think a whale is coming, and perhaps it will surface very close. . . ."

To my amazement everyone jumped into action, although none had seen or heard anything except Igruk's words. Only he stayed behind, while the others rushed for the water's edge. I was last to leave the tent. Seconds after I stepped outside, a broad, shining back cleaved the still water near the opposite side of the opening, accompanied by the burst of a whale's blow.

Later, when I asked how he'd known, Igruk said, "There was a ringing inside my ears." I have no explanation other than his; I can only report what I saw. None of the Inupiaq crew members even commented afterward, as if nothing out of the ordinary had happened.

Hunting, Gathering, and the Molimo*

Kevin Duffy

A bubbling sound awakened me in the darkness just before dawn. I reached out and felt the sticks and leaves of my shelter, reassured that it was not a dream. I really was lying in an Mbuti hut in the center of a primeval African forest. Abruptly, the bubbling was interrupted by a hacking cough, and I knew then that somebody with a water pipe was having an early morning smoke of bangi in the hut next to mine. Leafy walls do little to impede sounds between huts in a camp of nomadic Mbuti Pygmies, especially during the still hours between dusk and dawn.

I rolled over on the rough, earthen floor and peered out the open doorway at the dim shapes of the other huts. The bubbling noise had stopped, and from another direction an infant began to cry and was soon soothed by an attentive mother. From another hut came the first sounds of conversation, a man and woman talking, their every word carrying clearly into the neighboring huts. That seemed to be the signal for the camp to wake up. The light was stronger now, and one by one people wandered out of their huts and began their day in much the same way their ancestors—and mine—had for thousands of years. There were neighbors to greet, infants to wash, food to prepare, plans to discuss. I felt that I shared their humanity and was a part of it, for their world was fundamentally my world too.

But here there would be no children

to get ready for school, no rush-hour traffic to fight, no bus, train, or airplane to catch, no time clock to punch. For these nomadic Mbuti Pygmies, this would be just another day without name, number, or written record. In the daily quest for food, it would be remembered only as long as events made it memorable.

It takes little to create a cheerful mood in an Mbuti camp, only a dry, friendly forest and signs that the hunting is good—everything that a reasonable person could ask for. Children squealed and laughed as they chased each other around the huts. A group of larger boys and girls were taking turns swinging on a vine that hung from a tall tree. A young mother sang a gentle lullaby to her infant while her friends prepared foods, tended other small children, and brought smoldering logs outside from their huts to start fires for cooking.

It was the kind of morning the Mbuti like, with sunlight streaming through the trees above and no rain on the way. Soon the clinging moisture of the night would be gone, again leaving the forest a fit place in which to hunt and gather food. It was a happy camp, but only the women and children readily showed it with their bright mood and enthusiasm. The men and grown boys remained mostly reserved and aloof from the early morning activities of the women and girls. Only when the food was ready would they mingle again.

I followed a line of chatting women and girls leaving camp to fetch water. They laughed playfully when I joined them on a path through the trees, for usually men and women do not go to the river together. Yet as the Mbuti do not wash or bathe every day, the women were my surest way of finding the river. (Mbuti camps are usually built away from rivers and streams to avoid mosquitoes.) The older men were sitting at the communal fire

sharing a pipe of bangi. The young married hunters sat separately, passing around their own pipe of bangi, while the young bachelors stood talking in a group just outside the camp, glancing from time to time at the unmarried girls.

The women led me to a stream flowing gently beneath a vaulted archway of moss-covered trees, its clear water bubbling invitingly beneath a little waterfall. I wandered upstream alone and soon found a secluded spot for bathing. The deepest part only reached my knees, but it was refreshing to wash off the mud and sweat from the previous day's march. From downstream I could hear much laughing and splashing, and I wondered for how many thousands of years the forest had echoed with these delightful sounds. A movement caught my eye and I looked up at the bank to see two boys staring at me curiously. From then on, there would be no doubt in their minds; I was white all over, not just on my hands and face. I smiled and invited them into the water. They called into the trees behind them, and three other boys of various ages joined them in jumping into the stream beside me. I splashed water at them and they splashed back and at each other. They thought the entire affair hilarious, especially when my shoes and clothes were knocked off a rock into the water and I grimaced in mock disgust as I held them up, dripping wet.

Back at the camp, I watched the women prepare the morning meal, each in her own way. A woman peeled some bananas and neatly put the skins in a pile. Another woman carelessly flung plantain skins over her shoulder to land somewhere behind her hut. She then placed the newly skinned fruit directly on the fire to cook. One woman was peeling a cassava root, its wet pulp gleaming whitely in the shade of the trees. It was obvious that these Mbuti net hunters and their wives were efficient enough with their net hunting to produce more meat than they required for their own needs, for it was from the trading of such excess meat that they had acquired the cassava, bananas, and other cultivated foods from the villagers. Of the items that do not grow naturally in the forest, the ones the Mbuti like most are the banana and its coarser cousin, the plantain. Many an antelope has died in exchange for a bunch of bananas.

I was looking over my almost completed hut when Abeli came by, carrying an empty cooking pot. "Rice?" he asked. "Do you want some rice cooked?" I nodded and we crawled into the hut where I had slept the night before, a place that sheltered all my worldly goods of the moment. I handed Abeli a beer bottle filled with palm oil and corked with a rolled-up leaf and then gave him the bag of precious rice (precious because there was no place where I could purchase more when it ran out). I watched as he poured enough rice into the pot for about ten people.

"Is that for you, Kachelewa, Anziani, and myself?" I inquired.

"Yes." He shrugged as he went off to have the rice washed and cooked by Sangali and Anziani. Abeli was not one for unnecessary explanations, but I was glad that the rice and any other foods I gave him would apparently be shared among his relatives and friends, for I wanted to show my gratitude to these people who were allowing me to become a part of their daily lives.

Abeli was a serious young Mbuti caught between the worlds of the forest and the village. He liked to stay at Epulu and had somehow acquired a tattered shirt and short trousers. Yet his immediate relatives spent many months every year roaming the forest, the place where he was born and reared and that provided the meat that probably paid for his clothes. As an Mbuti, he could survive in the forest without the village, but not in the village without the forest. Only when he imitated the villagers and cultivated his own food would he be independent of the forest—and the villagers.

On a tree stump near me, a youth sat, lengthening his father's hunting net by

weaving in twine newly made from the kusa vine. The finished mesh was remarkably symmetrical and could well have been factory made. Altogether I counted about nine hunting nets about the camp, some of them neatly coiled and ready to be carried on a hunter's shoulder into the forest. Three of them were being repaired by hunters. Although both men and women may gather the bark of the kusa vine and roll it into twine, it is the man's task to weave the net and repair it when necessary, just as only he may make arrows or put a new string on a bow, or work on anything else that has to do with the tools of the hunter. In the same way, only women weave the baskets traditionally used by them to gather and carry food. The other main items of value in an Mbuti camp—cooking pots and metal knives—are acquired ready-made from the villagers, for the Mbuti have never learned to work with clay, stone, or iron.

From experience, I had brought a bag of salt into the forest, and it wasn't long before every family in the camp had come to me for a handful of this popular item. Like the rice, it would be used up all too soon. The Mbuti share their food willingly enough with other members of the band, and I believe that this generosity would have extended to me for a time if I had arrived in their camp without food, or without anything to offer in exchange for food. In the same way, they hoped that the foods I brought into the forest would be shared around, and not just among those who came with me as guides. So now the bag of rice that would have lasted me a month might be used up in a couple of days. This is one reason I have sometimes found myself sooner than expected eating an all-Mbuti diet, which may include such tasty items as elephant, pig, pangolin, monkey, rat, snake, grubs, termites, and several varieties of mushrooms, fruits, nuts, mbau seeds, roots, and vegetables, all of which exist wild in the forest for those skillful enough to find them.

When the inevitable time came that I ran out of my own food, I would offer either goods or money in exchange for Mbuti fare. The goods I carried on this occasion included pocket knives, magnifying glasses (my idea of waterproof

fire makers), nylon fishing line, and hooks. From time to time I would give money and empty containers, plastic bags, and the like to someone walking to the road. With luck they would bring back rice, oil, salt, bananas, and other items to eat with the venison or whatever meat was in camp, if any. The price I paid for this service included giving away more than half of the food soon after it arrived in the camp.

The road has been cut through the forest long enough for the Mbuti to know what paper money is, but not every Mbuti knows how to count into the higher numbers or to judge the real value of money. To enhance my acceptability as a guest of the community, I also brought two cartons of cigarettes, for I have yet to meet an Mbuti who does not smoke. Because they cannot afford to buy cigarettes from a roadside store, they usually smoke dried tobacco leaves acquired from the villagers who grow them. They smoke this in their pipes, sometimes mixing it with bangi. When I was present they learned to ask me for pieces of paper in which to roll the tobacco into cigarettes.

Soon everybody had settled down for breakfast. Among the foods I saw at the various family groups were boiled bananas, roasted plantains, cassava, stewed leafy vegetables gathered wild from the forest, and meat—altogether a better selection than usual for breakfast in an Mbuti camp. The cassava had been pounded into a coarse flour in the traditional way and boiled with very little water, creating a thick, puttylike substance to be eaten by hand. I took a plate from my pack and joined Abeli's group around their fire, where I was given a piece of the aging antelope leg presented to me by Makubasi the previous day and which I had passed on to Abeli, hoping never to see it again. The bottle of village-produced palm oil I had brought would be used to make it and the other food more palatable to us all.

We shared common dishes, each person taking a handful of cassava in turn, shaping it in one hand, and dipping it into the vegetables and juices. I had the only plate but ate with my fingers like the others. As guests, Abeli and I were privileged to have the only chairs, which had been simply made by lashing three sticks together in the middle with a piece of vine and spreading them into a kind of three-legged stool. There was no cushion or padding of any kind. One just somehow sat wedged between the three upright sticks. The others sat on logs or on little pieces of wood on the ground.

The meal was eaten in an agreeable, leisurely fashion. The plantains and meat were politely passed around so that everybody received a fair share. At first nobody reached for the biggest or best parts or gulped their food down. Instead, each person savored what he or she ate as if it were a new and exotic dish. Nearby, Makela and Kimbi were eating with another girl of about the same age. From time to time all three of them smiled in our direction. Abeli and Kachelewa returned their glances readily enough, but did not smile back.

I politely refused more of the antelope leg now offered by Sangali's husband and instead took a piece of banana. I had lived in Africa long enough to have contracted and thankfully recovered from several of the more serious diseases endemic to the area. After such hard-won experience, I no longer felt it necessary to prove I could eat anything that came my way.

When we had all finished, Sangali wrapped some of the cassava and meat in mongongo leaves and gave the food to her eldest child, a boy of about eleven. As an apprentice hunter, he would carry it into the forest for his father, where it would be eaten as a midday meal. Most boys and youths were supposed to stay with their fathers or perhaps an uncle during the hunt. In this way they learned by example and were also useful as an extra pair of hands at otherwise unguarded sections of net.

About two hours after sunrise the hunters began to walk into the forest. They went in small groups or one by one, some carrying nets over their shoulders. Several men carried spears, and one or two had a bow and some arrows. Contact was maintained with those ahead by shouting and listening for the call that came back. The sound was uniquely Pygmy and was the same as that I had heard from Pygmies a thousand miles to the west—a series of loud "ooohs" that

cheerfully echoed back and forth through the forest. The sound effectively transformed an awesome wilderness into a friendly place for a little band of humans who needed each other to survive.

I accompanied Kachelewa and Abeli to the kungya, a fire made in the forest some distance from the camp each morning before the hunt. Besides serving as a gathering place, its purpose was to honor the forest and to ask for its blessing on the hunt. The fire had been made earlier by one of the hunters while the others were having breakfast. Now all the hunters sat near this fire, some of them talking, others silent.

While they waited for the women to arrive, they burned small, fresh branches with green leaves still attached. From the burned ends of such sticks, they blackened parts of their faces, especially around the eyes. In this way, they wore a part of the hunting fire, which in turn had been made from the sacred forest, in order to bring good luck in the hunt. Painting this essence of the forest around their eyes was meant to magically help the hunters see the animals better.

The women began to arrive and wait nearby, most of them carrying large baskets in which they would collect mushrooms and other wild edibles along the way. If the hunt went well, these baskets would also be used to carry back any small antelope killed at the net. Back at the camp there remained a few people old enough to have grown sons to do their hunting for them. They would look after the children who were too young—or not young enough—to go on the hunt. Only children older than about ten and infants not yet weaned went on the hunt. Such an infant was slung from its mother's shoulder in a piece of animal skin and could be breast-fed even while its mother moved through the forest with the band of hunters.

Only when everybody had collected in the vicinity of the kungya did we all depart for the first place in the forest where the nets would be set up. From now on there was no shouting, and talking was done in whispers or not at all. Abeli had discarded his shirt and trousers and wore only the traditional Mbuti bark cloth. He seemed extraordinarily happy and grinned broadly when he said

that he was not going to stay with me, but would join the hunters ahead. Young and eager, he had lost the somber mask he had seemed to adopt in the world of the village. Here in the forest, showing one's emotions was natural, desirable, and expected. Abeli had grown up in the forest an Mbuti, yet was just as thrilled with the hunt as I was. In moments he had disappeared with his peers among the trees, leaving me with the less energetic Kachelewa, whose name meant "late" or "to be late" in at least two of the African languages I know.

The first area chosen to place the nets was about a mile from the camp and contained the sort of vegetation where some nocturnal antelopes like to hide during the day. Working quietly, the hunters uncoiled their nets and attached them end to end in a half-circle about three hundred yards in diameter. Made from natural materials and suspended or tied from bushes or trees, the thin strands of the net formed an almost invisible barrier among the shadows. It was only three and a half feet high, however, and was meant mainly for the smaller kinds of forest antelope and was generally useless against full-grown specimens of such animals as the giant forest hog, the forest buffalo, the bongo antelope, and the okapi.

The forest was almost silent now except for a shrill symphony of crickets. The only people Kachelewa and I could see were Usaute and his young son, who continued to adjust their net here and there so that a tiny antelope wouldn't be able to nudge beneath it and escape. All I had to do was wait, an easy task.

The notion of man as hunter and chief provider is nowhere better exposed as a myth than in Mbuti net hunting.

In their traditional role as beaters, it is the women who must outwit the animals being hunted. They do this with stealth as they first silently approach the animals hidden among the trees, then with noise as they drive the animals into the net. A faulty sense of direction or poor timing by the women and the animals could well escape before the women can close the trap.

In contrast, it takes no particular skill to wait at the net or to kill an animal that runs blindly into it and becomes entangled in its mesh. Sometimes a woman will help guard the section of net owned by her husband. She may do this because she is an older woman and chooses this less strenuous work, or because her husband has no close relatives available to help him with his section of the net. More than any other people I know in Africa, the Mbuti are willing to ignore traditional male and female roles when total coordination is required to obtain food.

I knew that by now the women were probably in a position from which they would begin their advance into the half-circle of nets, driving any hiding animals ahead of them toward the waiting hunters. I wondered what would happen if they surprised a buffalo or leopard.

Just then the unseen women started to shout and beat the bushes as they began their drive. Careful not to move, I strained to see any animal that might come bounding toward me. To the left, I heard the terrified squealing of an mboloko, the local name for the little blue duiker antelope. A sudden silence meant it had perhaps died when a spear found its mark, or else it had escaped from the net. But within moments the first drive was over, and it turned out that the mboloko I heard was the only animal killed.

We quietly walked another mile and the nets were set up once more. This time I found myself waiting expectantly with Anjuway and his wife, Sefini, who guarded their net together. For the moment, Kachelewa had apparently taken his position somewhere else.

Anjuway ran a finger over the sharp edge of his rusted iron spear and muttered something about having nobody to help him except a woman and a Muzungu (in many African languages the word for a European or fair-skinned person of any origin except an African albino).

Again the distant women began to chant and shout as they advanced into the circle of waiting nets. Beside me, Anjuway stood poised with his spear; he was almost invisible in the shadows. Unarmed, his wife stood apart at another section of the net, ready to tackle whatever might dash toward us.

Suddenly two mboloko came running out of the shadows directly into the net between us. Anjuway stabbed the one

nearest him with his spear, narrowly missing Sefini, who was gamely trying to grab the other one, a male with sharp little horns. She finally gripped it by the hind legs as it thrashed in the net, and lifted it off the ground as it squealed pathetically. Quickly, Anjuway slit its throat, using the blade of his spear as a knife. Sefini put both mboloko in her basket, a total weight of about fifty pounds, and began to help Anjuway roll up his net for the next drive. It was all quite efficient. Incidentally, among the various duiker antelopes, and including the okapi, of the Ituri forest, the females are larger than the males of their species, an interesting development for which I do not have an explanation.

In the next hunt, I joined the women beaters instead of waiting at the net. A young married woman named Miasa agreed to be my guide on this adventure. Both she and her friends thought it was an amusing idea to have me along, although there were two women who apparently thought I would scare the animals away.

Miasa was a cheerful, buxom young woman who was clearly popular among her peers. She seemed tireless in everything she did. During the walk to the next net-hunt location, I was fascinated to see her skill in gathering wild edible things along the way. In the dark shadows beneath a dense cover of foliage, she somehow spotted a cluster of mushrooms, which she quickly gathered and put in the basket on her back. Usually without slowing her pace, she collected handfuls of berries, kola nuts, and some green leaves. She did all this while apparently continuing to be aware of the location of everybody else, including the men, who were nowhere in sight. There was no shouting, but several times I saw Miasa pause to listen carefully for sounds I did not always hear or recognize. But I knew that at least a part of her apparent sense of direction was based on things and places familiar to her. To me, an outsider, the endless trees looked alike.

Each Mbuti band tended to spend its entire existence in one particular section of the forest, usually marked by natural boundaries such as streams, hills, and changes in the vegetation. In a lifetime of nomadic wandering through one's

large but clearly defined territory, certain landmarks and locations would become established—the place where Sangu killed the elephant, the tree where Madada fell while getting honey, the sunny clearing where the animals come to eat the earth with the salt in it. To the Mbuti, these were street names and place names imprinted only on memory and were ever changing over the generations as new events occurred and old ones were forgotten. To be an Mbuti was the only way to know them all.

Miasa wore a G-string made of faded bark cloth as her only adornment, and like the other women, her feet were bare. In the irresponsible days of my youth, when I had hunted elephants for their ivory, I had envied my African companions for their ability to walk barefoot while hunting. The game in the Ituri was smaller but just as sensitive to the dramatic crunch of a dried leaf or the painfully loud snap of a twig. To be noisy now meant to disgrace oneself and to justify the warnings of the two women who had objected to my joining the ranks of the beaters.

The best way to do all the right things was to follow Miasa and do everything she did. I stopped to listen only when she listened, and walked only where she walked. I did not want to be the one to step on a piece of dried wood, and so kept an eye carefully on the path directly ahead. Momentarily distracted by the dappled light playing on the rippling, glossy surface of my companion's bare glutei maximi, I eventually did step on a twig, but Miasa was polite enough to ignore it.

At the place where we found the men silently setting up the nets, the women divided into two groups, each group keeping pace with its end of the combined net as it quickly grew again into a large half-circle. When the last net was tied in place, I followed Miasa as she quietly led her companions in a line through the forest. In a few moments we met the first of the other women coming from the opposite end of the net, and the trap was set.

For me, it was a truly unique experience. I had always hunted alone or with other men. Women were the beings who cooked what the men killed and brought back to camp. But here the hunt depended on the skill of the women and their knowledge of the psychology of the animals they hunted. The results at the net would thus in large measure reflect the efforts of the women and not just of the men who mindlessly butchered whatever animals the women sent their way. And if a hunt went badly and no animals were killed, the food the women industriously collected in their baskets during the hunt would be all there was, and it would be shared with the men.

Miasa glanced along the line of women and girls as she waited with them. Now everything depended on an antelope or two hiding somewhere among the trees between us and the men. In the distance a troop of baboons jabbered excitedly, then there was silence again. From somewhere I heard a single call that was the signal we waited for. With lusty shouts and the beating of sticks, the women simultaneously began their advance toward the distant net and the silent, waiting hunters.

I saw Miasa reach for something hiding beneath a bush. It was a baby mboloko antelope, apparently left by its mother when the shouting began. When we reached the net, the only antelope I saw killed was a female that was probably the baby's mother. Miasa carried the struggling baby to her husband, who promptly killed it with Miasa's own knife before putting it in his wife's basket, which she had left at the net. The baby's mother ended up in the basket of the wife of the hunter in whose net it had been killed. Apparently there had been another antelope, but it had somehow jumped the net and escaped.

When Kachelewa appeared, I suggested to him that we head back toward the camp. This pleased him because he did not care much for the hard work involved in hunting; this is probably why I found him in Epulu. But like Abeli, he had been reared in the forest and was just as skilled in its lore as the hunters we were leaving behind.

During the walk back to Camp Ekale, it was Kachelewa who first heard the distant sound of chopping. He stopped in his tracks and cocked his head to listen. "Honey," he said dramatically. "Somebody has found a honey tree." He looked at me expectantly.

"Let's go and eat some honey," I told him, wanting to witness the event.

Kachelewa took off with more energy than he had shown all day, plunging northward through the trees, away from the track we had been following. Stopping every few minutes, he would again locate the sound and dash off again. Watching his enthusiastic behavior, I wondered what he would say if he could see the dozens of glass jars of honey on display in the average modern supermarket. In a short time the chopping stopped, but happily we could now hear the sound of voices, and minutes later we came out in a clearing to find the two girls Kimbi and Makela sitting on a log beneath a large buttress-rooted tree. From high above us came the sound of two men talking. They were so far up the tree that they couldn't be seen from the ground. I sat beside the girls and watched Kachelewa begin to climb the hanging vines that led up to where the two men were. About thirty feet off the ground, he changed his mind and came back down to flirt with the girls instead.

Soon a basket lined with leaves was lowered on a rope of tree bark through the overhead greenery. It was half full of honeycombs, and Kachelewa dashed to hold a cupped leaf beneath it to catch the precious stream of leaking honey. Minutes later, the two youths who had performed the dangerous raid on a high-altitude bees' nest climbed down the vines to join us in the feast. The boys' names were Sefu and Pushipush, and it was soon apparent that Pushipush was unable to talk or even make recognizable sounds. He was in fact dumb, and possibly a deaf mute. He also had the only buckteeth I had seen in the Ituri forest, and I wondered if this had anything to do with his condition. He was about eighteen years old, unmarried, and as I would subsequently learn, a kind of camp clown. Nobody took him seriously, especially Kachelewa, who teased him mercilessly by forever imitating the pathetic animal sounds he made, although it is doubtful if Pushipush was fully aware of the teasing. On the other hand, when I later tested his hearing by shouting his name when he had his back to me, he stopped walking two out of three times and looked around at me

with a puzzled expression on his face. On this scant evidence, I am forever left wondering whether he was partly deaf or if he was so accustomed to people not taking him seriously that he had learned to ignore the sincere but rare attempts to communicate with him.

When Pushipush produced a little rusted can and indicated with gestures and noises that he wanted some of the honey he had risked his life for, the others ignored him, and he was apparently too gentle to take it for himself. I hoped he had been clever enough to eat his share while still up in the tree.

Though Kachelewa had insisted that his friend was crazy, it was Pushipush we all followed without question as he unerringly led the way back to camp through the endless maze of trees, absently tapping a finger against his little rusted can as if it was a miniature drum.

This had been the second time in a week that I found honey being gathered in the Ituri. In the tropical Ituri forest, the presence of bees and their nests is constant despite a so-called "honey season." Only the quality and quantity of the honey may vary, depending on the seasonal flowering of certain trees, especially the mbau tree, which also produces a beanlike seed that both the Mbuti and the wild animals and even the fish in the river eat. The mbau bean is the same one that the Mbuti taught Stanley to eat when he was starving.

By midafternoon the hunters and women began arriving back at Camp Ekale. Several of the women carried mboloko in their baskets, and one young hunter proudly staggered back carrying a young yellow-backed duiker on his shoulders; next to the bongo, this is the largest species of antelope in the forest. It had been a good day's hunt, and the camp had a distinctively festive air about it. Both men and women returning from the hunt wore bunches of green leaves tucked into their belts as decoration. People laughed and shouted at one another across the camp, sometimes joking about events of the hunt, especially where somebody had missed an easy target or made a fool of himself in some way. But mistakes or not, there was an abundance of food and no need to hunt the next day. . . .

WHY WOMEN CHANGE

The winners of evolution's race are those who can leave behind the most offspring to carry on their progenitors' genes. So doesn't it seem odd that human females should be hobbled in their prime by menopause?

JARED DIAMOND

Jared Diamond is a contributing editor of DISCOVER, a professor of physiology at the UCLA School of Medicine, a recipient of a MacArthur genius award, and a research associate in ornithology at the American Museum of Natural History. Expanded versions of many of his DIS-COVER articles appear in his book The Third Chimpanzee: The Evolution and Future of the Human Animal, *which won Britain's 1992 COPUS prize for best science book and the* Los Angeles Times science book prize.

Most wild animals remain fertile until they die. So do human males: although some may eventually become less fertile, men in general experience no shutdown of fertility, and indeed there are innumerable well-attested cases of old men, including a 94-year-old, fathering children.

But for women the situation is different. Human females undergo a steep decline in fertility from around the age of 40 and within a decade or so can no longer produce children. While some women continue to have regular menstrual cycles up to the age of 54 or 55, conception after the age of 50 was almost unknown until the recent advent of hormone therapy and artificial fertilization.

Human female menopause thus appears to be an inevitable fact of life, albeit sometimes a painful one. But to an evolutionary biologist, it is a paradoxical aberration in the animal world. The essence of natural selection is that it promotes genes for traits that increase one's number of descendants bearing those genes. How could natural selection possibly result in every female member of a species carrying genes that throttle her ability to leave more descendants? Of course, evolutionary biologists (including me) are not implying that a woman's only proper role is to stay home and care for babies and to forget about other fulfilling experiences. Instead I am using standard evolutionary reasoning to try to understand how men's and women's bodies came to be the way they are. That reasoning tends to regard menopause as among the most bizarre features of human sexuality. But it is also among the most important. Along with the big brains and upright posture that every text of human evolution emphasizes, I consider menopause to be among the biological traits essential for making us distinctively human—something qualitatively different from, and more than, an ape.

Not everyone agrees with me about the evolutionary importance of human female menopause. Many biologists see no need to discuss it further, since they don't think it poses an unsolved problem. Their objections are of three types. First, some dismiss it as a result of a recent increase in human expected life span. That increase stems not just from public health measures developed within the last century but possibly also from the rise of agriculture 10,000 years ago, and even more likely from evolutionary changes leading to increased human survival skills within the last 40,000 years.

According to proponents of this view, menopause could not have been a frequent occurrence for most of the several million years of human evolution, because (supposedly) almost no women or men used to survive past the age of 45 or 50. Of course the female reproductive tract was programmed to shut down by age 50, since it would not have had the opportunity to operate thereafter anyway. The increase in human life span, these critics believe, has occurred much too recently in our evolutionary history for the female reproductive tract to have had time to adjust.

What this view overlooks, however, is that the human male reproductive tract and every other biological function of both women and men continue to function in most people for decades after age 50. If all other biological functions adjusted quickly to our new long life span, why was female reproduction uniquely incapable of doing so?

Furthermore, the claim that in the past few women survived until the age of menopause is based solely on paleodemography, which attempts to estimate age at time of death in ancient skeletons. Those estimates rest on unproven, implausible assumptions, such as that the recovered skeletons represent an unbiased sample of an entire ancient population, or that ancient adult skeletons' age of death can accurately be determined. While there's no question that paleodemographers can distinguish an ancient skeleton of a 10-year-old from that of a 25-year-old, they have never demonstrated that they can distinguish an ancient 40-year-old from a 55-year-old. One can hardly reason by comparison with skeletons of modern people, whose bones surely age at different rates from bones of ancients with different lifestyles, diets, and diseases.

A second objection acknowledges that human female menopause may be an ancient phenomenon but denies that it is unique to humans. Many wild animals undergo a decline in fertility with age. Some elderly individuals of many wild mammal and bird species are found to be infertile. Among animals in laboratory cages or zoos, with their lives considerably extended over expected spans in the wild by a gourmet diet, superb medical care, and protection from enemies, many elderly female rhesus monkeys and individuals of several strains of laboratory mice do become infertile. Hence some biologists object that human female menopause is merely part of a widespread phenomenon of animal menopause, not something peculiar to humans.

However, one swallow does not make a summer, nor does one sterile female constitute menopause. Establishing the existence of menopause as a biologically significant phenomenon in the wild requires far more than just coming upon the occasional sterile elderly individual in the wild or observing regular sterility in caged animals with artificially extended life spans. It requires finding a wild animal population in which a substantial proportion of females become sterile and spend a significant fraction of their life spans after the end of their fertility.

The human species does fulfill that definition, but only one wild animal species is known to do so: the short-finned pilot whale. One-quarter of all adult females killed by whalers prove to be postmenopausal, as judged by the condition of their ovaries. Female pilot whales enter menopause at the age of 30 or 40

years, have a mean survival of at least 14 years after menopause, and may live for over 60 years. Menopause as a biologically significant phenomenon is thus not strictly unique to humans, being shared at least with that one species of whale.

There is no obvious reason we had to evolve eggs that degenerate by the end of half a century. Eggs of elephants, baleen whales, and tortoises remain viable for at least 60 years.

But human female menopause remains sufficiently unusual in the animal world that its evolution requires explanation. We certainly did not inherit it from pilot whales, from whose ancestors our own ancestors parted company over 50 million years ago. In fact, we must have evolved it after we separated from the apes just 7 million to 5 million years ago, because we undergo menopause whereas chimps and gorillas appear not to (or at least not regularly).

The third and last objection acknowledges human menopause as an ancient phenomenon that is indeed unusual among animals. But these critics say that we need not seek an explanation for menopause, because the puzzle has already been solved. The solution, they say is the physiological mechanism of menopause: the senescence and exhaustion of a woman's egg supply, fixed at birth and not added to after birth. An egg is lost at each menstrual cycle. By the time a woman is 50 years old, most of that original egg supply has been depleted. The remaining eggs are half a century old and increasingly unresponsive to hormones.

But there is a fatal counterobjection to this objection. While the objection is not wrong, it is incomplete. Yes, exhaustion and aging of the egg supply are the immediate cause of human menopause, but why did natural selection program

women so that their eggs become exhausted or aged in their forties? There is no obvious reason we had to evolve eggs that degenerate by the end of half a century. Eggs of elephants, baleen whales, and tortoises remain viable for at least 60 years. A mutation only slightly altering how eggs degenerate might have sufficed for women to remain fertile until age 60 or 75.

The easy part of the menopause puzzle is identifying the physiological mechanism by which a woman's egg supply becomes depleted or impaired by the time she is around 50 years old. The challenging problem is understanding why we evolved that seemingly self-defeating detail of reproductive physiology. Apparently there was nothing physiologically inevitable about human female menopause, and there was nothing evolutionarily inevitable about it from the perspective of mammals in general. Instead the human female, but not the human male, was programmed by natural selection, at some time within the last few million years, to shut down reproduction prematurely. That premature senescence is all the more surprising because it goes against an overwhelming trend: in other respects, we humans have evolved to age more slowly, not more rapidly, than most other animals.

As a woman ages, she can do more to increase the number of people bearing her genes by devoting herself to her existing children and grandchildren than by producing yet another child.

Any theory of menopause evolution must explain how a woman's apparently counterproductive evolutionary strategy of making fewer babies could actually result in her making more. Evidently, as a woman ages, she can do more to increase the number of people bearing her genes by devoting herself to her existing children, her potential grandchildren, and her other relatives than by producing yet another child.

That evolutionary chain of reasoning rests on several cruel facts. One is that the human child depends on its parents for an extraordinarily long time, longer than in any other animal species. A baby chimpanzee, as soon as it starts to be weaned, begins gathering its own food, mostly with its own hands. (Chimpanzee use of tools, such as fishing for termites with blades of grass or cracking nuts with stones, is of great interest to human scientists but of only limited dietary significance to chimpanzees.) The baby chimpanzee also prepares its food with its own hands. But human hunter-gatherers acquire most food with tools (digging sticks, nets, spears), prepare it with other tools (knives, pounders, huskers), and then cook it in a fire made by still other tools. Furthermore, they use tools to protect themselves against dangerous predators, unlike other prey animals, which use teeth and strong muscles. Making and wielding all those tools are completely beyond the manual dexterity and mental ability of young children. Tool use and toolmaking are transmitted not just by imitation but also by language, which takes over a decade for a child to master.

As a result, human children in most societies do not become capable of economic independence until their teens or twenties. Before that, they remain dependent on their parents, especially on the mother, because mothers tend to provide more child care than do fathers. Parents not only bring food and teach tool-making but also provide protection and status within the tribe. In traditional societies, early death of either parent endangers a child's life even if the surviving parent remarries, because of possible conflicts with the stepparent's genetic interests. A young orphan who is not adopted has even worse chances of surviving.

Hence a hunter-gatherer mother who already has several children risks losing her genetic investment in them if she does not survive until the youngest is at least a teenager. That's one cruel fact underlying human female menopause. Another is that the birth of each successive child immediately jeopardizes a mother's previous children because the mother risks dying in childbirth. In most other animal species that risk is very low. For example, in one study of 401 rhesus monkey pregnancies, only three mothers died in childbirth. For humans in traditional societies, the risk is much higher and increases with age. Even in affluent twentieth-century Western societies, the risk of dying in childbirth is seven times higher for a mother over the age of 40 than for a 20-year-old. But each new child puts the mother's life at risk not only because of the immediate risk of death in childbirth but also because of the delayed risk of death related to exhaustion by lactation, carrying a young child, and working harder to feed more mouths.

Infants of older mothers are themselves increasingly unlikely to survive or be healthy, because the risks of abortion, stillbirth, low birth weight, and genetic defects rise as the mother grows older. For instance, the risk of a fetus's carrying the genetic condition known as Down syndrome increases from one in 2,000 births for a mother under 30, one in 300 for a mother between the ages of 35 and 39, and one in 50 for a 43-year-old mother to the grim odds of one in 10 for a mother in her late forties.

Thus, as a woman gets older, she is likely to have accumulated more children, and she has been caring for them longer, so she is putting a bigger investment at risk with each successive pregnancy. But her chances of dying in or after childbirth, and the chances that the infant will die, also increase. In effect, the older mother is risking more for less potential gain. That's one set of factors that would tend to favor human female menopause and that would paradoxically result in a woman's having more surviving children by giving birth to fewer children.

But a hypothetical nonmenopausal older woman who died in childbirth, or while caring for an infant, would thereby be throwing away even more than her investment in her previous children. That is because a woman's children eventually begin producing children of their own, and those children count as part of the woman's prior investment. Especially in traditional societies, a woman's survival is important not only to her children but also to her grandchildren.

That extended role of postmenopausal women has been explored by anthropologists Kristen Hawkes, James O'Connell, and Nicholas Blurton Jones, who studied foraging by women of different ages among the Hadza hunter-gatherers of Tanzania. The women who devoted the most time to gathering food (especially roots, honey, and fruit) were postmenopausal women. Those hardworking Hadza grandmothers put in an impressive seven hours per day, compared with a mere three hours for girls not yet pregnant and four and a half hours for women of childbearing age. As one might expect, foraging returns (measured in pounds of food gathered per hour) increased with age and experience, so that mature women achieved higher returns than teenagers. Interestingly, the grandmothers' returns were still as high as women in their prime. The combination of putting in more foraging hours and maintaining an unchanged foraging efficiency meant that the postmenopausal grandmothers brought in more food per day than women of any of the younger groups, even though their large harvests were greatly in excess of their own personal needs and they no longer had dependent young children of their own to feed.

Observations indicated that the Hadza grandmothers were sharing their excess food harvest with close relatives, such as their grandchildren and grown children. As a strategy for transforming food calories into pounds of baby, it's more efficient for an older woman to donate the calories to grandchildren and grown children than to infants of her own, because her fertility decreases with age anyway, while her children are young adults at peak fertility. Naturally, menopausal grandmothers in traditional societies contribute more to their offspring than just food. They also act as baby-sitters for grandchildren, thereby helping their adult children churn out more babies bearing Grandma's genes. And though they work hard for their grandchildren, they're less likely to die as a result of exhaustion than if they were nursing infants as well as caring for them.

Supposedly, natural selection can't weed out mutations that affect only old people, because old people are "postreproductive." But no humans, except hermits, are ever truly postreproductive.

But menopause has another virtue, one that has received little attention. That is the importance of old people to their entire tribe in preliterate societies, which means every human society in the world from the time of human origins until the rise of writing in Mesopotamia around 3300 B.C.

A common genetics argument is that natural selection cannot weed out mutations that do not damage people until they are old, because old people are supposedly "postreproductive." I believe that such statements overlook an essential fact distinguishing humans from most animal species. No humans, except hermits, are ever truly postreproductive, in the sense of being unable to aid in the survival and reproduction of other people bearing their genes. Yes, I grant that if any orangutans lived long enough in the wild to become sterile, they would count as postreproductive, since orangutans (other than mothers with one young offspring) tend to be solitary. I also grant that the contributions of very old people to modern literate societies tend to decrease with age. That new phenomenon of modern societies is at the root of the enormous problems that old

age now poses, both for the elderly themselves and for the rest of society. But we moderns get most of our information through writing, television, or radio. We find it impossible to conceive of the overwhelming importance of elderly people in preliterate societies as repositories of information and experience.

Here is an example of that role. During my field studies of bird ecology on New Guinea and adjacent southwestern Pacific islands, I live among people who traditionally were without writing, depended on stone tools, and subsisted by farming and fishing supplemented by hunting and gathering. I am constantly asking villagers to tell me the names of local birds, animals, and plants in their language, and to tell me what they know about each species. New Guineans and Pacific islanders possess an enormous fund of biological knowledge, including names for a thousand or more species, plus information about where each species occurs, its behavior, its ecology, and its usefulness to humans. All that information is important because wild plants and animals furnish much of the people's food and all their building materials, medicines, and decorations.

Again and again, when I ask about some rare bird, only the older hunters know the answer, and eventually I ask a question that stumps even them. The hunters reply, "We have to ask the old man [or the old woman]." They take me to a hut where we find an old man or woman, blind with cataracts and toothless, able to eat food only after someone else has chewed it. But that old person is the tribe's library. Because the society traditionally lacked writing, that old person knows more about the local environment than anyone else and is the sole person with accurate knowledge of events that happened long ago. Out comes the rare bird's name, and a description of it.

The accumulated experience that the elderly remember is important for the whole tribe's survival. In 1976, for instance, I visited Rennell Island, one of the Solomon Islands, lying in the southwestern Pacific's cyclone belt. When I asked about wild fruits and seeds that birds ate, my Rennellese informants named dozens of plant species by Ren-

nell language names, named for each plant species all the bird and bat species that eat its fruit, and said whether the fruit is edible for people. They ranked fruits in three categories: those that people never eat, those that people regularly eat, and those that people eat only in famine times, such as after—and here I kept hearing a Rennell term initially unfamiliar to me—the *hungi kengi*.

Those words proved to be the Rennell name for the most destructive cyclone to have hit the island in living memory—apparently around 1910, based on people's references to datable events of the European colonial administration. The hungi kengi blew down most of Rennell's forest, destroyed gardens, and drove people to the brink of starvation. Islanders survived by eating fruits of wild plant species that were normally not eaten. But doing so required detailed knowledge about which plants are poisonous, which are not poisonous, and whether and how the poison can be removed by some technique of food preparation.

When I began pestering my middle-aged Rennellese informants with questions about fruit edibility, I was brought into a hut. There, once my eyes had become accustomed to the dim light, I saw the inevitable frail old woman. She was the last living person with direct experience of which plants were found safe and nutritious to eat after the *hungi kengi*, until people's gardens began producing again. The old woman explained that she had been a child not quite of marriageable age at the time of the *hungi kengi*. Since my visit to Rennell was in 1976, and since the cyclone had struck 66 years before, the woman was probably in her early eighties. Her survival after the 1910 cyclone had depended on information remembered by aged survivors of the last big cyclone before the *hungi kengi*. Now her people's ability to survive another cyclone would depend on her own memories, which were fortunately very detailed.

Such anecdotes could be multiplied indefinitely. Traditional human societies face frequent minor risks that threaten a few individuals, and also face rare natural catastrophes or intertribal wars that threaten the lives of everybody in the society. But virtually everyone in a small traditional society is related to one another. Hence old people in a traditional society are essential to the survival not only of their children and grandchildren but also of hundreds of other people who share their genes. In preliterate societies, no one is ever postreproductive.

Any preliterate human societies that included individuals old enough to remember the last *hungi kengi* had a much better chance of surviving the next one than did societies without such old people. The old men were not at risk from childbirth or from exhausting responsibilities of lactation and child care, so they did not evolve protection by menopause. But old women who did not undergo menopause tended to be eliminated from the human gene pool because they remained exposed to the risk of childbirth and the burden of child care. At times of crises, such as a *hungi kengi,*

the prior death of such an older woman also tended to eliminate all the woman's relatives from the gene pool—a huge genetic price to pay just for the dubious privilege of continuing to produce another baby or two against lengthening odds. That's what I see as a major driving force behind the evolution of human female menopause. Similar considerations may have led to the evolution of menopause in female pilot whales. Like us, whales are long-lived, involved in complex social relationships and lifelong family ties, and capable of sophisticated communication and learning.

If one were playing God and deciding whether to make older women undergo menopause, one would do a balance sheet, adding up the benefits of menopause in one column for comparison with its costs in another column. The costs of menopause are the potential children of a woman's old age that she forgoes. The potential

benefits include avoiding the increased risk of death due to childbirth and parenting at an advanced age, and thereby gaining the benefit of improved survival for one's grandchildren, prior children, and more distant relatives. The sizes of those benefits depend on many details: for example, how large the risk of death is in and after childbirth, how much that risk increases with age, how rapidly fertility decreases with age before menopause, and how rapidly it would continue to decrease in an aging woman who did not undergo menopause. All those factors are bound to differ between societies and are not easy for anthropologists to estimate. But natural selection is a more skilled mathematician because it has had millions of years in which to do the calculation. It concluded that menopause's benefits outweigh its costs, and that women can make more by making less.

Keepers of the Oaks

California is wilder now than it was before Europeans arrived. Where there now are forests, there once were vast acorn orchards, painstakingly tended by Native Americans.

GLEN MARTIN

Glen Martin is a staff writer for the San Francisco Chronicle *who writes mostly about the environment and natural resources. "The idea for this story came to me by talking with people in diverse fields," he says. "Anthropologists, enthnoo-botanists—they were all saying the same thing couched in different terms."*

ONE THURSDAY IN NOVEMBER 1856, a *Marysville Herald* reporter visited the native people of Yuba City, California. "It is not necessary for us to speak of their filth, and other circumstances connected with their miserable condition," he wrote. "We would rather ask, is there no method by which they could be made to improve themselves? In their council hall, as it is called, but more properly a deep dirty pit, with poles for bunks, and everything else in keeping, we saw three chiefs, and a dozen or more captains, large, muscular men, squatted on the ground by bowls of acorn mush, lazily lying in their bunks, with a few unraveling a red comfort, to bedeck themselves for some imbecile fandango. There is to us something so utterly abhorrent in the thought that they must waste away life like that in inactivity, or by the more speedy process of dissipation, to which they are becoming addicted. Could not those who live among us by some law be required to bind out their children to farmers and others, for a given period, so as to make them useful, and thus induct them to habits of cleanliness and industry?"

While twentieth-century anthropologists emphatically reject the reporter's moral judgments, until recently they did agree that California's natives were no farmers. They held that California, like most of North America during neolithic times, was for millennia a wilderness populated by hunter-gatherers. Before Columbus landed, they believed, American agriculture was confined to southwestern and eastern tribes, who cultivated beans, corns, and squash. California's natives neither sowed nor reaped. They appeared to fit the hunter-gatherer profile precisely, subsisting entirely on what nature offered them—grass seed, salmon, game, and acorns.

But recent research suggests that California's natives weren't waiting for the manna of acorns to fall from the trees into their hands. Instead, anthropologists and ethnographers increasingly view the state's first inhabitants as agriculturists. True, they didn't plant grains or vegetables or cultivate fruit trees, but they employed intensive horticultural practices to ensure that oak trees would flourish. In their own way, they farmed oaks.

Anyone who has ever nibbled on a raw acorn might doubt that the things are edible, let alone worth cultivating. But once the nuts have been processed to remove their tannins, which are responsible for the acrid taste, acorns are an impressive source of nourishment. With up to 18 percent fat, 6 percent protein, and 68 percent carbohydrate, depending on the species, they compare favorably with modern grains—wheat and corn register about 2 percent fat, 10 percent protein, and 75 percent carbohydrate. The acorns' richness and abundance made them the staff of life for California's natives.

To get the materials they wanted, the Indians had to stimulate growth through fire. Redbud, for example, responds to burning by sending out the straight new shoots needed for baskets.

That abundance was largely the result of the careful use of one important tool: fire. Californians certainly didn't practice agriculture in the traditional sense. They didn't domesticate the oak, as Mediterraneans did the almond, by selecting and planting nuts with useful characteristics. Oaks may have to grow 20 years or more before yielding a good acorn crop—hardly a desirable trait in an orchard tree. But by employing fire as a horticultural tool, California's natives achieved a singular feat. No other people have ever bent the recalcitrant oak so effectively to the human will. Simply put, regular low-level wildfires encourage oaks in California. Stop the fires, and plants with low fire resistance, such as shade-tolerant conifers and brush, dominate. This fact, researchers are recognizing, was not lost on California's Indians.

Historical descriptions support this conclusion. Spanish missionaries in the eighteenth and nineteenth centuries, and American settlers in the nineteenth century, reported that natives regularly set fire to grass and forestlands. As one woman of the Karok tribe explained in 1933, "Our kind of people never used the plow.... All they used to do was burn the brush at various places so that some good things will grow up.... And sometimes they burn where the tan oak trees are lest it be brushy when they pick up the acorns.... Some kinds of trees are better when it is burned off. They come up better ones again."

Fires helped keep the trees healthy, ensured bigger crops, and made it easier to gather the nuts. "Naturally occurring oak seedlings form very thick stands," says Pamela Muick, a San Francisco State University ecologist who is conducting an oak habitat study at the Elkhorn Slough Sanctuary on Monterey Bay. "Burning thins them out, creating a density pattern that allows trees to grow large, healthy, and easy to walk through."

As late as the 1960s, recall surviving members of California's tribes, people were setting fire to the forests every year, just after the midfall acorn harvest. One member of the Wukchumni Yokuts tribe told a researcher that the burning was necessary to rid oak lands of acorn pests. "If left unchecked, filbert worms and weevils can destroy up to 95 percent of the acorn crop dropped by individual trees," agrees Kat Anderson, an ethnobotanist with the American Indian Studies Center at UCLA, who for the past ten years has been studying the influence of Native American cultural practices on plant distribution. "Fire breaks the life cycle of both pests, ensuring much better crops."

Setting fires wasn't the only native practice that kept oaks healthy. "The preferred method of gathering acorns was to knock them off the trees with long, flexible poles," says Anderson. "But when they were knocking acorns off, people would also knock off dead or diseased wood, a practice that stimulates new growth. I've talked to elders who say that the traditional knocking off

of old wood has the same effect as a big snowstorm, which breaks off dead and weak wood—it's good for the trees."

California's native people also performed another task critical to successful agriculture: weed removal. Galen Clark, a nineteenth-century Yosemite Valley resident and one of Yosemite National Park's first nonnative caretakers, reported that Indians diligently pulled cottonwood seedlings from meadows surrounding oak groves. Keeping those meadows open protected the oaks from harmful crown fires and encouraged light surface fires that would burn out only the undergrowth. Other modes of weeding may have been practiced as well, though solid evidence is lacking. "I've found that a quick removal of the grass around each seedling oak in the spring contributes tremendously to their vigor," says Muick. "Annual grasses are serious competitors with young oaks for water and nutrients. A few seconds of weeding for each tree during the first few seasons is all it takes—they respond tremendously. I can't believe that similar empirical observations weren't made by indigenous people."

Fire, though, was the primary horticultural tool. It was easily and quickly employed, and it could be used to work many acres. Applied regularly over a vast area for centuries, fire became a force as profound as weather in its impact on regional ecology.

Essentially, large portions of California tend to go one of two ways, depending on whether fire regularly burns across the landscape. In the Sierra foothills and other portions of the north, the choices are forests of conifers—dominated by incense cedar and white fir—or savannas of oaks. In the coastal central and the southern parts of the state, the choice is chaparral or oaks. Fires favor oak habitats in both areas. If fires aren't regularly introduced, the oaks gradually disappear.

For the past 70 years, the fires have been stopped, by California's fire-fighting agencies. As a result, much of California's forestland looks very different from the way it looked when European explorers first arrived. As late as 1844 when explorer John C. Fremont led an expedition to the Sacramento Valley, he

described the north state foothills as "smooth and grassy; [the woodlands] had no undergrowth; and in the open valleys of rivulets, or around spring heads, the low groves of oak give the appearance of orchards in an old cultivated country." Similarly, a nineteenth-century visitor to the middle fork of the Tuolumne River near Yosemite Valley found it "like an English park—a lovely valley, wide and grassy, broken with clumps of oak and cedar." Fire made the difference.

However much benefit the native people derived from oaks, it appears the stately trees weren't their original reason for burning off the land. Natives may have been setting fires in California for at least 5,000 years, speculates Anderson, judging by how long fire-loving giant sequoias have been expanding their range. But California's Indians didn't begin relying on acorns until at least 1,000 years later.

"At first, acorns seem to have been a food of opportunistic significance, not a staple," says anthropologist Helen McCarthy of the University of California at Davis, who has been studying the relationship between California's native people and plants for more than 25 years. "Natives buried them for a long time, and groundwater slowly removed the tannins. Then, we think, they were eaten one by one." Ambitious acorn processing, she says, is associated with stone mortars and pestles—and those that have been recovered are 4,000 years old at most. "It's just my opinion," says McCarthy, "but that leads me to believe acorns became a staple part of the diet around 4,000 years ago." For some parts of California, Anderson puts that date even later: 1,000 years ago.

Then why were California natives setting fires, when they weren't using acorns in quantity? "Archeologists have found milling stations where no oaks grow," says Anderson, "so it's apparent they were grinding something other than acorns. All evidence points to seeds of grasses and forbs—broad-leaved herbaceous plants—which also increase with burning. Grass and forb seed remained an important secondary food source throughout the acorn era. It now appears that the first thing that was important to natives in the oak and grass savannas they created through fire was the grass. The emphasis on acorns came later."

The mortars and pestles used to grind grass and forb seed into flour, which is called pinole, typically weren't as massive as those required for acorns, observes Anderson. "Pinole mortars were usually small enough to tote around, and the pestles were relatively small. But for acorns, you need big pestles and bedrock mortars—holes dug into the living rock, deep enough to allow you to pound the acorns vigorously without having the meal scatter everywhere. We only start finding those between 450 and 1,650 years ago. That's pretty significant, considering that Indians have lived in California for at least 10,000 years."

As well as encouraging grasses to grow; fires created ecotones—varied ecological communities within a relatively small area. "Wildland areas in California that haven't burned in a long time are low in species diversity," says McCarthy. "In the chaparral zones of California, for example, you can have huge expanses dominated almost completely by chamiso, a resinous shrub. On the other hand, regular burning produces an explosion in the diversity of plants." Such burning, she explains, creates "edges in the landscape—places where different communities can take hold. From the Indian perspective, that would be very valuable, because food sources would increase in both quantity and variety. Deer were particularly important to California's natives, and they like burned landscapes, where there's abundant forage."

Some of the plants that grew in burned areas were important not just as food but for making tools. California natives relied on deer grass and shrubs such as redbud for their basketry, which was used for everything from storing food and goods to cooking: acorn gruel was prepared by dropping heated stones into a basket containing a cold mixture of pounded acorn meal and water. Such baskets were marvels of aesthetics and function; cooking baskets, obviously, had to be so tightly woven that they could hold water. But the materials needed didn't just grow willy-nilly—

they had to be stimulated through fire. Redbud's immediate response to burning, for example, is to send out an abundant growth of straight new shoots of the dimensions needed for baskets. "Today, Maidu, Miwok, and Mono basket makers prune individual redbud bushes to get the shoots they need," says Anderson, "but they say that the traditional method is burning."

While it seems likely that tribespeople first burned for grass seed and basket materials rather than acorns, it's not clear what made acorns assume such an important role in the native diet. Compared with grass and forb seed, acorns are tough and time-consuming to prepare. A few swipes with a pestle in a mortar is all that's necessary to turn most herbaceous seeds into meal, but acorns take intense pounding. And the resultant meal still has to be leached of tannin. This was often accomplished by packing the meal into basins scooped from clean sand and pouring water over it several times. Sometimes cooks added yet another step, congealing the mush into a kind of bread by immersing it in cold water.

Though McCarthy doesn't know what made California's natives start looking to oaks as their primary food, she is sure of one thing: "Generally, people don't work any harder than they have to. We don't know if they turned to acorns big-time because a growing population made it necessary, or if the dissemination of the acorn processing allowed the population to grow because more food became available. One way or the other though, oaks ended up supporting a lot of people in California."

One well-regarded population study conducted in the 1950s correlated food resource bases, such as acres of oak groves and miles of salmon spawning grounds, with regional native populations, and came up with 350,000 people. Another study completed the following decade relied on Spanish mission records and native village reports, and put the population at 320,000. Either way, it's clear that at the height of its acorn-processing culture, California supported what was an anomalously high population density. By contrast, the Great Plains—stretching from mid-Canada to

the Gulf of Mexico—supported no more than 150,000 people during the late seventeenth and eighteenth centuries.

With so many people depending on oaks, it's not surprising that a complex of laws and lore grew up around them. For example, John Hudson, a northern California ethnographer, wrote early in this century that favored trees were marked to distinguish ownership: "An acorn-bearing tree was undisturbed when guarded by four sticks placed against it. An Indian believes it is sure death to disturb the sticks or their wards."

"Black oak is still the favorite among traditional tribal members. It has a nice big nut, it's high in fat so it's really tasty, the meat separates easily from the husk, and it stores well.

"Particularly valued trees could have several owners, each of whom had specific rights," observes historian Malcolm Margolin, the publisher of Heyday Books in Berkeley, which specializes in texts on California natives. "One person, for example, may have had the acorn franchise. Another may have held rights to hunt woodpeckers on the trees. Another would have had rights to collect deadwood for fuel."

Just as some individual trees were more valuable than others, so were some of California's 23 oak species. "Black oak is still the favorite among traditional tribal members," observes Walter Koenig, a research zoologist with the University of California at Berkeley whose work with acorn woodpeckers has led him into the related field of acorn production patterns. "It has a nice big nut, it's high in fat so it's really tasty, the meat separates easily from the husk, and it stores well." Nevertheless, observes Koenig, "if black oaks weren't producing well one year, the tribes would use varieties that were.

Oak diversity would have been insurance against hunger."

When white settlers took over the land where California's tribes lived with their oaks, they didn't abolish burning all at once. Early ranchers favored fires because they stimulated the bunch-grasses livestock loved, and acorns were a rich winter feed for cattle. By the 1920s, however, widespread wildland burning ground to a halt, the result of an aggressive fire-prevention policy instituted by state and federal forestry agencies (though some native people continued to burn on the sly until the early 1960s). Over the past seven decades, the conifers and brush have encroached across the state, and the oak savannas have retreated. Today the Sierra Nevada are cloaked with white fir and incense cedar; the coastal range is swathed in brush.

But things are again changing. The U.S. Forest Service and the California Division of Forestry and Fire Prevention have turned to a process called prescription burning to remove buildups of woody detritus and improve woodland diversity. Prescription burning uncannily mimics the native use of wildland fire. Forest Service fire scientists minutely monitor air temperature, humidity, and wind direction before igniting a burn, to make sure that it falls within the fire prescription. They want a blaze hot enough to destroy downed wood, but cool enough so little harm is done to standing timber. California's Indians had the same goal. "Natives typically burned during the fall," says Anderson. "The cool temperatures and high humidities produced low-lying fires that burned out the deadwood without harming the trees. They would burn river drainages with different exposures at different times, depending on the kind of burn they wanted."

Each of the last five years has seen bigger Forest Service budgets earmarked for prescription burning. And California's natives are part of that process. "There's a real resurgence in native awareness in this state, and concern for oaks is a big part of it," says Lorrie Planas, a member of the Western Mono and Choinumni tribes and a heritage resource specialist for the U.S. Forest Service Kings River Ranger District, in the Sierra Nevada. Planas oversees a Forest Service burning project on black-oak groves near the Kings River. "First," says Planas, "we want to invigorate the groves and prevent encroachment from other species. Second, we're maximizing access to the acorn crop for local tribespeople. The burning clears the underbrush so people can get at the acorns more easily."

So popular are acorn-based foods becoming among California's tribes that the merits of relative preparation methods are actively debated. "Some people feel that the only way to prepare mush is the traditional way—grinding the acorns with stone implements and cooking them with hot rocks in basketry," says Planas, laughing. "They say it makes the mush taste much better—more nutty and toasty. But most people opt for modern convenience—food processors, colanders, gas stoves, and metal cookware."

The growing awareness that California was a vast nut orchard for thousands of years changes the definition of *wilderness*. "Oak landscapes were manipulated landscapes. They were very rich biologically because of their patchiness—their differences from one small area to another," explains Anderson. "Ironically, the state's ecosystems were far richer than if there had been no human influence. California's wildlands are losing their biodiversity, their patchiness, because there is no longer a native influence on the land."

Anderson thinks that the evidence of historic native environmental impact in California will ultimately cause a sea change in the way ecological processes are defined. "One of the most significant environmental disturbance factors in North America has been indigenous peoples. In ecological circles, we've begun to change the classic metaphor for nature from 'balance' to 'flux.' But we need to recognize that the flux was caused by native people. Horticultural practices have been an inextricable part of nature in California and other parts of the continent since natives first arrived. California is more of a wilderness now than it ever was. It's like a feral garden, one that has gone to weeds through neglect."

Too Many Bananas, Not Enough Pineapples, and No Watermelon at All: Three Object Lessons in Living with Reciprocity

David Counts

McMaster University

NO WATERMELON AT ALL

The woman came all the way through the village, walking between the two rows of houses facing each other between the beach and the bush, to the very last house standing on a little spit of land at the mouth of the Kaini River. She was carrying a watermelon on her head, and the house she came to was the government "rest house," maintained by the villagers for the occasional use of visiting officials. Though my wife and I were graduate students, not officials, and had asked for permission to stay in the village for the coming year, we were living in the rest house while the debate went on about where a house would be built for us. When the woman offered to sell us the watermelon for two shillings, we happily agreed, and the kids were delighted at the prospect of watermelon after yet another meal of rice and bully beef. The money changed hands and the

seller left to return to her village, a couple of miles along the coast to the east.

It seemed only seconds later that the woman was back, reluctantly accompanying Kolia, the man who had already made it clear to us that he was the leader of the village. Kolia had no English, and at that time, three or four days into our first stay in Kandoka Village on the island of New Britain in Papua New Guinea, we had very little Tok Pisin. Language difficulties notwithstanding, Kolia managed to make his message clear: The woman had been outrageously wrong to sell us the watermelon for two shillings and we were to return it to her and reclaim our money immediately. When we tried to explain that we thought the price to be fair and were happy with the bargain, Kolia explained again and finally made it clear that we had missed the point. The problem wasn't that we had paid too much; it was that we had paid at all. Here he was, a leader, responsible for us while we were living in his village, and we had shamed him. How would it look if he let guests in his village *buy* food? If we wanted watermelons, or bananas, or anything else,

all that was necessary was to let him know. He told us that it would be all right for us to give little gifts to people who brought food to us (and they surely would), but *no one* was to sell food to us. If anyone were to try—like this woman from Lauvore—then we should refuse. There would be plenty of watermelons without us buying them.

The woman left with her watermelon, disgruntled, and we were left with our two shillings. But we had learned the first lesson of many about living in Kandoka. We didn't pay money for food again that whole year, and we did get lots of food brought to us . . . but we never got another watermelon. That one was the last of the season.

LESSON 1: *In a society where food is shared or gifted as part of social life, you may not buy it with money.*

TOO MANY BANANAS

In the couple of months that followed the watermelon incident, we managed to become at least marginally competent in Tok Pisin, to negotiate the construction of a house on what we hoped was neutral ground, and to settle into the routine of our fieldwork. As our village leader had predicted, plenty of food was brought to us. Indeed, seldom did a day pass without something coming in—some sweet potatoes, a few taro, a papaya, the occasional pineapple, or some bananas—lots of bananas.

We had learned our lesson about the money, though, so we never even offered to buy the things that were brought, but instead made gifts, usually of tobacco to the adults or chewing gum to the children. Nor were we so gauche as to haggle with a giver over how much of a return gift was appropriate, though the two of us sometimes conferred as to whether what had been brought was a "two-stick" or a "three-stick" stalk, bundle, or whatever. A "stick" of tobacco was a single large leaf, soaked in rum and then twisted into a ropelike form. This, wrapped in half a sheet of newsprint (torn for use as cigarette paper), sold in the local trade stores for a shilling. Nearly all of the adults in the village smoked a great deal, and they seldom had much cash, so our stocks of twist tobacco and stacks of the Sydney *Morning Herald* (all, unfortunately, the same day's issue) were seen as a real boon to those who preferred "stick" to the locally grown product.

We had established a pattern with respect to the gifts of food. When a donor appeared at our veranda we would offer our thanks and talk with them for a few minutes (usually about our children, who seemed to hold a real fascination for the villagers and for whom most of the gifts were intended) and then we would inquire whether they could use some tobacco. It was almost never refused, though occasionally a small bottle of kerosene, a box of matches, some laundry soap, a cup of rice, or a tin of meat would be requested instead of (or even in addition to) the tobacco. Everyone, even Kolia, seemed to think this arrangement had worked out well.

Now, what must be kept in mind is that while we were following their rules—or seemed to be—we were *re-*

ally still buying food. In fact we kept a running account of what came in and what we "paid" for it. Tobacco as currency got a little complicated, but since the exchange rate was one stick to one shilling, it was not too much trouble as long as everyone was happy, and meanwhile we could account for the expenditure of "informant fees" and "household expenses." Another thing to keep in mind is that not only did we continue to think in terms of our buying the food that was brought, we thought of them as *selling it.* While it was true they never quoted us a price, they also never asked us if we needed or wanted whatever they had brought. It seemed clear to us that when an adult needed a stick of tobacco, or a child wanted some chewing gum (we had enormous quantities of small packets of Wrigley's for just such eventualities) they would find something surplus to their own needs and bring it along to our "store" and get what they wanted.

By late November 1966, just before the rainy reason set in, the bananas were coming into flush, and whereas earlier we had received banana gifts by the "hand" (six or eight bananas in a cluster cut from the stalk), donors now began to bring bananas, "for the children," by the *stalk!* The Kaliai among whom we were living are not exactly specialists in banana cultivation—they only recognize about thirty varieties, while some of their neighbors have more than twice that many—but the kinds they produce differ considerably from each other in size, shape, and taste, so we were not dismayed when we had more than one stalk hanging on our veranda. The stalks ripen a bit at the time, and having some variety was nice. Still, by the time our accumulation had reached *four* complete stalks, the delights of variety had begun to pale a bit. The fruits were ripening progressively and it was clear that even if we and the kids ate nothing but bananas for the next week, some would still fall from the stalk onto the floor in a state of gross overripeness. This was the situation as, late one afternoon, a woman came bringing yet another stalk of bananas up the steps of the house.

Several factors determined our reaction to her approach: one was that there was literally no way we could possibly use the bananas. We hadn't quite reached the point of being crowded off our veranda by the stalks of fruit, but it was close. Another factor was that we were tired of playing the gift game. We had acquiesced in playing it—no one was permitted to sell us anything, and in turn we only gave things away, refusing under any circumstances to sell tobacco (or anything else) for money. But there had to be a limit. From our perspective what was at issue was that the woman wanted something and she had come to trade for it. Further, what she had brought to trade was something we neither wanted nor could use, and it should have been obvious to her. So we decided to bite the bullet.

The woman, Rogi, climbed the stairs to the veranda, took the stalk from where it was balanced on top of her head, and laid it on the floor with the word, "Here are some bananas for the children." Dorothy and I sat near her on the floor and thanked her for her thought but explained, "You know, we really have too many bananas—we can't use these; maybe you ought to give them to someone else. . . ." The woman looked mystified, then brightened and explained that she didn't want anything for them, she wasn't short of tobacco or anything. They were just a gift for the kids. Then she just sat there, and we sat there, and the bananas sat there, and we tried again. "Look," I said, pointing up to them and counting, "we've got four stalks already hanging here on the veranda— there are too many for us to eat now. Some are rotting already. Even if we eat only bananas, we can't keep up with what's here!"

Rogi's only response was to insist that these were a gift, and that she didn't want anything for them, so we tried yet another tack: "Don't *your* children like bananas?" When she admitted that they did, and that she had none at her house, we suggested that she should take them there. Finally, still puzzled, but convinced we weren't going to keep the bananas, she replaced them on her head, went down the stairs, and made her way back through the village toward her house.

As before, it seemed only moments before Kolia was making his way up the stairs, but this time he hadn't brought the woman in tow. "What was wrong with those bananas? Were they no good?" he demanded. We explained that there was nothing wrong with the bananas at all, but that we simply couldn't use them and it seemed foolish to take them when we had so many and Rogi's own children had none. We obviously didn't make ourselves clear because Kolia then took up the same refrain that Rogi had—he insisted that we shouldn't be worried about taking the bananas, because they were a gift for the children and Rogi hadn't wanted anything for them. There was no reason, he added, to send her away with them—she would be ashamed. I'm afraid we must have seemed as if we were hard of hearing or thought he was, for our only response was to repeat our reasons. We went through it again—there they hung, one, two, three, *four* stalks of bananas, rapidly ripening and already far beyond our capacity to eat—we just weren't ready to accept any more and let them rot (and, we added to ourselves, pay for them with tobacco, to boot).

Kolia finally realized that we were neither hard of hearing nor intentionally offensive, but merely ignorant. He stared at us for a few minutes, thinking, and then asked: "Don't you frequently have visitors during the day and evening?" We nodded. Then he asked, "Don't you usually offer them cigarettes and coffee or milo?" Again, we nodded. "Did it ever occur to you to suppose," he said, "that your visitors might be hungry?" It was at this point in the conversation, as we recall, that we began to see the depth of the pit we had dug for ourselves. We nodded, hesitantly. His last words to us before he went down the stairs and stalked away were just what we were by that time afraid they might be. "When your guests are hungry, *feed them bananas!*"

LESSON 2: *Never refuse a gift, and never fail to return a gift. If you cannot*

use it, you can always give it away to someone else—there is no such thing as too much—there are never too many bananas.*

NOT ENOUGH PINEAPPLES

During the fifteen years between that first visit in 1966 and our residence there in 1981 we had returned to live in Kandoka village twice during the 1970s, and though there were a great many changes in the village, and indeed for all of Papua New Guinea during that time, we continued to live according to the lessons of reciprocity learned during those first months in the field. We bought no food for money and refused no gifts, but shared our surplus. As our family grew, we continued to be accompanied by our younger children. Our place in the village came to be something like that of educated Kaliai who worked far away in New Guinea. Our friends expected us to come "home" when we had leave, but knew that our work kept us away for long periods of time. They also credited us with knowing much more about the rules of their way of life than was our due. And we sometimes shared the delusion that we understood life in the village, but even fifteen years was not long enough to relieve the need for lessons in learning to live within the rules of gift exchange.

In the last paragraph I used the word *friends* to describe the villagers intentionally, but of course they were not all our friends. Over the years some really had become friends, others were acquaintances, others remained consultants or informants to whom we turned when we needed information. Still others, unfortunately, we did not like at all. We tried never to make an issue of these distinctions, of course, and to be evenhanded and generous to all, as they were to us. Although we almost never actually refused requests that were made of us, over the long term our reciprocity in the village was balanced. More was given to those who helped us the most, while we gave assistance or donations of small items even to those who were not close or helpful.

One elderly woman in particular was a trial for us. Sara was the eldest of a group of siblings and her younger brother and sister were both generous, informative, and delightful persons. Her younger sister, Makila, was a particularly close friend and consultant, and in deference to that friendship we felt awkward in dealing with the elder sister.

Sara was neither a friend nor an informant, but she had been, since she returned to live in the village at the time of our second trip in 1971, a constant (if minor) drain on our resources. She never asked for much at a time. A bar of soap, a box of matches, a bottle of kerosene, a cup of rice, some onions, a stick or two of tobacco, or some other small item was usually all that was at issue, but whenever she came around it was always to ask for something—or to let us know that when we left, we should give her some of the furnishings from the house. Too, unlike almost everyone else in the village, when she came, she was always empty-handed. We ate no taro from her gardens, and the kids chewed none of her sugarcane. In short, she was, as far as we could tell, a really grasping, selfish old woman—and we were not the only victims of her greed.

Having long before learned the lesson of the bananas, one day we had a stalk that was ripening so fast we couldn't keep up with it, so I pulled a few for our own use (we only had one stalk at the time) and walked down through the village to Ben's house, where his five children were playing. I sat down on his steps to talk, telling him that I intended to give the fruit to his kids. They never got them. Sara saw us from across the open plaza of the village and came rushing over, shouting, "My bananas!" Then she grabbed the stalk and went off gorging herself with them. Ben and I just looked at each other.

Finally it got to the point where it seemed to us that we had to do something. Ten years of being used was long enough. So there came the afternoon when Sara showed up to get some tobacco—again. But this time, when we gave her the two sticks she had demanded, we confronted her.

3. THE ORGANIZATION OF SOCIETY AND CULTURE

First, we noted the many times she had come to get things. We didn't mind sharing things, we explained. After all, we had plenty of tobacco and soap and rice and such, and most of it was there so that we could help our friends as they helped us, with folktales, information, or even gifts of food. The problem was that she kept coming to get things, but never came to talk, or to tell stories, or to bring some little something that the kids might like. Sara didn't argue—she agreed. "Look," we suggested, "it doesn't have to be much, and we don't mind giving you things—but you can help us. The kids like pineapples, and we don't have any—the next time you need something, bring something—like maybe a pineapple." Obviously somewhat embarrassed, she took her tobacco and left, saying that she would bring something soon. We were really pleased with ourselves. It had been a very difficult thing to do, but it was done, and we were convinced that either she would start bringing things or not

come. It was as if a burden had lifted from our shoulders.

It worked. Only a couple of days passed before Sara was back, bringing her bottle to get it filled with kerosene. But this time, she came carrying the biggest, most beautiful pineapple we had seen the entire time we had been there. We had a friendly talk, filled her kerosene container, and hung the pineapple up on the veranda to ripen just a little further. A few days later we cut and ate it, and whether the satisfaction it gave came from the fruit or from its source would be hard to say, but it was delicious. That, we assumed, was the end of that irritant.

We were wrong, of course. The next afternoon, Mary, one of our best friends for years (and no relation to Sara), dropped by for a visit. As we talked, her eyes scanned the veranda. Finally she asked whether we hadn't had a pineapple there yesterday. We said we had, but that we had already eaten it. She commented that it had been a really nice-looking one, and we

told her that it had been the best we had eaten in months. Then, after a pause, she asked, "Who brought it to you?" We smiled as we said, "Sara!" because Mary would appreciate our coup—she had commented many times in the past on the fact that Sara only *got* from us and never gave. She was silent for a moment, and then she said, "Well, I'm glad you enjoyed it—my father was waiting until it was fully ripe to harvest it for you, but when it went missing I thought maybe it was the one you had here. I'm glad to see you got it. I thought maybe a thief had eaten it in the bush."

LESSON 3: *Where reciprocity is the rule and gifts are the idiom, you cannot demand a gift, just as you cannot refuse a request.*

It says a great deal about the kindness and patience of the Kaliai people that they have been willing to be our hosts for all these years despite our blunders and lack of good manners. They have taught us a lot, and these three lessons are certainly not the least important things we learned.

From Shells to Money

Ceremonial Exchange among the Simbu of Papua New Guinea

High in the mountains of New Guinea, a transformation is taking place as money becomes increasingly important for the formerly secluded Simbu tribespeople

Karl F. Rambo

Karl F. Rambo is currently conducting research in the Papua New Guinea highlands on the economic consequences of rural migration.

While conducting fieldwork among the Simbu in 1985 and 1986, I occasionally encountered people in the small roadside markets selling crescents of large, old pearl shells, to be worn around the neck. Although the price for these was generally only about U.S. $5, the once highly prized shells drew few interested purchasers. In my discussions with the sellers, they invariably mentioned how—in the past—one such shell would form a substantial portion of the bride-price given by the groom's family to the bride's family in the ceremonial gift given at a marriage. Now money equal to thousands of dollars, collected from many people and displayed on tall bamboo poles, is the valuable supplementing traditional items such as pork. Gifts of purchased cartons of beer, stacked and displayed at the ceremonies, are now much more frequent than the once-common ceremonial gifts of colorful bird of paradise plumes.

This adoption of cash into the ceremonial system has affected the course of economic change and development in the New Guinea highlands in an unusual way. Although the Simbu people now eagerly desire money, what

motivates their actions is more than a desire for material goods.

Until relatively recently, these people were remote from any of the effects of the market economies that link together much of the rest of the world. Prior to contact with the outside world, the Simbu relied almost solely on the products they themselves produced. At that time the New Guinea highlands lay at the end of multistaged trading systems that extended hundreds of kilometers to the coasts, the source of a most precious traditional valuable—seashells. The source of the shells was so remote that some highlanders believed they grew on trees. Prior to the arrival of Australian colonialists, small quantities of shells passed through many hands on their way to the highlands. There, they became one of the most important items needed for the ceremonial gift exchanges.

These ceremonial exchanges were, and continue to be, essential for establishing and maintaining social relationships between the individual members of the small tribes of the region. Today however, this area no longer remains as isolated from the rest of the world as in the past. Money, and goods purchased with money, has for the most part replaced shells and many other traditional goods previously used in these exchanges. The advent of money in the Papua New Guinea highlands and its incorporation into the ceremonial exchange system have resulted in the amalgamation of elements of two

sometimes conflicting economic value systems.

The recent changes in the highlands of Papua New Guinea are of particular interest to anthropologists and other social scientists in that these changes are recent and well documented. People who were for all intents completely isolated from the industrialized and industrializing world become involved in a worldwide economy when they produce goods or sell their labor in a money-linked market. The last three centuries are replete with examples of incorporation of cultures into such a worldwide economy. In many ways, each case recapitulates the earlier adoption of money by peoples who now rely almost exclusively on a monied, market economy. Money has facilitated the incorporation of many far-flung peoples by providing a medium of exchange that translates the value of many material things and services into a common system. Often, however, with the development of a money economy come greatly increased economic stratification and a loss of economic independence. But because the Simbu have maintained their interest in ceremonial exchanges, they have ameliorated some of the negative effects associated with involvement in the cash-oriented market economy.

But before one can understand this interesting economic transformation, one should know something about the environment, culture, and history of the Simbu. The interaction of these

KARL RAMBO

In preparation for a final marriage ceremony, long bamboo poles, covered in money, are placed in the ground. In the wedding ceremony the groom's relatives give money, pigs, and store-bought goods to the bride's relatives.

elements with the introduced cash economy has resulted in a melding of the old with the new to produce a monied economy unlike those commonly found in the industrialized world.

CEREMONIAL EXCHANGE IN TRADITIONAL SIMBU SOCIETY

Lying at the heart of the central highlands of the now independent country of Papua New Guinea, Simbu is the most densely populated province in the country, with more than 180,000 people living in an area slightly larger than the state of Delaware. The majority ethnic group, named the Simbu (or Chimbu) by the first Australian patrol that entered the area, live along the slopes of the mountains bordering the Wahgi River, which runs past some of the highest mountains in the country. In 1933, Australian gold miners and colo-

nial government patrol officers were the first representatives of the outside, Europeanized world to enter the New Guinea mountain valleys the Simbu inhabited. Although little gold was discovered in the area, thousands of tribespeople were found in a locale previously thought to be too rugged for human habitation.

The mountainous, high-altitude terrain that isolated the Simbu and other highland peoples is also responsible for an environment unlike those of the hot coastal and lowland areas with their infertile soils. The climate of this area is temperate, with cool evenings and warm days. Drought conditions are rare. A year-round springlike climate and a lack of many of the tropical diseases found elsewhere in New Guinea contribute to a relatively densely settled population. In most of the northern areas of the province, population densities exceed 150 people per square kilometer.

"Simbu" is the word in the local language first heard by the initial Australian patrol. It is an expression of astonishment called out by the local people when they saw their first white men. Initially, the Simbu people thought the explorers were the reincarnated spirits of their dead relatives. The physical appearance of the early patrol members, as well as their control of a vast quantity of wealth in the form of shells, made them seem otherworldly.

The Simbu like many other cultural groups in the central highlands, are not traditionally a single political group but rather are divided into many tribal units of twenty-five hundred to five thousand people, each identified with discrete territories. The membership of each tribe is further subdivided into patrilineal clans and subclans. Although parliamentary democracy has been practiced for some time, tribal identification and loyalty remain very strong. Today, as in precontact times, warfare breaks out between neighboring tribes. Members of any single clan must find marriage partners outside their own clan. Through marriage, clan members are linked by kinship to members of other clans in their own tribe as well as to people in clans in other tribes. These political, economic, and social links between people are created and maintained through a complex web of ceremonial exchanges of valuables. All important events are marked by the giving of prestations (valuables). The kind of valuables given in these ceremonies has changed over the years with the introduction of money and items purchased with money. Although the Simbu are connected to the rest of the world through the market economy of which they are now a part, the introduction of money and markets has not meant the total abandonment of previously existing economic practices. It is important to

look at the nature and form of these ceremonial exchanges before discussing the changes brought through the introduction of money.

For the Simbu, the bestowing of goods that accompanies ceremonies helps to create social obligations and reciprocal relations with other people and with other clans and tribes. The ceremonies are held in conjunction with a number of events such as marriages, funerals, and the seasonal harvest of particular fruits and vegetables. These events are held regularly. The largest of such events, called *bugla ingu* in the local language, is held once every seven to ten years. In the bugla ingu, entire clans and tribes organize to hold a series of gift prestations culminating in an enormous pig kill, in which thousands of pigs are killed, cooked, and given away to visiting friends and relatives. For the Simbu, maintaining good social relationships

with others, both within and outside the patrilineal clans, is inseparable from such gift exchanges. The amounts given in many such ceremonies require the cooperation of many people.

It is useful to contrast the type of economic transactions that take place in Simbu ceremonial exchange with the types of transaction most familiar to Westerners—barter and trade. Barter and trade consist of discrete economic transactions completed with the giving and receiving of goods, services, or money. Social relationships are often independent of such transactions and, once the deal is completed, there are few continuing social obligations between the parties involved. In addition, forces other than social relationships between the transactors (i.e., supply and demand) regulate the amount of goods or services changing hands.

In ceremonial exchanges such as those in Simbu, however, the exchange

A Simbu man rests from his work in a newly planted sweet potato garden. The slopes on mountain gardens can be as steep as 45 degrees.

is not independent of the social relationship between transactors. Each individual demonstrates his prosperity and ability to produce and shows his willingness and ability to maintain social obligations with each item he gives to an exchange partner. Although there is a general expectation that the recipient will reciprocate with a return presentation at an unspecified future date (and therefore continue the relationship), the purpose of participating in such exchanges is not to maximize a material return from the original gift. In fact, the opposite is closer to reality. Great prestige is gained by giving valuables to an exchange partner. The partner, to maintain the relationship, must return to the original giver at least as much as originally received plus, if he wishes to garner prestige, slightly

more. This amount, over and above the original gift, then becomes debt that must be repaid. Added to this will be any additional goods that become debts incurred by the exchange partner. The competitive nature of these exchanges is acknowledged by the men involved.

In addition to the absence of separation between the giving of the ceremonial prestation and the social relationship between the participants, there is an attempt not to maximize one's economic holdings but to maximize prestige in the community by participating often and generously in the many prestations. Not only is prestige gained, but social ties are maintained with a network of individuals, many of them the affinal relatives (in-laws) acquired at marriage. Although men are the transactors in these situa-

tions, the women are the central links to many of the social/exchange relationships, for it is with the wives' male kin that many of the transactions are arranged.

Each marriage establishes a new exchange relationship between the groom and his close relatives and the bride's father, brothers, and close kin. Gifts must be made to the bride's family at marriage, and this is followed by a lifetime of exchanges at the birth of children, the death of children or the wife, at various points in the wife's children's lives, and at any vegetable exchange (*mogena biri*) or bugla ingu where the wife's group (clan or subclan) is invited. In addition to the relationships with wives' relatives, similar relationships exist with the men's mothers' male kin, their sisters' husbands, and their daughters' husbands. The valuables given in these ceremonies are expected to be returned in the future. An immediate exact equivalence is not expected, but eventually food or goods deemed at least similar in value should be repaid.

The relationships between these men are multi-functional. Ceremonial exchanges serve to distribute certain scarce resources that are not available in a territory—giving forest products and fruits that grow only at lower altitudes, for instance, to people who otherwise would not have access to these things. Mutual aid in work is sometimes extended between exchange partners.

Very important is the support given to men in other tribes in times of war. This is particularly true when there are many such interpersonal relationships between men of two groups. Without the support of others beyond one's clan and tribe, there is danger that if hostilities arise one would not have enough allies to prevent being chased off one's land. If the relationships to men outside one's clan and tribe are not maintained with frequent contributions to ceremonial exchanges, one faces the possibility of not having adequate allies in time of conflict. In fact, long delays in returning goods can add to hostility over other issues, such as marriage disputes and conflicting land claims,

Coffee cherries, the berries containing coffee beans, are handpicked when ripe. Coffee is the major cash crop that finances ceremonial gift presentations. This man's shirt reflects the influence of Christian missions in Simbu.

more than 85 percent of the Simbu people's diet, and pork was the most important item given in the ceremonial exchanges. It was rarely eaten on other occasions. Prior to the arrival of Christian missions, ceremonial sacrifice of pigs not only provided meat to be given to one's exchange partners but also served to appease the ancestral spirits.

MOVEMENT TOWARD A CASH ECONOMY

The initial Western contact with the Simbu was quickly followed by the establishment of a patrol post with a single Australian government officer in residence, and several Catholic and Lutheran missions. Although before the Second World War the changes they brought about were not extreme for most Simbu people, these Westerners did introduce a large quantity of high-quality pearl shell that was flown into the area from the coasts and traded for food and services.

Large-scale economic change did not occur until after the war, when men began to be sent to the coasts to work as laborers on plantations. After finishing their labor contracts, usually after two years, the men returned to their Simbu homes carrying imported manufactured goods such as cloth, metal tools, and cooking pots. These items were valued for their novelty as well as their usefulness.

Opportunities to acquire these sought-after imported goods were limited during this early period because the Simbu lacked the means to earn enough locally for their purchase. This problem was greatly alleviated when, in the late 1950s, coffee was introduced as a cash crop into the Simbu area. Coffee growing was particularly suited to the social and ecological situation of Simbu, and it was quickly adopted by the local people. The cool, temperate conditions were perfect for growing high-quality *arabica* coffee varieties. The poor road network had hampered development by placing delays and weight restrictions on export crops. Dried coffee beans, being durable and of high value for their weight, were perfect for such

An unmarried woman, dressed to participate in a dance competition at an Independence Day celebration, surrounded by spectators in modern dress.

turning previous allies into warring enemies.

Although the ceremonial exchange of items is between individuals, individuals are representatives of their clans and subclans. Often the individual prestations are organized and combined so that the men of one clan give goods to their ceremonial exchange partners in another clan in one large display. For example, at a mogena biri, the valuables are placed in a huge pile, twenty to forty feet in diameter, and the recipients, decorated in traditional finery of bird-plume headdresses, dance around the pile chanting, beating drums, and brandishing spears. Speeches are made relating past exchanges and the close relationships between members of each group, and then the entire pile

is disassembled and each parcel given to the proper recipient.

Before contact with the colonial government, most of the items used in ceremonial exchanges were of local origin. Although shells, feathers, stone ax blades, and salt were often imported over long distances, pigs and other locally produced foods predominated in prestations. Each tribe was politically, and in large measure economically, self-contained. Money was unknown in the area. Although in some other non-Western societies shells were used in much the same way we use money, nothing served as such a universal medium of exchange for the precontact Simbu. Pigs, one of the few domesticated animals, were raised on the same sweet potatoes that made up a situation. In addition, coffee requires relatively little year-round labor and does well as a subsidiary crop to subsistence food crops.

Coffee is still today by far the most important cash crop for the Simbu and the source of most of their money. Other sources of monetary income include growing cardamom, selling vegetables at small markets, and receiving occasional remittances from employed relatives. Average annual household income today approximates U.S. $250 per year.

Although their income is low by American standards, many of the Simbu's basic subsistence needs are satisfied without resorting to the marketplace. Most of the food consumed is produced in family gardens, and many other material needs, like housing and firewood, are obtained with little or no cash expenditure. Much of the money that does pass through the hands of the average Simbu is not spent directly on consumer goods but is channeled first through the now monetized ceremonial gifts.

Because it now requires cash to properly participate in many ceremonial exchange obligations, a man who wishes to obtain a modicum of prestige must have some source of money income. Those who do not contribute to prestations soon become known as insignificant "rubbish" men. The emphasis is, therefore, not on earning cash so as to acquire material goods for oneself, but rather to earn the money necessary to contribute cash to marriage, bride-price, or death compensations, or to buy cartons of beer to present to one's exchange partners at ceremonies. If too much of an individual's income is spent on himself without adequate compensation's being paid to supporters, he gains a reputation as being stingy. In addition to gaining a bad reputation, such an individual may have difficulty obtaining financial and other types of help when needed.

Although the monetization of ceremonial exchanges now encourages participation in activities with cash rewards, for the most part it discourages the accumulation of capital by individuals

for reinvestment into money-making ventures. Small business ventures, such as stores, cattle projects, or commercial trucks, are generally begun with financial help and labor donated by kin and other associates. This help is given like a ceremonial prestation and is treated as such. Great pressure is then put on the leader of a venture to pay back these investments.

Often the response of the owner of a small venture such as a rural trade store is to slowly deplete the stock of the store by giving away store goods or cash receipts to his exchange partners. Since prestige is gained by reimbursing the network of investors, the organizer gains status and maintains a network of content exchange partners even though the business venture fails. Since the Simbu are rarely dependent on money-producing ventures for basic necessities such as food, the economic failure of such enterprises does not have serious consequences for the organizer. In fact, since success in the community depends on maintaining ceremonial exchange relations with other people, the economic failure of a business through its dismantlement and distribution of its assets often has a positive result.

In addition to leveling individual wealth by discouraging accumulation, channeling cash into prestations distributes wealth to a wide circle of people. Thousands of dollars often change hands at such events as weddings or funerals (when death compensation payments, a form of "blood money," are given to a dead person's relatives by the relatives of the person accused of causing the death). After the money is removed from the bamboo poles on which it is displayed, it is distributed widely by the initial receiver, with many individuals receiving only small amounts. So although theoretically as much money is received from the ceremonial exchanges as is put into them, the funds received are often in smaller (but more frequent) amounts. These smaller amounts of money are more prone to be spent quickly on items such as canned fish and bottled beer.

To be sure, there are a few Simbu men who have managed to become

quite wealthy. By being politically savvy and practicing good management, these people have been able to satisfy the demands of their local supporters and exchange partners and succeed in business. In other areas of the Papua New Guinea highlands, where lower population densities allow for greater availability of land and therefore greater individual economic opportunity, other social scientists have reported on a number of such wealthy men. But even in these areas, such people are only a tiny fraction of the population.

So although the pearl shells sold in the markets no longer have the value they once did, and money has become predominant in the Simbu economy, indigenous institutions such as ceremonial gift exchange are maintained. Shells and other imported valuables of the past have been supplanted by another import—cash. But in many ways the economic strategy of maximizing social relationships rather than individual wealth remains intact.

As long as this remains the case, the opportunities for many individuals to achieve long-term capitalistic success, to develop businesses by turning profits back into the businesses rather than toward ceremonial exchanges, remain remote. But the importance of tribal social ties, and the ceremonial prestations that maintain those ties, serves to ameliorate many of the negative side effects of incorporation into the world money-based economy.

ADDITIONAL READING

Paula Brown, *The Chimbu: A Study of Change in the New Guinea Highlands,* Schenkman Press, Cambridge, Mass., 1972.

————, *Highland Peoples of New Guinea,* Cambridge University Press, U.K., 1978.

Bob Connolly and Robin Anderson, *First Contact,* Viking Penguin Inc., New York, 1987.

Ben R. Finney, *Big-Men and Business: Entrepreneurship and Economic Growth in the New Guinea Highlands,* University of Hawaii Press, Honolulu, 1973.

————, *Business Development in the Highlands of New Guinea,* East-West Center, Honolulu, 1987.

Allen Johnson, In Search of the Affluent Society," *Human Nature* 1(9), 1978.

Andrew Strathern, ed., *Inequality in New Guinea Highlands Societies,* Cambridge University Press, 1982.

Life Without Chiefs

Are we forever condemned to a world of haves and have-nots, rulers and ruled?
Maybe not, argues a noted anthropologist—if we can relearn some ancient lessons.

Marvin Harris

Marvin Harris is a graduate research professor of anthropology at the University of Florida and chair of the general anthropology division of the American Anthropological Association. His seventeen books include Cows, Pigs, Wars and Witches *and* Cannibals and Kings.

Can humans exist without some people ruling and others being ruled? To look at the modern world, you wouldn't think so. Democratic states may have done away with emperors and kings, but they have hardly dispensed with gross inequalities in wealth, rank, and power.

However, humanity hasn't always lived this way. For about 98 percent of our existence as a species (and for four million years before then), our ancestors lived in small, largely nomadic hunting-and-gathering bands containing about 30 to 50 people apiece. It was in this social context that human nature evolved. It has been only about ten thousand years since people began to settle down into villages, some of which eventually grew into cities. And it has been only in the last two thousand years that the majority of people in the world have not lived in hunting-and-gathering societies. This brief period of time is not nearly sufficient for noticeable evolution to have taken place. Thus, the few remaining foraging societies are the closest analogues we have to the "natural" state of humanity.

To judge from surviving examples of hunting-and-gathering bands and villages, our kind got along quite well for the greater part of prehistory without so much as a paramount chief. In fact, for tens of thousands of years, life went on without kings, queens, prime ministers, presidents, parliaments, congresses, cabinets, governors, and mayors—not to mention the police officers, sheriffs, marshals, generals, lawyers, bailiffs, judges, district attorneys, court clerks, patrol cars, paddy wagons, jails, and penitentiaries that help keep them in power. How in the world did our ancestors ever manage to leave home without them?

Small populations provide part of the answer. With 50 people per band or 150 per village, everybody knew everybody else intimately. People gave with the expectation of taking and took with the expectation of giving. Because chance played a great role in the capture of animals, collection of wild foodstuffs, and success of rudimentary forms of agriculture, the individuals who had the luck of the catch on one day needed a handout on the next. So the best way for them to provide for their inevitable rainy day was to be generous. As expressed by anthropologist Richard Gould, "The greater the amount of risk, the greater the extent of sharing." Reciprocity is a small society's bank.

In reciprocal exchange, people do not specify how much or exactly what they expect to get back or when they expect to get it. That would besmirch the quality of that transaction and make it similar to mere barter or to buying and selling. The distinction lingers on in societies dominated by other forms of exchange, even capitalist ones. For we do carry out a give-and-take among close kin and friends that is informal, uncalculating, and imbued with a spirit of generosity. Teen-agers do not pay cash for their meals at home or for the use of the family car, wives do not bill their husbands for cooking a meal, and friends give each other birthday gifts and Christmas presents. But much of this is marred by the expectation that our generosity will be acknowledged with expression of thanks.

Where reciprocity really prevails in daily life, etiquette requires that generosity be taken for granted. As Robert Dentan discovered during his field-work among the Semai of Central Malaysia, no one ever says "thank you" for the meat received from another hunter. Having struggled all day to lug the carcass of a pig home through the jungle heat, the hunter allows his prize to be cut up into exactly equal portions, which he then gives away to the entire group. Dentan explains that to express gratitude for the portion received indicates that you are the kind of ungenerous person who calculates how much you give and take: "In this con-

From *New Age Journal*, November/December 1989, pp. 42-45, 205-209. Excerpted from *Our Kind* by Marvin Harris. © 1989 by Marvin Harris. Reprinted by permission of HarperCollins Publishers, Inc.

text, saying 'thank you' is very rude, for it suggests, first, that one has calculated the amount of a gift and, second, that one did not expect the donor to be so generous." To call attention to one's generosity is to indicate that others are in debt to you and that you expect them to repay you. It is repugnant to egalitarian peoples even to suggest that they have been treated generously.

Canadian anthropologist Richard Lee tells how, through a revealing incident, he learned about this aspect of reciprocity. To please the !Kung, the "bushmen" of the Kalahari desert, he decided to buy a large ox and have it slaughtered as a present. After days of searching Bantu agricultural villages for the largest and fattest ox in the region, he acquired what appeared to be a perfect specimen. But his friends took him aside and assured him that he had been duped into buying an absolutely worthless animal. "Of course, we will eat it," they said, "but it won't fill us up—we will eat and go home to bed with stomachs rumbling." Yet, when Lee's ox was slaughtered, it turned out to be covered with a thick layer of fat. Later, his friends explained why they had said his gift was valueless, even though they knew better than he what lay under the animal's skin:

"Yes, when a young man kills much meat he comes to think of himself as a chief or a big man, and he thinks of the rest of us as his servants or inferiors. We can't accept this, we refuse one who boasts, for someday his pride will make him kill somebody. So we always speak of his meat as worthless. This way we cool his heart and make him gentle."

Lee watched small groups of men and women returning home every evening with the animals and wild fruits and plants that they had killed or collected. They shared everything equally, even with campmates who had stayed behind and spent the day sleeping or taking care of their tools and weapons.

"Not only do families pool that day's production, but the entire camp—residents and visitors alike—shares equally in the total quantity of food available," Lee observed. "The evening meal of

any one family is made up of portions of food from each of the other families resident. There is a constant flow of nuts, berries, roots, and melons from one family fireplace to another, until each person has received an equitable portion. The following morning a different combination of foragers moves out of camp, and when they return late in the day, the distribution of foodstuffs is repeated."

In small, prestate societies, it was in everybody's best interest to maintain each other's freedom of access to the natural habitat. Suppose a !Kung with a lust for power were to get up and tell his campmates, "From now on, all this land and everything on it belongs to me. I'll let you use it but only with my permission and on the condition that I get first choice of anything you capture, collect, or grow." His campmates, thinking that he had certainly gone crazy, would pack up their few belongings, take a long walk, make a new camp, and resume their usual life of egalitarian reciprocity. The man who would be king would be left by himself to exercise a useless sovereignty.

THE HEADMAN: LEADERSHIP, NOT POWER

To the extent that political leadership exists at all among band-and-village societies, it is exercised by individuals called headmen. These headmen, however, lack the power to compel others to obey their orders. How can a leader be powerful and still lead?

The political power of genuine rulers depends on their ability to expel or exterminate disobedient individuals and groups. When a headman gives a command, however, he has no certain physical means of punishing those who disobey. So, if he wants to stay in "office," he gives few commands. Among the Eskimo, for instance, a group will follow an outstanding hunter and defer to his opinion with respect to choice of hunting spots. But in all other matters, the leader's opinion carries no more weight than any other man's. Similarly, among the !Kung, each band has its recognized leaders, most of whom are males. These men speak out more than others and are listened to

with a bit more deference. But they have no formal authority and can only persuade, never command. When Lee asked the !Kung whether they had headmen—meaning powerful chiefs—they told him, "Of course we have headmen! In fact, we are all headmen. Each one of us is headman over himself."

Headmanship can be a frustrating and irksome job. Among Indian groups such as the Mehinacu of Brazil's Zingu National Park, headmen behave something like zealous scoutmasters on overnight cookouts. The first one up in the morning, the headman tries to rouse his companions by standing in the middle of the village plaza and shouting to them. If something needs to be done, it is the headman who starts doing it, and it is the headman who works harder than anyone else. He sets an example not only for hard work but also for generosity: After a fishing or hunting expedition, he gives away more of his catch than anyone else does. In trading with other groups, he must be careful not to keep the best items for himself.

In the evening, the headman stands in the center of the plaza and exhorts his people to be good. He calls upon them to control their sexual appetites, work hard in their gardens, and take frequent baths in the river. He tells them not to sleep during the day or bear grudges against each other.

COPING WITH FREELOADERS

During the reign of reciprocal exchange and egalitarian headmen, no individual, family, or group smaller than the band or village itself could control access to natural resources. Rivers, lakes, beaches, oceans, plants and animals, the soil and subsoil were all communal property.

Among the !Kung, a core of people born in a particular territory say that they "own" the water holes and hunting rights, but this has no effect on the people who happen to be visiting and living with them at any given time. Since !Kung from neighboring bands are related through marriage, they often visit each other for months at a time and have free use of whatever resources they need without having to ask permission. Though people from distant bands must make a request to use another band's territory, the "owners" seldom refuse them.

The absence of private possession in land and other vital resources means that a form of communism probably existed among prehistoric hunting and collecting bands and small villages. Perhaps I should emphasize that this did not rule out the existence of private property. People in simple band-and-village societies own personal effects such as weapons, clothing, containers, ornaments, and tools. But why should anyone want to steal such objects? People who have a bush camp and move about a lot have no use for extra possessions. And since the group is small enough that everybody knows everybody else, stolen items cannot be used anonymously. If you want something, better to ask for it openly, since by the rules of reciprocity such requests cannot be denied.

I don't want to create the impression that life within egalitarian band-and-village societies unfolded entirely without disputes over possessions. As in every social group, nonconformists and malcontents tried to use the system for their own advantage. Inevitably there were freeloaders, individuals who consistently took more than they gave and lay back in their hammocks while others did the work. Despite the absence of a criminal justice system, such behavior eventually was punished. A widespread belief among band-and-village peoples attributes death and misfortune to the malevolent conspiracy of sorcerers. The task of identifying these evildoers falls to a group's shamans, who remain responsive to public opinion during their divinatory trances. Well-liked individuals who enjoy strong support from their families need not fear the shaman. But quarrelsome, stingy people who do not give as well as take had better watch out.

FROM HEADMAN TO BIG MAN

Reciprocity was not the only form of exchange practiced by egalitarian band-and-village peoples. Our kind long ago found other ways to give and take. Among them the form of exchange known as redistribution played a crucial role in creating distinctions of rank during the evolution of chiefdoms and states.

Redistribution occurs when people turn over food and other valuables to a prestigious figure such as a headman, to be pooled, divided into separate portions, and given out again. The primordial form of redistribution was probably keyed to seasonal hunts and harvests, when more food than usual became available.

True to their calling, headmen-redistributors not only work harder than their followers but also give more generously and reserve smaller and less desirable portions for themselves than for anyone else. Initially, therefore, redistribution strictly reinforced the political and economic equality associated with reciprocal exchange. The redistributors were compensated purely with admiration and in proportion to their success in giving bigger feasts, in personally contributing more than anybody else, and in asking little or nothing for their effort, all of which initially seemed an innocent extension of the basic principle of reciprocity.

But how little our ancestors understood what they were getting themselves into! For if it is a good thing to have a headman give feasts, why not have several headmen give feasts? Or, better yet, why not let success in organizing and giving feasts be the measure of one's legitimacy as a headman? Soon, where conditions permit, there are several would-be headmen vying with each other to hold the most lavish feasts and redistribute the most food and other valuables. In this fashion there evolved the nemesis that Richard Lee's !Kung informants had warned about: the youth who wants to be a "big man."

A classic anthropological study of big men was carried out by Douglas Oliver among the Siuai, a village people who live on the South Pacific island of Bougainville, in the Solomon Islands. In the Siuai language, big men were known as *mumis*. Every Siuai boy's highest ambition was to become a mumi. He began by getting married, working hard, and restricting his own consumption of meats and coconuts. His wife and parents, impressed with the seriousness of his intentions, vowed to help him prepare for his first feast. Soon his circle of supporters widened and he began to construct a clubhouse in which his male followers could lounge about and guests could be entertained and fed. He gave a feast at the consecration of the clubhouse; if this was a success, the circle of people willing to work for him grew larger still, and he began to hear himself spoken of as a mumi. Larger and larger feasts meant that the mumi's demands on his supporters became more irksome. Although they grumbled about how hard they had to work, they remained loyal as long as their mumi continued to maintain and increase his renown as a "great provider."

Finally the time came for the new mumi to challenge the older ones. He did this at a *muminai* feast, where both sides kept a tally of all the pigs, coconut pies, and sago-almond puddings given away by the host mumi and his followers to the guest mumi and his followers. If the guests could not reciprocate with a feast as lavish as that of the challengers, their mumi suffered a great social humiliation, and his fall from mumihood was immediate.

At the end of a successful feast, the greatest of mumis still faced a lifetime of personal toil and dependence on the moods and inclinations of his followers. Mumihood did not confer the power to coerce others into doing one's bidding, nor did it elevate one's standard of living above anyone else's. In fact, because giving things away was the essence of mumihood, great mumis consumed less meat and other delicacies than ordinary men. Among the Kaoka, another Solomon Islands group, there is the saying, "The giver of the feast takes the bones and the stale cakes; the meat and the fat go to the others." At one great feast attended by 1,100 people, the host mumi, whose name was Soni, gave away thirty-two pigs and a large quantity of sago-almond puddings. Soni himself and some of his closest followers went hungry. "We shall eat Soni's renown," they said.

FROM BIG MAN TO CHIEF

The slide (or ascent?) toward social stratification gained momentum wherever extra food produced by the inspired diligence of redistributors could be stored while awaiting muminai feasts, potlatches, and other occasions of redistribution. The more concentrated and abundant the harvest and the less perishable the crop, the greater its potential for endowing the big man with power. Though others would possess some stored-up foods of their own, the redistributor's stores would be the largest. In times of scarcity, people would come to him, expecting to be fed; in return, he could call upon those who had special skills to make cloth, pots, canoes, or a fine house for his own use. Eventually, the redistributor no longer needed to work in the fields to gain and surpass big-man status. Management of the harvest surpluses, a portion of which continued to be given to him for use in communal feasts and other communal projects (such as trading expeditions and warfare), was sufficient to validate his status. And, increasingly, people viewed this status as an office, a sacred trust, passed on from one generation to the next according to the rules of hereditary succession. His dominion was no longer a small, autonomous village but a large political community. The big man had become a chief.

Returning to the South Pacific and the Trobriand Islands, one can catch a glimpse of how these pieces of encroaching stratification fell into place. The Trobrianders had hereditary chiefs who held sway over more than a dozen villages containing several thousand people. Only chiefs could wear certain shell ornaments as the insignia of high rank, and it was forbidden for commoners to stand or sit in a position that put a chief's head at a lower elevation. British anthropologist Bronislaw Malinowski tells of seeing all the people present in the village of Bwoytalu drop from their verandas "as if blown down by a hurricane" at the sound of a drawn-out cry warning that an important chief was approaching.

Yams were the Trobrianders' staff of life; the chiefs validated their status by storing and redistributing copious quantities of them acquired through donations from their brothers-in-law at harvest time. Similar "gifts" were received by husbands who were commoners, but chiefs were polygymous and, having as many as a dozen wives, received many more yams than anyone else. Chiefs placed their yam supply on display racks specifically built for this purpose next to their houses. Commoners did the same, but a chief's yam racks towered over all the others.

This same pattern recurs, with minor variations, on several continents. Striking parallels were seen, for example, twelve thousand miles away from the Trobrianders, among chiefdoms that flourished throughout the southeastern region of the United States—specifically among the Cherokee, former inhabitants of Tennessee, as described by the eighteenth-century naturalist William Bartram.

At the center of the principal Cherokee settlements stood a large circular house where a council of chiefs discussed issues involving their villages and where redistributive feasts were held. The council of chiefs had a paramount who was the principal figure in the Cherokee redistributive network. At the harvest time a large crib, identified as the "chief's granary," was erected in each field. "To this," explained Bartram, "each family carries and deposits a certain quantity according to his ability or inclination, or none at all if he so chooses." The chief's granaries functioned as a public treasury in case of crop failure, a source of food for strangers or travelers, and as military store. Although every citizen enjoyed free access to the store, commoners had to acknowledge that it really belonged to the supreme chief, who had "an exclusive right and ability . . . to distribute comfort and blessings to the necessitous."

Supported by voluntary donations, chiefs could now enjoy lifestyles that set them increasingly apart from their followers. They could build bigger and finer houses for themselves, eat and dress more sumptuously, and enjoy the sexual favors and personal services of several wives. Despite these harbingers, people in chiefdoms voluntarily invested unprecedented amounts of labor on behalf of communal projects. They dug moats, threw up defensive earthen embankments, and erected great log palisades around their villages. They heaped up small mountains of rubble and soil to form platforms and mounds on top of which they built temples and big houses for their chief. Working in teams and using nothing but levers and rollers, they moved rocks weighing fifty tons or more and set them in precise lines and perfect circles, forming sacred precincts for communal rituals marking the change of seasons.

If this seems remarkable, remember that donated labor created the megalithic alignments of Stonehenge and Carnac, put up the great statues on Easter Island, shaped the huge stone heads of the Olmec in Vera Cruz, dotted Polynesia with ritual precincts set on great stone platforms, and filled the Ohio, Tennessee, and Mississippi valleys with hundreds of large mounds. Not until it was too late did people realize that their beautiful chiefs were about to keep the meat and fat for themselves while giving nothing but bones and stale cakes to their followers.

IN THE END

As we know, chiefdoms would eventually evolve into states, states into empires. From peaceful origins, humans created and mounted a wild beast that ate continents. Now that beast has taken us to the brink of global annihilation.

Will nature's experiment with mind and culture end in nuclear war? No one knows the answer. But I believe it is essential that we understand our past before we can create the best possible future. Once we are clear about the roots of human nature, for example, we can refute, once and for all, the notion that it is a biological imperative for our kind to form hierarchical groups. An observer viewing human life shortly after cultural takeoff would easily have concluded that our species was destined to be irredeemably egalitarian except for distinctions of sex and age. That someday the world would be divided into aristocrats and commoners, masters and slaves, billionaires and homeless beggars would have seemed wholly contrary to human nature as evidenced in the affairs of every human society then on Earth.

Of course, we can no more reverse the course of thousands of years of cultural evolution than our egalitarian ancestors could have designed and built the space shuttle. Yet, in striving for the preservation of mind and culture on Earth, it is vital that we recognize the significance of cultural takeoff and the great difference between biological and cultural evolution. We must rid ourselves of the notion that we are an innately aggressive species for whom war is inevitable. We must reject as unscientific claims that there are superior and inferior races and that the hierarchical divisions within and between societies are the consequences of natural selection rather than of a long process of cultural evolution. We must struggle to gain control over cultural selection through objective studies of the human condition and the recurrent process of history. Not only a more just society, but our very survival as a species may depend on it.

From peaceful origins, humans created and mounted a wild beast that ate continents. Now that beast has taken us to the brink of global annihilation.

Other Families,
Other Ways

Since most people in small-scale societies of the past spent their whole lives within a local area, it is understandable that their primary interactions—economic, religious, and otherwise—were with their relatives. It also makes sense that through marriage customs, they strengthened those kinship relationships that clearly defined their mutual rights and obligations. Indeed, the resulting family structure may be surprisingly flexible and adaptive, as witnessed in the essay "When Brothers Share a Wife," by Melvyn Goldstein, and in Serena Nanda's presentation "Arranging a Marriage in India." For these reasons, anthropologists have looked upon family and kinship as the key mechanisms for transmitting culture from one generation to the next. Social changes may have been slow to take place throughout the world, but as social horizons have widened, family relationships and community alliances are increasingly based upon new principles. Kinship networks have diminished in size and strength as people have increasingly become involved with others as coworkers in a market economy. Our associations depend more and more upon factors such as personal aptitudes, educational backgrounds, and job opportunities. Yet the family is still there. It is smaller, but it still functions in its age-old nurturing and protective role, even under conditions of extreme poverty and a high infant mortality rate (see "Death without Weeping" by Nancy Scheper-Hughes). Beyond the immediate family, the situation is in a state of flux. Certain ethnic groups, especially those in poverty, still have a need for the broader network, and in some ways seem to be reformulating those ties.

Where the changes described in this section will lead us and which ones will ultimately prevail, we do not know. One thing is certain: anthropologists will be there to document the trends, for the discipline of anthropology has had to change as well. One important feature of the essays in this section is the growing interest of anthropologists in the study of complex societies, where old theoretical perspectives are increasingly inadequate.

Current trends do not necessarily mean the eclipse of the kinship unit, however, as Enid Schildkrout illustrates in "Young Traders of Northern Nigeria." The message is that the large family network is still the best guarantee of individual survival and well-being in an urban setting.

Looking Ahead: Challenge Questions

Why do you think "fraternal polyandry" is socially acceptable in Tibet but not in our society?

What are the implications of Western education for the ability of Hausa women to earn an income?

How do differences in child care relate to economic circumstances?

What are the pros and cons of arranged marriages versus freedom of choice?

but finally one of my brothers helped me take it to her.

"When I returned, my mother was busy pounding some grain, and she sent me out to have some locust beans pounded. She then sent me to pick up three bowls of pounded guinea corn, and she gave me money to take to the woman who had pounded it. The woman told me to remind my mother that she still owed money from the day before.

"When I came home I was sent out to trade again, this time with salt, bouillon cubes, and laundry detergent in small packets. Afterward I prepared some pancakes using ingredients I bought myself—ten kobo worth of flour, one kobo worth of salt, five kobo worth of palm oil, and ten kobo worth of firewood. I took this food outside to sell it to children.

"My mother then gave me a calabash of guinea corn to take for grinding; my younger sister also gave me two calabashes of corn to take. The man who ran the grinding machine advised me that I should not carry so large a load, so I made two trips on the way back. He gave me and my younger brothers, who accompanied me, one kobo each.

"I was then told to take a bath, which I did. After that I was sent to visit a sick relative who was in the hospital. On the way I met a friend, and we took the bus together. I also bought some cheese at the market for five kobo. I met another friend on the way home, and she bought some fish near the market for ten kobo and gave me some. I played on the way to the hospital. When I got home, I found the women of the house preparing a meal. One of them was already eating, and I was invited to eat with her.

"After nightfall, I was sent to take some spices for pounding, and I wasted a lot of time there. The other children and I went to a place where some fruits and vegetables are sold along the street. We bought vegetables for soup for fifty kobo, as my mother had asked me to do. By the time I got home it was late, so I went to sleep."

Binta's many responsibilities are typical for a girl her age. Like many women, Binta's mother relies upon her children in carrying out an occupation at home. Although purdah implies that a woman will be supported by her husband and need not work, most Hausa women do work, keeping their incomes distinct from the household budget. Women usually cook one main meal a day and purchase their other meals from other women. In this way they are able to use their time earning a living instead of performing only unpaid domestic labor.

Among the Hausa, men and women spend relatively little time together, eating separately and, except in certain ritual contexts, rarely doing the same things. Differences in gender are not as important among children, however. In fact, it is precisely because children's activities are not rigidly defined by sex that they are able to move between the world of women, centered in the inner courtyard of the house, and the world of men, whose activities take place mainly outside the home. Children of both sexes care for younger children, go to the market, and help their mothers cook.

Both boys and girls do trading, although it is more common for girls. From the age of about five until marriage, which is very often at about age twelve for girls, many children like Binta spend part of every day selling such things as fruits, vegetables, and nuts; bouillon cubes, bread, and small packages of detergent, sugar, or salt; and bowls of steaming rice or *tuwo*. If a woman embroiders, children buy the thread and later take the finished product to the client or to an agent who sells it.

Women in purdah frequently change their occupations depending on the availability of child helpers. In Kano, women often trade in small commodities that can be sold in small quantities, such as various kinds of cooked food. Sewing, embroidery, mat weaving, and other craft activities (including, until recently, spinning) are less remunerative occupations, and women pursue them when they have fewer children around to help. Unlike the situation common in the United States, where children tend to hamper a woman's ability to earn money, the Hausa woman finds it difficult to earn income without children's help. Often, if a woman has no children of her own, a relative's child will come to live with her.

Child care is another service children perform that benefits women. It enables mothers to devote themselves to their young infants, whom they carry on their backs until the age of weaning, between one and two. Even though women are always at home, they specifically delegate the care of young children to older ones. The toddler moves from the mother's back into a group of older children, who take the responsibility very seriously. Until they are old enough, children do not pick up infants or very young children, but by the age of nine, both boys and girls bathe young children, play with them, and take them on errands. The older children do a great deal of direct and indirect teaching of younger ones. As soon as they can walk, younger children accompany their older siblings to Arabic school. There the children sit with their age-mates, and the teacher gives them lessons according to their ability.

Much of a child's activity is directed toward helping his or her parents, but other relatives—grandparents, aunts, uncles, and stepmothers—and adults living in the same house as servants or tenants may call on a child for limited tasks without asking permission of the parents. Like other Muslims, Hausa men may have up to four wives, and these women freely call on each other's children to perform household chores. Even strangers in the street sometimes ask a child to do an errand, such as delivering a message, particularly if the chore requires entering a house to which the adult does not have access. The child will be rewarded with a small amount of money or food.

Adults other than parents also reprimand children, who are taught very early to obey the orders of grownups. Without ever directly refusing to obey a command, however, children do devise numerous strategies of non-compliance, such as claiming that another adult has already co-opted their time or simply leaving the scene and ignoring the command. Given children's greater mobility, there is little an adult can do to enforce compliance.

4. OTHER FAMILIES, OTHER WAYS

Besides working on behalf of adults, children also participate in a "children's economy." Children have their own money—from school allowances given to them daily for the purchase of snacks, from gifts, from work they may have done, and even from their own investments. For example, boys make toys for sale, and they rent out valued property, such as slide viewers or bicycles. Just as women distinguish their own enterprises from the labor they do as wives, children regard the work they do for themselves differently from the work they do on behalf of their mothers. When Binta cooks food for sale, using materials she has purchased with her own money, the profits are entirely her own, although she may hand the money over to her mother for safekeeping.

Many girls begin to practice cooking by the age of ten. They do not actually prepare the family meals, for this heavy and tedious work is primarily the wives' responsibility. But they do carry out related chores, such as taking vegetables out for grinding, sifting flour, and washing bowls. Many also cook food for sale on their own. With initial help from their mothers or other adult female relatives, who may given them a cooking pot, charcoal, or a small stove, children purchase small amounts of ingredients and prepare various snacks. Since they sell their products for less than the adult women do, and since the quantities are very small, their customers are mainly children. Child entrepreneurs even extend credit to other children.

Aisha is a ten-year-old girl who was notoriously unsuccessful as a trader. She disliked trading and regularly lost her mother's investment. Disgusted, her mother finally gave her a bit of charcoal, some flour and oil, and a small pot. Aisha set up a little stove outside her house and began making small pancakes, which she sold to very young children. In three months she managed to make enough to buy a new dress, and in a year she bought a pair of shoes. She had clearly chosen her occupation after some unhappy trials at street trading.

Hausa women usually engage in some form of enterprise; most of their profits are invested in their children's marriage expenses. Working at home, a woman weaves a mat for sale.

In the poorest families, as in Aisha's, the profit from children's work goes toward living expenses. This may occur in households that are headed by divorced or widowed women. It is also true for the *almajirai*, or Arabic students, who often live with their teachers. The proceeds of most children's economic activity, however, go to the expenses of marriage. The income contributes to a girl's dowry and to a boy's bridewealth, both of which are considerable investments.

The girl's dowry includes many brightly painted enamel, brass, and glass bowls, collected years before marriage. These utensils are known as *kayan daki*, or "things of the room." After the wedding they are stacked in a large cupboard beside the girl's bed. Very few of them are used, but they are always proudly displayed, except during the mourning period if the husband dies. *Kayan daki* are not simply for conspicuous display, however. They remain the property of the woman unless she sells them or gives them away. In the case of divorce or financial need, they can provide her most important and immediate source of economic security.

Kayan daki traditionally consisted of brass bowls and beautifully carved calabashes. Today the most common form is painted enamel bowls manufactured in Nigeria or abroad. The styles and designs change frequently, and the cost is continually rising.

Among the wealthier urban women and the Western-educated women, other forms of modern household equipment, including electric appliances and china tea sets, are becoming part of the dowry.

The money a young girl earns on her own, as well as the profits she brings home through her trading, are invested by her mother or guardian in *kayan daki* in anticipation of her marriage. Most women put the major part of their income into their daughters' *kayan daki* as well as helping their sons with marriage expenses. When a woman has many children, the burden can be considerable.

For girls, marriage, which ideally coincides with puberty, marks the transition to adult status. If a girl marries as early as age ten, she does not cook for her husband or have sexual relations with him for some time, but she enters purdah and loses the freedom of childhood. Most girls are married by age fifteen, and for many the transition is a difficult one.

Boys usually do not marry until they are over twenty and are able to support a family. They also need to have raised most of the money to cover the cost of getting married. Between the ages of eight and ten, however, they gradually begin to move away from the confines of the house and to regard it as a female domain. They begin taking their food outside and eating it with friends, and they roam much farther than girls in their play activities. By the onset of puberty, boys have begun to observe the rules of purdah by refraining from entering the houses of all but their closest relatives. In general, especially if they have sisters, older boys spend less time than girls doing chores and errands and more time playing and, in recent years, going to school. Traditionally, many boys left home to live and study with an Arabic teacher. Today many also pursue Western education, sometimes in boarding school. Although the transition to adulthood is less abrupt for boys, childhood for both sexes ends by age twelve to fourteen.

As each generation assumes the responsibilities of adulthood and the restrictions of sexual separation, it must rely on the younger members of society who can work around the purdah system. Recently, however, the introduction of Western education has begun to threaten this traditional arrangement, in part just by altering the pattern of children's lives.

The Nigerian government is now engaged in a massive program to provide Western education to all school-age children. This program has been undertaken for sound economic and political reasons. During the colonial period, which ended in the early 1960s, the British had a "hands-off"
policy regarding education in northern Nigeria. They ruled through the Islamic political and judicial hierarchy and supported the many Arabic schools, where the Koran and Islamic law, history, and religion were taught. The British discouraged the introduction of Christian mission schools in the north and spent little on government schools.

The pattern in the rest of Nigeria was very different. In the non-Muslim areas of the country, mission and government schools grew rapidly during the colonial period. The result of this differential policy was the development of vast regional imbalances in the extent and level of Western education in the country. This affected the types of occupational choices open to Nigerians from different regions. Despite a longer tradition of literacy in Arabic in the north, few northerners were eligible for those civil service jobs that required literacy in English, the language of government business. This was one of the many issues in the tragic civil war that tore Nigeria apart in the 1960s. The current goal of enrolling all northern children in public schools, which offer training in English and secular subjects, has, therefore, a strong and valid political rationale.

Western education has met a mixed reception in northern Nigeria. While
it has been increasingly accepted for boys—as an addition to, not a substitute for, Islamic education—many parents are reluctant to enroll their daughters in primary school. Nevertheless, there are already more children waiting to get into school than there are classrooms and teachers to accommodate them. If the trend continues, it will almost certainly have important, if unintended, consequences for purdah and the system of child enterprise that supports it.

Children who attend Western school continue to attend Arabic school, and thus are removed from the household for much of the day. For many women this causes considerable difficulty in doing daily housework. It means increased isolation and a curtailment of income-producing activity. It creates a new concern about where to obtain the income for children's marriages. As a result of these practical pressures, the institution of purdah will inevitably be challenged. Also, the schoolgirl of today may develop new skills and new expectations of her role as a woman that conflict with the traditional ways. As Western education takes hold, today's young traders may witness a dramatic change in Hausa family life— for themselves as adults and for their children.

Death Without Weeping

Has poverty ravaged mother love in the shantytowns of Brazil?

Nancy Scheper-Hughes

Nancy Scheper-Hughes is a professor in the Department of Anthropology at the University of California, Berkeley. She has written Death Without Weeping: Violence of Everyday Life in Brazil *(1992).*

I have seen death without weeping
The destiny of the Northeast is death
Cattle they kill
To the people they do something worse
  —Anonymous Brazilian singer (1965)

"Why do the church bells ring so often?" I asked Nailza de Arruda soon after I moved into a corner of her tiny mud-walled hut near the top of the shantytown called the Alto do Cruzeiro (Crucifix Hill). I was then a Peace Corps volunteer and a community development/health worker. It was the dry and blazing hot summer of 1965, the months following the military coup in Brazil, and save for the rusty, clanging bells of N. S. das Dores Church, an eerie quiet had settled over the market town that I call Bom Jesus da Mata. Beneath the quiet, however, there was chaos and panic. "It's nothing," replied Nailza, "just another little angel gone to heaven."

Nailza had sent more than her share of little angels to heaven, and sometimes at night I could hear her engaged in a muffled but passionate discourse with one of them, two-year-old Joana. Joana's photograph, taken as she lay propped up in her tiny cardboard coffin, her eyes open, hung on a wall next to one of Nailza and Ze Antonio taken on the day they eloped.

Nailza could barely remember the other infants and babies who came and went in close succession. Most had died unnamed and were hastily baptized in their coffins. Few lived more than a month or two. Only Joana, properly baptized in church at the close of her first year and placed under the protection of a powerful saint, Joan of Arc, had been expected to live. And Nailza had dangerously allowed herself to love the little girl.

In addressing the dead child, Nailza's voice would range from tearful imploring to angry recrimination: "Why did you leave me? Was your patron saint so greedy that she could not allow me one child on this earth?" Ze Antonio advised me to ignore Nailza's odd behavior, which he understood as a kind of madness that, like the birth and death of children, came and went. Indeed, the premature birth of a stillborn son some months later "cured" Nailza of her "inappropriate" grief, and the day came when she removed Joana's photo and carefully packed it away.

More than fifteen years elapsed before I returned to the Alto do Cruzeiro, and it was anthropology that provided the vehicle of my return. Since 1982 I have returned several times in order to pursue a problem that first attracted my attention in the 1960s. My involvement with the people of the Alto do Cruzeiro now spans a quarter of a century and three generations of parenting in a community where mothers and daughters are often simultaneously pregnant.

The Alto do Cruzeiro is one of three shantytowns surrounding the large market town of Bom Jesus in the sugar plantation zone of Pernambuco in Northeast Brazil, one of the many zones of neglect that have emerged in the shadow of the now tarnished economic miracle of Brazil. For the women and children of the Alto do Cruzeiro the only miracle is that some of them have managed to stay alive at all.

The Northeast is a region of vast proportions (approximately twice the size of Texas) and of equally vast social and developmental problems. The nine states that make up the region are the poorest in the country and are representative of the Third World within a dynamic and rapidly industrializing nation. Despite waves of migrations from the interior to the teeming shantytowns of coastal cities, the majority still live in rural areas on farms and ranches, sugar plantations and mills.

Life expectancy in the Northeast is only forty years, largely because of the appallingly high rate of infant and child mortality. Approximately one million children in Brazil under the age of five die each year. The children of the Northeast, especially those born in shantytowns on the periphery of urban life, are at a very high risk of death. In these areas, children are born without the traditional protection of breast-feeding, subsistence gardens, stable marriages, and multiple adult caretakers that exists in the interior. In the hillside shantytowns that spring up around cities or, in this case, interior market towns, marriages are brittle, single parenting is the norm, and women are

From *Natural History,* October 1989, pp. 8, 10, 12, 14, 16. © 1989 by Nancy Scheper-Hughes. Reprinted by permission of the author.

frequently forced into the shadow economy of domestic work in the homes of the rich or into unprotected and oftentimes "scab" wage labor on the surrounding sugar plantations, where they clear land for planting and weed for a pittance, sometimes less than a dollar a day. The women of the Alto may not bring their babies with them into the homes of the wealthy, where the often-sick infants are considered sources of contamination, and they cannot carry the little ones to the river-banks where they wash clothes because the river is heavily infested with schistosomes and other deadly parasites. Nor can they carry their young children to the plantations, which are often several miles away. At wages of a dollar a day, the women of the Alto cannot hire baby sitters. Older children who are not in school will sometimes serve as somewhat indifferent care-takers. But any child not in school is also expected to find wage work. In most cases, babies are simply left at home alone, the door securely fastened. And so many also die alone and unattended.

Bom Jesus da Mata, centrally located in the plantation zone of Pernambuco, is within commuting distance of several sugar plantations and mills. Consequently, Bom Jesus has been a magnet for rural workers forced off their small subsistence plots by large landowners wanting to use every available piece of land for sugar cultivation. Initially, the rural migrants to Bom Jesus were squatters who were given tacit approval by the mayor to put up temporary straw huts on each of the three hills overlooking the town. The Alto do Cruzeiro is the oldest, the largest, and the poorest of the shanty-towns. Over the past three decades many of the original migrants have become permanent residents, and the primitive and temporary straw huts have been replaced by small homes (usually of two rooms) made of wattle and daub, sometimes covered with plaster. The more affluent residents use bricks and tiles. In most Alto homes, dangerous kerosene lamps have been replaced by light bulbs. The once tattered rural garb, often fashioned from used sugar sacking, has likewise been replaced by store-bought clothes, often castoffs from a wealthy *patrão* (boss). The trappings are modern, but the hunger, sickness, and death that they conceal are traditional, deeply rooted in a history of feudalism, exploitation, and institutionalized dependency.

My research agenda never wavered. The questions I addressed first crystallized during a veritable "die-off" of Alto babies during a severe drought in 1965. The food and water shortages and the political and economic chaos occasioned by the military coup were reflected in the handwritten entries of births and deaths in the dusty, yellowed pages of the ledger books kept at the public registry office in Bom Jesus. More than 350 babies died in the Alto during 1965 alone—this from a shanty-town population of little more than 5,000. But that wasn't what surprised me. There were reasons enough for the deaths in the miserable conditions of shantytown life. What puzzled me was the seeming indifference of Alto women to the death of their infants, and their willingness to attribute to their own tiny offspring an aversion to life that made their death seem wholly natural, indeed all but anticipated.

Although I found that it was possible, and hardly difficult, to rescue infants and toddlers from death by diarrhea and dehydration with a simple sugar, salt, and water solution (even bottled Coca-Cola worked fine), it was more difficult to enlist a mother herself in the rescue of a child she perceived as ill-fated for life or better off dead, or to convince her to take back into her threatened and besieged home a baby she had already come to think of as an angel rather than as a son or daughter.

I learned that the high expectancy of death, and the ability to face child death with stoicism and equanimity, produced patterns of nurturing that differentiated between those infants thought of as thrivers and survivors and those thought of as born already "wanting to die." The survivors were nurtured, while stigmatized, doomed infants were left to die, as mothers say, *a mingua,* "of neglect." Mothers stepped back and allowed nature to take its course. This pattern, which I call mortal selective neglect, is called passive infanticide by anthropologist Marvin Harris. The Alto situation, although culturally specific in the form that it takes, is not unique to Third World shantytown communities and may have its correlates in our own impoverished urban communities in some cases of "failure to thrive" infants.

I use as an example the story of Zezinho, the thirteen-month-old toddler of one of my neighbors, Lourdes. I became involved with Zezinho when I was called in to help Lourdes in the delivery of another child, this one a fair and robust little tyke with a lusty cry. I noted that while Lourdes showed great interest in the newborn, she totally ignored Zezinho who, wasted and severely malnourished, was curled up in a fetal position on a piece of urine- and feces-soaked cardboard placed under his mother's hammock. Eyes open and vacant, mouth slack, the little boy seemed doomed.

When I carried Zezinho up to the community day-care center at the top of the hill, the Alto women who took turns caring for one another's children (in order to free themselves for part-time work in the cane fields or washing clothes) laughed at my efforts to save Ze, agreeing with Lourdes that here was a baby without a ghost of a chance. Leave him alone, they cautioned. It makes no sense to fight with death. But I did do battle with Ze, and after several weeks of force-feeding (malnourished babies lose their interest in food), Ze began to succumb to my ministrations. He acquired some flesh across his taut chest bones, learned to sit up, and even tried to smile. When he seemed well enough, I returned him to Lourdes in her miserable scrap-material lean-to, but not without guilt about what I had done. I wondered whether returning Ze was at all fair to Lourdes and to his little brother. But I was busy and washed my hands of the matter. And Lourdes did seem more interested in Ze now that he was looking more human.

When I returned in 1982, there was Lourdes among the women who formed my sample of Alto mothers—still struggling to put together some semblance of life for a now grown Ze and her five other surviving children. Much was made of my reunion with Ze in 1982, and everyone enjoyed retelling the story of Ze's rescue and of how his mother had given him up for dead. Ze would laugh the loudest when told how I had had to force-feed him like a fiesta turkey. There was no hint of guilt on the part of Lourdes and no resentment on the part of Ze. In fact, when questioned in private as to who was the best friend he ever had in life, Ze took a long drag on his cigarette and answered without a trace of irony, "Why my mother, of course." "But of course," I replied.

Part of learning how to mother in the Alto do Cruzeiro is learning when to let go of a child who shows that it "wants" to die or that it has no "knack" or no "taste" for life. Another part is learning when it is safe to let oneself love a child. Frequent child death remains a powerful shaper of maternal thinking and practice. In the absence of firm expectation that a child will survive, mother love as we conceptualize it (whether in popular terms or in the psychobiological notion of maternal bonding) is attenuated and delayed with consequences for infant survival. In an environment already precarious to young life, the emotional detachment of mothers toward some of their babies contributes even further to the spiral of high mortality—high fertility in a kind of macabre lock-step dance of death.

The average woman of the Alto experiences 9.5 pregnancies, 3.5 child deaths, and 1.5 stillbirths. Seventy percent of all child deaths in the Alto occur in the first six months of life, and 82 percent by the end of the first year. Of all deaths in the community each year, about 45 percent are of children under the age of five.

Women of the Alto distinguish between child deaths understood as natural (caused by diarrhea and communicable diseases) and those resulting from sorcery, the evil eye, or other magical or supernatural afflictions. They also recognize a large category of infant deaths seen as fated and inevitable. These hopeless cases are classified by mothers under the folk terminology "child sickness" or "child attack." Women say that there are at least fourteen different types of hopeless child sickness, but most can be subsumed under two categories—chronic and acute. The chronic cases refer to infants who are born small and wasted. They are deathly pale, mothers say, as well as weak and passive. They demonstrate no vital force, no liveliness. They do not suck vigorously; they hardly cry. Such babies can be this way at birth or they can be born sound but soon show no resistance, no "fight" against the common crises of infancy: diarrhea, respiratory infections, tropical fevers.

The acute cases are those doomed infants who die suddenly and violently. They are taken by stealth overnight, often following convulsions that bring on head banging, shaking, grimacing, and shrieking. Women say it is horrible to look at such a baby. If the infant begins to foam at the mouth or gnash its teeth or go rigid with its eyes turned back inside its head, there is absolutely no hope. The infant is "put aside"— left alone—often on the floor in a back room, and allowed to die. These symptoms (which accompany high fevers, dehydration, third-stage malnutrition, and encephalitis) are equated by Alto women with madness, epilepsy, and worst of all, rabies, which is greatly feared and highly stigmatized.

Most of the infants presented to me as suffering from chronic child sickness were tiny, wasted famine victims, while those labeled as victims of acute child attack seemed to be infants suffering from the deliriums of high fever or the convulsions that can accompany electrolyte imbalance in dehydrated babies.

Local midwives and traditional healers, praying women, as they are called, advise Alto women on when to allow a baby to die. One midwife explained: "If I can see that a baby was born unfortuitously, I tell the mother that she need not wash the infant or give it a cleansing tea. I tell her just to dust the infant with baby powder and wait for it to die." Allowing nature to take its course is not seen as sinful by these often very devout Catholic women. Rather, it is understood as cooperating with God's plan.

Often I have been asked how consciously women of the Alto behave in this regard. I would have to say that consciousness is always shifting between allowed and disallowed levels of awareness. For example, I was awakened early one morning in 1987 by two neighborhood children who had been sent to fetch me to a hastily organized wake for a two-month-old infant whose mother I had unsuccessfully urged to breast-feed. The infant was being sustained on sugar water, which the mother referred to as *soro* (serum), using a medical term for the infant's starvation regime in light of his chronic diarrhea. I had cautioned the mother that an infant could not live on *soro* forever.

The two girls urged me to console the young mother by telling her that it was "too bad" that her infant was so weak that Jesus had to take him. They were coaching me in proper Alto etiquette. I agreed, of course, but asked, "And what do *you* think?" Xoxa, the eleven-year-old, looked down at her dusty flip-flops and blurted out, "Oh, Dona Nanci, that baby never got enough to eat, but you must never say that!" And so the death of hungry babies remains one of the best kept secrets of life in Bom Jesus da Mata.

Most victims are waked quickly and with a minimum of ceremony. No tears are shed, and the neighborhood children form a tiny procession, carrying the baby to the town graveyard where it will join a multitude of others. Although a few fresh flowers may be scattered over the tiny grave, no stone or wooden cross will mark the place, and the same spot will be reused within a few months' time. The mother will never visit the grave, which soon becomes an anonymous one.

What, then, can be said of these women? What emotions, what sentiments motivate them? How are they able to do what, in fact, must be done? What does mother love mean in this inhospitable context? Are grief, mourning, and melancholia present, although deeply repressed? If so, where shall we look for them? And if not, how are we to understand the moral visions and moral sensibilities that guide their actions?

I have been criticized more than once for presenting an unflattering portrait of poor Brazilian women, women who are, after all, themselves the victims of severe social and institutional neglect. I have described these women as allowing some of their children to die, as if this were an unnatural and inhuman act rather than, as I would assert, the way any one of us might act, reasonably and rationally, under similarly desperate conditions. Perhaps I have not emphasized enough the real pathogens in this environment of high risk: poverty, deprivation, sexism, chronic hunger, and economic exploitation. If mother love is, as many psychologists and some feminists believe, a seemingly natural and universal maternal script, what does it mean to women for whom scarcity, loss, sickness, and deprivation have made that love frantic and robbed them of their grief, seeming to turn their hearts to stone?

Throughout much of human history— as in a great deal of the impoverished Third World today—women have had to give birth and to nurture children under ecological conditions and social arrangements hostile to child survival, as well as to their own well-being. Under circumstances of high childhood mortality, patterns of selective neglect and passive infanticide may be seen as active survival strategies.

They also seem to be fairly common practices historically and across cultures. In societies characterized by high childhood mortality and by a correspondingly high (replacement) fertility, cultural practices of infant and child care tend to be organized primarily around survival goals. But what this means is a pragmatic recognition that not all of one's children can be expected to live. The nervousness about child survival in areas of northeast Brazil, northern India, or Bangladesh, where a 30 percent or 40 percent mortality rate in the first years of life is common, can lead to forms of delayed attachment and a casual or benign neglect that serves to weed out the worst

bets so as to enhance the life chances of healthier siblings, including those yet to be born. Practices similar to those that I am describing have been recorded for parts of Africa, India, and Central America.

Life in the Alto do Cruzeiro resembles nothing so much as a battlefield or an emergency room in an overcrowded inner-city public hospital. Consequently, morality is guided by a kind of "lifeboat ethics," the morality of triage. The seemingly studied indifference toward the suffering of some of their infants, conveyed in such sayings as "little critters have no feelings," is understandable in light of these women's obligation to carry on with their reproductive and nurturing lives.

In their slowness to anthropomorphize and personalize their infants, everything is mobilized so as to prevent maternal overattachment and, therefore, grief at death. The bereaved mother is told not to cry, that her tears will dampen the wings of her little angel so that she cannot fly up to her heavenly home. Grief at the death of an angel is not only inappropriate, it is a symptom of madness and of a profound lack of faith.

Infant death becomes routine in an environment in which death is anticipated and bets are hedged. While the routinization of death in the context of shantytown life is not hard to understand, and quite possible to empathize with, its routinization in the formal institutions of public life in Bom Jesus is not as easy to accept uncritically. Here the social production of indifference takes on a different, even a malevolent, cast.

In a society where triplicates of every form are required for the most banal events (registering a car, for example), the registration of infant and child death is informal, incomplete, and rapid. It requires no documentation, takes less than five minutes, and demands no witnesses other than office clerks. No questions are asked concerning the circumstances of the death, and the cause of death is left blank, unquestioned and unexamined. A neighbor, grandmother, older sibling, or common-law husband may register the

death. Since most infants die at home, there is no question of a medical record.

From the registry office, the parent proceeds to the town hall, where the mayor will give him or her a voucher for a free baby coffin. The full-time municipal coffinmaker cannot tell you exactly how many baby coffins are dispatched each week. It varies, he says, with the seasons. There are more needed during the drought months and during the big festivals of Carnaval and Christmas and São Joao's Day because people are too busy, he supposes, to take their babies to the clinic. Record keeping is sloppy.

Similarly, there is a failure on the part of city-employed doctors working at two free clinics to recognize the malnutrition of babies who are weighed, measured, and immunized without comment and as if they were not, in fact, anemic, stunted, fussy, and irritated starvation babies. At best the mothers are told to pick up free vitamins or a health "tonic" at the municipal chambers. At worst, clinic personnel will give tranquilizers and sleeping pills to quiet the hungry cries of "sick-to-death" Alto babies.

The church, too, contributes to the routinization of, and indifference toward, child death. Traditionally, the local Catholic church taught patience and resignation to domestic tragedies that were said to reveal the imponderable workings of God's will. If an infant died suddenly, it was because a particular saint had claimed the child. The infant would be an angel in the service of his or her heavenly patron. It would be wrong, a sign of a lack of faith, to weep for a child with such good fortune. The infant funeral was, in the past, an event celebrated with joy. Today, however, under the new regime of "liberation theology," the bells of N. S. das Dores parish church no longer peal for the death of Alto babies, and no priest accompanies the procession of angels to the cemetery where their bodies are disposed of casually and without ceremony. Children bury children in Bom Jesus da Mata. In this most Catholic of communities, the coffin is handed to the disabled and irritable municipal gravedigger, who often chides the children for one reason or another. It may be that the coffin is larger than expected and the gravedigger can find no appropriate space. The children do not wait for the gravedigger to complete his task. No prayers are recited and no sign of the cross made as the tiny coffin goes into its shallow grave.

When I asked the local priest, Padre Marcos, about the lack of church ceremony surrounding infant and childhood death today in Bom Jesus, he replied: "In the old days, child death was richly celebrated. But those were the baroque customs of a conservative church that wallowed in death and misery. The new church is a church of hope and joy. We no longer celebrate the death of child angels. We try to tell mothers that Jesus doesn't want all the dead babies they send him." Similarly, the new church has changed its baptismal customs, now often refusing to baptize dying babies brought to the back door of a church or rectory. The mothers are scolded by the church attendants and told to go home and take care of their sick babies. Baptism, they are told, is for the living; it is not to be confused with the sacrament of extreme unction, which is the anointing of the dying. And so it appears to the women of the Alto that even the church has turned away from them, denying the traditional comfort of folk Catholicism.

The contemporary Catholic church is caught in the clutches of a double bind. The new theology of liberation imagines a kingdom of God on earth based on justice and equality, a world without hunger, sickness, or childhood mortality. At the same time, the church has not changed its official position on sexuality and reproduction, including its sanctions against birth control, abortion, and sterilization. The padre of Bom Jesus da Mata recognizes this contradiction intuitively, although he shies away from discussions on the topic, saying that he prefers to leave questions of family planning to the discretion and the "good consciences" of his impoverished parishioners. But this, of course, sidesteps the extent to which those good consciences have been shaped by traditional church teachings in Bom Jesus, especially by his recent predecessors. Hence, we can begin to see that the seeming indifference of Alto mothers toward the death of some of their infants is but a pale reflection of the official indifference of church and state to the plight of poor women and children.

Nonetheless, the women of Bom Jesus are survivors. One woman, Biu, told me her life history, returning again and again to the themes of child death, her first husband's suicide, abandonment by her father and later by her second husband, and all the other losses and disappointments she had suffered in her long forty-five years. She concluded with great force, reflecting on the days of Carnaval '88 that were fast approaching:

No, Dona Nanci, I won't cry, and I won't waste my life thinking about it from morning to night. . . . Can I argue with God for the state that I'm in? No! And so I'll dance and I'll jump and I'll play Carnaval! And yes, I'll laugh and people will wonder at a *pobre* like me who can have such a good time.

And no one did blame Biu for dancing in the streets during the four days of Carnaval—not even on Ash Wednesday, the day following Carnaval '88 when we all assembled hurriedly to assist in the burial of Mercea, Biu's beloved *casula*, her last-born daughter who had died at home of pneumonia during the festivities. The rest of the family barely had time to change out of their costumes. Severino, the child's uncle and godfather, sprinkled holy water over the little angel while he prayed: "Mercea, I don't know whether you were called, taken, or thrown out of this world. But look down at us from your heavenly home with tenderness, with pity, and with mercy." So be it.

Arranging a Marriage in India

Serena Nanda

John Jay College of Criminal Justice

Sister and doctor brother-in-law invite correspondence from North Indian professionals only, for a beautiful, talented, sophisticated, intelligent sister, 5′ 3″, slim, M.A. in textile design, father a senior civil officer. Would prefer immigrant doctors, between 26–29 years. Reply with full details and returnable photo.

A well-settled uncle invites matrimonial correspondence from slim, fair, educated South Indian girl, for his nephew, 25 years, smart, M.B.A., green card holder, 5′ 6″. Full particulars with returnable photo appreciated.

Matrimonial Advertisements,
India Abroad

In India, almost all marriages are arranged. Even among the educated middle classes in modern, urban India, marriage is as much a concern of the families as it is of the individuals. So customary is the practice of arranged marriage that there is a special name for a marriage which is not arranged: It is called a "love match."

On my first field trip to India, I met many young men and women whose parents were in the process of "getting them married." In many cases, the bride and groom would not meet each other before the marriage. At most they might meet for a brief conversation, and this meeting would take place only after their parents had decided that the match was suitable. Parents do not compel their children to marry a person who either marriage partner finds objectionable. But only after one match is refused will another be sought.

As a young American woman in India for the first time, I found this custom of arranged marriage oppressive. How could any intelligent young person agree to such a marriage without great reluctance? It was contrary to everything I believed about the importance of romantic love as the only basis of a happy marriage. It also clashed with my strongly held notions that the choice of such an intimate and permanent relationship could be made only by the individuals involved. Had anyone tried to arrange my marriage, I would have been defiant and rebellious!

At the first opportunity, I began, with more curiosity than tact, to question the young people I met on how they felt about this practice. Sita, one of my young informants, was a college graduate with a degree in political science. She had been waiting for over a year while her parents were arranging a match for her. I found it difficult to accept the docile manner in which this well-educated young woman awaited the outcome of a process that would result in her spending the rest of her life with a man she hardly knew, a virtual stranger, picked out by her parents.

"How can you go along with this?" I asked her, in frustration and distress. "Don't you care who you marry?"

"Of course I care," she answered. "This is why I must let my parents choose a boy for me. My marriage is too important to be arranged by such an inexperienced person as myself. In such matters, it is better to have my parents' guidance."

I had learned that young men and women in India do not date and have very little social life involving members of the opposite sex. Although I could not disagree with Sita's reasoning, I continued to pursue the subject.

"But how can you marry the first man you have ever met? Not only have you missed the fun of meeting a lot of different people, but you have not given yourself the chance to know who is the right man for you."

"Meeting with a lot of different people doesn't sound like any fun at all," Sita answered. "One hears that in America the girls are spending all their time worrying about whether they will meet a man and get married. Here we have the chance to enjoy our life and let our parents do this work and worrying for us."

She had me there. The high anxiety of the competition to "be popular" with the opposite sex certainly was the most prominent feature of life as an American teenager in the late fifties. The endless worrying about the rules that governed our behavior and about our popularity ratings sapped both our self-esteem and our enjoyment of adolescence. I reflected that absence of this competition in India most certainly may have contributed to the self-confidence and natural charm of so many of the young women I met.

And yet, the idea of marrying a perfect stranger, whom one did not know and did not "love," so offended my American ideas of individualism and romanticism, that I persisted with my objections.

"I still can't imagine it," I said. "How can you agree to marry a man you hardly know?"

"But of course he will be known. My parents would never arrange a marriage for me without knowing all about the boy's family background. Naturally we will not rely only on what the family tells us. We will check the particulars out ourselves. No one will want their daughter to marry into a family that is not good. All these things we will know beforehand."

Impatiently, I responded, "Sita, I don't mean know the family, I mean, know the man. How can you marry someone you don't know personally and don't love? How can you think of spending your life with someone you may not even like?"

"If he is a good man, why should I not like him?" she said. "With you people, you know the boy so well before you marry, where will be the fun to get married? There will be no mystery and no romance. Here we have the whole of our married life to get to know and love our husband. This way is better, is it not?"

Her response made further sense, and I began to have second thoughts on the matter. Indeed, during months of meeting many intelligent young Indian people, both male and female, who had the same ideas as Sita, I saw arranged marriages in a different light. I also saw the importance of the family in Indian life and realized that a couple who took their marriage into their own hands was taking a big risk, particularly if their families were irreconcilably opposed to the match. In a country where every important resource in life—a job, a house, a social circle—is gained through family connections, it seemed foolhardy to cut oneself off from a supportive social network and depend solely on one person for happiness and success.

Six years later I returned to India to again do fieldwork, this time among the middle class in Bombay, a modern, sophisticated city. From the experience of my earlier visit, I decided to include a study of arranged marriages in my project. By this time I had met many Indian couples whose marriages had been arranged and who seemed very happy. Particularly in contrast to the fate of many of my married friends in the United States who were already in the process of divorce, the positive aspects of arranged marriages appeared to me to outweigh the negatives. In fact, I thought I might even participate in arranging a marriage myself. I had been fairly successful in the United States in "fixing up" many of my friends, and I was confident that my matchmaking skills could be easily applied to this new situation, once I learned the basic rules. "After all," I thought, "how complicated can it be? People want pretty much the same things in a marriage whether it is in India or America."

An opportunity presented itself almost immediately. A friend from my previous Indian trip was in the process of arranging for the marriage of her eldest son. In India there is a perceived shortage of "good boys," and since my friend's family was eminently respectable and the boy himself personable, well educated, and nice looking, I was sure that by the end of my year's fieldwork, we would have found a match.

The basic rule seems to be that a family's reputation is most important.

It is understood that matches would be arranged only within the same caste and general social class, although some crossing of subcastes is permissible if the class positions of the bride's and groom's families are similar. Although dowry is now prohibited by law in India, extensive gift exchanges took place with every marriage. Even when the boy's family do not "make demands," every girl's family nevertheless feels the obligation to give the traditional gifts, to the girl, to the boy, and to the boy's family. Particularly when the couple would be living in the joint family—that is, with the boy's parents and his married brothers and their families, as well as with unmarried siblings—which is still very common even among the urban, uppermiddle class in India, the girl's parents are anxious to establish smooth relations between their family and that of the boy. Offering the proper gifts, even when not called "dowry," is often an important factor in influencing the relationship between the bride's and groom's families and perhaps, also, the treatment of the bride in her new home.

In a society where divorce is still a scandal and where, in fact, the divorce rate is exceedingly low, an arranged marriage is the beginning of a lifetime relationship not just between the bride and groom but between their families as well. Thus, while a girl's looks are important, her character is even more so, for she is being judged as a prospective daughter-in-law as much as a prospective bride. Where she would be living in a joint family, as was the case with my friend, the girl's ability to get along harmoniously in a family is perhaps the single most important quality in assessing her suitability.

My friend is a highly esteemed wife, mother, and daughter-in-law. She is religious, soft-spoken, modest, and deferential. She rarely gossips and never quarrels, two qualities highly desirable in a woman. A family that has the reputation for gossip and conflict among its womenfolk will not find it easy to get good wives for their sons. Parents will not want to send their daughter to a house in which there is conflict.

My friend's family were originally from North India. They had lived in Bombay, where her husband owned a business, for forty years. The family had delayed in seeking a match for their eldest son because he had been an Air Force pilot for several years, stationed in such remote places that it had seemed fruitless to try to find a girl who would be willing to accompany him. In their social class, a military career, despite its economic security, has little prestige and is considered a drawback in finding a suitable bride. Many families would not allow their daughters to marry a man in an occupation so potentially dangerous and which requires so much moving around.

The son had recently left the military and joined his father's business. Since he was a college graduate, modern, and well traveled, from such a good family, and, I thought, quite handsome, it seemed to me that he, or rather his family, was in a position to pick and choose. I said as much to my friend.

While she agreed that there were many advantages on their side, she also said, "We must keep in mind that my son is both short and dark; these are drawbacks in finding the right match." While the boy's height had not escaped my notice, "dark" seemed to me inaccurate; I would have called him "wheat" colored perhaps, and in any case, I did not realize that color would be a consideration. I discovered, however, that while a boy's skin color is a less important consideration than a girl's, it is still a factor.

An important source of contacts in trying to arrange her son's marriage was my friend's social club in Bombay. Many of the women had daughters of the right age, and some had already expressed an interest in my friend's son. I was most enthusiastic about the possibilities of one particular family who had five daughters, all of whom were pretty, demure, and well educated. Their mother had told my friend, "You can have your pick for your son, whichever one of my daughters appeals to you most."

I saw a match in sight. "Surely," I said to my friend, "we will find one there. Let's go visit and make our choice." But my friend held back; she did not seem to share my enthusiasm, for reasons I could not then fathom.

When I kept pressing for an explanation of her reluctance, she admitted, "See, Serena, here is the problem. The family has so many daughters, how will they be able to provide nicely for any of them? We are not making any demands, but still, with so many daughters to marry off, one wonders whether she will even be able to make a proper wedding. Since this is our eldest son, it's best if we marry him to a girl who is the only daughter, then the wedding will truly be a gala affair." I argued that surely the quality of the girls themselves made up for any deficiency in the elaborateness of the wedding. My friend admitted this point but still seemed reluctant to proceed.

"Is there something else," I asked her, "some factor I have missed?" "Well," she finally said, "there is one other thing. They have one daughter already married and living in Bombay. The mother is always complaining to me that the girl's in-laws don't let her visit her own family often enough. So it makes me wonder, will she be that kind of mother who always wants her daughter at her own home? This will prevent the girl from adjusting to our house. It is not a good thing." And so, this family of five daughters was dropped as a possibility.

Somewhat disappointed, I nevertheless respected my friend's reasoning and geared up for the next prospect. This was also the daughter of a woman in my friend's social club. There was clear interest in this family and I could see why. The family's reputation was excellent; in fact, they came from a subcaste slightly higher than my friend's own. The girl, who was an only daughter, was pretty and well educated and had a brother studying in the United States. Yet, after expressing an interest to me in this family, all talk of them suddenly died down and the search began elsewhere.

"What happened to that girl as a prospect?" I asked one day. "You

Even today, almost all marriages in India are arranged. It is believed that parents are much more effective at deciding who their daughters should marry.

never mention her any more. She is so pretty and so educated, what did you find wrong?"

"She is too educated. We've decided against it. My husband's father saw the girl on the bus the other day and thought her forward. A girl who 'roams about' the city by herself is not the girl for our family." My disappointment this time was even greater, as I thought the son would have liked the girl very much. But then I thought, my friend is right, a girl who is going to live in a joint family cannot be too independent or she will make life miserable for everyone. I also learned that if the family of the girl has even a slightly higher social status than the family of the boy, the bride may think herself too good for them, and this too will cause problems. Later my friend admitted to me that this had been an important factor in her decision not to pursue the match.

The next candidate was the daughter of a client of my friend's husband. When the client learned that the family was looking for a match for their son, he said, "Look no further, we have a daughter." This man then invited my friends to dinner to see the girl. He had already seen their son at the office and decided that "he liked the boy." We all went together for tea, rather than dinner—it was less of a commitment—and while we were there, the girl's mother showed us around the house. The girl was studying for her exams and was briefly introduced to us.

After we left, I was anxious to hear my friend's opinion. While her husband liked the family very much and was impressed with his client's business accomplishments and reputation, the wife didn't like the girl's looks. "She is short, no doubt, which is an important plus point, but she is also fat and wears glasses." My friend obviously thought she could do better for her son and asked her husband to make his excuses to his client by saying that they had decided to postpone the boy's marriage indefinitely.

By this time almost six months had passed and I was becoming impatient. What I had thought would be an easy matter to arrange was turning out to be quite complicated. I began to believe that between my friend's desire for a girl who was modest enough to fit into her joint family, yet attractive and educated enough to be an acceptable partner for her son, she would not find anyone suitable. My friend laughed at my impatience: "Don't be so much in a hurry," she said. "You Americans want everything done so quickly. You get married quickly and then just as quickly get divorced. Here we take marriage more seriously. We must take all the factors into account. It is not enough for us to learn by our mistakes. This is too serious a business. If a mistake is made we have not only ruined the life of our son or daughter, but we have spoiled the reputation of our family as well. And that will make it much harder for their brothers and sisters to get married. So we must be very careful."

What she said was true and I promised myself to be more patient, though it was not easy. I had really hoped and expected that the match would be made before my year in India was up. But it was not to be. When I left India my friend seemed no further along in finding a suitable match for her son than when I had arrived.

Two years later, I returned to India and still my friend had not found a girl for her son. By this time, he was close to thirty, and I think she was a little worried. Since she knew I had friends all over India, and I was going to be there for a year, she asked me to "help her in this work" and keep an eye out for someone suitable. I was flattered that my judgment was respected, but knowing now how complicated the process was, I had lost my earlier confidence as a matchmaker. Nevertheless, I promised that I would try.

It was almost at the end of my year's stay in India that I met a family with a marriageable daughter whom I felt might be a good possibility for my friend's son. The girl's father was related to a good friend of mine and by coincidence came from the same village as my friend's husband. This new family had a successful business in a medium-sized city in central India and were from the same subcaste as my friend. The daughter was pretty and chic; in fact, she had studied fashion design in college. Her parents would not allow her to go off by herself to any of the major cities in India where she could make a career, but they had compromised with her wish to work by allowing her to run a small dressmaking boutique from their home. In spite of her desire to have a career, the daughter was both modest and home-loving and had had a traditional, sheltered upbringing. She had only one other sister, already married, and a brother who was in his father's business.

I mentioned the possibility of a match with my friend's son. The girl's parents were most interested. Although their daughter was not eager to marry just yet, the idea of living in Bombay—a sophisticated, extremely fashion-conscious city where she could continue her education in clothing design—was a great inducement. I gave the girl's father my friend's address and suggested that when they went to Bombay on some business or whatever, they look up the boy's family.

Returning to Bombay on my way to New York, I told my friend of this newly discovered possibility. She seemed to feel there was potential but, in spite of my urging, would not make any moves herself. She rather preferred to wait for the girl's family to call upon them. I hoped something would come of this introduction, though by now I had learned to rein in my optimism.

A year later I received a letter from my friend. The family had indeed come to visit Bombay, and their daughter and my friend's daughter, who were near in age, had become very good friends. During that year, the two girls had frequently visited each other. I thought things looked promising.

Last week I received an invitation to a wedding: My friend's son and the girl were getting married. Since I had found the match, my presence was particularly requested at the wedding. I was thrilled. Success at last! As I prepared to leave for India, I began thinking, "Now, my friend's younger son, who do I know who has a nice girl for him . . .?"

Who Needs Love! In Japan, Many Couples Don't

Nicholas D. Kristof

OMIYA, Japan—Yuri Uemura sat on the straw tatami mat of her living room and chatted cheerfully about her 40-year marriage to a man whom, she mused, she never particularly liked.

"There was never any love between me and my husband," she said blithely, recalling how he used to beat her. "But, well, we survived."

A 72-year-old midwife, her face as weathered as an old baseball and etched with a thousand seams, Mrs. Uemura said that her husband had never told her that he liked her, never complimented her on a meal, never told her "thank you," never held her hand, never given her a present, never shown her affection in any way. He never calls her by her name, but summons her with the equivalent of a grunt or a "Hey, you."

"Even with animals, the males cooperate to bring the females some food," Mrs. Uemura said sadly, noting the contrast to her own marriage. "When I see that, it brings tears to my eyes."

In short, the Uemuras have a marriage that is as durable as it is unhappy, one couple's tribute to the Japanese sanctity of family.

The divorce rate in Japan is at a record high but still less than half that of the United States, and Japan arguably has one of the strongest family structures in the industrialized world. As the United States and Europe fret about the disintegration of the traditional family, most Japanese families remain as solid as the small red table on which Mrs. Uemura rested her tea.

A study published last year by the Population Council, an international non-profit group based in New York, suggested that the traditional two-parent household is on the wane not only in America but throughout most of the world. There was one prominent exception: Japan.

In Japan, for example, only 1.1 percent of births are to unwed mothers—virtually unchanged from 25 years ago. In the United States, the figure is 30.1 percent and rising rapidly.

Yet if one comes to a little Japanese town like Omiya to learn the secrets of the Japanese family, the people are not as happy as the statistics.

"I haven't lived for myself," Mrs. Uemura said, with a touch of melancholy, "but for my kids, and for my family, and for society."

Mrs. Uemura's marriage does not seem exceptional in Japan, whether in the big cities or here in Omiya. The people of Omiya, a community of 5,700 nestled in the rain-drenched hills of the Kii Peninsula in Mie Prefecture, nearly 200 miles southwest of Tokyo, have spoken periodically to a reporter about various aspects of their daily lives. On this visit they talked about their families.

Survival Secrets

Often, the Couples Expect Little

Osamu Torida furrowed his brow and looked perplexed when he was asked if he loved his wife of 33 years.

"Yeah, so-so, I guess," said Mr. Torida, a cattle farmer. "She's like air or water. You couldn't live without it, but most of the time, you're not conscious of its existence."

The secret to the survival of the marriage, Mr. Torida acknowledged, was not mutual passion.

"Sure, we had fights about our work," he explained as he stood beside his barn. "But we were preoccupied by work and our debts, so we had no time to fool around."

That is a common theme in Omiya. It does not seem that Japanese families survive because husbands and wives love each other more than American couples, but rather because they perhaps love each other less.

"I think love marriages are more fragile than arranged marriages," said Tomika Kusukawa, 49, who married her high-school sweetheart and now runs a car repair shop with him. "In love marriages, when something happens or if the couple falls out of love, they split up."

If there is a secret to the strength of the Japanese family it consists of three ingredients: low expectations, patience, and shame.

The advantage of marriages based on low expectations is that they have built in shock absorbers. If the couple discover that they have nothing in common, that they do not even like each other, then that is not so much a reason for divorce as it is par for the course.

Even the discovery that one's spouse is having an affair is often not as traumatic in a Japanese marriage as it is in the West. A little sexual infidelity on the part of a man (though not on the part of his wife) was traditionally tolerated, so long as he did not become so besotted as to pay his mistress more than he could afford.

Tsuzuya Fukuyama, who runs a convenience store and will mark her 50th wedding anniversary this year, toasted her hands on an electric heater in the front of the store and declared that a woman would be wrong to get angry if her husband had an affair.

"It's never just one side that's at fault," Mrs. Fukuyama said sternly. "Maybe the husband had an affair because his wife wasn't so hot herself. So she should look at her own faults."

Mrs. Fukuyama's daughter came to her a few years ago, suspecting that her husband was having an affair and asking what to do.

"I told her, 'Once you left this house, you can only come back if you divorce; if you're not prepared to get a divorce, then you'd better be patient,'" Mrs. Fukuyama recalled. "And so she was patient. And then she got pregnant and had a kid, and now they're close again."

The word that Mrs. Fukuyama used for patience is "gaman," a term that comes up whenever marriage is discussed in Japan. It means toughing it out, enduring hardship, and many Japanese regard gaman with pride as a national trait.

Many people complain that younger folks divorce because they do not have enough gaman, and the frequency with which the term is used suggests a rather bleak understanding of marriage.

"I didn't know my husband very well when we married, and afterward we used to get into bitter fights," said Yoshiko Hirowaki, 56, a store owner. "But then we had children, and I got very busy with the kids and with this shop. Time passed."

Now Mrs. Hirowaki has been married 34 years, and she complains about young people who do not stick to their vows.

"In the old days, wives had more gaman," she said. "Now kids just don't have enough gaman."

The durability of the Japanese family is particularly wondrous because couples are, by international standards, exceptionally incompatible.

One survey asked married men and their wives in 37 countries how they felt about politics, sex, religion, ethics and

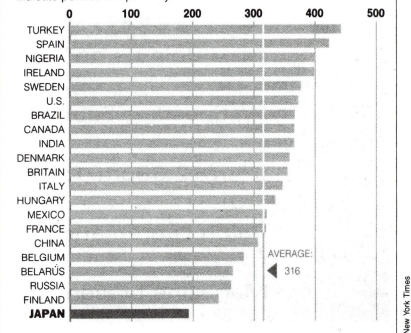

GETTING ALONG

Matchmaker, Matchmaker

How countries compare on an index of compatibility of spouses, based on answers to questions about politics, sex, social issues, religion and ethics, from a survey by the Dentsu Research Institute and Leisure Development Center in Japan. A score of 500 would indicate perfect compatibility.

TURKEY
SPAIN
NIGERIA
IRELAND
SWEDEN
U.S.
BRAZIL
CANADA
INDIA
DENMARK
BRITAIN
ITALY
HUNGARY
MEXICO
FRANCE
CHINA
BELGIUM
BELARUS
RUSSIA
FINLAND
JAPAN

AVERAGE: 316

New York Times

social issues. Japanese couples ranked dead last in compatibility of views, by a huge margin. Indeed, another survey found that if they were doing it over again, only about one-third of Japanese would marry the same person.

Incompatibility might not matter so much, however, because Japanese husbands and wives spend very little time talking to each other.

"I kind of feel there's nothing new to say to her," said Masayuki Ogita, an egg farmer, explaining his reticence.

In a small town like Omiya, couples usually have dinner together, but in Japanese cities there are many "7-11 husbands," so called because they leave at 7 A.M. and return after 11 P.M.

Masahiko Kondo now lives in Omiya, working in the chamber of commerce, but he used to be a salesman in several big cities. He would leave work each morning at 7, and about four nights a week would go out for after-work drinking or mah-jongg sessions with buddies.

"I only saw my baby on Saturdays or Sundays," said Mr. Kondo, a lanky good-natured man of 37. "But in fact, I really enjoyed that life. It didn't bother me that I never spent time with my kid on weekdays."

Mr. Kondo's wife, Keiko, had her own life, spent with her child and the wives of other workaholic husbands.

"We had birthday parties, but they were with the kids and the mothers," she remembers. "No fathers ever came."

A national survey found that 30 percent of fathers spend less than 15 minutes a day on weekdays talking with or playing with their children. Among eighth graders, 51 percent reported that they never spoke with their fathers on weekdays.

As a result, the figures in Japan for single-parent households can be deceptive. The father is often more a theoretical presence than a homework-helping reality.

Still, younger people sometimes want to see the spouses in daylight, and a result is a gradual change in focus of lives from work to family. Two decades ago, nearly half of young people said in surveys that they wanted their fathers to put priority on work rather than family. Now only one-quarter say that.

Social Pressures
Shame Is Keeping Bonds in Place

For those who find themselves desperately unhappy, one source of pressure to keep plugging is shame.

"If you divorce, you lose face in society," said Tatsumi Kinoshita, a tea farmer. "People say, 'His wife escaped.' So folks remain married because they hate to be gossiped about."

Shame is a powerful social sanction in Japan, and it is not just a matter of gossip. Traditionally, many companies were reluctant to promote employees who had divorced or who had major problems at home.

"If you divorce, it weakens your position at work," said Akihiko Kanda, 27, who works in a local government office. "Your bosses won't give you such good ratings, and it'll always be a negative factor."

The idea, Mr. Kanda noted, is that if an employee cannot manage his own life properly, he should not be entrusted with important corporate matters.

Financial sanctions are also a major disincentive for divorce. The mother gets the children in three-quarters of divorces, but most mothers in Japan do not have careers and have few financial resources. Fathers pay child support in only 15 percent of all divorces with children, partly because women often hesitate to go to court to demand payments and partly because men often fail to pay even when the court orders it.

"The main reason for lack of divorce is that women can't support themselves," said Mizuko Kanda, a 51-year-old housewife. "My friends complain about their husbands and say that they'd divorce if they could, but they can't afford to."

The result of these social and economic pressures is clear.

Even in Japan, there are about 24 divorces for every 100 marriages, but that compares with 32 in France, and 42 in England, and 55 in the United States.

The Outlook
Change Creeps In, Imperiling Family

But society is changing in Japan, and it is an open question whether these changes will undermine the traditional family as they have elsewhere around the globe.

The nuclear family has already largely replaced the extended family in Japan, and shame is eroding as a sanction. Haruko Okumura, for example, runs a kindergarten and speaks openly about her divorce.

"My Mom was uneasy about it, but I never had an inferiority complex about being divorced," said Mrs. Okumura, as dozens of children played in the next room. "And people accepted me easily."

Mrs. Okumura sees evidence of the changes in family patterns every day: fathers are playing more of a role in the kindergarten. At Christmas parties and sports contests, fathers have started to show up along with mothers. And Mrs. Okumura believes that divorce is on the upswing.

"If there's a weakening of the economic and social pressures to stay married," she said, "surely divorce rates will soar."

Already divorce rates are rising, approximately doubling over the last 25 years. But couples are very reluctant to divorce when they have children, and so single-parent households account for exactly the same proportion today as in 1965.

Shinsuke Kawaguchi, a young tea farmer, is one of the men for whom life is changing. Americans are not likely to be impressed by Mr. Kawaguchi's open-mindedness, but he is.

"I take good care of my wife," he said. "I may not say 'I love you,' but I do hold her hand. And I might say, after she makes dinner, 'This tastes good.' "

"Of course," Mr. Kawaguchi quickly added, "I wouldn't say that unless I'd just done something really bad."

Even Mrs. Uemura, the elderly woman whose husband used to beat her, said that her husband was treating her better.

"The other day, he tried to pour me a cup of tea," Mrs. Uemura recalled excitedly. "It was a big change. I told all my friends."

Gender and Status

The feminist movement in the United States has had a significant impact upon the development of anthropology. Feminists have rightly charged that anthropologists have tended to gloss over the lives of women in studies of society and culture. In part, this is because, until recent times, most anthropologists have been men. The result has been an undue emphasis upon male activities as well as male perspectives in descriptions of particular societies.

These charges, however, have proven to be a firm corrective. In the last few years, anthropologists have begun to study women and, more particularly, the sexual division of labor and its relation to biology as well as to social and political status. In addition, these changes in emphasis have been accompanied by an increase in the number of women in the field.

Feminist anthropologists have begun to critically attack many of the established anthropological beliefs. They have shown, for example, that field studies of nonhuman primates, which were often used to demonstrate the evolutionary basis of male dominance, distorted the actual evolutionary record by focusing primarily on baboons. (Male baboons are especially dominant and aggressive.) Other, less-quoted primate studies show how dominance and aggression are highly situational phenomena, sensitive to ecological variation. Feminist anthropologists have also shown that the subsistence contribution of women has likewise been ignored by anthropologists. A classic case is that of the !Kung, a hunting and gathering people in southern Africa, where women provide the bulk of the foodstuffs, including most of the available protein, and who, not coincidentally, enjoy a more egalitarian relationship than usual with men. Even when the issue is premarital virginity for women, Alice Schlegel, in "Status, Property, and the Value on Virginity," shows that the concern for biological paternity may have more to do with maintaining or enhancing a family's social status than with male domination per se.

The most common occurrence, at least in recent history, has been male domination over women. Recent studies have concerned themselves with why there has been such gender inequality. Although the subordination of women can be extreme, as seen in "The Little Emperors" by Daniela Deane, Ernestine Friedl, in "Society and Sex Roles," explains that the sex that controls the valued goods of exchange in a society is the dominant one. Thus, since this control is a matter of cultural variation, male authority is not biologically predetermined. Indeed, women have played visibly prominent roles in many cultures, as addressed by Leslie Marmon Silko in "Yellow Woman and a Beauty of the Spirit." Even so, the essay "The War against Women" shows that sexual equality is still far from being a reality in many parts of the world. And, as we see in "The Initiation of a Maasai Warrior" and in "Bundu Trap," gender relationships are deeply embedded in social experience.

Looking Ahead: Challenge Questions

What is it about foraging societies that encourages an egalitarian relationship between the sexes? Why are the Eskimos an exception?

What kinds of shifts in the social relations of production are necessary for women to achieve equality with men?

What was meant by "beauty" in the old-time Pueblo culture? How and why is diversity valued in Pueblo culture?

What are bridewealth and dowry, and under what circumstances do they occur?

How does female circumcision differ from male circumcision in terms of its social functions?

What kinds of personal dilemmas do women face in a changing society?

What kinds of historical, religious, and legal legacies have contributed to violence against women around the world?

How may a culture's political and religious ideology serve to justify sex role differences?

What have been the unforeseen consequences of China's one-child policy? Does this policy represent the wave of the future for the world? Why or why not?

Sometimes she read the Bible stories that we kids liked because of the illustrations of Jonah in the mouth of a whale and Daniel surrounded by lions. Grandma A'mooh would send me home when she took her nap, but when the sun got low and the afternoon began to cool off, I would be back on the porch swing, waiting for her to come out to water the plants and to haul in firewood for the evening. When Grandma was 85, she still chopped her own kindling. She used to let me carry in the coal bucket for her, but she would not allow me to use the ax. I carried armloads of kindling too, and I learned to be proud of my strength.

I was allowed to listen quietly when Aunt Susie or Aunt Alice came to visit Grandma. When I got old enough to cross the road alone, I went and visited them almost daily. They were vigorous women who valued books and writing. They were usually busy chopping world or cooking but never hesitated to take time to answer my questions. Best of all they told me the "hummah-hah" stories, about an earlier time when animals and humans shared a common language. In the old days, the Pueblo people had educated their children in this manner; adults took time out to talk to and teach young people. Everyone was a teacher, and every activity had the potential to teach the child.

But as soon as I started kindergarten at the Bureau of Indian Affairs day school, I began to learn more about the difference between the Laguna Pueblo world and the outside world. It was at school that I learned just how different I looked from my classmates. Sometimes tourists driving past on Route 66 would stop by Laguna Day School at recess time to take photographs of us kids. One day, when I was in the first grade, we all crowded around the smiling white tourists who peered at our faces. We all wanted to be in the picture because afterward the tourists sometimes gave us each a penny. Just as we were all posed and ready to have our picture taken, the tourist man looked at me. "Not you," he said and motioned for me to step away from my classmates. I felt so embarrassed that I wanted to disappear. My classmates were puzzled by the tourists' behavior, but I knew the tourists didn't want me in their snapshot because I looked different, because I was part white.

In the view of the old-time people, we are all sisters and brothers because the Mother Creator made all of us—all colors and all sizes. We are sisters and brothers, clanspeople of all the living beings around us. The plants, the birds, fish, clouds, water, even the clay—they all are related to us. The old-time people believe that all things, even rocks and water, have spirit and being. They understood that all things only want to continue being as they are; they need only to be left as they are. Thus the old folks used to tell us kids not to disturb the earth unnecessarily. All things as they were created exist already in harmony with one another as long as we do not disturb them.

As the old story tells us, Tse'its'i'na-ko, Thought Woman, the Spider, thought of her three sisters, and as she thought of them, they came into being. Together with Thought Woman, they thought of the sun and the stars and the moon. The Mother Creators imagined the earth and the oceans, the animals and the people, and the kat'sina spirits that reside in the mountains. The Mother Creators imagined all the plants that flower and the trees that bear fruit. As Thought Woman and her sisters thought of it, the whole universe came into being. In this universe, there is no absolute good or absolute bad; there are only balances and harmonies that ebb and flow. Some years the desert receives abundant rain, other years there is too little rain, and sometimes there is so much rain that floods cause destruction. But rain itself is neither innocent or guilty. The rain is simply itself.

My great-grandmother was dark and handsome. Her expression in photographs is one of confidence and strength. I do not know if white people then or now would consider her beautiful. I do not know if the old-time Laguna Pueblo people considered her beautiful or if the old-time people even thought in those terms. To the Pueblo way of thinking, the act of comparing one living being with another was silly, because each being or thing is unique and therefore incomparably valuable because it is the only one of its kind. The old-time people thought it was crazy to attach such importance to a person's appearance. I understood very early that there were two distinct ways of interpreting the world. There was the white people's way, and there was the Laguna way. In the Laguna way, it was bad manners to make comparisons that might hurt another person's feelings.

In everyday Pueblo life, not much attention was paid to one's physical appearance or clothing. Ceremonial clothing was quite elaborate but was used only for the sacred dances. The traditional Pueblo societies were communal and strictly egalitarian, which means that no matter how well or how poorly one might have dressed, there was no "social ladder" to fall from. All food and other resources were strictly shared so that no one person or group had more than another. I mention social status because it seems to me that most of the definitions of beauty in contemporary Western culture are really codes for determining social status. People no longer hide their face-lifts, and they discuss their liposuctions because the point of the procedures isn't just cosmetic, it is social. It says to the world, "I have enough spare cash that I can afford surgery for cosmetic purposes."

In the old-time Pueblo world, beauty was manifested in behavior and in one's relationships with other living beings. Beauty was as much a feeling of harmony as it was a visual, aural or sensual effect. The whole person had to be beautiful, not just the face or the body; faces and bodies could not be separated from hearts and souls. Health was foremost in achieving this sense of well-being and harmony; in the old-time Pueblo world, a person who did not look healthy inspired feelings of worry and anxiety, not feelings of well-being. A healthy person, of course, is in harmony with the world around her; she is at peace with herself too. Thus an unhappy person or spiteful person would not be considered beautiful.

In the old days, strong, sturdy women were most admired. One of my most vivid preschool memories is of the crew of Laguna women, in their 40s and 50s, who came to cover our house with adobe plaster. They handled the ladders with great ease, and while two women ground the adobe mud on stones and added straw, another woman loaded the hod with mud and passed it up to the two women on ladders, who were smoothing the plaster on the wall with their hands. Since women owned the houses, they did the plastering. At Laguna, men did the basket-making and the weaving of fine textiles; men helped a great deal with the child-care too. Because the Creator is female, there is no stigma on being female; gender is not used to control behavior. No job was a "man's job" or a "woman's job"; the most able person did the work.

My Grandma Lily had been a Ford Model A mechanic when she was a teen-ager. I remember when I was young, she was always fixing broken lamps and appliances. She was small and wiry, but she could lift her weight in rolled roofing or boxes of nails. When she was 75, she was still repairing washing machines in my uncle's coin-operated laundry.

The old-time people paid no attention to birthdays. When a person was ready to do something, she did it. When she no longer was able, she stopped. Thus the traditional Pueblo people did not worry about aging or about looking old because there were no social boundaries drawn by the passage of years. It was not remarkable for young men to marry women as old as their mothers. I never heard anyone talk about "women's work" until after I left Laguna for college. Work was there to be done by any able-bodied person who wanted to do it. At the same time, in the old-time Pueblo world, identity was acknowledged to be always in a flux; in the old stories, one minute Spider Woman is a little spider under a yucca plant, and the next instant she is a spritely grandmother walking down the road.

When I was growing up, there was a young man from a nearby village who wore nail polish and women's blouses and permed his hair. People paid little attention to his appearance; he was always part of a group of other young men from his village. No one ever made fun of him. Pueblo communities were, and still are, very interdependent, but they also have to be tolerant of individual eccentricities because survival of the group means everyone has to cooperate.

In the old Pueblo world, differences were celebrated as signs of the Mother Creators' grace. Persons born with exceptional physical or sexual differences were highly respected and honored because their physical differences gave them special positions as mediators between this world and the spirit world. The great Navajo medicine man of the 1920s, the Crawler, had a hunchback and could not walk upright, but he was able to heal even the most difficult cases. Before the arrival of Christian missionaries, a man could dress as a woman and work with the women and even marry a man without any fanfare. Likewise, a woman was free to dress like a man, to hunt and go to war with the men and to marry a woman. In the old Pueblo world view, we are all a mixture of male and female, and this sexual identity is changing constantly. Sexual inhibition did not begin until the Christian missionaries arrived. For the old-time people, marriage was about teamwork and social relationships, not about sexual excitement. In the days before the Puritans came, marriage did not mean an end to sex with people other than your spouse. Women were just as likely as men to have a "si'ash," or lover.

New life was so precious that pregnancy was always appropriate, and pregnancy before marriage was celebrated as a good sign. Since the children belonged to the mother and her clan, and women owned and bequeathed the houses and farmland, the exact determination of paternity wasn't critical. Although fertility was prized, infertility was no problem because mothers with unplanned pregnancies gave their babies to childless couples

within the clan in open adoption arrangements. Children called their mother's sisters "mother" as well, and a child became attached to a number of parent figures.

In the sacred kiva ceremonies, men mask and dress as women to pay homage and to be possessed by the female energies of the spirit beings. Because differences in physical appearance were so highly valued, surgery to change one's face and body to resemble a model's face and body would be unimaginable. To be different, to be unique was blessed and was best of all.

The traditional clothing of Pueblo women emphasized a woman's sturdiness. Buckskin leggings wrapped around the legs protected her from scratches and injuries while she worked. The more layers of buckskin, the better. All those layers gave her legs the appearance of strength, like sturdy tree trunks. To demonstrate sisterhood and brotherhood with the plants and animals, the old-time people make masks and costumes that transform the human figures of the dancers into the animal beings they portray. Dancers paint their exposed skin; their postures and motions are adapted from their observations. But the motions are stylized. The observer sees not an actual eagle or actual deer dancing, but witnesses a human being, a dancer, gradually changing into a woman/buffalo or a man/deer. Every impulse is to reaffirm the urgent relationships that human beings have with the plant and animal world.

In the high desert plateau country, all vegetation, even weeds and thorns, becomes special, and all life is precious and beautiful because without the plants, the insects and the animals, human beings living here cannot survive. Perhaps human beings long ago noticed the devastating impact human activity can have on the plants and animals; maybe this is why tribal cultures devised the stories about humans and animals intermarrying, and the clans that bind humans to animals and plants through a whole complex of duties.

We children were always warned not to harm frogs or toads, the beloved children of the rain clouds, because terrible floods would occur. I remember in the summer the old folks used to stick big bolls of cotton on the outside of their screen doors as bait to keep the flies from going in the house when the door was opened. The old folks staunchly resisted the killing of flies because once, long, long ago, when human beings were in a great deal of trouble, green bottle fly carried the desperate messages of human beings to the Mother Creator in the Fourth World below this one. Human beings had outraged the Mother Creator by neglecting the Mother Corn altar while they dabbled with sorcery and magic. The Mother Creator disappeared, and with her disappeared the rain clouds, and the plants and the animals too. The people began to starve, and they had no way of reaching the Mother Creator down below. The green bottle fly took the message to the Mother Creator, and the people were saved. To show their gratitude, the old folks refused to kill any flies.

The old stories demonstrate the interrelationships that the Pueblo people have maintained with their plant and animal clanspeople. Kochininako, Yellow Woman, represents all women in the old stories. Her deeds span the spectrum of human behavior and are mostly heroic acts, though in at least one story, she chooses to join the secret Destroyer Clan, which worships destruction and death. Because Laguna Pueblo cosmology features a female creator, the status of women is equal with the status of men, and women appear as often as men in the old stories as hero figures. Yellow Woman is my favorite because she dares to cross traditional boundaries of ordinary behavior during times of crisis in order to save the Pueblo; her power lies in her courage and in her uninhibited sexuality, which the old-time Pueblo stories celebrate again and again because fertility was so highly valued.

The old stories always say that Yellow Woman was beautiful, but remember that the old-time people were not so much thinking about physical appearances. In each story, the beauty that Yellow Woman possesses is the beauty of her passion, her daring and her sheer strength to act when catastrophe is imminent.

In one story, the people are suffering during a great drought and accompanying famine. Each day, Kochininako has to walk farther and farther from the village to find fresh water for her husband and children. One day she travels far, far to the east, to the plains, and she finally locates a freshwater spring. But when she reaches the pool, the water is churning violently as if something large had just gotten out of the pool. Kochininako does not want to see what huge creature had been at the pool, but just as she fills her water jar and turns to hurry away, a strong, sexy man in buffalo skin leggings appears by the pool. Little drops of water glisten on his chest. She cannot help but look at him because he is so strong and so good to look at. Able to transform himself from human to buffalo in the wink of an eye, Buffalo Man gallops away with her on his back. Kochininako falls in love with Buffalo Man, and because of this liaison, the Buffalo People agree to give their bodies to the hunters to feed the starving Pueblo. Thus Kochininako's fearless sensuality results in the salvation of the people of her village, who are saved by the meat the Buffalo people "give" to them.

My father taught me and my sisters to shoot .22 rifles when we were 7; I went hunting with my father when I was 8, and I killed my first mule deer buck when I was 13. The Kochininako stories were always my favorite because Yellow Woman had so many adventures. In one story, as she hunts rabbits to feed her family, a giant monster pursues her, but she has the courage and presence of mind to outwit it.

In another story, Kochininako has a fling with Whirlwind Man and returns to her husband 10 months later with twin baby boys. The twin boys grow up to be great heroes of the people. Once again, Kochininako's vibrant sexuality benefits her people.

The stories about Kochininako made me aware that sometimes an individual must act despite disapproval, or concern for "appearances" or "what others may say." From Yellow Woman's adventures, I learned to be comfortable with my differences. I even imagined that Yellow Woman had yellow skin, brown hair and green eyes like mine, although her name does not refer to her color, but rather to the ritual color of the East.

There have been many other moments like the one with the camera-toting tourist in the schoolyard. But the old-time people always say, remember the stories, the stories will help you be strong. So all these years I have depended on Kochininako and the stories of her adventures.

Kochininako is beautiful because she has the courage to act in times of great peril, and her triumph is achieved by her sensuality, not through violence and destruction. For these qualities of the spirit, Yellow Woman and all women are beautiful.

Status, Property, and the Value on Virginity

Alice Schlegel

One way to assess a woman's autonomy is to ask whether she controls her own sexuality. Thus, the prohibition on premarital sex for females is often considered a measure of men's control over women's lives. There are certain difficulties with this assumption, however. First, the way a people feels about premarital sex is not necessarily consonant with its attitude toward extramarital sex, as many people allow premarital freedom but condemn adultery, while others, such as the South African Lovedu (Sacks 1979), insist on premarital virginity but turn a blind eye to discreet extramarital affairs.

Second, this assumption fails to recognize that in most societies, the value placed on virginity applies to adolescent girls, not to adult women. With few exceptions worldwide, girls are still physically adolescent when they marry, generally within three or four years after puberty. More important, young people are generally not social adults until they marry, so that the premarital female is socially an adolescent girl. Some societies, such as our own and that of 17th-century England (Stone 1977), for example, are exceptions to this, having a stage that I call "youth" intervening between adolescence and full adulthood. However, in most parts of the world the bride is a teenage girl who in most aspects of her life is still very much under the authority of her parents.

If virginity is not, then, a very good measure of female subordination, we must look for other aspects of girls' and young women's lives that are associated with the proscription of premarital sex. One common notion is that virginity is valued when men have to "pay" for wives by transferring goods in the form of bridewealth to the women's families. This notion is based on the assumption that there is some innate preference for virgins which can be activated when men have the upper hand, so to speak, because they are paying for the bride. It must be noted, of course, that there is no universal preference for virgin brides. Such an assumption projects onto other cultures the attitudes that have developed historically in our own. Moreover, the belief that when men give bridewealth they pay for virgin brides is shaken when we read in Goody (1973:25) that dowry-giving societies, in which the bride's family pays, are generally intolerant of premarital sex for girls. Here the family pays to give, not to receive, a virgin bride.

There is a connection between marriage transactions—the movement of goods or services at the time of a marriage—and the value on virginity, but it is not obvious what that connection is. In this paper, I argue that the virginity of daughters protects the interests of brides' families when they use marital alliances to maintain or enhance their social status. To illuminate this issue, it is necessary to understand the varying effects that marriage transactions have on the transmission or retention of property and on the social debts thus incurred.

MARRIAGE TRANSACTIONS

The form of marriage transaction that has received the most attention in the anthropological literature is *bridewealth,* goods given by the groom, usually with the assistance of his kin, to the family of the bride. Bridewealth generally does not remain with the family that receives it: it or its equivalent is used to obtain wives for brothers of the bride or an additional wife for her father. Thus, goods and women circulate and countercirculate. In the large majority of bridewealth-giving societies, which are patrilocal, households end up with as many women as they have produced, by replacing daughters with daughters-in-law and sisters with wives.

Women exchange is also a form of replacement, the exchange being direct rather than mediated by a transfer of property. Women exchange and bridewealth are most frequently found where women have economic value through their large contribution to subsistence (cf. Schlegel and Barry 1986). In each case the result is a kind of social homeostasis, both among the families through which women and goods circulate and within the household that sooner or later gains a woman to replace each one it has lost.

Brideservice is often considered to be analogous to bridewealth, with payment in labor rather than goods. They differ significantly, however, in that the benefit of brideservice goes directly to the bride's household and is not circulated as are bridewealth goods. Thus, families with many daughters receive much free labor, while families with few get little.

While *gift exchange,* in which relatively equal amounts are exchanged between the families of the bride and groom, can occur at all levels of social complexity, it is often found in societies with important status differences in rank or wealth; it occurs most often in Asia, native North America, and the Pacific. Since residence is predominantly patrilocal in gift-exchanging societies, the bride-receiving household is socially, although not economically, in debt to the bride-giving one. The exchange of equivalent goods is a way of ensuring that the intermarrying families are of the same social status, as indicated by the wealth that they own or can call up from among their kin and dependents.

Status is a major consideration in dowry-giving societies. The bride's dowry is sometimes matched against the groom's settlement, thus ensuring equivalence, a usual practice among European land-owning peasants or elites. Dowry can also be used to "buy" a high status son-in-law, a common practice in South Asia and one also known in Europe. Dowry or a bride's anticipated inheritance can be used to attract a poor but presentable groom, a client son-in-law whose allegiance will be primarily to the house into which he has married and on which he is dependent. This strategy seems to have been practiced by mercantile families in Europe and Latin America. Dowry was associated historically with the property-owning classes of the Old High Culture areas such as the Mediterranean (ancient Mesopotamia, Greece, and Rome) and Asia (India, China, and Japan), and was the common form throughout Europe until recently.

The final form of marriage transaction to be examined here is *indirect dowry,* which contains some features of both bridewealth, in that goods are given by the groom's family, and dowry, in that the goods end up with the new conjugal couple. Sometimes the groom's kin give goods directly to the bride, but more often they give goods to her father, who then gives goods to the new couple. The latter form has frequently been confused with bridewealth, as in the Islamic *mahr.* Indirect dowry tends to be found both on the fringes of and within the Old High Culture areas, such as Egypt, where it has been introduced along with conversion to Islam, replacing the simple dowry of earlier times. In its classic form, indirect dowry appears to be a way of establishing the properly rights of the conjugal couples that make up larger households, in anticipation of eventual fission. In addition, it allows for status negotiation without either family being put in the other's economic or social debt.

There are variations within these major types, and there are additional features (such as the European dower) that are secondary and limited in distribution. In complex societies, the form of transaction may vary according to region or class. In prerevolutionary China, for example, the landed or mercantile elite gave dowry while the landless peasantry gave indirect dowry. In modern China, marriage transactions have disappeared from urban areas, whereas bridewealth has replaced indirect dowry among peasants (Fang 1990).

WHY VALUE VIRGINITY?

Since the burden of controlling a girl's sexuality through socialization or surveillance falls upon her family, it is instructive to consider what benefits are to be derived from preserving the virginity of daughters and sisters. Goody (1976) sees restrictiveness as a way of avoiding inappropriate marriages: by controlling a girl's sexuality, her family can better control her marriage choice, for the loss of virginity may "diminish a girl's honour and reduce her marriage chances" (Goody 1976:14). However, this presupposes that preserving virginity has some inherent value, whereas that value is precisely what needs to be explained.

I argue that virginity is valued in those societies in which young men may seek to better their chances in life by allying themselves through marriage to a wealthy or powerful family. In preserving a daughter's virginity, a family is protecting her from seduction, impregnation, and paternity claims on her child. This is most critical when certain kinds of property transactions are involved. In societies in which dowry is given (or daughters inherit), it would be attractive to seduce a dowered daughter (or heiress), demanding her as wife along with her property. Her parents would be reluctant to refuse, since the well-being of their grandchildren would depend upon their inheritance from both of their parents, and another man would be unlikely to marry the mother if it meant that he had not only to support her children but also to make them his heirs. (The widow with children would be a different matter, since these children would have received property through their father and would make no claims on their stepfather beyond support, for which their labor would provide compensation.)

To illustrate that upward mobility through marriage with a dowered daughter or heiress is known in dowry-giving societies, let us consider a common theme of European fairy tales. A poor but honest young man goes through trials to win the hand of the princess, who inherits her father's kingdom. Or, he wins her heart, and through the good offices of a fairy godmother or other spirit helper, they evade her wrathful father and are eventually reconciled with him. This more or less legitimate means to upward mobility is not so different from the illegitimate one, by which he wins the girl through seduction.

This line of reasoning was familiar to the seventeenth- and eighteenth-century English, as Trumbach tells it:

Stealing a son . . . was not the great crime. It was, rather, the theft of a daughter that was the real nightmare. For a woman's property became her husband's and she took his social standing. . . . To steal an heiress was therefore the quickest way to make a man's fortune—this was the common doctrine of the stage before 1710—and it had a special appeal to younger sons (1978:101–102).

As the table shows, the value on virginity is statistically associated with the type of economic exchange linked to the marriage transaction.

All of the dowry-giving societies in the sample value virginity except the Haitians. Nevertheless, as Herskovits, writing about Haiti, points out: "Even though pre-marital relations are commonplace, . . . the pregnancy of an unmarried girl is regarded as both reprehensible and unfortunate, and she is severely beaten for it by her family" (1971:111). Their fear of her seduction is well founded, for if they disapprove of a suitor and reject him, the young man "uses all persuasion to give her a child and, this achieved, abandons her to show his contempt for the family that has formally refused to accept him as a son-in-law" (Herskovits 1971:110). To avoid childbearing, women and girls resort to magical means of contraception and the more effective abortion.

The majority of societies that exchange gifts and give indirect dowry also expect brides to be virgins. This is particularly true in the case of gift exchange, in which a bride's family gives quantities of property along with her, receiving a more or less equivalent amount from the family of the groom. As noted earlier, gift exchange is a way of ensuring that the two families are of equal wealth or of equal social power. Impregnating a girl would give a boy and his family a claim on that girl and an alliance with her family, even though they would have to come up with something themselves for the exchange (not necessarily equivalent to what a more appropriate suitor would give; see the case of the Omaha, discussed below). As in dowry-giving societies, an emphasis on virginity discourages a man who is tempted to jump the status barrier by claiming fatherhood of a woman's child. The sample does, however, include three exceptions to the general requirement of virginity in gift-exchanging societies, and it is instructive to examine these deviant cases.

Malinowski (1932) has discussed at some length the sexual freedom of girls

in the Trobriand Islands in Melanesia. However, we must recall that the Trobriand Islanders do not, at least ideologically, associate sexual intercourse with pregnancy. Weiner (1976:122) relates two cases in which pregnancy was attributed to magic, and her informants maintained that women could conceive without male assistance. No boy, then, can make a claim on a girl simply because he has been sleeping with her and she has become pregnant. Fatherhood can only be attained after marriage, when it is socially defined.

Among the Omaha Indians of the Great Plains, virginity was not considered important for most girls (as coded in Broude and Greene [1980]), but according to Fletcher and LaFlesche (1911), virgins were held in greater esteem than those who had lost their virginity. It was a special privilege to marry a girl who had been tattooed with the "mark of honor," which was given to a virgin of a prominent family on the occasion of her father's or another close relative's initiation into one of the ceremonial societies. Only the marriages in prominent families involved significant gift exchange. In ordinary marriages, the young husband was expected to work a year or two for his father-in-law, making brideservice a more common feature than gift exchange. Thus, it was in the important marriages, accompanied by the exchange of goods of much value, that the bride was expected to be a virgin. Omaha elite families faced the danger that a daughter might be seduced by a youth who would persuade her to elope. As long as his family recognized the marriage and brought some gifts to the bride's father, the marriage was legitimate in the eyes of the community. Maintaining the virginity of high-status girls protected their families from unwanted alliances.

In the Polynesian islands of Samoa, similarly, girls from untitled families had sexual freedom (as coded in Broude and Greene [1980]) but the daughters of titled chiefs did not. Samoa had an ambilineal descent system, in that children could be affiliated either to the mother's or the father's group. If the mother's rank was higher

than the father's, the children's status would be elevated above their father's. High-status families would wish to guard their daughters against potential social climbers, who might be tempted to improve their children's position in life by seducing and marrying socially superior girls. It appears that only the arranged marriages, generally of high-status people, involved much gift exchange. Most marriages were of the "elopement" type and were much less expensive than the arranged ones (Shore 1981). Thus, as in the case of the Omaha, intracultural comparison demonstrates a correlation between the type of marriage transaction and the value on virginity.

It is clear that when no property accompanies the marriage, virginity is of little interest. If the groom gives goods or labor, the picture is mixed, but fewer societies are restrictive than permissive. In societies in which the bride's side gives considerable property, as with gift exchange, dowry, and, in many cases, indirect dowry, virginity is most likely to be valued. Thus, there is an association between the giving of property, particularly from the bride's side, and control of the girl's sexuality. I have interpreted this as a means by which the families of girls prevent their being seduced by ineligible boys, resulting in alliances that could be an embarrassment. This is particularly the case when status negotiation is a prominent feature of marital alliances, in those societies in which families use the marriages of their daughters to maintain or enhance their social position. Such considerations are likely to be found only in rank or class societies.

VIRGINITY AND FATHERHOOD

The question of the value on virginity revolves around two issues: whether premarital sexual intercourse leads to pregnancy, and whether biological fatherhood alone gives a man a claim on a child and its mother. There should be less concern over virginity when sexual intercourse is not likely to lead to pregnancy than when it is. Safe, so-

Correlations of value on virginity with type of marriage transaction[1]

| Virginity valued | Marriage transaction | | | | | |
	None	Bride-wealth[2]	Bride-service	Gift exchange	Dowry and indirect dowry	Total
Yes	3	16	6	9	18	52
No	26	27	10	3	7	73

N = 125; Chi-square = 27.13; p <.0001

[1] Information on attitudes toward premarital sex for females comes primarily from the code "Attitude Toward Premarital Sex (Female)" in Broude and Greene (1980), which is based on the Standard Sample of 186 preindustrial societies. I have altered the code established by Broude and Greene for four societies based on the ethnographic literature. The second source is a body of data collected by Herbert Barry and me on adolescent socialization in Standard Sample societies not coded by Broude and Greene.

[2] Includes token bridewealth.

cially condoned abortion is a reliable way of preventing unwanted births, and virginity is not such an issue if abortion is freely available, as it has been in Southeast Asia since at least the sixteenth century. Even there, however, the elite have secluded their daughters, possibly in imitation of the Hindu, Buddhist, or Moslem aristocrats whom they have emulated in other ways (cf. Reid 1988:163).

Although abortive techniques are widely known and practiced, even where proscribed (Devereux 1976), there is little evidence to indicate the extent to which illicit abortions are available to unmarried girls. Desperate girls, with the help of their mothers, surely must resort to them, as anecdotal information indicates; but whether or not they are successful, and whether or not the girls can keep them secret, are open to question. Illicit abortion is a last-ditch measure for preventing unwanted births and must take a distant second place to the maintenance of virginity.

Impregnating a girl does not automatically give a boy or man a claim to her child or to her. In the Trobriand Islands, as we have seen, biological fatherhood alone is simply not recognized. In other places, it may be recognized without giving the impregnator a paternity claim. Such a claim may have to be paid for either directly or indirectly through bridewealth and marriage to the mother; if it is not, the child is absorbed into the mother's kin group. This practice appears to be more common in Africa than in other regions, although the question requires a study in its own right. I suggest that the acceptance of illegitimate children is greater when children are a distinct economic asset. They are likely to be so in underpopulated areas, such as are found throughout much of Africa (Kopytoff 1987). In such places, the availability of labor rather than of land is the major constraint on the economic success and expansion of the productive unit, the family and the kin group, and illegitimate origins do not detract from the potential labor value of a child. A similar explanation may hold for some European peasantries.

Where land is in short supply in preindustrial societies and family resources consist of private property, heirship is a central concern. A bastard is less likely to be welcomed, since it is totally dependent on the mother's family and does not draw in resources from the father. Bastards may be better received when the father is of much higher status than the mother—when he is, for example, a king or the noble impregnator of a peasant girl. In such cases, so long as paternity is acknowledged, the child provides a left-handed link to wealth and power, one that otherwise would be beyond the reach of the mother's family.

If children are not an unqualified asset to the mother's family, the rules of social life are likely to include the prescription that fathers take responsibility for their children, thus bringing biological and social fatherhood closer together. The responsibility for one's child can be restated as the right to that child, and biological fatherhood becomes a claim on social fatherhood. When the status of the mother is equal to or lower than that of the impregnator, it is to her advantage to use the rule of responsibility to press for marriage or at least support, so long as the impregnator is willing (or is unable to escape). Turning this on its head, when the mother is of greater wealth or higher status, particularly when her status or property will be inherited by her child, it is to the advantage of the impregnator to use the rule of responsibility to press *his* claim on the child and its mother. It is in precisely such situations, I propose, that virginity is valued, as it is the surest way of preventing such claims.

This is not to deny that virginity may acquire secondary meanings. In its extreme form, a value on virginity can lead to a value on chastity so great that widows are discouraged from remarriage. Such was the case in India for the higher castes (Ullrich 1977), throughout prerevolutionary China (Chiao 1971), and in early Christian Europe (Verdon 1988). In such places celibacy comes to be seen as a spiritually higher state than married sexuality. In this form, the ideal of virginity has been incorporated into some religions and has been diffused along with conversion.

While the eighteenth-century English, living at a time of expanding wealth and social mobility, were aware of the social advantage of seducing an heiress and spoke freely about it, it is improbable that most peoples would give this as the reason for keeping their daughters virginal. In Eurasia, at any rate, one is much more likely to get explanations involving purity and the shame that follows its loss. We weave significance around the hard facts of existence, and virginity, a practical concern, can be a sign of spiritual purity when the invasion of the body implies the invasion of the spirit or when the seduction of female kin comes to symbolize the violability of the lineage.

The idealization of virginity is most common in Eurasia, and it is found in some other areas, such as Polynesia or native North America, where certain categories of girls are expected to be virginal. It is noteworthy that belief in the purity or spiritual power of virginity, chastity, and celibacy developed in those regions where dowry or gift-exchange was the established form or the form practiced by the elite and aspired to by those who would imitate them. Ideology does not arise *de novo* but is grounded in existential concerns and issues. I suggest that the ideology of virginity has its source in pragmatic concerns about status maintenance and improvement.

As a practical matter, ensuring that daughters and sisters remain virginal puts a heavy burden of surveillance on parents and brothers. The effort required is worthwhile when the stakes are high, as when considerable property and status are involved, or the secondary meanings of virginity are such that the purity of the girl and thus the honor of her family are at issue. In many parts of the Mediterranean world, control over female sexuality is a lived metaphor for control over social relations. The transgressing girl is defying her male kin and giving away what only they have the right to bestow (cf. Schneider 1971).

Elsewhere, particularly among poorer people in societies that value virginity, the daughter's choice of husband is of minor consequence. Thus, there is no point in restricting her. Even when virginity is generally accorded a high value, it may be an ideal to which only a minority aspire. Recognizing this makes it easier to reconcile the seeming contradiction between the high value placed on virginity and the high rate of bastardy at various times and places throughout European history.

IMPLICATIONS OF THE PROPOSITION

Regarding a value on virginity is a way of forestalling male social climbing through seduction causes us to take a fresh look at the interest, in some places, in seducing virgins and the self-congratulation or acclaim by peers that accompanies the successful boy or man in this pursuit. It has nothing to do with sexual pleasure, for the experienced girl or woman is a more satisfying sexual partner than the virgin. What, then, is the point?

First, of course, is the thrill of the forbidden. However, seducing a virgin can be as much of a coup in sexually permissive societies like Samoa as it is in the restrictive ones. In a discussion of adolescent sexuality in the Trobriand Islands, Weiner (1988:71) has pointed out that attracting lovers is not a frivolous pastime but rather "the first step toward entering the adult world of strategies, where the line between influencing others while not allowing others to gain control of oneself must be carefully learned." If the game of seduction is serious business, then how much more is this true when seduction can lead to status improvement. We can understand the Cinderella story and its variants as a tale of upward mobility for women through sexual attraction—but what about upwardly mobile men?

Winning the heart of a high-status woman as a path to a better life may be a male fantasy in all societies that are divided by rank or class, or at least those in which men will not be killed or severely punished for the attempt. Boys and youths have nothing to lose and much to gain if they can make a paternity claim on the child of a high-status girl. In such a setting, where only a few can succeed, all boys will be tempted to refine their skills with virgins of their own rank while hoping for their big chance with a *taupou* (the Samoan "village princess") or her equivalent.

It is well recognized that women use their sexual attractiveness to try to improve their position through a socially advantageous marriage or liaison, when such possibilities are open to them. (The seclusion of girls not only protects daughters against seduction but also protects sons against inconvenient romantic attachments, thus reinforcing parental control over the marriages of children of both sexes.) It should not surprise us that men and boys do the same if the opportunity arises. When sexual success can be translated into social success, it is predictable that men and boys will make themselves attractive to women and that sexual exploits will become a major topic of discussion, teasing, and boasting. In such cases, male competitiveness is channeled into overt sexual competition. The man who seduces a dowered virgin has his fortune made.

CONCLUSION

The trend in the modern world follows the pattern established for the preindustrial societies in the sample. With readily available contraception and abortion, extramarital sexual relations do not have to result in pregnancy or illegitimate birth. Even if a paternity claim is pressed, there is no obligation in our individual-centered society to honor it, as economic opportunities for women as well as welfare payments by the state make it possible to support a child without a husband.

Equally important, the dowry has lapsed in most European and European-derived cultures. Parental investment in daughters is increasingly in the form of education, not dowry. Furthermore, the daughter's choice of a husband does not have the significance for the family today that it did in earlier times. For most people in the industrial world, there is little in the way of a family estate to preserve. Even among the rich, a rebellious daughter and her husband can be cut out of the will, since in modern societies the disposal of assets is up to the individual with legal ownership of them. Thus, a daughter's choice of a husband is not critical to the well-being of the family and the maintenance of its assets.

Most commentators on the "sexual revolution" point to the availability of new contraception and abortion technology as the deciding factor in the changing of our sexual habits. But contraception and abortion have a long history in civilization; techniques to reduce fertility have been known and used in Europe and elsewhere for centuries, albeit clandestinely. Technology alone, without significant changes in social relations, is not enough to alter such deep-seated cultural values as the value on virginity. As marriage transactions disappear and social status is gained more through achievement than through the family into which one is born or marries, parental control over marriage declines and disappears. The choice of a son-in-law is no longer a central concern, and the virginity of daughters loses its salience.

Bundu Trap

I still remember the stories my sister told me about girls whose parents fooled them to get them into the hands of Mami Sowe.

Memuna M. Sillah

In West Africa, initiation of girls into a secret society of women centers on circumcision, and preparations may take months. Planning is handled exclusively by women within the family because it is considered inappropriate to discuss the subject with men. Several families may have their children initiated together to reduce costs and for solidarity and comfort. The girls usually leave home to stay in a hut, called a Bundu bush in Sierra Leone, with other girls their age for months—and sometimes years—while they receive instructions and training in wifely and motherly duties that have been prescribed by the community and handed down to generations of women before them.

The most important decision for a mother is the choice of a circumciser—called a sowe *in Sierra Leone—usually an old, experienced "professional" who has studied under a superior for years. The community sees her as endowed with special powers to perform the surgery. The instrument of the profession is a small penknife or a blade, considered a sacred object given by the gods especially for the circumcision.*

Although a girl may be given only a few weeks' or days' notice of the ceremony, she grows up knowing that she will someday be initiated into society. Envying the fuss made over older sisters and female cousins during their initiation period, she longs for the deferential treatment they receive on returning home: Parental supervision then is lax, and new and permissive wardrobes—in essence, advertisements to potential husbands—are usually provided.

While a few girls have gone so far as to run away from home in protest of the operation, most abandon their initial resistance after being told of the elaborate gifts they will receive from relatives. Nonetheless, the weeks before the ceremony are charged with apprehension. The story that follows is based on my own childhood experiences in Sierra Leone and, to a lesser extent, on those of girls I knew.

For all my eight years, I've been conditioned to fear the Bundu[1] bush; by Mother, my aunties, my older sister, Fanta, and many more. I've heard horror stories of young girls being circumcised without their parents' consent because they unwittingly strayed into a Bundu bush. And simply hearing the name of a certain Mami Sowe after sunset keeps me awake half the night.

Almost every circumcised girl in Freetown has a story to tell about how she was lured into the Bundu bush. Most of the younger girls know that the bush is only a tent built with straw mats, not the thick, faraway bushes where Bundu activities used to take place. Still, few walk in voluntarily—except, of course, girls in the small villages, who look forward to circumcision with great expectation and joy. Mother says they must get married as early as possible because that's all they have to look forward to.

Suddenly, Mother wants me to go to the bush. She has fixed food for Fanta and my three cousins who were circumcised four weeks ago and wants me to take it over. Now she's changing the entire story.

"Nobody will touch you. They don't want little girls like you."

"But they've caught little girls before. Remember the story you told me about the girl who was there three weeks before her parents knew where she was?"

"OK," she says, smiling. "You don't have to go inside. You can stand outside and call out Granny's name. She'll send to get you."

"What if someone pushes me inside?"

"Nobody will do that when you're carrying a tray of food on your head. Go wash your feet and get dressed before the food gets cold."

"Maybe this is just a plot to get me to Mami Sowe like they did to Fanta." My mother shrugs me off and leaves the kitchen. I want to see how my sister and cousins look in the Bundu wraps my mother bought them and in the necklaces of cloves and spices they'll be wearing as jewelry. But I still remember the stories Fanta's been telling me about girls whose parents fool them to get them into the hands of Mami Sowe. Like the one about one girl who was asked to deliver some expensive gold jewelry into her auntie's hands. The girl waited at the appointed place for about thirty minutes before her auntie appeared with two other women. Fanta said that had this girl frequented Bundu bushes before, she would have recognized the women as Mami Sowe's assistants. Minutes later one of the women forced a large piece of cloth into the girl's mouth. By the time the girl was

---

1. Circumcision; secret society of circumcised women.

able to breathe through her mouth again, she was bleeding profusely. Fanta never told me where the bleeding came from, although my brother Amadu said they broke the girl's teeth when they forced the cloth into her mouth.

My mother returns to the kitchen, holding a tray and kitchen towel. She busies herself packing two large bowls into the tray. I help her wipe excess oil off the covers and try some last-ditch delaying tactics.

"I don't know where the bush is or how to get there," I say.

My mother smiles softly. "They're expecting you. Now, change your clothes before the food gets cold."

"Why shouldn't Amadu take the food? He's the older one."

"Go get dressed before I get angry." She is shouting now as she goes down the kitchen steps. I follow her into the house. She pushes me into her bedroom and points to a dress lying on the bed. "Put that on before you come out." She gives the orders as she pulls a red-and-white checkered towel from the basket on the floor. I am getting nervous, but I don't want her to notice. I figure if it is decided I should be circumcised this summer, Mother will figure out a way to get me out of the house, will or woe. But I am not going to make it easy for her.

I feign a struggle, pulling the dress down over my face. She ignores me. I try conversation.

"How have they been, Fanta and Mbalia and Yanati and Seray? How have they been since they've been at the bush?"

"They look very nice in the cotton material I bought them, and they've all put on weight."

"What do they eat there?" I ask with great interest.

"Every kind of food you can think of. Last Friday, Mbalia asked for *sattie*,[2] and Auntie Mbalia prepared it for them in the morning. Then Auntie Seray prepared couscous and salads for Yanati in the afternoon, and Auntie Fanta roasted a whole duck for dinner. It's been like that every day."

This is my favorite part of the entire Bundu process—the eating and drinking to the heart's content. The thought actu-ally calms me down a little as I begin to imagine cassava leaves, potato leaves, *obiata*,[3] jollof rice,[4] plantains, okra, and *foofo*,[5] all lined up in front of my diet-conscious sister and cousins.

"What did you cook?" I ask, following my mother back to the kitchen.

She replies, "Yanati said she wanted to eat some fried fish with plantains before the ceremony tonight. So that's . . ."

"What ceremony?" I ask jumpily, wondering if it has anything to do with me.

"We're going to do a small ceremony tonight, so the girls will be able to come outside and walk around the yard. Maybe in a few weeks they can go out into the streets."

"I'll just leave the tray at Granny's house, and somebody else will take it to the bush."

"You have nothing to worry about. Granny is there. She won't let them touch you," Mother says as she spreads the towel over the food and places the tray on my head.

I grab the sides of the heavy tray with both hands and bite my lower lip as I make my way out toward the gate.

"Keep both hands on the tray," Mother shouts as I leave the confines of her gate.

As the women work, they sing. They move their heads and wave the knives in their hands to the rhythm of the song.

Before I reach the empty lot next to Granny's house, I hear the sound of women singing and clapping. The women sit in clusters of five to seven—one group is peeling onions, another is skinning fowls, another pounding flour in large mortars, another cutting meat. As the women work, they sing, moving their heads or waving the knives in their hands to the rhythm of the song. I try to weave my way through the enormous pots and bowls, the white powder from the mortars, the obese legs sprawled between one bowl and an other. Auntie Ole, Haja[6] Khadi, Auntie Memuna, Haja Fatmata, Miss Conteh, Haja Alari. I call out those names I remember and smile broadly to the others.

It doesn't seem as bad as I had imagined. I feel as though I could leave the food with one of these aunties or hajas and return home safely, but I move on, even quickening my now light steps until suddenly I see it. Spiked stalks of dried bamboo leaves protrude from the roof of a dark hut standing ahead of me on the farthest end of the yard. Its fragile walls of straw mats are square in shape, and from where I am standing, I can see no doors. Just as I begin to imagine being locked up inside with Mami Sowe, with no way of escape, I see a woman sitting by what finally is beginning to look like a doorway to the bush. She is cutting cloth—the same cloth my mother said she bought for Fanta and the others. I remember mother saying they looked good in it, so why is it only being cut now? I don't have time to answer my own question. The woman's voice cuts its way through my thoughts like a butcher's knife on brisket.

"Send her over here."

My blood stops cold, my legs weaken under me, and my head begins to spin. Voices murmur around me. Ear-piercing clanks cause my head to feel as though every piece of flesh is suddenly scalpeled from the inside. A wet piece of cloth passes through my mouth. I feel the soaked sponge of red fluid on my face and neck—and then a soft voice.

"Your mother is not going to be pleased."

Other voices intervene. "You were not paying attention. What happened to you?"

"Leave her alone, she was just afraid, coming to a Bundu bush."

"You mean she is still not . . . ?"

"Oh yes, don't you know her? She's Siminie, Mariatu's daughter."

---

2. Rice porridge.
3. Sisal leaves cooked in West African sauce.
4. Senegal-style red rice.
5. Cooked cassava dough.
6. Title of honor for a woman who has been on a pilgrimage to Mecca.

"Take her in to Granny Yamakoro. She's inside."

"Wait, let her rest a little out here first."

"No, let her go inside and rest."

"Let her take the empty bowls with her."

"No, let her go for now."

"Where's the food?" I gasp when I manage to remove the palm-oil-soaked towel from my face. Just as I am asking the question, I see Mother's bowls, bottoms up on the floor, mud-red pieces of fish and plantain on the ground.

The voices continue: "Let her go wash her face."

"Someone give her some soap."

"No, just water will do."

Inside the Bundu bush is the smell of burned, perfumed palm oil and the sound of the women's Mandingo songs.

The setting inside the Bundu bush is similar to the one outside, except for the strong smell of burned, perfumed palm oil and the vivacious claps accompanying the Mandingo[7] songs. About a dozen more aunties sit on the mud floor, which is covered with straw mats similar to those used to panel the windowless bush. Granny is sitting on her special wide bench, the only seat that can contain all of her behind. As soon as she sees me, she motions for me to enter. Still mute from the food accident, I enter like one drugged. Granny places my skinny body between her thick legs. The warmth relaxes me a little, and my eyes begin to search for Fanta and my cousins.

They're all sitting on the floor, with straightened backs and stretched-out legs, like Barbie dolls. The tallest of the four, Fanta, sits at the far end of the room. Mbalia is sitting next to her, then Seray; Yanati, the shortest, is at the other extreme end. They're all topless to their

waists, which are wrapped in the black-and-blue cotton cloth Mother had bought. Their heads are tied with the same cloth. Between the head-tie and the waist wrap, their bare breasts—full and firm, garnished with palm oil and dried, beaded cloves—jump up and down as the girls clap their hands. The girls' breasts carry the same vigorous rhythm of the dancing heads of the women sitting opposite them. While the aunties seem to be enjoying the songs, the girls look as though they would be happy to leave any time.

I notice my cousins have all put on weight. Fanta's face looks sour, the way it does when she's eating tamarinds. I'm dying to ask her why, in all her seventeen years, she did not suspect anything when Auntie Iye came to take her shopping. But I dare not leave the security of Granny's legs.

Standing in front of the Bundu girls is a short, fleshy woman with extremely tiny eyes and sharp, almost loony eyeblinks, leading the song with a long, thin stick that she waves over their heads. She is dressed in ordinary, even dirty-looking, clothes, but something about her holds me hostage. Maybe it is her baritone voice, which supports the song when the other women forget a line, or the looks she throws out when the girls mispronounce an old Mandingo word. Or, maybe it is her grandly gesticulating manner and the flabby piece of extra flesh waving under her arm, or the way she uses the stick to control the song and at the same time separate Fanta's tightly set legs or straighten Yanati's slouch. As soon as the song ends, the woman with the stick starts another, pausing slightly to look over to where Granny is sitting. When Granny smiles and nods her head, the woman continues with added confidence, then gives the silent girls on the mat a strong look. Seray slouches and lowers her head on her chest. The woman gives her three quick taps on the shoulder, and her back straightens again. Fanta frowns, and Auntie Mbalia admonishes her with a tight wink. Yanati and Mbalia mouth the words, anxiety crowding their faces. Sensing the impending judgment, the mothers and aunties quickly double their enthusiasm and, adding to Granny's frail

voice, carry off the song. The girls begin to clap again, their breasts following energetically. I can actually feel the relief I see on their faces. Yanata and Mbalia smile at each other.

I find myself thinking that I will get Granny to teach me all the Bundu songs before my time comes, because I wouldn't want to offend this peculiar woman. I'm thinking I'll ask Fanta to teach me all she has learned when she returns home. That way. . . . "Come this way with me, Siminie."

A large hand grabs mine, axing my thoughts at the same time. I turn around to see the face of one of three women in the bush I do not recognize. Something about her face cuts a vein in my heart. I try to climb onto Granny's chest, clutching at her.

"Don't let her take me away, Granny."

Granny peels my fingers off her clothes.

"You're going to choke me."

My aunties and cousins, meanwhile, are rolling over one another with laughter. Only Fanta looks worried. The woman with the stick allows a smile to escape.

"What are you afraid of?" she asks aggressively, feigning a confrontation.

"She's lucky we've waited this long. At her age, I had already forgotten what Bundu was like," Auntie Mbalia says.

"Don't listen to them," Granny says, putting her arms around me. "I am your father's mother. While I'm alive, I'm the only person who can give consent for you to be brought into this Bundu society."

"Oh, but I'm your father's sister. I can do it too," Auntie Mbalia insists.

"No, you cannot. Granny is older than you. She won't let you," I scream from the safety of Granny's lap. Everybody laughs again.

I notice that the girls on the mat are beginning to lose their straight backs and Barbie legs. Fanta is resting on the palms of both hands behind her back, Yanati is slouching, Seray has one hand on Yanati's shoulder; only Mbalia maintains a straight back. Even the woman with the thin rod now seems more interested in me than in her pupils.

---

7. A minority tribe of Sierra Leone.

"The little girl understands things well," she says, nodding to Auntie Mbalia.

"Oh, but if her granny is not around, I will be the one in charge. I hope she knows that."

Then turning to me, Auntie Mbalia adds, "Just pray for your granny to be alive until you finish school."

Granny puts her arms around me. I know that I have been saved so far only because she, like my mother, believes in education.

Even though Auntie Mbalia loves to tease me, I know she is serious about having me circumcised as soon as possible. Her own three daughters were all circumcised only a few days after birth. Auntie Mbalia believes in doing things "the way our people did." I know I have been saved so far only because Granny, like my mother, believes in education. Granny single-handedly put her two sons through school after her husband died, when my father, the elder, was only six years old. She has not regretted the sacrifice; her children provide adequately for her today.

"I'm not dying yet. I won't die until I've seen all my granddaughters circumcised," Granny says defensively.

"*Amin,*[8] Amin, Amin," the women chorus, including Auntie Mbalia. The woman with the stick sets herself down on the floor.

"That's the dream of every grandmother. Allah will answer your prayers." She is almost whispering now, her face changing into the same serious mold it had when she scrutinized her pupils. She settles the rod on the ground beside her, pulls her clothes together and tucks them between her legs. "That was my grandmother's biggest dream," she begins. "She was a *sowe* herself in my village, and she taught me everything I

know today. I used to go with her to the bushes to pick the leaves she used. We would wake up early in the morning, before even the fowls began to crow, to set off for the bushes. Even though I was only about six or seven years old, she only had to say my name once, and I was jumping out of the mat. I used to sleep on the ground beside her. There would be nobody on the paths from the moment we left the hut until we returned from the depth of the bushes. My grandmother liked it that way—she tried to avoid bad spirits who might spoil the power of the leaves. She knew the strength of every leaf in the bush, the old woman. All her life as a *sowe,* almost forty years, she never once lost a child in operation. Not a single one."

The women punctuate the story with impressive *Alhamdudilais.*[9]

"And remember, with us Temne[10] people, we put our children through society at a very early age, sometimes as young as five years, for both girls and boys. You know the sooner we were prepared for marriage, the better it was for our parents. . . ."

"But in Freetown, most Temne girls who go to school don't go through society until after they finish school," Fanta argues. I had almost forgotten what Fanta's voice sounded like. It is the first time I've heard any of the girls speak since I entered the bush.

I don't know how the thin stick got from the floor to the air. I just see it there, flying about.

"Did I ask any of my girls a question?" The woman with the stick is talking to the bamboo ceiling. She turns to the other women and asks, "People, did I give Fanta permission to talk? Is Fanta allowed to talk when society women are talking? Fanta who is still not healed, Fanta who still has more than half the trials of society to pass through—can she talk when the rest of us are talking? Women, please tell me."

I notice Auntie Fanta vehemently loosening a small knot at the edge of her clothes. Hiding behind her namesake, she unfolds a small stack of bills and retrieves two notes, which she folds up into an even smaller stack. She ties her wrap again and stands up.

"Mami Sowe, you did not throw any words at Fanta, and Fanta should not have the mind to talk before she's asked to do so. But she's only been here three weeks. Let us please forgive her. In time, she'll learn the ways of a woman. That's the reason. . . ." I do not hear the rest of Auntie Fanta's words. The name Mami Sowe has just taken effect on me.

"Is she Mami Sowe?" I ask in Granny's ears.

Granny does not answer.

Auntie Fanta tries to press the folded notes into the woman's hand.

"Let this pay the fine."

"But did I ask for a fine yet? You Fantas are all alike. You think I'm cheap? Don't you know that if there's a fine, I should tell you what the fine should be? This is the problem with Bundu in towns. There is no respect for the *sowe.* Get away from me." She pushes Auntie Fanta with her elbow.

The women are laughing, and I suddenly find them all very strange. I am actually standing in Mami Sowe's presence, and I did not know it, just as Fanta did not suspect the shopping expedition with Auntie Iye would end up in the Bundu bush. Me, finally in the hands of Mami Sowe. Even as the women laugh, they're nodding their heads in agreement with Mami Sowe. They all agree with everything she says.

Auntie Fanta stands up and playfully pulls at the extra flesh under Mami Sowe's armpit.

"What do you expect? We're in Freetown; this is British Bundu."

Mami Sowe points a hand at Auntie Fanta. "Then maybe you should have taken your children to the British so they can circumcise them."

"Oh, they can do that in hospitals nowadays, you know, and you don't even have to go through all the expenses. You do it quietly there, everything is faster, and you bring them home sooner."

This is the first time I'm hearing this. There's Bundu in the hospitals too? First there was injection, now there's circumcision. I must remember that next time

---

8. "Amen."
9. "Thanks be to God."
10. A majority tribe in Sierra Leone.

mother asks me to accompany her to visit some relative at the hospital. But I'm not the only person who is shocked.

Mami Sowe's mouth is agape. She recovers soon enough and takes on Auntie Fanta.

"Can the hospitals perform the different ceremonies? Can they teach your daughters to fetch water from a well, to cook, to know when to talk, to know how to address elders? Can the hospitals prepare them for marriage? Can the hospitals find them husbands? Only a fool like you will put your daughters through all that pain without teaching them anything. Just move out of my way."

Everybody laughs again. One of the laughs from the mat is so loud that it startles Mami Sowe. She turns around and addresses the girls in a commanding tone. "Who laughed like that?" The girls on the mat look at one another and maintain a cold silence. "I want to know the person who laughed so loud just now. I want her to sell me some raw fish."[11]

The silence is beginning to freeze.

"If you all think you will leave my bush without good manners, then my name is not Mami Sowe."

Mami Sowe's countenance has taken an even sterner look than the one it had when I first walked into the bush. She now looks like what I'd always imagined her to be—a heartless, merciless inflicter of pain on little girls. She pans the faces of her pupils from one end of the room to another. Auntie Mbalia cuts through the silence.

"You have to learn to adjust your behavior in this bush. Whatever loose ways you have acquired during your lifetime, this is the place where you offload them and leave them on these mats."

Auntie Seray adjusts her head-tie to deliver her portion of the speech: "You must listen to instructions and learn to comport yourselves well in this bush. This is the beginning of your adult life, your life as a woman, a respectable woman in society. The skills you learn here will be with you for the rest of your lives. If you cannot own up to your responsibilities here, where else will you be able to do that?"

Mami Sowe is now looking so pleased, I almost think the speeches were meant to please her and were not for the girls.

Auntie Seray moves closely to her namesake and, rubbing her legs, whispers a few words into her ear.

Seray adjusts herself on the mat.

"OK, I was the one who laughed," she says. Then, as if angered by her own confession, she tosses her chin up and adds, "What's wrong with laughing, anyway?"

Seray barely finishes her sentence before her mother in some magical way gets the stick from Granny's hands and starts hitting Seray incessantly on the head.

"What's wrong with this child? She should have been circumcised long before this."

I wriggle my small body between Granny's legs to hide my presence, lest they decide to have me circumcised before I become like Seray.

Granny is crying and swaying her behind from side to side, unable to get up from her bench, and wanting everyone to see her distress. "All these witches walking around this bush ever since these children were brought here, trying to destroy my grandchildren, trying to distract them from the lessons they should be learning." Then wiping her tears, she says decisively, "Tomorrow, first thing in the morning, I am sending for Pa Morlia[12] to drive out the bad spirits. I will put an end to this, or my name is not Yamakoro."

The attention of everyone now turns to calming down Granny. They remind her of her high blood pressure, ask her to look to God, assure her that Seray will change, show her examples of wild girls who changed and ended up getting good husbands. Mami Sowe is rubbing Granny's back; a soft look now blankets her face.

The conciliatory mood in the room is interrupted by the entrance of one of the women who were cutting meat outside. She walks over and kneels down beside Mami Sowe, then whispers something in her ears. Mami Sowe in turn whispers into Granny's ear, and Granny straightens up, then makes a hand movement I do not understand to Auntie Mbalia. The latter looks at me, then at Auntie Fanta, then back at me.

"Granny, can I go to the bathroom?" I ask quietly.

"Not yet," she answers, then points to the meat-cutting woman. "Go with Auntie Zainab. She will take you home," she says, and she continues whispering with Mami Sowe.

I know one day I will be circumcised. But I also know that when the time comes, I will not surrender without a fight.

Confused, I try to remember how I arrived here. I had told mother I didn't know how to get to the Bundu bush, but that was only an excuse not to come. In fact, I had located the bush the very first week my sister and cousins started their confinement here, and I'd increased considerably my reasons for passing by Granny's house during every errand I ran. While I usually give all Bundu bushes a wide berth, it has been difficult to distance myself from this one holding Fanta and my cousins within. Sometimes, while standing in front of it, I was petrified and mesmerized at the same time. All the women in my family are Bundu women. I know that one day, with or without my consent, I will be circumcised. But I also know that when the time comes, I will not give in without a fight.

My mother is sitting on the kitchen steps, her face in her hands. As soon as she sees me, she stands up.

"If you didn't want to take the food for me, you should have said so."

I do not believe my mother is talking like that. I cannot contest her now so I just let her talk while I catch my breath.

"All that food I spent the whole day preparing; for you to go and throw it all away like that, in the blink of an eye."

---

11. "She sounds like a fishwife."
12. A shaman who will cast out "bad spirits."

"I was afraid," I manage to add through breaths. "I thought. . . ."

"I don't want to know what you thought. I warned you to keep your hands on the tray. I don't know why you think you can keep a tray on your head without your hands on it."

"I was holding it. I held it all the way to Granny's house."

"And what were you standing in the bush for? What business did you have there when they wanted to start the ceremonies?"

"Granny wanted a strange woman to take me away," I reply.

"You were standing there like a dead body. She was going to bring you home."

"I know my way home," I answer defensively.

"You know your way home, and you couldn't keep a tray of food on your head."

"I told you I was afraid they were going to catch me."

The way Mother is looking at me, I know that if a garbage truck for children came along at this moment, she would happily throw me in.

"They should have just circumcised you then so you could stay there. Maybe they'll find you a husband after that. You're no use to me."

I know my mother is just upset, so I don't say anything. I go inside the house and change my clothes, happy I came back—at least for now.

Born in Sierra Leone, Memuna M. Sillah grew up "in the midst of quiet, yet constant, revolts, especially by teenage girls, against the unnecessary pain caused by genital mutilation." Sillah came to the United States eight years ago, after living in London, Paris, and Kingston, Jamaica. Now a graduate student in sociology at City College of the City University of New York (CUNY), she has been actively concerned with the problem of female genital mutilation since 1993, when she chose the topic for a term paper in Asha Samad's course on violations of women's rights. "I then learned," Sillah writes, "how widespread the practice is in Africa and other parts of the world—and the drastic forms it can take. This knowledge awakened my old teenage passions against the practice." Sillah is now at work on a novel about immigrant African women in the United States.

Afterword

Asha Samad

Worldwide, some 80 to 100 million women have undergone an operation first recorded in Egypt more than 4,000 years ago. Since then, "female circumcision" in various forms has been customary in many African and in some Asian, Middle Eastern, and indigenous Central and South American cultures. Very different from male circumcision (the removal of the foreskin of the penis), female circumcision can involve the partial or total removal of the clitoris and/or "infibulation," surgical modification and suturing together of the labia. In some areas (Chad, Somalia, Sudan), "decircumcisions" are necessary to open infibulations before marriage and childbirth. While many associate female circumcision with Muslim tradition, it predates Judaism, Christianity, and Islam. It has also been practiced by Jewish communities and Christians living in regions where circumcision is customary.

Condemned by African women's groups and the World Health Organization as abusive and often dangerous, female circumcision persists even where modern African governments seek to limit or prohibit it. While most women survive these mutilating operations, they may suffer immediate and lasting physical effects. Hemorrhaging, infection, and infertility are among the serious complications. The inability to pass urine normally, pain during sexual intercourse, and excessively difficult deliveries are common results. Although harder to measure, emotional and psychological effects may also ensue.

All groups circumcising females also circumcise males. Such groups regard the rite as an essential part of a child's socialization. The operation is done at different ages in different societies—ranging from a few days after birth until puberty. However, among some ethnic groups it is done just prior to marriage, or, as in Rivers state, Nigeria, in the seventh month of the woman's first pregnancy. The rite can symbolize the stability of the group as expressed in the faithfulness of its females—the passers-on of its customs and the maintainers of its families. The custom also reinforces respect and authority. The day of circumcision thus involves not only pain but also recognition for having become a full adult and a marriageable member of society.

Other obvious functions of female circumcision include control of female sexuality and marital chastity. In patrilineal societies, authority over the bride is transferred at marriage to the spouse's patriline. The bride's moral and economic value to her patriline and to her spouse is dependent upon her unquestioned virginity as demonstrated by the intact infibulation.

Many groups feel that attempts to prevent them from practicing circumcision represent an attack on their cultural integrity by "colonial," Western interests and westernized African governments. (The Masai, for instance, are loath to change customs at the behest of a government that has moved them out of their traditional lands.) They may fear that loss of a cohesive tradition, with nothing to replace it, will result in daughters who are as "loose" as uncircumcised African and Western women are perceived to be. More generally, they believe that an uncircumcised daughter may become centered on herself, rather than family, home, and group.

Some westernized Africans now debate the value of female circumcision. But fear that uncircumcised daughters will not be acceptable as brides in their communities spurs many to perpetuate the custom. Some parents may seek modi-

fied forms of the operation for their daughters and may have the procedure performed in private clinics or at home under anesthesia and in antiseptic conditions.

Some—usually Western-educated African women, often of independent means, or those living in the immigrant and refugee communities of Europe and North America—have fully rejected the procedure and are educating women about its deleterious effects and organizing to end the custom. At the same time, other women protest what they consider outside interference in the most intimate aspects of their culture. They ask why Western women—whose own culture often leads them to radically alter their appearance, even through surgery—are so intolerant of the practices of others.

What African women on both sides of the issue resent most is being looked upon by the rest of the world as self-mutilating primitives. Even opponents of circumcision feel that women from the ethnic groups practicing this ancient custom should be the ones leading the fight to eradicate it.

The War Against Women

*In much of the world, political and economic 'progress'
has been dragging them backward*

Twenty-five years ago, a band of militant women picketed the Miss America Pageant in Atlantic City, tossed bras, girdles and other "boob-girlie symbols" into the trash and added an epithet (bra burners) and a rallying cry (women's liberation) to the English language. A quarter of a century later, few countries are without a women's movement; few governments are immune to women's demands. Traditional notions of a woman's place are eroding, and gender gaps are narrowing.

Yet much of the world is still waging war against women. In 1980, the United Nations summed up the burden of inequality: Women, half the world's population, did two thirds of the world's work, earned one tenth of the world's income and owned one hundredth of the world's property. Fourteen years later, despite the fall of repressive regimes, a decade of high growth, the spread of market economics and the rise of female prime ministers and CEOs, women remain victims of abuse and discrimination just about everywhere. The 1993 U.N. Human Development Report found that there still is no country that treats its women as well as its men.

Not only have the political and economic gains of the past decade not always benefited women; in many places "progress" has dragged them backward:

■ **Victims of freedom.** The collapse of communism in the former Soviet Union has thrown women out of work in disproportionate numbers, chan-

neled them into second-rate jobs and revived prerevolutionary attitudes about a woman's place. Women applying for office jobs in the new Russia often are told that their duties include sleeping with the boss.

■ **Victims of democracy.** The new democratically elected assemblies of Eastern Europe have far fewer women members than their puppet predecessors did, and abortion rights are under fire in Germany, Poland and Romania.

■ **Victims of prosperity.** China's economy is growing at a double-digit clip, but most of the workers in the sweatshops that are helping to power the boom are women. And Beijing has subordinated women's health, employment and education needs to its goal of keeping the birthrate low.

■ **Victims of holy war.** Islamic militants are crusading against Western-style women's rights, issuing death threats against feminists and making headway even in traditionally tolerant Muslim lands such as Egypt.

■ **Victims of progress.** In China, India and other nations where sons are still valued more highly than daughters, medical technology has provided a new means of disposing of unwanted baby girls.

■ **Victims of violence.** Despite the toppling of military dictatorships in Latin America, the deregulation of India's economy and the end of apartheid in South Africa, there has been no halt to what the U.N. has called "a global epidemic of violence against women."

■ **Victims of success.** In America and Western Europe, women have made great strides in politics and in some professions. But even in Norway, where women now dominate the political scene, women are still hired last, fired first, paid less than men and held back from the top jobs. In America, a growing number of "separate sisters," including black women and other minorities, women in traditional "women's jobs" and both elderly and young women, charge that the feminist movement has ignored them and their concerns.

The collapse of communism, unlamented almost everywhere, has hurt women in unexpected ways. Gender equality was always more rhetorical than real under Marxism, but women have been hard hit by the implosion of old command economies, the end of guaranteed employment and the unraveling of the social safety net. In Russia, 70 percent of those laid off in the first two post-Communist years were women.

Birthrates in Russia and eastern Germany have dropped to all-time lows as benefits have evaporated and state-financed kindergartens have closed. Abortion rights are under fire in Germany and have been all but extinguished in Poland. In Romania, where abortion was banned for 23 years, abortion rates have hit a global high and the Orthodox Church is pushing to restore the ban.

Even robust economic growth is no guarantee that women will prosper. In China, where Communists still rule but capitalism is taking command, women are no longer being hired for secure, benefit-buffered jobs in state enterprises. Instead, they are being channeled into jobs as secretaries, tour guides and hostesses, for which they dress in traditional, tight *cheongsams* with thigh-high slits. Prof. Ma Xiaonian of the Beijing Women's Hotline says that when women ask how to deal with sexual harassment on the job he advises them to give in if they want to get ahead.

Small bandwagon. Even where female politicians have made gains, women's rights have not always followed. Twenty-five years ago, only three women had run a modern country: India's Indira Gandhi, Israel's Golda Meir and Sri Lanka's Sirimavo Bandaranaike. Since then, 25 more women have been elected head of state or government. Six women prime ministers and three presidents hold office today, as do 300 women ministers in 142 countries. But until recently, when Pakistan's Benazir Bhutto jumped on their small bandwagon, only Prime Minister Gro Harlem Brundtland of Norway and President Mary Robinson of Ireland had strongly pushed women's causes or candidacies.

Bhutto, the first woman to lead a Muslim country, was criticized in her first term for failing women. Back in power, she has a women's agenda, including separate women's police stations and courts, a 10 percent quota for government jobs and the expansion of education for girls. But a litmus test

will be whether she challenges an Islamic ordinance that allows rape victims to be charged with adultery; some 2,000 women languish in Pakistani jails under the law.

Across the Muslim world, women are feeling the heat from Islamic militants. The government of Bangladesh's female Prime Minister Khaleda Zia took away the passport of the country's leading feminist writer, Taslima Nasreen, because "her books were against religion." This encouraged local Islamic zealots to issue a Salman Rushdie-style *fatwa,* or religious edict, calling for Nasreen, who writes about taboo subjects such as sexual abuse, to be put to death for blasphemy. Two Egyptian feminists have received similar death threats.

Western feminists have learned to be cautious about rushing to the aid of endangered women where oppressors can claim cultural or religious sanction. Even local women activists sometimes turn defensive when traditional practices such as genital mutilation in Africa come under foreign attack. The U.N.'s Human Rights Commission tiptoed into that minefield earlier this month by calling for "the eradication of the harmful effects of certain traditional or customary practices." Next month, the commission will name a special investigator to look into violence against women.

As a club of governments, the U.N. is an unlikely catalyst for a feminist revolution. Three U.N. women's con-

ferences, in 1975, 1980 and 1985, served as transmission belts for the message of women s liberation. Now the world is gearing up for a fourth women's conference in Beijing next year and a fourth global plan for righting wrongs against the second sex.

High among them is what Health and Human Services Secretary Donna Shalala calls "terrorism in the home." Anthropology confirms that if there is anything universal about the female condition it is vulnerability to assault. In the United States in 1991, the FBI recorded 106,593 rapes. And a survey of Third World women's groups in the late 1980s found violence the top common concern. A woman is raped in South Africa every 83 seconds. In Latin America, where macho culture breeds high levels of abuse, more than 100 women's projects are dedicated to fighting it.

Violence has been a potent mobilizing force for feminists. Indian women date the takeoff of their movement to protests against rape and "bride burning" in the late 1970s. Today some American women's groups are promoting an antiviolence campaign that would replace abortion rights as the unifying thrust of the feminist movement.

The National Organization for Women is planning a national march against violence this summer while Congress considers a bill that would make violence against women a civil rights offense. But some prominent dissenters oppose making violence a priority be-

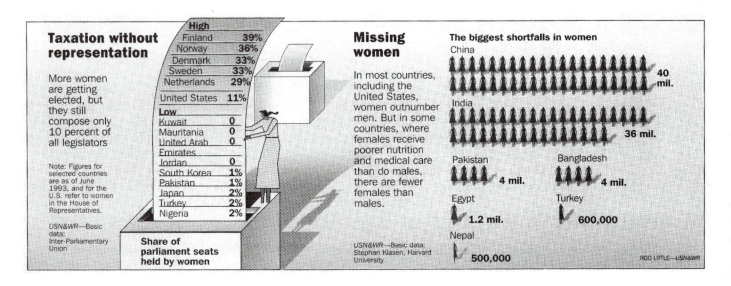

Taxation without representation

More women are getting elected, but they still compose only 10 percent of all legislators

Note: Figures for selected countries are as of June 1993, and for the U.S. refer to women in the House of Representatives.

USN&WR—Basic data: Inter-Parliamentary Union

High		
Finland	39%	
Norway	36%	
Denmark	33%	
Sweden	33%	
Netherlands	29%	
United States	11%	
Low		
Kuwait	0	
Mauritania	0	
United Arab Emirates	0	
Jordan	0	
South Korea	1%	
Pakistan	1%	
Japan	2%	
Turkey	2%	
Nigeria	2%	

Share of parliament seats held by women

Missing women

In most countries, including the United States, women outnumber men. But in some countries, where females receive poorer nutrition and medical care than do males, there are fewer females than males.

USN&WR—Basic data: Stephan Klasen, Harvard University

The biggest shortfalls in women

China — 40 mil.

India — 36 mil.

Pakistan — 4 mil.

Bangladesh — 4 mil.

Egypt — 1.2 mil.

Turkey — 600,000

Nepal — 500,000

ROD LITTLE—*USN&WR*

cause, like the drives against pornography and sexual harassment, it fosters "victim feminism."

While rape, harassment and battering hog the headlines, the vital issues for most women in most countries continue to be bread-and-butter ones. A recent survey by *Ms.* magazine found equal pay and job discrimination the top concerns of American women.

More women are working: They do so in industrial nations at 77 percent of the men's rate in 1991, up from 59 percent 20 years earlier. But women's pay still averages two thirds of men's, mainly because women are clustered in low-wage "women's jobs." In the United States, year-round full-time working women earned 71 percent of the male wage in 1992, up from 62 percent a decade earlier. But women high school graduates earn slightly less than do men who dropped out of school before ninth grade.

Basic burdens. For poor women—and the majority of women are poor—needs are more basic: food, shelter, work. Third World women get nothing like equal pay. Most of their work, on family farms or crafts, does not even count as paid labor, and they rarely inherit or control property. Their burdens have eased somewhat as birth control has become widely available. Mothers are producing fewer children, but every year half a million women still die from pregnancy-related problems, including botched abortions.

The other big shackle on poor women is illiteracy. Although the literacy gap is shrinking, two thirds of the world's illiterates are female; 600 million women cannot read, and 90 million school-age girls are not in school. Uneducated women everywhere have high birthrates, low earnings and short lives. Yet even a few years of education for girls can be a magic bullet, leading to smaller, healthier families, less economic dependence and less vulnerability to abusive husbands.

Natural hardiness has made females the majority in all Western countries and in most of the poorest. But nearly half the world's women live in countries where males are more numerous. In these places, as Harvard economist Amartya Sen points out, girls and women get less food and health care than their brothers and husbands and often die of neglect.

A measure of this extreme prejudice is the number of missing women. China and India together have 75 million fewer women than they should have, according to calculations by Harvard scholar Stephan Klasen. Premature death from neglect is the main cause, but there are others. In China, many girls are not counted because their families hide them from the birth control police. Both Asian giants have traditions of female infanticide, which continues in small pockets. And now technology offers a modern alternative in the form of sex-selective abortions.

Even villagers have access to ultrasound machines that can detect the sex of a fetus in time for a late abortion. Selective abortion is producing a big deficit in newborn girls, but it also leaves feminists in a moral quandary: Can abortion-rights advocates demand that limits be placed on a woman's right to choose? This dilemma may be the international abortion hot potato of the 1990s.

Now that American feminists are looking beyond abortion, their priorities may be more relevant to the forgotten women at home and overseas. Since feisty women tend to flourish best where speech is free, it may be that a rising tide of political and economic freedom eventually will lift women's boats, too. Russian women are beginning to meet in informal groups similar to those that coalesced into America's women's movement three decades ago. South African women are beginning to fight for equal rights now that majority rights are nearly won. In China, where women are just raising their heads above the parapet, there was not even a word for feminism until a few weeks ago, when women academics in Beijing settled on *nuquanzhuyi*—"women's rightsism." Just in time, too, before regiments of women's rightsists descend on Beijing for the womanpower fest next year.

BY EMILY MACFARQUHAR WITH JENNIFER SETER, SUSAN V. LAWRENCE IN BEIJING, ROBIN KNIGHT IN LONDON AND JOANNIE M. SCHROF

Poor, powerless and pregnant

While women in industrialized countries are generally able to control the number of children they bear, some 250 million women in developing countries face unplanned pregnancies and dangerous abortion options.

USN&WR—Basic data: Population Reference Bureau, Population Action International

Average number of children born in a woman's lifetime

High (selected countries)

Gaza Strip	7.9
Malawi	7.7
Yemen	7.5
Ethiopia	7.5
Ivory Coast	7.4

Low

Hong Kong	1.2
Italy	1.3
Spain	1.3
Germany	1.4
Greece	1.4

Average of:

Africa	6.1
South Asia	4.4
Latin America	3.2
United States	2.0
East Asia	1.8
Europe	1.6

Maternal mortality

Women in developing countries continue to face risks from complications of pregnancy, childbirth and botched abortions. For each woman who dies in these countries, 10 times as many suffer serious illness.

Note: Figures are for selected countries from 1988.

USN&WR—Basic data: United Nations, Population Action International

Deaths from childbirth
(per 100,000 live births)

High

Sierra Leone	1,000
Guinea	1,000
Congo	900
Ethiopia	900
Angola	900
Somalia	900

Low

Iceland	2
Ireland	3
Belgium	4
Denmark	4
Norway	4
Australia	5

Average of:

Sub-Saharan Africa	690
All developing countries	420
Industrialized countries	26
North America	12

The Initiation of a Maasai Warrior

Tepilit Ole Saitoti

"Tepilit, circumcision means a sharp knife cutting into the skin of the most sensitive part of your body. You must not budge; don't move a muscle or even blink. You can face only one direction until the operation is completed. The slightest movement on your part will mean you are a coward, incompetent and unworthy to be a Maasai man. Ours has always been a proud family, and we would like to keep it that way. We will not tolerate unnecessary embarrassment, so you had better be ready. If you are not, tell us now so that we will not proceed. Imagine yourself alone remaining uncircumcised like the water youth [white people]. I hear they are not circumcised. Such a thing is not known in Maasailand; therefore, circumcision will have to take place even if it means holding you down until it is completed."

My father continued to speak and every one of us kept quiet. "The pain you will feel is symbolic. There is a deeper meaning in all this. Circumcision means a break between childhood and adulthood. For the first time in your life, you are regarded as a grownup, a complete man or woman. You will be expected to give and not just to receive. To protect the family always, not just to be protected yourself. And your wise judgment will for the first time be taken into consideration. No family affairs will be discussed without your being consult-

ed. If you are ready for all these responsibilities, tell us now. Coming into manhood is not simply a matter of growth and maturity. It is a heavy load on your shoulders and especially a burden on the mind. Too much of this—I am done. I have said all I wanted to say. Fellows, if you have anything to add, go ahead and tell your brother, because I am through. I have spoken."

After a prolonged silence, one of my half-brothers said awkwardly, "Face it, man . . . it's painful. I won't lie about it, but it is not the end. We all went through it, after all. Only blood will flow, not milk." There was laughter and my father left.

My brother Lellia said, "Men, there are many things we must acquire and preparations we must make before the ceremony, and we will need the cooperation and help of all of you. Ostrich feathers for the crown and wax for the arrows must be collected."

"Are you *orkirekenyi?*" one of my brothers asked. I quickly replied no, and there was laughter. *Orkirekenyi* is a person who has transgressed sexually. For you must not have sexual intercourse with any circumcised woman before you yourself are circumcised. You must wait until you are circumcised. If you have not waited, you will be fined. Your father, mother, and the circumciser will take a cow from you as punishment.

Just before we departed, one of my closest friends said, "If you kick the knife, you will be in trouble." There was laughter. "By the way, if you have decided to kick the circumciser, do it well. Silence him once and for all." "Do it the way you kick a football in school." "That will fix him," another added, and we all laughed our heads off again as we departed.

The following month was a month of preparation. I and others collected wax, ostrich feathers, honey to be made into honey beer for the elders to drink on the day of circumcision, and all the other required articles.

Three days before the ceremony my head was shaved and I discarded all my belongings, such as my necklaces, garments, spear, and sword. I even had to shave my pubic hair. Circumcision in many ways is similar to Christian baptism. You must put all the sins you have committed during childhood behind and embark as a new person with a different outlook on a new life.

The circumciser came the following day and handed the ritual knives to me. He left drinking a calabash of beer. I stared at the knives uneasily. It was hard to accept that he was going to use them on my organ. I was to sharpen them and protect them from people of ill will who might try to blunt them, thus rendering them inefficient during the ritual and thereby bringing shame on our family. The knives threw a chill down my spine; I was not sure I was sharpening them properly, so I took them to my closest brother for him to check out, and he assured me that the knives were all right. I hid them well and waited.

Tension started building between me and my relatives, most of whom worried that I wouldn't make it through the ceremony valiantly. Some even snarled at me, which was their way of encouraging me. Others threw insults and abusive words my way. My sister Loiyan in particular was more troubled by the whole affair than anyone in the whole family. She had to assume my mother's role during the circumcision. Were I to fail my initiation, she would have to face the consequences. She would be spat upon and even beaten for representing the mother of an unworthy son. The same fate would befall my father, but he seemed unconcerned. He had this weird belief that because I was not particularly handsome, I must be brave. He kept saying, "God is not so bad as to have made him ugly and a coward at the same time."

Failure to be brave during circumcision would have other unfortunate consequences: the herd of cattle belonging to the family still in the compound would be beaten until they stampeded; the slaughtered oxen and honey beer prepared during the month before the ritual would go to waste; the initiate's food would be spat upon and he would have to eat it or else get a severe beating. Everyone would call him Olkasiodoi, the knife kicker.

Kicking the knife of the circumciser would not help you anyway. If you struggle and try to get away during the ritual, you will be held down until the operation is completed. Such failure of nerve would haunt you in the future. For example, no one will choose a person who kicked the knife for a position of leadership. However, there have been instances in which a person who failed to go through circumcision successfully became very brave afterwards because he was filled with anger over the incident; no one dares to scold him or remind him of it. His agemates, particularly the warriors, will act as if nothing had happened.

During the circumcision of a woman, on the other hand, she is allowed to cry as long as she does not hinder the operation. It is common to see a woman crying and kicking during circumcision. Warriors are usually summoned to help hold her down.

For woman, circumcision means an end to the company of Maasai warriors. After they recuperate, they soon get married, and often to men twice their age.

The closer it came to the hour of truth, the more I was hated, particularly by those closest to me. I was deeply troubled by the withdrawal of all the support I needed. My annoyance turned into anger and resolve. I decided not to budge or blink, even if I were to see my intestines flowing before me. My resolve was hardened when newly circumcised warriors came to sing for me. Their songs were utterly insulting, intended to annoy me further. They tucked their wax arrows under my crotch and rubbed them on my nose. They repeatedly called me names.

By the end of the singing, I was fuming. Crying would have meant I was a coward. After midnight they left me alone and I went into the house and tried to sleep but could not. I was exhausted and numb but remained awake all night.

At dawn I was summoned once again by the newly circumcised warriors. They piled more and more insults on me. They sang their weird songs with even more vigor and excitement than before. The songs praised warriorhood and encouraged one to achieve it at all costs. The songs continued until the sun shone on the cattle horns clearly. I was summoned to the main cattle gate, in my hand a ritual cowhide from a cow that had been properly slaughtered during my naming ceremony. I went past Loiyan, who was milking a cow, and she muttered something. She was shaking all over. There was so much tension that people could hardly breathe.

I laid the hide down and a boy was ordered to pour ice-cold water, known as *engare entolu* (ax water), over my head. It dripped all over my naked body and I shook furiously. In a matter of seconds I was summoned to sit down. A large crowd of boys and men formed a semicircle in front of me; women are

not allowed to watch male circumcision and vice-versa. That was the last thing I saw clearly. As soon as I sat down, the circumciser appeared, his knives at the ready. He spread my legs and said, "One cut," a pronouncement necessary to prevent an initiate from claiming that he had been taken by surprise. He splashed a white liquid, a ceremonial paint called *enturoto*, across my face. Almost immediately I felt a spark of pain under my belly as the knife cut through my penis' foreskin. I happened to choose to look in the direction of the operation. I continued to observe the circumciser's fingers working mechanically. The pain became numbness and my lower body felt heavy, as if I were weighed down by a heavy burden. After fifteen minutes or so, a man who had been supporting from behind pointed at something, as if to assist the circumciser. I came to learn later that the circumciser's eyesight had been failing him and that my brothers had been mad at him because the operation had taken longer than was usually necessary. All the same, I remained pinned down until the operation was over. I heard a call for milk to wash the knives, which signaled the end, and soon the ceremony was over.

With words of praise, I was told to wake up, but I remained seated. I waited for the customary presents in appreciation of my bravery. My father gave me a cow and so did my brother Lillia. The man who had supported my back and my brother-in-law gave me a heifer. In all I had eight animals given to me. I was carried inside the house to my own bed to recuperate as activities intensified to celebrate my bravery.

I laid on my own bed and bled profusely. The blood must be retained within the bed, for according to Maasai tradition, it must not spill to the ground. I was drenched in my own blood. I stopped bleeding after about half an hour but soon was in intolerable pain. I was supposed to squeeze my organ and force blood to flow out of the wound, but no one had told me, so the blood coagulated and caused unbearable pain. The circumciser was brought to my aid and showed me what to do, and soon the pain subsided.

The following morning, I was escorted by a small boy to a nearby valley to walk and relax, allowing my wound to drain. This was common for everyone who had been circumcised, as well as for women who had just given birth. Having lost a lot of blood, I was extremely weak. I walked very slowly, but in spite of my caution I fainted. I tried to hang on to bushes and shrubs, but I fell, irritating my wound. I came out of unconsciousness quickly, and the boy who was escorting me never realized what had happened. I was so scared that I told him to lead me back home. I could have died without there being anyone around who could have helped me. From that day on, I was selective of my company while I was feeble.

In two weeks I was able to walk and was taken to join other newly circumcised boys far away from our settlement. By tradition Maasai initiates are required to decorate their headdresses with all kinds of colorful birds they have killed. On our way to the settlement, we hunted birds and teased girls by shooting them with our wax blunt arrows. We danced and ate and were well treated wherever we went. We were protected from the cold and rain during the healing period. We were not allowed to touch food, as we were regarded as unclean, so whenever we ate we had to use specially prepared sticks instead. We remained in this pampered state until our wounds healed and our headdresses were removed. Our heads were shaved, we discarded our black cloaks and bird headdresses and embarked as newly shaven warriors, Irkeleani.

As long as I live I will never forget the day my head was shaved and I emerged a man, a Maasai warrior. I felt a sense of control over my destiny so great that no words can accurately describe it. I now stood with confidence, pride, and happiness of being, for all around me I was desired and loved by beautiful, sensuous Maasai maidens. I could now interact with women and even have sex with them, which I had not been allowed before. I was now regarded as a responsible person.

In the old days, warriors were like gods, and women and men wanted only to be the parent of a warrior. Everything else would be taken care of as a result. When a poor family had a warrior, they

ceased to be poor. The warrior would go on raids and bring cattle back. The warrior would defend the family against all odds. When a society respects the individual and displays confidence in him the way the Maasai do their warriors, the individual can grow to his fullest potential. Whenever there was a task requiring physical strength or bravery, the Maasai would call upon their warriors. They hardly ever fall short of what is demanded of them and so are characterized by pride, confidence, and an extreme sense of freedom. But there is an old saying in Maasai: "You are never a free man until your father dies." In other words, your father is paramount while he is alive and you are obligated to respect him. My father took advantage of this principle and held a tight grip on all his warriors, including myself. He always wanted to know where we all were at any given time. We fought against his restrictions, but without success. I, being the youngest of my father's five warriors, tried even harder to get loose repeatedly, but each time I was punished severely.

Roaming the plains with other warriors in pursuit of girls and adventure was a warrior's pastime. We would wander from one settlement to another, singing, wrestling, hunting, and just playing. Often I was ready to risk my father's punishment for this wonderful freedom.

One clear day my father sent me to take sick children and one of his wives to the dispensary in the Korongoro Highlands. We rode in the L.S.B. Leakey lorry. We ascended the highlands and were soon attended to in the local hospital. Near the conservation offices I met several acquaintances, and one of them told me of an unusual circumcision that was about to take place in a day or two. All the local warriors and girls were preparing to attend it.

The highlands were a lush green from the seasonal rains and the sky was a purple-blue with no clouds in sight. The land was overflowing with milk, and the warriors felt and looked their best, as they always did when there was plenty to eat and drink. Everyone was at ease. The demands the community usually made on warriors during the dry sea-

son when water was scarce and wells had to be dug were now not necessary. Herds and flocks were entrusted to youths to look after. The warriors had all the time for themselves. But my father was so strict that even at times like these he still insisted on overworking us in one way or another. He believed that by keeping us busy, he would keep us out of trouble.

When I heard about the impending ceremony, I decided to remain behind in the Korongoro Highlands and attend it now that the children had been treated. I knew very well that I would have to make up a story for my father upon my return, but I would worry about that later. I had left my spear at home when I boarded the bus, thinking that I would be coming back that very day. I felt lighter but now regretted having left it behind; I was so used to carrying it wherever I went. In gales of laughter resulting from our continuous teasing of each other, we made our way toward a distant kraal. We walked at a leisurely pace and reveled in the breeze. As usual we talked about the women we desired, among other things.

The following day we were joined by a long line of colorfully dressed girls and warriors from the kraal and the neighborhood where we had spent the night, and we left the highland and headed to Ingorienito to the rolling hills on the lower slopes to attend the circumcision ceremony. From there one could see Oldopai Gorge, where my parents lived, and the Inaapi hills in the middle of the Serengeti Plain.

Three girls and a boy were to be initiated on the same day, an unusual occasion. Four oxen were to be slaughtered, and many people would therefore attend. As we descended, we saw the kraal where the ceremony would take place. All those people dressed in red seemed from a distance like flamingos standing in a lake. We could see lines of other guests heading to the settlements. Warriors made gallant cries of happiness known as *enkiseer*. Our line of warriors and girls responded to their cries even more gallantly.

In serpentine fashion, we entered the gates of the settlement. Holding spears in our left hands, we warriors walked proudly, taking small steps, swaying like palm trees, impressing our girls, who walked parallel to us in another line, and of course the spectators, who gazed at us approvingly.

We stopped in the center of the kraal and waited to be greeted. Women and children welcomed us. We put our hands on the children's heads, which is how children are commonly saluted. After the greetings were completed, we started dancing.

Our singing echoed off the kraal fence and nearby trees. Another line of warriors came up the hill and entered the compound, also singing and moving slowly toward us. Our singing grew in intensity. Both lines of warriors moved parallel to each other, and our feet pounded the ground with style. We stamped vigorously, as if to tell the next line and the spectators that we were the best.

The singing continued until the hot sun was overhead. We recessed and ate food already prepared for us by other warriors. Roasted meat was for those who were to eat meat, and milk for the others. By our tradition, meat and milk must not be consumed at the same time, for this would be a betrayal of the animal. It was regarded as cruel to consume a product of the animal that could be obtained while it was alive, such as milk, and meat, which was only available after the animal had been killed.

After eating we resumed singing, and I spotted a tall, beautiful *esiankiki* (young maiden) of Masiaya whose family was one of the largest and richest in our area. She stood very erect and seemed taller than the rest.

One of her breasts could be seen just above her dress, which was knotted at the shoulder. While I was supposed to dance generally to please all the spectators, I took it upon myself to please her especially. I stared at and flirted with her, and she and I danced in unison at times. We complemented each other very well.

During a break, I introduced myself to the *esiankiki* and told her I would like to see her after the dance. "Won't you need a warrior to escort you home later when the evening threatens?" I said. She replied, "Perhaps, but the evening is still far away."

I waited patiently. When the dance ended, I saw her departing with a group of other women her age. She gave me a sidelong glance, and I took that to mean come later and not now. With so many others around, I would not have been able to confer with her as I would have liked anyway.

With another warrior, I wandered around the kraal killing time until the herds returned from pasture. Before the sun dropped out of sight, we departed. As the kraal of the *esiankiki* was in the lowlands, a place called Enkoloa, we descended leisurely, our spears resting on our shoulders.

We arrived at the woman's kraal and found that cows were now being milked. One could hear the women trying to appease the cows by singing to them. Singing calms cows down, making it easier to milk them. There were no warriors in the whole kraal except for the two of us. Girls went around into warriors' houses as usual and collected milk for us. I was so eager to go and meet my *esiankiki* that I could hardly wait for nightfall. The warriors' girls were trying hard to be sociable, but my mind was not with them. I found them to be childish, loud, bothersome, and boring.

As the only warriors present, we had to keep them company and sing for them, at least for a while, as required by custom. I told the other warrior to sing while I tried to figure out how to approach my *esiankiki*. Still a novice warrior, I was not experienced with women and was in fact still afraid of them. I could flirt from a distance, of course. But sitting down with a woman and trying to seduce her was another matter. I had already tried twice to approach women soon after my circumcision and had failed. I got as far as the door of one woman's house and felt my heart beating like a Congolese drum; breathing became difficult and I had to turn back. Another time I managed to get in the house and succeeded in sitting on the bed, but then I started trembling until the whole bed was shaking, and conversation became difficult. I left the house and the woman, amazed and speechless, and never went back to her again.

Tonight I promised myself I would be brave and would not make any silly, ridiculous moves. "I must be mature

and not afraid," I kept reminding myself, as I remembered an incident involving one of my relatives when he was still very young and, like me, afraid of women. He went to a woman's house and sat on a stool for a whole hour; he was afraid to awaken her, as his heart was pounding and he was having difficulty breathing.

When he finally calmed down, he woke her up, and their conversation went something like this:

"Woman, wake up."

"Why should I?"

"To light the fire."

"For what?"

"So you can see me."

"I already know who you are. Why don't *you* light the fire, as you're nearer to it than me?"

"It's your house and it's only proper that you light it yourself."

"I don't feel like it."

"At least wake up so we can talk, as I have something to tell you."

"Say it."

"I need you."

"I do not need one-eyed types like yourself."

"One-eyed people are people too."

"That might be so, but they are not to my taste."

They continued talking for quite some time, and the more they spoke, the braver he became. He did not sleep with her that night, but later on he persisted until he won her over. I doubted whether I was as strong-willed as he, but the fact that he had met with success encouraged me. I told my warrior friend where to find me should he need me, and then I departed.

When I entered the house of my *esiankiki,* I called for the woman of the house, and as luck would have it, my lady responded. She was waiting for me. I felt better, and I proceeded to talk to her like a professional. After much talking back and forth, I joined her in bed.

The night was calm, tender, and loving, like most nights after initiation ceremonies as big as this one. There must have been a lot of courting and lovemaking.

Maasai women can be very hard to deal with sometimes. They can simply reject a man outright and refuse to change their minds. Some play hard to get, but in reality are testing the man to see whether he is worth their while. Once a friend of mine while still young was powerfully attracted to a woman nearly his mother's age. He put a bold move on her. At first the woman could not believe his intention, or rather was amazed by his courage. The name of the warrior was Ngengeiya, or Drizzle.

"Drizzle, what do you want?"

The warrior stared her right in the eye and said, "You."

"For what?"

"To make love to you."

"I am your mother's age."

"The choice was either her or you."

This remark took the woman by surprise. She had underestimated the saying "There is no such thing as a young warrior." When you are a warrior, you are expected to perform bravely in any situation. Your age and size are immaterial.

"You mean you could really love me like a grown-up man?"

"Try me, woman."

He moved in on her. Soon the woman started moaning with excitement, calling out his name. "Honey Drizzle, Honey Drizzle, you *are* a man." In a breathy, stammering voice, she said, "A real man."

Her attractiveness made Honey Drizzle ignore her relative old age. The Maasai believe that if an older and a younger person have intercourse, it is the older person who stands to gain. For instance, it is believed that an older woman having an affair with a young man starts to appear younger and healthier, while the young man grows older and unhealthy.

The following day when the initiation rites had ended, I decided to return home. I had offended my father by staying away from home without his consent, so I prepared myself for whatever punishment he might inflict on me. I walked home alone.

The Little Emperors

A generation of spoiled brats, a tidal wave of abortions and thousands of missing girls—these are some of the unintended consequences of China's revolutionary one-child policy

Daniela Deane

Daniela Deane, who has two sons and lives in Hong Kong, is a free-lance writer who contributes to the Washington Post *and* Newsweek. *Her last article for this magazine was "The Vanishing Border," about the growing integration of southern China and Hong Kong.*

XU MING SITS ON THE WORN SOFA WITH his short, chubby arms and legs splayed, forced open by fat and the layers of padded clothing worn in northern China to ward off the relentless chill. To reach the floor, the tubby 8-year-old rocks back and forth on his big bottom, inching forward slowly, eventually ending upright. Xu Ming finds it hard to move.

"He got fat when he was about 3," says his father, Xu Jianguo, holding the boy's bloated, dimpled hand. "We were living with my parents and they were very good to him. He's the only grandson. It's a tradition in China that boys are very loved. They love him very much, and so they feed him a lot. They give him everything he wants."

Xu Ming weighs 135 pounds, about twice what he should at his age. He's one of hundreds of children who have sought help in the past few years at the Beijing Children's Hospital, which recently began the first American-style fat farm for obese children in what was once the land of skin and bones.

"We used to get a lot of cases of malnutrition," says Dr. Ni Guichen, director of endocrinology at the hospi-

tal and founder of the weight-reduction classes. "But in the last 10 years, the problem has become obese children. The number of fat children in China is growing very fast. The main reason is the one-child policy," she says, speaking in a drab waiting room. "Because parents can only have one child, the families take extra good care of that one child, which means feeding him too much."

Bulging waistlines are one result of China's tough campaign to curb its population. The one-child campaign, a strict national directive that seeks to limit each Chinese couple to a single son or daughter, has other dramatic consequences: millions of abortions, fewer girls and a generation of spoiled children.

The 10-day weight-reduction sessions—a combination of exercise, nutritional guidance and psychological counseling—are very popular. Hundreds of children—some so fat they can hardly walk—are turned away for each class.

According to Ni, about 5% of children in China's cities are obese, with two obese boys for every overweight girl, the traditional preference toward boys being reflected in the amount of attention lavished on the child. "Part of the course is also centered on the parents. We try to teach them how to bring their children up properly, not just by spoiling them," Ni says.

Ming's father is proud that his son, after two sessions at the fat farm, has managed to halve his intake of *jiaozi,*

the stodgy meat-filled dumplings that are Ming's particular weakness, from 30 to 15 at a sitting. "Even if he's not full, that's all he gets," he says. "In the beginning, it was very difficult. He would put his arms around our necks and beg us for more food. We couldn't bear it, so we'd give him a little more."

Ming lost a few pounds but hasn't been able to keep the weight off. He's a bit slimmer now, but only because he's taller. "I want to lose weight," says Ming, who spends his afternoons snacking at his grandparents' house and his evenings plopped in front of the television set at home. "The kids make fun of me, they call me a fat pig. I hate the nicknames. In sports class, I can't do what the teacher says. I can run a little bit, but after a while I have to sit down. The teacher puts me at the front of the class where all the other kids can see me. They all laugh and make fun of me."

The many fat children visible on China's city streets are just the most obvious example of 13 years of the country's one-child policy. In the vast countryside, the policy has meant shadowy lives as second-class citizens for thousands of girls, or, worse, death. It has made abortion a way of life and a couple's sexual intimacy the government's concern. Even women's menstrual cycles are monitored. Under the directive, couples literally have to line up for permission to procreate. Second children are sometimes possible, but only on payment of a heavy fine.

The policy is an unparalleled intrusion into the private lives of a nation's citizens, an experiment on a scale never attempted elsewhere in the world. But no expert will argue that China—by far the world's most populous country with 1.16 billion people—could continue without strict curbs on its population.

China's communist government adopted the one-child policy in 1979 in response to the staggering doubling of the country's population during Mao Tse-tung's rule. Mao, who died in 1976, was convinced that the country's masses were a strategic asset and vigorously encouraged the Chinese to produce even-larger families.

But large families are now out for the Chinese—20% of the world's population living on just 7% of the arable land. "China has to have a population policy," says Huang Baoshan, deputy director of the State Family Planning Commission. With the numbers ever growing, "how can we feed these people, clothe them, house them?"

DINNER TIME FOR ONE 5-YEAR-OLD GIRL consists of granddad chasing her through the house, bowl and spoon in hand, barking like a dog or mewing like a cat. If he performs authentically enough, she rewards him by accepting a mouthful of food. No problem, insists granddad, "it's good exercise for her."

An 11-year-old boy never gets up to go to the toilet during the night. That's because his mother, summoned by a shout, gets up instead and positions a bottle under the covers for him. "We wouldn't want him to have to get up in the night," his mother says.

Another mother wanted her 16-year-old to eat some fruit, but the teen-ager was engrossed in a video game. Not wanting him to get his fingers sticky or daring to interrupt, she peeled several grapes and popped one after another into his mouth. "Not so fast," he snapped. "Can't you see I have to spit out the seeds?"

Stories like these are routinely published in China's newspapers, evidence that the government-imposed birth-control policy has produced an emerging generation of spoiled, lazy, selfish, self-centered and overweight children. There are about 40 million only chil-

dren in China. Dubbed the country's "Little Emperors," their behavior toward their elders is likened to that of the young emperor Pu Yi, who heaped indignities on his eunuch servants while making them cater to his whims, as chronicled in Bernardo Bertolucci's film "The Last Emperor."

Many studies on China's only children have been done. One such study confirmed that only children generally are not well liked. The study, conducted by a team of Chinese psychologists, asked a group of 360 Chinese children, half who have siblings and half who don't, to rate each other's behavior. The only children were, without fail, the least popular, regardless of age or social background. Peers rated them more uncooperative and selfish than children with brothers and sisters. They bragged more, were less helpful in group activities and more apt to follow their own selfish interests. And they wouldn't share their toys.

The Chinese lay a lot of blame on what they call the "4-2-1" syndrome—four doting grandparents, two overindulgent parents, all pinning their hopes and ambitions on one child.

Besides stuffing them with food, Chinese parents have very high expectations of their one *bao bei,* or treasured object. Some have their still-in-strollers babies tested for IQ levels. Others try to teach toddlers Tang Dynasty poetry. Many shell out months of their hard-earned salaries for music lessons and instruments for children who have no talent or interest in playing. They fill their kids' lives with lessons in piano, English, gymnastics and typing.

The one-child parents, most of them from traditionally large Chinese families, grew up during the chaotic, 10-year Cultural Revolution, when many of the country's cultural treasures were destroyed and schools were closed for long periods of time. Because many of that generation spent years toiling in the fields rather than studying, they demand—and put all their hopes into—academic achievement for their children.

"We've already invested a lot of money in his intellectual development," Wang Zhouzhi told me in her Spartan home in a tiny village of Changping

county outside Beijing, discussing her son, Chenqian, an only child. "I don't care how much money we spend on him. We've bought him an organ and we push him hard. Unfortunately, he's only a mediocre student," she says, looking toward the 10-year-old boy. Chenqian, dressed in a child-sized Chinese army uniform, ate 10 pieces of candy during the half-hour interview and repeatedly fired off his toy pistol, all without a word of reproach from his mother.

Would Chenqian have liked a sibling to play with? "No," he answers loudly, firing a rapid, jarring succession of shots. His mother breaks in: "If he had a little brother or sister, he wouldn't get everything he wants. Of course he doesn't want one. With only one child, I give my full care and concern to him."

But how will these children, now entering their teen-age years and moving quickly toward adulthood, become the collectivist-minded citizens China's hard-line communist leadership demands? Some think they never will. Ironically, it may be just these overindulged children who will change Chinese society. After growing up doing as they wished, ruling their immediate families, they're not likely to obey a central government that tells them to fall in line. This new generation of egotists, who haven't been taught to take even their parents into consideration, simply may not be able to think of the society as a whole—the basic principle of communism.

THE NEED FOR FAMILY PLANNING IS OBvious in the cities, where living space is limited and the one-child policy is strictly enforced and largely successful. City dwellers are slowly beginning to accept the notion that smaller families are better for the country, although most would certainly want two children if they could have them. However, in the countryside, where three of every four Chinese live—nearly 900 million people—the goal of limiting each couple to only one child has proved largely elusive.

In the hinterlands, the policy has become a confusing patchwork of special cases and exceptions. Provincial authorities can decide which couples can have a second child. In the southern province of Guangdong, China's richest, two children are allowed and many couples can afford to pay the fine to have even a third or fourth child. The amounts of the fines vary across the country, the highest in populous Sichuan province, where the fine for a second child can be as much as 25% of a family's income over four years. Special treatment has been given to China's cultural minorities such as the Mongolians and the Tibetans because of their low numbers. Many of them are permitted three or four children without penalty, although some Chinese social scientists have begun to question the privilege.

"It's really become a two-child policy in the countryside," says a Western diplomat. "Because of the traditional views on labor supply, the traditional bias toward the male child, it's been impossible for them to enforce a one-child policy outside the cities. In the countryside, they're really trying to stop that third child."

Thirteen years of strict family planning have created one of the great mysteries of the vast and remote Chinese countryside: Where have all the little girls gone? A Swedish study of sex ratios in China, published in 1990, and based on China's own census data, concluded that several million little girls are "missing"—up to half a million a year in the years 1985 to 1987—since the policy was introduced in late 1979.

In the study, and in demographic research worldwide, sex ratio at birth in humans is shown to be very stable, between 105 and 106 boys for every 100 girls. The imbalance is thought to be nature's way of compensating for the higher rates of miscarriage, stillbirth and infant mortality among boys.

In China, the ratio climbed consistently during the 1980s, and it now rests at more than 110 boys to 100 girls. "The imbalance is evident in some areas of the country," says Stirling Scruggs, director of the United Nations Population Fund in China. "I don't think the reason is widespread

infanticide. They're adopting out girls to try for a boy, they're hiding their girls, they're not registering them. Throughout Chinese history, in times of famine, and now as well, people have been forced to make choices between boys and girls, and for many reasons, boys always win out."

With the dismantling of collectives, families must, once again, farm their own small plots and sons are considered necessary to do the work. Additionally, girls traditionally "marry out" of their families, transferring their filial responsibilities to their in-laws. Boys carry on the family name and are entrusted with the care of their parents as they age. In the absence of a social security system, having a son is the difference between starving and eating when one is old. To combat the problem, some innovative villages have begun issuing so-called "girl insurance," an old-age insurance policy for couples who have given birth to a daughter and are prepared to stop at that.

"People are scared to death to be childless and penniless in their old age," says William Hinton, an American author of seven books chronicling modern China. "So if they don't have a son, they immediately try for another. When the woman is pregnant, they'll have a sex test to see if it's a boy or a girl. They'll abort a girl, or go in hiding with the girl, or pay the fine, or bribe the official or leave home. Anything. It's a game of wits."

Shen Shufen, a sturdy, round-faced peasant woman of 33, has two children—an 8-year-old girl and a 3-year-old boy—and lives in Sihe, a dusty, one-road, mud-brick, village in the countryside outside Beijing. Her husband is a truck driver. "When we had our girl, we knew we had to have another child somehow. We saved for years to pay the fine. It was hard giving them that money, 3,000 yuan ($550 in U.S. dollars), in one night. That's what my husband makes in three years. I was so happy when our second child was a boy."

The government seems aware of the pressure its policies put on expectant parents, and the painful results, but has not shown any flexibility. For instance,

Beijing in 1990 passed a law forbidding doctors to tell a couple the results of ultrasound tests that disclose the sex of their unborn child. The reason: Too many female embryos were being aborted.

And meanwhile, several hundred thousand women—called "guerrilla moms"—go into hiding every year to have their babies. They become part of China's 40-million-strong floating population that wanders the country, mostly in search of work, sleeping under bridges and in front of railway stations. Tens of thousands of female children are simply abandoned in rural hospitals.

And although most experts say female infanticide is not widespread, it does exist. "I found a dead baby girl," says Hinton. "We stopped for lunch at this mountain ravine in Shaanxi province. We saw her lying there, at the bottom of the creek bed. She was all bundled up, with one arm sticking out. She had been there a while, you could tell, because she had a little line of mold growing across her mouth and nostrils."

Death comes in another form, too: neglect. "It's female neglect, more than female infanticide, neglect to the point of death for little girls," says Scruggs of the U.N. Population Fund. "If you have a sick child, and it's a girl," he says, "you might buy only half the dose of medicine she needs to get better."

Hundreds of thousands of unregistered little girls—called "black children"—live on the edge of the law, unable to get food rations, immunizations or places in school. Many reports are grim. The government-run China News Service reported last year that the drowning of baby girls had revived to such an extent in Guangxi province that at least 1 million boys will be unable to find wives in 20 years. And partly because of the gender imbalance, the feudalistic practice of selling women has been revived.

The alarming growth of the flesh trade prompted authorities to enact a law in January that imposes jail sentences of up to 10 years and heavy fines for people caught trafficking. The government also recently began broadcasting a television dramatization to warn women against the practice. The public-service message shows two women, told that they would be given high-paying jobs, being lured to a suburban home. Instead, they are locked in a small, dark room, and soon realize that they have been sold.

LI WANGPING IS NERVOUS. SHE KEEPS looking at the air vents at the bottom of the office door, to see if anyone is walking by or, worse still, standing there listening. She rubs her hands together over and over. She speaks in a whisper. "I'm afraid to get into trouble talking to you," Li confides. She says nothing for a few minutes.

"After my son was born, I desperately wanted another baby," the 42-year-old woman finally begins. "I just wanted to have more children, you understand? Anyway, I got pregnant three times, because I wasn't using any birth control. I didn't want to use any. So, I had to have three abortions, one right after the other. I didn't want to at all. It was terrible killing the babies I wanted so much. But I had to."

By Chinese standards, Li (not her real name) has a lot to lose if she chooses to follow her maternal yearnings. As an office worker at government-owned CITIC, a successful and dynamic conglomerate, she has one of the best jobs in Beijing. Just being a city-dweller already puts her ahead of most of the population.

"One of my colleagues had just gotten fired for having a second child. I couldn't afford to be fired," continues Li, speaking in a meeting room at CITIC headquarters. "I had to keep everything secret from the family-planning official at CITIC, from everyone at the office. Of course, I'm supposed to be using birth control. I had to lie. It was hard lying, because I felt so bad about everything."

She rubs her hands furiously and moves toward the door, staring continuously at the air slats. "I have to go now. There's more to say, but I'm afraid to tell you. They could find me."

China's family-planning officials wield awesome powers, enforcing the policy through a combination of incentives and deterrents. For those who comply, there are job promotions and small cash awards. For those who resist, they suffer stiff fines and loss of job and status within the country's tightly knit and heavily regulated communities. The State Family Planning Commission is the government ministry entrusted with the tough task of curbing the growth of the world's most populous country, where 28 children are born every minute. It employs about 200,000 full-time officials and uses more than a million volunteers to check the fertility of hundreds of millions of Chinese women.

"Every village or enterprise has at least one family-planning official," says Zhang Xizhi, a birth-control official in Changping county outside Beijing. "Our main job is propaganda work to raise people's consciousness. We educate people and tell them their options for birth control. We go down to every household to talk to people. We encourage them to have only one child, to marry late, to have their child later."

China's population police frequently keep records of the menstrual cycles of women of childbearing age, on the type of birth control they use and the pending applications to have children. If they slip up, street committees—half-governmental, half-civilian organizations that have sprung up since the 1949 Communist takeover—take up the slack. The street committees, made up mostly of retired volunteers, act as the central government's ear to the ground, snooping, spying and reporting on citizens to the authorities.

When a couple wants to have a child—even their first, allotted one—they must apply to the family-planning office in their township or workplace, literally lining up to procreate. "If a woman gets pregnant without permission, she and her husband will get fined, even if it's their first," Zhang says. "It is fair to fine her, because she creates a burden on the whole society by jumping her place in line."

If a woman in Nanshao township, where Zhang works, becomes pregnant with a second child, she must terminate her pregnancy unless she or her husband or their first child is disabled or if both parents are only children. Her local family-planning official will repeatedly visit her at home to pressure her to comply. "Sometimes I have to go to people's homes five or six times to explain everything to them over and over to get them to have an abortion," says Zhang Cuiqing, the family-planning official for Sihe village, where there are 2,900 married women of childbearing age, of which 2,700 use some sort of birth control. Of those, 570 are sterilized and 1,100 have IUDs. Zhang recites the figures proudly, adding, "If they refuse, they will be fined between 20,000 and 50,000 yuan (U.S. $3,700 to $9,500)." The average yearly wage in Sihe is 1,500 yuan ($285).

The lack of early sexual education and unreliable IUDs are combining to make abortion—which is free, as are condoms and IUDs—a cornerstone of the one-child policy. Local officials are told not to use force, but rather education and persuasion, to meet their targets. However, the desire to fulfill their quotas, coupled with pressure from their bosses in Beijing, can lead to abuses by overzealous officials.

"Some local family-planning officials are running amok, because of the targets they have to reach," a Western health specialist says, "and there are a bunch of people willing to turn a blind eye to abuses because the target is so important."

The official Shanghai Legal Daily last year reported on a family-planning committee in central Sichuan province that ordered the flogging of the husbands of 10 pregnant women who refused to have abortions. According to the newspaper, the family-planning workers marched the husbands one by one into an empty room, ordered them to strip and lie on the floor and then beat them with a stick, once for every day their wives were pregnant.

"In some places, yes, things do happen," concedes Huang of the State Family Planning Commission. "Sometimes, family-planning officials do carry it too far."

THE YOUNG WOMAN LIES STILL ON THE narrow table with her eyes shut and her legs spread while the doctor quickly performs a suction abortion. A few moments, and the fetus is removed. The woman lets out a short, sharp yell. "OK, next," the doctor says.

She gets off the table and, holding a piece of cloth between her legs to catch the blood and clutching her swollen womb, hobbles over to a bed and collapses. The next patient gets up and walks toward the abortion table. No one notices a visitor watching. "It's very quick, it only takes about five minutes per abortion," says Dr. Huang Xiaomiao, chief physician at Beijing's Maternity Hospital. "No anesthetic. We don't use anesthetic for abortions or births here. Only for Cesarean sections, we use acupuncture."

Down the hall, 32-year-old Wu Guobin waits to be taken into the operating room to have her Fallopian tubes untied—a reversal of an earlier sterilization. "After my son was killed in an accident last year, the authorities in my province said I could try for another." In the bed next to Wu's, a dour-faced woman looks ready to cry. "She's getting sterilized," the nurse explains. "Her husband doesn't want her to, but her first child has mental problems."

Although it's a maternity hospital, the Family Planning Unit—where abortions, sterilizations, IUD insertions and the like are carried out—is the busiest department. "We do more abortions than births," says Dr. Fan Huimin, head of the unit. "Between 10 and 20 a day."

Abortions are a way of life in China, where about 10.5 million pregnancies are terminated each year. (In the United States, 1.6 million abortions are performed a year, but China's population is four to five times greater than the United States'.) One fetus is aborted for about every two children born and Chinese women often have several abortions. Usually, abortions are performed during the first trimester. But because some women resist, only to cave in under mental bullying further into their terms, abortions are also done in the later months of pregnancy, sometimes up till the eighth month.

Because of their population problem, the Chinese have become pioneers in contraceptive research. China will soon launch its own version of the controversial French abortion pill RU-486, which induces a miscarriage. They have perfected a non-scalpel procedure for male sterilization, with no suture required, allowing the man to "ride his bicycle home within five minutes." This year, the government plans to spend more than the $34 million it spent last year on contraception. The state will also buy some 961 million condoms to be distributed throughout the country, 11% more than in 1991.

But even with a family-planning policy that sends a chill down a Westerner's spine and touches every Chinese citizen's life, 64,000 babies are born every day in China and overpopulation continues to be a paramount national problem. Officials have warned that 24 million children will be born in 1992—a number just slightly less than the population of Canada. "The numbers are staggering," says Scruggs, the U.N. Population Fund official, noting that "170 million people will be added

in the 1990s, which is the current population of England, France and Italy combined. There are places in China where the land can't feed that many more people as it is."

China estimates that it has prevented 200 million births since the one-child policy was introduced. Women now are having an average of 2.4 children as compared to six in the late '60s. But the individual sacrifice demanded from every Chinese is immense.

Large billboards bombard the population with images of happy families with only one child. The government is desperately trying to convince the masses that producing only one child leads to a wealthier, healthier and happier life. But foreigners in China tell a different story, that the people aren't convinced. They tell of being routinely approached—on the markets, on the streets, on the railways—and asked about the contraceptive policies of their countries. Expatriate women in Beijing all tell stories of Chinese women enviously asking them how many sons they have and how many children they plan to have. They explain that they only have one child because the government allows them only one.

"When I'm out with my three children on the weekend," says a young American father who lives in Beijing, "people are always asking me why am I allowed to have three children. You can feel when they ask you that there is envy there. There's a natural disappointment among the people. They just want to have more children. But there's a resigned understanding, an acceptance that they just can't."

Religion, Belief, and Ritual

The anthropological interest in religion, belief, and ritual is not concerned with the scientific validity of such phenomena, but rather the way in which people relate various concepts of the supernatural to their everyday lives. With this practical perspective, some anthropologists have found that traditional spiritual healing is just as helpful in the treatment of illness as modern medicine, that voodoo is a form of social control, and that the ritual and spiritual preparation for playing the game of baseball can be just as important as spring training.

Every society is composed of feeling, thinking, and acting human beings who at one time or another are either conforming to or altering the social order into which they were born. Religion is an ideological framework that gives special legitimacy and validity to human experience within any given sociocultural system. In this way, monogamy as a marriage form or monarchy as a political form ceases to be simply one of many alternative ways in which a society can be organized, but becomes, for the believer, the only legitimate way. Religion renders certain human values and activities as sacred and inviolable. It is this mythic function that helps to explain the strong ideological attachments that some people have regardless of the scientific merits of their points of view.

While under some conditions religion may in fact be "the opiate of the masses," under other conditions such a belief system may be a rallying point for social and economic protest. A contemporary example of the former might be the "Moonies" (members of the Unification Church founded by Sun Myung Moon), while a good example of the latter is the role of the black church in the American civil rights movement, along with the prominence of such religious figures as Martin Luther King Jr. and Jesse Jackson.

A word of caution must be set forth concerning attempts to understand belief systems of other cultures. At times the prevailing attitude seems to be, "What I believe in is religion, and what you believe in is superstition." While anthropologists generally do not subscribe to this view, some tend to explain behavior that seems, on the surface, to be incomprehensible and impractical as some form of religious ritual. The articles in this unit should serve as a strong warning concerning the pitfalls of that approach.

"Psychotherapy in Africa" shows how important traditional belief systems, combined with community involvement, can be to the physical and psychological well-being of the individual. This perspective is so important that the treatment of illness is hindered without it. "The Mbuti Pygmies: Change and Adaptation" describes ritual that is subtle, informal, and yet absolutely necessary for social harmony and stability. The emphasis in the essay "The Secrets of Haiti's Living Dead" is upon both individual conformity and community solidarity.

Mystical beliefs and ritual are not absent from the modern world. "Rituals of Death" draws striking parallels between capital punishment in the United States and human sacrifice among the Aztecs of Mexico. "Body Ritual among the Nacirema" reveals that even our daily routines have mystic overtones. Finally, "Superstition and Ritual in American Baseball" examines the need for ritual and taboo in the "great American pastime."

In summary, the writings in this unit show religion, belief, and ritual in relationship to practical human affairs.

Looking Ahead: Challenge Questions

How can modern medicine be combined with traditional healing to take advantage of the best aspects of both?

In what respects do perceptions of disease affect treatment and recovery?

How does ritual contribute to a sense of personal security, individual responsibility, and social equality?

How has voodoo become such an important form of social control in rural Haiti?

In what ways can capital punishment be seen as a ritual with social functions?

In what ways are magic rituals practical and rational?

How do rituals and taboos get established in the first place?

How important are ritual and taboo in our modern industrial society?

sacrilege of killing. Yet they, the hunters, could not light the fire themselves. After all, they were already contaminated by death. Even youths, who daily joined the hunt at the edges, catching any game that escaped the nets, by hand, if they could, were not pure enough to invoke the spirits of forestness. But young children were uncontaminated, as yet untainted by contact with the original sin of the Mbuti. It was their responsibility to light the fire, and if it was not lit then the hunt would not take place, or as the Mbuti put it, the hunt *could* not take place.

In this way even the children in Mbuti society, at the first of the four age levels that dominate Mbuti social structure, are given very real social responsibility and see themselves as a part of that structure, by virtue of their purity. After all, they have just been born from the source of all purity, the forest itself. By the same reasoning, the elders, who are about to return to that ultimate source of all being, through death, are at least closer to purity than the adults, who are daily contaminated by killing. Elders no longer go on the hunt. So, like the children, the elders have important sacred ritual responsibilities in the Mbuti division of labor by age.

In the *bopi* the children play, but they have no "games" in the strict sense of the word. Levi-Strauss has perceptively compared games with rituals, suggesting that whereas in a game the players start theoretically equal but end up unequal, in a ritual just the reverse takes place. All are equalized. Mbuti children could be seen every day playing in the *bopi*, but not once did I see a game, not one activity that smacked of any kind of competition, except perhaps that competition that it is necessary for us all to feel from time to time, competition with our own private and personal inadequacies. One such pastime (rather than game) was tree climbing. A dozen or so children would climb up a young sapling. Reaching the top, their weight brought the sapling bending down until it almost touched the ground. Then all the children leapt off together, shrieking as the young tree sprang upright again with a rush. Sometimes one child, male or female, might stay on a

little too long, either out of fear, or out of bravado, or from sheer carelessness or bad timing. Whatever the reason, it was a lesson most children only needed to be taught once, for the result was that you got flung upward with the tree, and were lucky to escape with no more than a few bruises and a very bad fright.

Other pastimes taught the children the rules of hunting and gathering. Frequently elders, who stayed in camp when the hunt went off, called the children into the main camp and enacted a mock hunt with them there. Stretching a discarded piece of net across the camp, they pretended to be animals, showing the children how to drive them into the nets. And, of course, the children played house, learning the patterns of cooperation that would be necessary for them later in life. They also learned the prime lesson of egality, other than for purposes of division of labor making no distinction between male and female, this nuclear family or that. All in the *bopi* were *apua'i* to each other, and so they would remain throughout their lives. At every age level—childhood, youth, adulthood, or old age—everyone of that level is *apua'i* to all the others. Only adults sometimes (but so rarely that I think it was only done as a kind of joke, or possibly insult) made the distinction that the Bira do, using *apua'i* for male and *amua'i* for female. Male or female, for the Mbuti, if you are the same age you are *apua'i*, and that means that you share everything equally, regardless of kinship or gender.

YOUTH AND POLITICS

Sometime before the age of puberty boys or girls, whenever they feel ready, move back into the main camp from the *bopi* and join the youths. This is when they must assume new responsibilities, which for the youths are primarily political. Already, in the *bopi*, the children become involved in disputes, and are sometimes instrumental in settling them by ridicule, for nothing hurts an adult more than being ridiculed by children. The art of reason, however, is something they learn from the youths,

and it is the youths who apply the art of reason to the settlement of disputes.

When puberty comes it separates them, for the first time in their experience, from each other as *apua'i*. Very plainly girls are different from boys. When a girl has her first menstrual period the whole camp celebrates with the wild *elima* festival, in which the girl, and some of her chosen girl friends, are the center of all attention, living together in a special *elima* house. Male youths sit outside the *elima* house and wait for the girls to come out, usually in the afternoon, for the *elima* singing. They sing in antiphony, the girls leading, the boys responding. Boys come from neighboring territories all around, for this is a time of courtship. But there are always eligible youths within the camp as well, and the *elima* girl may well choose girls from other territories to come and join her, so there is more than enough excuse for every youth to carry on several flirtations, legitimate or illegitimate. I have known even first cousins to flirt with each other, but learned to be prudent enough not to pull out my kinship charts and point this out—well, not in public anyway.

The *elima* is more than a premarital festival, more than a joint initiation of youth into adulthood, and more than a rite of passage through puberty, though it is all those things. It is a public recognition of the opposition of male and female, and every *elima* is used to highlight the *potential* for conflict that lies in that opposition. As at other times of crisis, at puberty, a time of change and uncertainty, the Mbuti bring all the major forms of conflict out into the open. And the one that evidently most concerns them is the male/female opposition.

The adults begin to play a special form of "tug of war" that is clearly a ritual rather than a game. All the men are on one side, the women on the other. At first it looks like a game, but quickly it becomes clear that the objective is for *neither* side to win. As soon as the women begin to win, one of them will leave the end of the line and run around to join the men, assuming a deep male voice and in other ways ridicul-

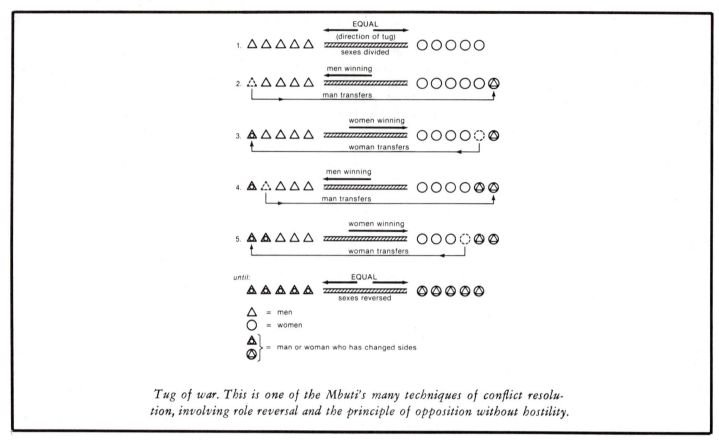

Tug of war. This is one of the Mbuti's many techniques of conflict resolution, involving role reversal and the principle of opposition without hostility.

ing manhood. Then, as the men begin to win, a male will similarly join the women, making fun of womanhood as he does so. Each adult on changing sides attempts to outdo all the others in ridiculing the opposite sex. Finally, when nearly all have switched sides, and sexes, the ritual battle between the genders simply collapses into hysterical laughter, the contestants letting go of the rope, falling onto the ground, and rolling over with mirth. Neither side wins, both are equalized very nicely, and each learns the essential lesson, that there should be *no* contest. . . .

the charm-box, before which the body rituals are conducted, will in some way protect the worshipper.

Beneath the charm-box is a small font. Each day every member of the family, in succession, enters the shrine room, bows his head before the charm-box, mingles different sorts of holy water in the font, and proceeds with a brief rite of ablution. The holy waters are secured from the Water Temple of the community, where the priests conduct elaborate ceremonies to make the liquid ritually pure.

In the hierarchy of magical practitioners, and below the medicine men in prestige, are specialists whose designation is best translated "holy-mouth-men." The Nacirema have an almost pathological horror and fascination with the mouth, the condition of which is believed to have a supernatural influence on all social relationships. Were it not for the rituals of the mouth, they believe that their teeth would fall out, their gums bleed, their jaws shrink, their friends desert them, and their lovers reject them. (They also belive that a strong relationship exists between oral and moral characteristics. For example, there is a ritual ablution of the mouth for children which is supposed to improve their moral fiber.)

The daily body ritual performed by everyone includes a mouth-rite. Despite the fact that these people are so punctilious about care of the mouth, this rite involves a practice which strikes the uninitiated stranger as revolting. It was reported to me that the ritual consists of inserting a small bundle of hog hairs into the mouth, along with certain magical powders, and then moving the bundle in a highly formalized series of gestures.

In addition to the private mouth-rite, the people seek out a holy-mouth-man once or twice a year. These practitioners have an impressive set of paraphernalia, consisting of a variety of augers, awls, probes, and prods. The use of these objects in the exorcism of the evils of the mouth involves almost unbelievable ritual torture of the client. The holy-mouth-man opens the client's mouth and, using the above mentioned tools, en-

larges any holes which decay may have created in the teeth. Magical materials are put into these holes. If there are no naturally occurring holes in the teeth, large sections of one or more teeth are gouged out so that the supernatural substance can be applied. In the client's view, the purpose of these ministrations is to arrest decay and to draw friends. The extremely sacred and traditional character of the rite is evident in the fact that the natives return to the holy-mouth-men year after year, despite the fact that their teeth continue to decay.

It is to be hoped that, when a thorough study of the Nacirema is made, there will be a careful inquiry into the personality structure of these people. One has but to watch the gleam in the eye of a holy-mouthman, as he jabs an awl into an exposed nerve, to suspect that a certain amount of sadism is involved. If this can be established, a very interesting pattern emerges, for most of the population shows definite masochistic tendencies. It was to these that Professor Linton referred in discussing a distinctive part of the daily body ritual which is performed only by men. This part of the rite involves scraping and lacerating the surface of the face with a sharp instrument. Special women's rites are performed only four times during each lunar month, but what they lack in frequency is made up in barbarity. As part of this ceremony, women bake their heads in small ovens for about an hour. The theoretically interesting point is that what seems to be a preponderantly masochistic people have developed sadistic specialists.

The medicine men have an imposing temple, or *latipso*, in every community of any size. The more elaborate ceremonies required to treat very sick patients can only be performed at this temple. These ceremonies involve not only the thaumaturge but a permanent group of vestal maidens who move sedately about the temple chambers in distinctive costume and headdress.

The *latipso* ceremonies are so harsh that it is phenomenal that a fair

proportion of the really sick natives who enter the temple ever recover. Small children whose indoctrination is still incomplete have been known to resist attempts to take them to the temple because "that is where you go to die." Despite this fact, sick adults are not only willing but eager to undergo the protracted ritual purification, if they can afford to do so. No matter how ill the supplicant or how grave the emergency, the guardians of many temples will not admit a client if he cannot give a rich gift to the custodian. Even after one has gained admission and survived the ceremonies, the guardians will not permit the neophyte to leave until he makes still another gift.

The supplicant entering the temple is first stripped of all his or her clothes. In every-day life the Nacirema avoids exposure of his body and its natural functions. Bathing and excretory acts are performed only in the secrecy of the household shrine, where they are ritualized as part of the body-rites. Psychological shock results from the fact that body secrecy is suddenly lost upon entry into the *latipso*. A man, whose own wife has never seen him in an excretory act, suddenly finds himself naked and assisted by a vestal maiden while he performs his natural functions into a sacred vessel. This sort of ceremonial treatment is necessitated by the fact that the excreta are used by a diviner to ascertain the course and nature of the client's sickness. Female clients, on the other hand, find their naked bodies are subjected to the scrutiny, manipulation and prodding of the medicine men.

Few supplicants in the temple are well enough to do anything but lie on their hard beds. The daily ceremonies, like the rites of the holy-mouth-men, involve discomfort and torture. With ritual precision, the vestals awaken their miserable charges each dawn and roll them about on their beds of pain while performing ablutions, in the formal movements of which the maidens are highly trained. At other times they insert magic wands in the supplicant's mouth or force him to eat substances which are supposed to be healing. From time to time the medicine men come to their clients and jab magically treated needles into their flesh. The fact that these temple ceremonies may not cure, and may even kill the neophyte, in no way decreases the people's faith in the medicine men.

There remains one other kind of practioner, known as a "listener." This witch-doctor has the power to exorcise the devils that lodge in the heads of people who have been bewitched. The Nacirema believe that parents bewitch their own children. Mothers are particularly suspected of putting a curse on children while teaching them the secret body rituals. The counter-magic of the witch-doctor is unusual in its lack of ritual. The patient simply tells the "listener" all his troubles and fears, beginning with the earliest difficulties he can remember. The memory displayed by the Nacirema in these exorcism sessions is truly remarkable. It is not uncommon for the patient to bemoan the rejection he felt upon being weaned as a babe, and a few individuals even see their troubles going back to the traumatic effects of their own birth.

In conclusion, mention must be made of certain practices which have their base in native esthetics but which depend upon the pervasive aversion to the natural body and its functions. There are ritual fasts to make fat people thin and ceremonial feasts to make thin people fat. Still other rites are used to make women's breasts large if they are small, and smaller if they are large. General dissatisfaction with breast shape is symbolized in the fact that the ideal form is virtually outside the range of human variation. A few women afflicted with almost inhuman hyper-mammary development are so idolized that they make a handsome living by simply going from village to village and permitting the natives to stare at them for a fee.

Reference has already been made to the fact that excretory functions are ritualized, routinized, and relegated to secrecy. Natural reproductive functions are similarly distorted. Intercourse is taboo as a topic and scheduled as an act. Efforts are made to avoid pregnancy by the use of magical materials or by limiting intercourse to certain phases of the moon. Conception is actually very infre-

quent. When pregnant, women dress so as to hide their condition. Parturition takes place in secret, without friends or relatives to assist, and the majority of women do not nurse their infants.

Our review of the ritual life of the Nacirema has certainly shown them to be a magic-ridden people. It is hard to understand how they have managed to exist so long under the burdens which they have imposed upon themselves. But even such exotic customs as these take on real meaning when they are viewed with the insight provided by Malinowski when he wrote (1948:70):

Looking from far and above, from our high places of safety in the developed civilization, it is easy to see all the crudity and irrelevance of magic. But without its power and guidance early man could not have mastered his practical difficulties as he has done, nor could man have advanced to the higher stages of civilization.

REFERENCES

Linton, Ralph. 1936. *The Study of Man*. New York, D. Appleton-Century Co.
Malinowski, Bronislaw. 1948. *Magic, Science, and Religion*. Glencoe, The Free Press.
Murdock, George P. 1949. *Social Structure*. New York, The Macmillan Co.

Superstition and Ritual in American Baseball

George Gmelch

George Gmelch teaches anthropology at Union College in Schenectady, New York. He has just completed a book on Caribbean migration, Double Passage, *from the University of Michigan Press. He is currently doing research for a book tentatively entitled* Culture Change and Professional Baseball in America: 1960–1990.

On each pitching day for the first three months of a winning season, Dennis Grossini, a pitcher on a Detroit Tiger farm team, arose from bed at exactly 10:00 A.M. At 1:00 P.M. he went to the nearest restaurant for two glasses of iced tea and a tuna fish sandwich. Although the afternoon was free he changed into the sweatshirt and supporter he wore during his last winning game, and one hour before the game he chewed a wad of Beech-Nut chewing tobacco. During the game he touched his letters (the team name on his uniform) after each pitch and straightened his cap after each ball. Before the start of each inning he replaced the pitcher's rosin bag next to the spot where it was the inning before. And after every inning in which he gave up a run, he would wash his hands.

I asked him which part of the ritual was most important. He responded, "You can't really tell what's most important so it all becomes important. I'd be afraid to change anything. As long

as I'm winning, I do everything the same. Even when I can't wash my hands (this would occur when he had to bat), it scares me going back to the mound. . . . I don't feel quite right."

Trobriand Islanders, according to anthropologist Bronislaw Malinowski, felt the same way about their fishing magic. Among the Trobrianders, fishing took two forms. In the inner lagoon fish were plentiful and there was little danger; on the open sea fishing was dangerous and yields varied widely. Malinowski found that magic was not used in lagoon fishing, where men could rely solely on their knowledge and skill. But when fishing on the open sea, Trobrianders used a great deal of magical ritual to ensure safety and increase their catch.

Baseball, the American national sport, is an arena in which the players behave remarkably like Malinowski's Trobriand fishermen. To professional baseball players, baseball is more than a game. It is an occupation. Since their livelihood depends on how well they perform, they use magic to try to control or eliminate the chance and uncertainty built into baseball.

To control uncertainty Chicago White Sox shortstop Ozzie Guillen doesn't wash his underclothes after a good game. The Boston Red Sox's Wade Boggs eats chicken before every game (that's 162 meals of chicken per year). Ex-San Francisco Giant pitcher Ron Bryant added a new stick of bubble gum to the collection in his bulging

back pocket after each game he won. Jim Ohms, my teammate on the Daytona Beach Islanders in 1966, used to put another penny in the pouch of his supporter after each win. Clanging against the hard plastic genital cup, the pennies made an audible sound as the pitcher ran the bases toward the end of a winning season.

Whether they are professional baseball players, Trobriand fishermen, soldiers, or farmers, people resort to magic in situations of chance, when they believe they have limited control over the success of their activities. In technologically advanced societies that pride themselves on a scientific approach to problem solving, as well as in simple societies, rituals of magic are common. Magic is a human attempt to impose order and certainty on a chaotic, uncertain situation. This attempt is irrational in that there is no causal connection between the instruments of magic and the desired consequences of the magical practice. But it is rational in that it creates in the practitioner a sense of confidence, competence, and control, which in turn is important to successfully executing a specific activity and achieving a desired result.

I have long had a close relationship with baseball, first as a participant and then as an observer. I devoted much of my youth to the game and played professionally as first baseman for five teams in the Detroit Tiger organization over three years. I also spent two years in the Quebec Provincial League. For

Originally appeared in *Elysian Fields Quarterly: The Baseball Review,* All Star Issue, 1992, Vol. 11, No. 3, pp. 25-36, P.O. Box 45618, Madison, WI 53744, 1-800-273-1444. © 1992 by George Gmelch. Reprinted by permission.

additional information about baseball magic I interviewed twenty-eight professional ballplayers and sportswriters.

There are three essential activities in baseball—pitching, hitting, and fielding. The first two, pitching and hitting, involve a great deal of chance and are comparable to the Trobriand fishermen's open sea; in them, players use magic and ritual to increase their chances for success. The third activity, fielding, involves little uncertainty and is similar to the Trobriander inner lagoon; fielders find it unnecessary to resort to magic.

The pitcher is the player least able to control the outcome of his own efforts. His best pitch may be hit for a home run, and his worst pitch may be hit directly into the hands of a fielder for an out or be swung at and missed for a third strike. He may limit the opposing team to a few hits yet lose the game, or he may give up a dozen hits and win. Frequently pitchers perform well and lose, and perform poorly and win. One has only to look at the frequency with which pitchers end a season with poor won-lost records but good earned run averages, or vice versa. For example, in 1990 Dwight Gooden gave up more runs per game than his teammate Sid Fernandez but had a won-lost record nearly twice as good. Gooden won nineteen games and lost only seven, one of the best in the National League, while Sid Fernandez won only nine games while losing fourteen. They pitched for the same team—the New York Mets—and therefore had the same fielders behind them. Regardless of how well he performs, on every outing the pitcher depends upon the proficiency of his teammates, the inefficiency of the opposition, and caprice.

An incredible example of bad luck in pitching occurred some years ago involving former Giant outfielder Willie Mays. Mays intentionally "dove for the dirt" to avoid being hit in the head by a fastball. While he was falling the ball hit his bat and went shooting down the left field line. Mays jumped up and ran, turning the play into a double. Players shook their heads in amazement—most players can't hit when they try to, but Mays couldn't avoid

hitting even when he tried not to. The pitcher looked on in disgust.

Hitting is also full of risk and uncertainty—Red Sox outfielder and Hall of Famer Ted Williams called it the most difficult single task in the world of sports. Consider the forces and time constraints operating against the batter. A fastball travels from the pitcher's mound to the batter's box, just sixty and one-half feet, in three to four tenths of a second. For only three feet of the journey, an absurdly short two-hundredths of a second, the ball is in a position where it can be hit. And to be hit well the ball must be neither too close to the batter's body nor too far from the "meat" of his bat. Any distraction, any slip of a muscle or change in stance, can throw a swing off. Once the ball is hit chance plays a large role in determining where it will go—into a waiting glove, whistling past a fielder's diving stab, or into the wide open spaces. While the pitcher who threw the fastball to Mays was suffering, Mays was collecting the benefits of luck.

Batters also suffer from the fear of being hit by a pitch—specifically, by a fastball that often travels at speeds exceeding ninety miles per hour. Throughout baseball history the great fastball pitchers like Sandy Koufax, Bob Gibson, Nolan Ryan, and Roger Clemens have thrived on this fear and on the level of distraction it causes hitters. The well-armed pitcher inevitably captures the advantage in the psychological war of nerves that characterizes the ongoing tension between pitcher and hitter, and that determines who wins and loses the game. If a hitter is crowding the plate in order to reach balls on the outside corner, or if the batter has been hitting unusually well, pitchers try to regain control of their territory. Indeed, many pitchers intentionally throw at or "dust" a batter in order to instill this sense of fear (what hitters euphemistically call "respect") in him. On one occasion Dock Ellis of the Pittsburgh Pirates, having become convinced that the Cincinnati Reds were dominating his team, intentionally hit the first three Reds batters he faced before his manager removed him from the game.

In fielding, on the other hand, the player has almost complete control over the outcome. Once a ball has been hit in his direction, no one can intervene and ruin his chances of catching it for an out. Infielders have approximately three seconds in which to judge the flight of the fall, field it cleanly, and throw it to first base. Outfielders have almost double that amount of time to track down a fly ball. The average fielding percentage (or success rate) of .975, compared with a .250 success rate for hitters (the average batting percentage), reflects the degree of certainty in fielding. Compared with the pitcher or the hitter, the fielder has little to worry about. He knows that in better than 9.7 times out of 10, he will execute his task flawlessly.

In keeping with Malinowski's hypothesis about the relationship between magic and uncertainty, my research shows that baseball players associate magic with hitting and pitching, but not with fielding. Despite the wide assortment of magic—which includes rituals, taboos, and fetishes—associated with both hitting and pitching, I have never observed any directly connected to fielding. In my experience I have known only one player, a shortstop with fielding problems, who reported any ritual even remotely connected with fielding.

The most common form of magic in professional baseball is personal ritual—a prescribed form of behavior that players scrupulously observe in an effort to ensure that things go their way. These rituals, like those of Malinowski's Trobriand fishermen, are performed in a routine, unemotional manner, much as players do nonmagical things to improve their play: rubbing pine tar on the hands to improve a grip on the bat, or rubbing a new ball to make it more comfortable and responsive to the pitcher's grip. Rituals are infinitely varied since ballplayers may formalize any activity that they consider important to performing well.

Rituals usually grow out of exceptionally good performances. When a player does well he seldom attributes his success to skill alone. Although his skill remains constant, he may go hit-less in one game and in the next get three or four hits. Many players attribute the inconsistencies in their performances to an object, item of food, or form of behavior outside their play. Through ritual, players seek to gain control over their performance. In the 1920s and 1930s sportswriters reported that a player who tripped en route to the field would often retrace his steps and carefully walk over the stumbling block for "insurance."

The word taboo comes from a Polynesian term meaning prohibition. Failure to observe a taboo or prohibition leads to undesirable consequences or bad luck. Most players observe a number of taboos. Taboos usually grow out of exceptionally poor performances, which players often attribute to a particular behavior or food. Certain uniform numbers may become taboo. If a player has a poor spring training season or an unsuccessful year, he may refuse to wear the same number again. During my first season of professional baseball I ate pancakes before a game in which I struck out four times. Several weeks later I had a repeat performance, again after eating pancakes. The result was a pancake taboo—I never ate pancakes during the season from that day on. Another personal taboo, against holding a baseball during the national anthem (the usual practice for first basemen, who must warm up the other infielders), had a similar origin.

In earlier decades some baseball players believed that it was bad luck to go back and fasten a missed buttonhole after dressing for a game. They simply left missed buttons on shirts or pants undone. This taboo is not practiced by modern ballplayers.

Fetishes or charms are material objects believed to embody supernatural powers that aid or protect the owner. Good luck fetishes are standard equipment for many ballplayers. They include a wide assortment of objects: horsehide covers from old baseballs, coins, crucifixes, and old bats. Ordinary objects acquire power by being connected to exceptionally hot batting or pitching streaks, especially ones in which players get all the breaks. The

object is often a new possession or something a player finds and holds responsible for his new good fortune. A player who is in a slump might find a coin or an odd stone just before he begins a hitting streak, attribute an improvement in his performance to the influence of the new object, and regard it as a fetish.

While playing for Spokane, a Dodger farm team, Alan Foster forgot his baseball shoes on a road trip and borrowed a pair from a teammate. That night he pitched a no-hitter, which he attributed to the borrowed shoes. After he bought them from his teammate, they became a prized possession.

During World War II American soldiers used fetishes in much the same way. Social psychologist Samuel Stouffer and his colleagues found that in the face of great danger and uncertainty, soldiers developed magical practices, particularly the use of protective amulets and good-luck charms (crosses, Bibles, rabbits' feet, medals), and jealously guarded articles of clothing they associated with past experiences of escape from danger. Stouffer also found that prebattle preparations were carried out in a fixed "ritual" order, much as ballplayers prepare for a game.

Because most pitchers play only once every four days, they perform rituals less frequently than hitters. The rituals they do perform, however, are just as important. A pitcher cannot make up for a poor performance the next day, and having to wait three days to redeem oneself can be miserable. Moreover, the team's win or loss depends more on the performance of the pitcher than on any other single player. Considering the pressures to do well, it is not surprising that pitchers' rituals are often more complex than those of hitters.

A seventeen-game winner in the Texas Rangers organization, Mike Griffin begins his ritual preparation a full day before he pitches, by washing his hair. The next day, although he does not consider himself superstitious, he eats bacon for lunch. When Griffin dresses for the game he puts on his clothes in the same order, making certain he puts the slightly longer of his

two outer, or "stirrup," socks on his right leg. "I just wouldn't feel right mentally if I did it the other way around," he explains. He always wears the same shirt under his uniform on the day he pitches. During the game he takes off his cap after each pitch, and between innings he sits in the same place on the dugout bench.

Tug McGraw, formerly a relief pitcher for the Phillies, slapped his thigh with his glove with each step he took leaving the mound at the end of an inning. This began as a means of saying hello to his wife in the stands, but it then became ritual as McGraw slapped his thigh whether his wife was there or not.

Many of the rituals pitchers engage in—tugging their caps between pitches, touching the rosin bag after each bad pitch, smoothing the dirt on the mound before each new batter or inning—take place on the field. Most baseball fans observe this behavior regularly, never realizing that it may be as important to the pitcher as actually throwing the ball.

Uniform numbers have special significance for some pitchers. Many have a lucky number which they request. Since the choice is usually limited, pitchers may try to get a number that at least contains their lucky number, such as fourteen, four, thirty-four, or forty-four for the pitcher whose lucky number is four. Oddly enough, there is no consensus about the effect of wearing number thirteen. Some pitchers will not wear it; others such as the Mets' David Cone and Oakland's John "Blue Moon" Odom prefer it. (During a pitching slump, however, Odom asked for a new number. Later he switched back to thirteen.)

The way in which number preferences emerge varies. Occasionally a pitcher requests the number of a former professional star, hoping that—in a form of imitative magic—it will bring him the same measure of success. Or he may request a favorite number that he has always associated with good luck. Vida Blue, former Athletic and Giant, changed his uniform number from thirty-five to fourteen, the number he wore as a high-school quarterback. When the new number did not produce the better pitching performance he was looking for, he switched back to his old number.

One of the sources of his good fortune, Blue believed, was the baseball hat he had worn—since 1974. Several American League umpires refused to let him wear the faded and soiled cap. When Blue persisted he was threatened with a fine and suspension from a game. Finally he conceded, but not before he ceremoniously burned the hat on the field before a game. On the days they are scheduled to appear, many pitchers avoid activities that they believe sap their strength and therefore detract from their effectiveness, or that they otherwise generally link with poor performance. (Many pitchers avoid eating certain foods on their pitching days; actually, some food taboos make good physiological sense). Some pitchers do not shave on the day of a game. In fact, Oakland's Dave Stewart and St. Louis's Todd Worrell don't shave as long as they are winning. Early in the 1989 season Stewart had six consecutive victories and a beard before he finally lost. Ex-St. Louis Cardinal Al Hrabosky took this taboo to extreme lengths; Samsonlike, he refused to cut his hair or beard during the entire season—hence part of the reason for his nickname, the "Mad Hungarian." Many hitters go through a series of preparatory rituals before stepping into the batter's box. These include tugging on their caps, touching their uniform letters or medallions, crossing themselves, tapping or bouncing the bat on the plate, swinging the weighted warm-up bat a prescribed number of times, and smoothing the dirt in the box.

There were more than a dozen individual elements in the batting ritual of Mike Hargrove, former Cleveland Indian first baseman. And after each pitch he would step out of the batter's box and repeat the entire sequence. His rituals were so time consuming that he was called "the human rain delay."

Clothing, both the choice of clothes and the order in which they are put on, is often ritualized. During a batting streak many players wear the same clothes and uniforms for each game and put them on in exactly the same order. Once I changed sweatshirts midway through the game for seven consecutive games to keep a hitting streak going. During a sixteen-game winning streak in 1954, the New York Giants wore the same clothes in each game and refused to let them be cleaned for fear that their good fortune might be washed away with the dirt. Taking this ritual to the extreme, Leo Durocher, managing the Brooklyn Dodgers to a pennant in 1941, spent three and a half weeks in the same black shoes, gray slacks, blue coat, and knitted blue tie.

The opposite may also occur. Several of the Oakland A's players bought new street clothing in an attempt to break a fourteen-game losing streak. Most players, however, single out one or two lucky articles or quirks of dress rather than ritualizing all items of clothing. After hitting two home runs in a game, infielder Jim Davenport of the San Francisco Giants discovered that he had missed a buttonhole while dressing for the game. For the remainder of his career he left the same button undone.

A popular ritual associated with hitting is tagging a base when leaving and returning to the dugout during each inning. Mickey Mantle was in the habit of tagging second base on the way to or from the outfield. During a successful month of the season, one player stepped on third base on his way to the dugout after the third, sixth, and ninth innings of each game. Asked if he ever purposely failed to step on the bag, he replied, "Never! I wouldn't dare. It would destroy my confidence to hit." A hitter who is playing poorly may try different combinations of tagging and not tagging particular bases in an attempt to find a successful combination.

When their players are not hitting some managers will rattle the bat bin, the large wooden box containing the team's bats, as if the bats were in a stupor and could be aroused by a good shaking. Similarly, some hitters rub their hands along the handles of the bats protruding from the bin, presumably in hopes of picking up some power or luck from bats that are getting hits for their owners.

There is a taboo against crossing bats, against permitting one bat to rest on top of another. Although this superstition appears to be dying out among ballplayers today, it was religiously observed by some of my teammates. And in some cases it was elaborated even further. One former Detroit minor leaguer became quite annoyed when a teammate tossed a bat from the batting cage and it landed on top of his bat. Later he explained that the top bat might steal hits from the lower one. In his view, bats contained a finite number of hits, a sort of baseball "image of limited good." For Pirate shortstop Honus Wagner, a charter member of baseball's Hall of Fame, each bat contained only a certain number of hits, and never more than 100. Regardless of the quality of the bat, he would discard it after its 100th hit.

Hall of Famer Johnny Evers, of the Cub double-play trio Tinker to Evers to Chance, believed in saving his luck. If he was hitting well in practice, he would suddenly stop and retire to the bench to "save" his batting for the game. One player told me that many of his teammates on the Asheville Tourists in the Class A Western Carolinas League would not let pitchers touch or swing their bats, not even to loosen up. The traditionally poor-hitting pitchers were believed to pollute or weaken the bats.

Food often forms part of a hitter's ritual repertoire. Eating certain foods before a game is supposed to give the ball "eyes," that is, the ability to seek the gaps between fielders after being hit. In hopes of maintaining a batting streak I once ate chicken every day at 4:00 P.M. until the streak ended. Yankee catcher Jim Leyritz eats turkey before every game. Hitters, like pitchers, also avoid certain foods that are believed to sap their strength during the game.

There are other examples of hitters' ritualized behavior. I once kept my eyes closed during the national anthem in an effort to prolong a batting streak. A friend of mine refused to read anything on the day of a game because he believed that reading weakened his eyesight when batting.

These are personal taboos. There are some taboos, however, that all players hold and that do not develop out of individual experiences or misfortunes. These taboos are learned, some as early as Little League. Mentioning a no-hitter while one is in progress is a widely known example. It is believed that if a pitcher hears the words "no-hitter," the spell will be broken and the no-hitter lost. This taboo is still observed by many sports broadcasters, who use various linguistic subterfuges to inform their listeners that the pitcher had not given up a hit, never mentioning "no-hitter."

But superstitions, like most everything else, change over time. Many of the rituals and beliefs of early baseball are no longer remembered. A century ago players spent time off the field and on looking for items that would bring them luck. For example, to find a hairpin on the street assured a batter of hitting safely in that day's game (today women don't wear hairpins—a good reason why the belief has died out). To catch sight of a white horse or a wagonload of barrels were also good omens. In 1904 the manager of the New York Giants, John McGraw, hired a driver and a team of white horses to drive past the Polo Grounds around the time his players were arriving at the ballpark. He knew that if his players saw white horses they'd have more confidence and that could only help them play better. Belief in the power of white horses survived in a few backwaters until the 1960s. A gray haired manager of a team I played for in Quebec would drive around the countryside before important games and during the playoffs looking for a white horse. When he was successful, he'd announce it to everyone in the clubhouse before the game.

Today most professional baseball coaches or managers will not step on the chalk foul lines when going onto the field to talk to their pitcher. Detroit's manager Sparky Anderson jumps over the line. Others follow a different ritual. They intentionally step on the lines when they are going to take a pitcher out of a game.

How do these rituals and taboos get established in the first place? B. F. Skinner's early research with pigeons provides a clue. Like human beings, pigeons quickly learn to associate their behavior with rewards or punishment. By rewarding the birds at the appropriate time, Skinner taught them such elaborate games as table tennis, miniature bowling, or to play simple tunes on a toy piano.

On one occasion he decided to see what would happen if pigeons were rewarded with food pellets every fifteen seconds, regardless of what they did. He found the birds tended to associate the arrival of the food with a particular action—tucking the head under a wing, hopping from side to side, or turning in a clockwise direction. About ten seconds after the arrival of the last pellet, a bird would begin doing whatever it had associated with getting the food and keep it up until the next pellet arrived.

In the same way, baseball players tend to believe there is a causal connection between two events that are linked only temporally. If a superstitious player touches his crucifix and then gets a hit, he may decide the gesture was responsible for his good fortune and follow the same ritual the next time he comes to the plate. If he should get another hit, the chances are good that he will begin touching the crucifix each time he bats and that he will do so whether or not he hits safely each time.

The average batter hits safely approximately one quarter of the time. And if the behavior of Skinner's pigeons—or of gamblers at a Las Vegas slot machine—is any guide, that is more often than necessary to keep him believing in a ritual. Skinner found that once a pigeon associated one of its actions with the arrival of food or water, sporadic rewards would keep the connection going. One pigeon, apparently believing that hopping from side to side brought pellets into its feeding cup, hopped ten thousand times without a pellet before it gave up.

Since the batter associates his hits at least in some degree with his ritual touching of a crucifix, each hit he gets reinforces the strength of the ritual. Even if he falls into a batting slump and the hits temporarily stop, he will persist in touching the crucifix in the hope that this will change his luck.

Skinner's and Malinowski's explanations are not contradictory. Skinner focuses on how the individual comes to develop and maintain a particular ritual, taboo, or fetish. Malinowski focuses on why human beings turn to magic in precarious or uncertain situations. In their attempts to gain greater control over their performance, baseball players respond to chance and uncertainty in the same way as do people in simple societies. It is wrong to assume that magical practices are a waste of time for either group. The magic in baseball obviously does not make a pitch travel faster or more accurately, or a batted ball seek the gaps between fielders. Nor does the Trobriand brand of magic make the surrounding seas calmer and more abundant with fish. But both kinds of magic give their practitioners a sense of control—and an important element in any endeavor is confidence. —EFQ

An earlier version of this essay was originally published in *Human Nature* magazine. This version is printed with permission of the author.

Sociocultural Change: The Impact of the West

The origins of academic anthropology lie in the colonial and imperial ventures of the nineteenth and twentieth centuries. During these periods, many people of the world were brought into a relationship with Europe and the United States that was usually exploitative and often socially and culturally disruptive. For almost a century, anthropologists have witnessed this process and the transformations that have taken place in those social and cultural systems brought under the umbrella of a world economic order. Early anthropological studies—even those widely regarded as pure research—directly or indirectly served colonial interests. Many anthropologists certainly believed that they were extending the benefits of Western technology and society while preserving the cultural rights of those people whom they studied. But representatives of poor nations challenge this view and are far less generous in describing the past role of the anthropologist. Most contemporary anthropologists, however, have a deep moral commitment to defending the legal, political, and economic rights of the people with whom they work.

When anthropologists discuss social change, they usually mean change brought about in preindustrial societies through long-standing interaction with the nation-states of the industrialized world. In early anthropology, contact between the West and the remainder of the world was characterized by the terms "acculturation" and "culture contact." These terms were used to describe the diffusion of cultural traits between the developed and less-developed countries. Often this was analyzed as a one-way process in which cultures of the Third World were seen, for better or worse, as receptacles for Western cultural traits. Nowadays, many anthropologists believe that the diffusion of cultural traits across social, political, and economic boundaries was emphasized at the expense of the real issues of dominance, subordinance, and dependence that characterized the colonial experience. Just as importantly, many anthropologists recognize that the present-day forms of cultural, economic, and political interaction between the developed and the so-called underdeveloped world are best characterized as neocolonial.

Most of the authors represented in this unit take the perspective that anthropology should be critical as well as descriptive. They raise questions about cultural contact and subsequent economic and social disruption. (This is demonstrated best in the essays "Pastoralism and the Demise of Communal Property in Tanzania" and "Paavahu and Paanaqawu: The Wellsprings of Life and the Slurry of Death.")

In keeping with the notion that the negative impact of the West on traditional cultures began with colonial domination, this unit opens with "Heart of Darkness, Heart of Light," "Why Can't People Feed Themselves?" and "The Arrow of Disease." These articles show that "progress" for the West has often meant poverty, hunger, and death for traditional peoples.

The following essays emphasize a different aspect of culture affected by the impact of the West. The article "Growing Up as a Fore" points to the problems of maintaining individual identity in a changing society. "Last Chance for First Peoples" helps us to understand that traditional peoples are not the only losers in the process of cultural destruction. All of humanity stands to suffer as a vast store of human knowledge, embodied in tribal subsistence practices, medicine, and folklore, is obliterated, in a manner not unlike the burning of the library of Alexandria 1,600 years ago.

Finally, on a positive note, the essay "From Hammock to Health" shows one way to maintain a cultural heritage while accommodating to the exigencies of social change.

Looking Ahead: Challenge Questions

What is a subsistence system?

What have been the effects of colonialism on formerly subsistence-oriented socioeconomic systems?

How do cash crops inevitably lead to class distinctions and poverty?

How can a nation with great ethnic diversity prevent a democracy from becoming a tyranny of the majority?

How can one nation help another without being ethnocentric?

What was it about their culture that made the Fore people so vulnerable to the harmful effects of the change from a subsistence economy to a cash crop economy?

In what ways are traditional peoples struggling to maintain their cultures?

What ethical obligations do industrial societies have toward respecting the human rights and cultural diversity of traditional communities?

What ecological lessons should we be learning from the past?

What happened to Easter Island civilization?

Heart of Darkness, Heart of Light

The Saga of Alvar Núñez Cabeza de Vaca, the First American

Michael Ventura

Michael Ventura's most recent novel is "The Zoo Where You're Fed to God" (Simon & Schuster).

Alvar Núñez Cabeza de Vaca was and is a dangerous man. Not because he was violent (for he is perhaps the gentlest person of the American saga), but because he stands as a challenge to our reflexive beliefs and our tidy categories. Though he was the first European on record to spend significant time in North America, and the first to write a book about this land, even most well-educated people haven't heard of him because his story is too strange, too disturbing to be taught in schools. To encounter him is to encounter our own limits and possibilities. To tell his story is to challenge our taboos. To invoke his time is to reveal our own.

Cabeza de Vaca was born in 1490 and died in 1557. To Americans, whose sense of the past fades every year, he can't help but seem remote. The media constantly enshrine the cliché that our era has seen the greatest change in human history, but judge for yourself whether or not the changes in Cabeza de Vaca's lifetime were equally transformative:

Columbus discovered the Americas for Europe, beginning the greatest mass migration the world has ever seen (a migration that created no less than,

at present, 45 new nations and protectorates in the Americas alone); 800,000 Jews were expelled from Spain; Cortés conquered the Aztecs of Mexico and Pizarro the Incas of Peru, ending two civilizations; Michelangelo painted the ceiling of the Sistine Chapel; Leonardo da Vinci made the Mona Lisa; the painters Hieronymus Bosch, Dürer, Raphael, Titian and Bruegel were active; the first modern clock was built; the first pawnshop was opened; the first political cartoon was drawn; the German priest Martin Luther and the English King Henry VIII broke from the Church of Rome, ending 1,500 years of Roman domination; Machiavelli wrote "The Prince," initiating the modern view of politics; Copernicus developed the theory of the solar system—the first huge step in modern scientific development; the slave trade began, and with it the destruction of millennia of African traditions; the first insurance policies were written; Queen Elizabeth I was born; the first theory of germs was formulated; the first game of billiards was played; the Spanish Inquisition burned Protestants as heretics, and Nostradamus wrote his prophecies.

So Cabeza de Vaca lived as we live, in that his was a time when the certainties of many centuries suddenly dissolved. Like many of us, when he tried to fit into his time, he became something he never expected to become.

And like us, he lived in an era of gruesome, widespread violence, much

of which he saw firsthand. In 1512, at the age of 22, he was a soldier at the Battle of Ravenna, where 20,000 men were killed. He continued soldiering with distinction until, in 1527, at the advanced age of 37 (the average European life span was only about 40), he was respected enough to be appointed second-in-command to Pámfilo de Narváez for what was supposed to be the conquest of Florida.

Narváez was a vicious soul. Red-bearded and one-eyed, as governor of Cuba he had won the approval of his king (and the clout to mount this expedition) by such acts as ordering his men to slaughter 2,500 Indians who had come bringing them food. The fact that Cabeza de Vaca accepted a commission with such a killer tells us that he was quite willing to be your average murderous Spanish conquistador.

But he quickly revealed himself to be something more. The memoir he left us is called, in Spanish, "La Relación"; the most accessible American translation is titled "Cabeza de Vaca's Adventures in the Unknown Interior of America" (University of New Mexico Press). In it, he details an incident in Cuba in the summer of 1527: Narváez and he, with five ships and 460 men, were gathering provisions for the conquest of Florida. But a great storm came up.

"All the houses and churches went down," he wrote in the first published description of a West Indies hurricane. "We had to walk seven or eight together, locking arms to keep from being blown away. Walking in the woods gave us as much fear as the tumbling houses, for the trees were falling, too, and could have killed us. We wandered all night in this raging tempest. . . . Particularly from midnight on, we heard a great roaring and the sound of many voices, of little bells, also flutes, tambourines, and other instruments, most of which lasted till morning, when the storm ceased."

What was this music in the storm? A writer's touch? What literary critics call "magical realism"? From novelists like Gabriel García Márquez we expect flutes and voices on the winds, but Cabeza de Vaca was not a novelist; he was writing what he considered a factual account. He was aware that this and much else in his narrative would be hard to believe. "La Relación" is addressed to the King of Spain—Cabeza de Vaca's commander-in-chief, as we would say. He cautioned his king from the first page: "I have written very exactly. Novel or, for some persons, difficult to believe though the things narrated may be, I assure you they can be accepted without hesitation as strictly factual."

Most of us don't hear music in storms, and science would not only doubt but also scoff at the possibility. Let's say, then, that the music was in Cabeza de Vaca's head—which doesn't necessarily mean that he was crazy. His record of endurance and clear-headedness argues against that. Rather, his hurricane story shows that, in extreme situations, some strange inner sense opened in him. Catastrophes that caused others to go rigid with fear caused Cabeza de Vaca to experience a deepened, wild, even spiritual awareness. In the midst of a hurricane, and while fighting for his life, he could hear music.

This is the signature of the man. Even this early in his tale you can begin to see why he isn't taught much in classrooms. Few teachers want to deal with questions—from students or from contentious school boards—about guys who hear flutes in the wind.

The Narváez expedition finally reached the west coast of Florida in

1528. Drive that country now and all you see is a mall, a housing development, a mall, a mall, a development, a mall—on and on. Cabeza de Vaca, in his day, saw "immense trees and open woods," "three kinds of deer," "bears and lions [cougars]," a profusion of birds.

Florida was lush, but there wasn't much to conquer. Its small tribes were primitive, apprehensive and hostile. They possessed nothing that any European would want to steal. Yet they were no fools. Fearing the Spaniards and eager to see them leave, they told grand lies about rich tribes inland and to the north—lies that Pámfilo de Narváez was eager to believe. Here he made the disastrous decision to split his forces: The infantry and cavalry would explore inland while the ships headed up the coast, to rendezvous later. Cabeza de Vaca was furious. Even in known territory the tactic was foolish; in unknown territory, it was mad. The land force could be lost forever.

Narváez called Cabeza de Vaca a coward and ordered him to remain with the ships. He refused, writing later: "I would rather hazard the danger that lay ahead in the interior than give any occasion for questioning my honor by remaining safely aboard behind." This man who heard music in the wind cared more about his honor than his life.

If we allow the possibility that Cabeza de Vaca's music in the wind showed an aptitude for spirituality rather than, as they say now, "disassociative tendencies," then we're beginning to see a rare breed of the spiritual man: not a meditator, a recluse or a teacher; not a priest, an evangel or a mild or wild man; but a man of action, a decisive man with classical notions of honor who, if he heard music in the wind, simply said so. And if his comrades were going to their doom, he tried to dissuade them, but when he could not dissuade, he stood with them.

Native Americans have such models in their history, visionary warriors like Cochise, Geronimo and Crazy Horse. But it is hard to think of another European-American with these particular dimensions—as though we admire these

qualities in others but are afraid to admit them in ourselves. Again we see why Cabeza de Vaca is a stranger to our textbooks. History is always taught as a reflection of the present, and he is more paradoxical than we want to believe we are.

It happened as Cabeza de Vaca feared it would. Narváez, with Cabeza de Vaca still second-in-command, got lost inland and couldn't find his ships. The terrain supplied little food, and the Spaniards could hardly hunt because they had to conserve their scarce ammunition for Indians who attacked guerrilla-style, killing many. Disease killed many more. Those who survived were exhausted and ill, and almost all (including Cabeza de Vaca) had been wounded. "You can imagine what it would be like," he wrote, "in a strange, remote land, destitute of means either to remain or to get out."

In a cove of what is now called Apalachicola Bay, on the west coast of Florida, they decided to build barges and try to make it around the coast toward the Río Grande, hoping to find the Spaniards in Mexico. Narváez picked the strongest men for his raft and said that it was every man for himself. His stronger men paddled swiftly away—and that's the last anyone ever saw of Narváez. Cabeza de Vaca was now in command.

They followed the coast as well as they could in bad weather, around the Florida Panhandle and to the waters of the Mississippi River near what is now New Orleans. They were the first Europeans to see the Mississippi, and Cabeza de Vaca was the first to write of it. They continued at the mercy of storms until they beached on what they called the Island of Doom, what is now Galveston, Tex. On the voyage, many died of hunger, thirst and disease. Remembering their state shortly before landfall, Cabeza de Vaca revealed his uncommon endurance when he wrote that "not five could stand. When night fell, only the navigator and I remained able to tend the barge."

When they landed on Galveston Island, they were "so emaciated we could easily count every bone and looked the very picture of death."

And now the story takes a turn. Indians came upon them. "Whatever their stature, they looked like giants to us in our fright. We could not hope to defend ourselves." What happened went against all expectations and stereotypes. "The Indians, understanding our full plight, sat down and lamented for half an hour so loudly they could have been heard a long way off. It was amazing to see these wild, untaught savages howling like brutes in compassion for us."

They had come to change the land, but the land changed them. This doesn't fit the prevailing heroic vision of Westerners.

By now, there were only about 80 survivors. The Indians cared for them. From this point on Cabeza de Vaca called his people "the Christians," to differentiate them from the pagan Indians. Here he recorded the first known cannibalism in North America: "Five Christians," cut off from the others on the coast, "came to the extremity of eating each other. . . . The Indians were so shocked at this cannibalism that, if they had seen it sometime earlier, they surely would have killed every one of us. In a very short while as it was, only 15 of the 80 who had come survived. . . . Then half the natives died from a disease of the bowels . . . and blamed us."

The Indians were probably right. The Spaniards had communicated the diseases they were dying of. We should pause for a moment. Imagine yourself one of those Indians, with half the people you've known all your life dead within days. Not surprisingly, the surviving Indians sought to kill the Spaniards. "When they came to kill us, the Indian who kept me interceded. He said: If we had so much power of sorcery we would not have let all but a few of our own perish."

It speaks of the stature of these Indians that, amid all this grief and death, one person had the power to reason and others had the capacity to listen. The Spaniards were not only spared but also tended to. Cabeza de Vaca had come to conquer Indians. Now he owed his life to one. For the remainder of his eight years in North America, he would never kill, or even fight, another Indian. (A century later, Puritans, whom Indians saved from starvation on Thanksgiving Day would have no such compunctions.)

Time passed. The Spaniards, with no means to leave, lived among the Capoques and the Han tribes. Then things took another extraordinary turn. Cabeza de Vaca relates wryly that the Indians "wanted to make physicians of us without examination or a review of diplomas."

"Their method of cure," he relates, "is to blow on the sick, the breath and the laying-on of hands supposedly casting out the infirmity. They insisted we should do this too and be of some use to them. We scoffed at their cures and at the idea that we knew how to heal." The dialogue between Cabeza de Vaca (who could now speak the tribal language) and the Indians was apparently intense. "An Indian [probably a medicine man] told me I knew not whereof I spoke in saying their methods had no effect." The Indians denied them food until the Spaniards complied with their request. "Hunger forced us to obey, but disclaiming any responsibility for our failure or success."

They had come to subdue, and now they were commanded to heal. Not only was it a complete reversal of roles, it presented a sticky theological problem. According to their religion, if these Spanish Catholics practiced paganism, they would lose their souls; but according to the Indians, if they did nothing they'd lose their lives. And what if the attempt failed? Then, too, they might lose their lives. So they added Catholicism to the ceremony. "Our method . . . was to bless the sick, breathe upon them, recite a paternoster and Ave María and pray earnestly to God our Lord for their recovery."

No one was more surprised than Cabeza de Vaca when their method worked.

Here Cabeza de Vaca passes the point where history is prepared to accept him. He ceases to be a conquistador, ceases even to be an explorer, and enters what Joseph Conrad called "the heart of darkness"—by which Conrad meant a realm of the psyche in which civilized certitudes collapse. But Cabeza de Vaca, as we shall see, might have called the same realm "the heart of light."

More time passed, the Spanish healers became ill again. At this, the tribes lost faith in their healing and treated them harshly. "My life had become unbearable. . . . In addition to much other work, I had to grub roots in the water or from underground in the canebrakes. . . . The broken canes often slashed my flesh; I had to work amid them without benefit of clothes." This proud Spanish soldier, so devoted to his own honor, had become a naked slave. Yet note how he writes of this slavery with pain but no bitterness, no anger, no blame. You cannot find in this narrative one disrespectful word about his captors—without whom, after all, he would have long since died. Again, it's as though catastrophe somehow freed him. He accepted the blows of fate without succumbing to them.

More years passed, with many hardships, adventures and deaths. Some Spaniards were killed only because an Indian had bad dreams about them. (The Indians sometimes killed each other this way, too.) Finally, of the 80 who made it to Galveston Island, only four remained: Cabeza de Vaca, Alonso del Castillo, Andrés Dorantes and Dorantes' slave, the first black man to set foot in what is now the United States, a Moroccan Moor converted to Christianity named Estevánico. (Our African American history begins with this man, nearly a century before the Pilgrims.)

After much planning and many disappointments, in the autumn of 1534 they escaped the tribes that held them as slaves and made their way west. Now they were taken in by a tribe in the vicinity of Austin and San Antonio.

"They lodged Dorantes and the Negro in the house of one medicine man, and Castillo and me in that of another."

This is a significant sentence. They had become the province not of the chiefs or the tribe as a whole, but of the shamans. These Indians had "heard of us and the wonders [healings] our Lord worked by us." Note that this tribe threatened neither violence nor enslavement. We should also remember that by now these Christians didn't look like Europeans. They wore what Indians wore, could live off the land like the Indians and speak their languages.

They had come to change the land, but the land had changed them. This, too, doesn't fit the prevailing heroic vision of Westerners as people who molded the wilderness with their own desires. By this point in Cabeza de Vaca's journey, heroism consisted of something very different: the ability to survive on the land's own terms.

"The very evening of our arrival, some Indians came to Castillo begging him to cure them of terrible headaches." Castillo prayed over them, and they claimed to be healed. And here follows the most amazing passage of Cabeza de Vaca's narrative:

"Since the Indians all through the region talked only of the wonders which God our Lord worked through us, individuals sought us from many parts in hopes of healing. The evening of the second day after our arrival . . . some of the Susolas came to us and pressed Castillo to go treat their ailing kinsmen—one wounded, the others sick and, among them, a fellow very near his end. Castillo happened to be a timid practitioner—the more so, the more serious and dangerous the case—feeling that his sins would weigh and some day impede his performing cures. The Indians urged me to go heal them. . . . So I had to go with them. Dorantes brought Estevánico and accompanied me. As we drew near the huts of the afflicted, I saw that the man we hoped to save was dead: . . . I found his eyes rolled up, his pulse gone, and every appearance of death, as Dorantes agreed. Taking off the mat that covered him, I supplicated our Lord in his behalf and in behalf of the rest who ailed, as fervently as I could . . . blessing and breathing on him many times. . . .

"The natives then took me to treat many others, who had fallen into a stupor. . . . When [we] got back that evening, they brought the tidings that the 'dead' man I had treated had got up whole and walked . . . all I had ministered to had recovered and were glad. Throughout the land the effect was a profound wonder and fear. People talked of nothing else, and wherever the fame of it reached, people set out to find us so we should cure them and bless their children. . . .

"Up to now, Dorantes and his Negro had not attempted to practice; but under the soliciting pressure of these pilgrims from diverse places, we all became physicians, of whom I was the boldest and most venturous in trying to cure anything . . . If anyone did not actually recover, he still contended he would. What they who did recover related caused general rejoicing and dancing; so we got no sleep."

Before anyone gets too skeptical of these events, it should be noted that several years later, when Coronado's expedition passed through New Mexico, Indians told them of "four great doctors, one of them black, the other three white, who gave blessings [and] healed the sick." Historians and journalists call that "independent corroboration."

Were the healings real? Cabeza de Vaca himself admits that not all were healed. But the phenomenon, let us say, was real enough to be remembered by independent witnesses. There have been many witnessings, both ancient and modern, in every known culture, to healings very like these. It's a subject that discomforts scientists, because they've been able neither to prove nor disprove it conclusively, but there's too much documentation for the phenomenon to be dismissed. And if even only a few of these phenomena are genuine—if healings such as Cabeza de Vaca described are part of the human possibility—then the present civilized consensus, and its description of existence, is not only incomplete but also inaccurate.

Though they were the first to explore North America and leave a record, and though their reports inspired the Coronado expedition, which resulted in the European settlement of the Southwest, still Cabeza de Vaca and his companions are lost to history because they challenge our consensus, our description, of reality. To teach of them at all is to at least consider the possibility that what they did was real.

Their healings can be contested, but what cannot be disputed is that the Indians of the Southeast adored them. Cabeza de Vaca, Dorantes, Castillo and Estevánico, hoping to run into Spaniards whom they thought might be exploring north from Mexico, proceeded into West Texas and New Mexico (some researchers think they got as far as Arizona). Thousands of Indians followed them. As Cabeza de Vaca writes, "we had been badly hampered by the hordes of Indians following us . . . they pursued so closely just to touch us. . . . Every Indian brought his portion to us to be breathed on and blessed before he would dare touch it. When you consider that we were frequently accompanied by 3,000 or 4,000 Indians and were obliged to sanctify the food and drink of each one, as well as grant permission for the many things they asked to do, you can appreciate our inconvenience."

Cabeza de Vaca attributed these wonders neither to himself nor to his friends. He gave all the credit to divine powers working through them. He was as much in awe of the events as the Indians themselves; therefore, though he found their adoration "inconvenient," he never looked down on the tribes. In fact, his verdict on the natives of this land was unique in his day and would be considered radical for the next several centuries: "They are a substantial people with a capacity for unlimited development."

That statement alone makes his story out of place in an education system that taught, until fairly recently, that tribal peoples were not the equals of Europeans. Cabeza de Vaca, writing to his king, added a note that would go against the future Indian policies of all governments, including the United States: "Clearly, to bring all these people to Christianity and subjection to Your Imperial Majesty, they must be won by kindness, the only certain way."

But when he finally came upon Spaniards, he found anything but kindness: "With heavy hearts we looked out over the lavishly watered and fertile, beautiful land, now abandoned and burned and the people thin and weak, scattering or hiding in fright. . . . [They] told us how the [Spaniards] had come through razing the towns and carrying off half the men and all the women and boys. . . . We told the natives we were going after those men to order them to stop killing, enslaving and dispossessing the Indians; which made our friends very glad."

As you can guess, they had no success with this project. When they found the Spaniards who had done those things, Cabeza de Vaca got into "a hot argument," for those Spaniards "meant to make slaves of the Indians in our train." The commander of those conquistadors, one Diego de Alcaraz, "bade his interpreter tell the Indians that we [Cabeza de Vaca and his friends] were members of his race who had been long lost; that his group were the lords of the land who must be obeyed and served, while we were inconsequential. The Indians paid no attention to this. Conferring among themselves, they replied that the Christians lied: We had come from the sunrise, they from the sunset; we healed the sick, they killed the sound; we came naked and barefoot, they clothed, horsed and lanced; we coveted nothing but gave whatever we were given, while they robbed whomever they found and bestowed nothing on anyone."

He added: "To the last I could not convince the Indians that we were of the same people as the Christian slavers."

Finally it was time for Cabeza de Vaca, Dorantes, Estevánico and Castillo to take their leave from the Indians—both those who had followed them for so long and those who had come to them for protection. Here Cabeza de Vaca added his most direct and defiant note to his king: "When the Indians took their leave of us they said they would do as we commanded and rebuild their towns, if the Christians let them. And I solemnly swear that if they have not done so it is the fault of the Christians."

Cabeza de Vaca and his companions journeyed south, accompanied by Spanish soldiers, and met with the governor of Mexico, Nuño de Guzmán, in Compostela, where he made his report to Guzmán and to the now aging Cortés. "The Governor received us graciously and outfitted us from his wardrobe. I could not stand to wear any clothes for some time, or to sleep anywhere but on the bare floor."

I think of him in that interim—of how strange clothing felt to him after eight years of nakedness, and of how he could not bring himself to sleep on a civilized bed. If he ever used his healing powers again, he made no record of it. In 1540, Cabeza de Vaca was appointed governor of the South American provinces of the Río de la Plata, where he prohibited the slaving, raping and looting of Indians. This caused deep resentment among the soldiers in his command, and finally, in 1543, they imprisoned him and sent him back to Spain in chains. He remained in prison for about eight years (almost as long as he'd spent in North America), until his wife spent the better part of her fortune to free him. He died in 1557, at the age of 67 and, despite the writings he left, virtually disappeared from history because history could accept neither his actions nor his message.

Had he actually been given the gift of healing? In answer we have to ask ourselves: Why else would Indians have followed him by the thousands? It is certain that they did, for many Spaniards in Mexico witnessed it. Since this is the only incidence in the entire history of the meeting of Europeans and Native Americans when a white man had such an effect without military coercion, we must assume an extraordinary cause. That is what leads me to believe Cabeza de Vaca's account credible.

But if he had such powers, why did they leave him when he was back among his own people? Perhaps because among his own kind his powers were neither wanted nor accepted; or perhaps because he had to wear again not only civilization's clothing but civilization's assumptions, and only when all trappings of civilization had been stripped away could the healing powers rise in him. Perhaps that is why he sought to return to the New World so soon. But as essentially a military governor in South America, he could not re-create the conditions that existed for him on his first journey.

Whatever the reason, it is clear that where others found, in the wilderness, Joseph Conrad's heart of darkness, Alvar Núñez Cabeza de Vaca experienced the heart of light. Is that heart of light still among us? Is it still reachable in this land that is no longer a wilderness—this land where society is in such turmoil, and where people feel so frightened, angry and insecure?

It may be because Cabeza de Vaca's journey raises this question that he has been, and is still, avoided in schools. Across the centuries he comes to suggest that being human may be a state of more possibilities that we have usually dared to dream. He tells us that only kindness, generosity and devotion are ultimately convincing—that they are "the only certain way" to reach across the barriers of our differences. He stands as a kindly, mysterious, courageous, yet disturbing figure, dangerous to our assumptions, challenging our limits.

He had begged that his story "be received as homage, since it is the most one could bring who returned thence naked." Instead we have ignored him. Yet it may be that, more than ever, we need him now—need to tell his story among ourselves and teach it to our children, meeting his challenge, giving consideration to his mysteries and living up to his example.

or sword wounds. All those military histories glorifying Alexander the Great and Napoleon ignore the ego-deflating truth: the winners of past wars were not necessarily those armies with the best generals and weapons, but those bearing the worst germs with which to smite their enemies.

The grimmest example of the role of germs in history is much on our minds this month, as we recall the European conquest of the Americas that began with Columbus's voyage of 1492. Numerous as the Indian victims of the murderous Spanish conquistadores were, they were dwarfed in number by the victims of murderous Spanish microbes. These formidable conquerors killed an estimated 95 percent of the New World's pre-Columbian Indian population.

Why was the exchange of nasty germs between the Americas and Europe so unequal? why didn't the reverse happen instead, with Indian diseases decimating the Spanish invaders, spreading back across the Atlantic, and causing a 95 percent decline in *Europe's* human population?

Similar questions arise regarding the decimation of many other native peoples by European germs, and regarding the decimation of would-be European conquistadores in the tropics of Africa and Asia.

Naturally, we're disposed to think about diseases from our own point of view: What can we do to save ourselves and to kill the microbes? Let's stamp out the scoundrels, and never mind what *their* motives are!

In life, though, one has to understand the enemy to beat him. So for a moment, let's consider disease from the microbes' point of view. Let's look beyond our anger at their making us sick in bizarre ways, like giving us genital sores or diarrhea, and ask why it is that they do such things. After all, microbes are as much a product of natural selection as we are, and so their actions must have come about because they confer some evolutionary benefit.

Basically, of course, evolution selects those individuals that are most effective at producing babies and at helping those babies find suitable places to live. Microbes are marvels at this latter requirement. They have evolved diverse ways of spreading from one person to another, and from animals to people. Many of our symptoms of disease actually represent ways in which some clever bug modifies our bodies or our behavior such that we become enlisted to spread bugs.

The most effortless way a bug can spread is by just waiting to be transmitted passively to the next victim. That's the strategy practiced by microbes that wait for one host to be eaten by the next—salmonella bacteria, for example, which we contract by eating already-infected eggs or meat; or the worm responsible for trichinosis, which waits for us to kill a pig and eat it without properly cooking it.

As a slight modification of this strategy, some microbes don't wait for the old host to die but instead hitchhike in the saliva of an insect that bites the old host and then flies to a new one. The free ride may be provided by mosquitoes, fleas, lice, or tsetse flies, which spread malaria, plague, typhus, and sleeping sickness, respectively. The dirtiest of all passive-carriage tricks is perpetrated by microbes that pass from a woman to her fetus—microbes such as the ones responsible for syphilis, rubella (German measles), and AIDS. By their cunning these microbes can already be infecting an infant before the moment of its birth.

Other bugs take matters into their own hands, figuratively speaking. They actively modify the anatomy or habits of their host to accelerate their transmission. From our perspective, the open genital sores caused by venereal diseases such as syphilis are a vile indignity. From the microbes' point of view, however, they're just a useful device to enlist a host's help in inoculating the body cavity of another host with microbes. The skin lesions caused by smallpox similarly spread microbes by direct or indirect body contact (occasionally very indirect, as when U.S. and Australian whites bent on wiping out "belligerent" native peoples sent

them gifts of blankets previously used by smallpox patients).

From our viewpoint, diarrhea and coughing are "symptoms" of disease. From a bug's viewpoint, they're clever evolutionary strategies to broadcast the bug. That's why it's in the bug's interests to make us "sick."

More vigorous yet is the strategy practiced by the influenza, common cold, and pertussis (whooping cough) microbes, which induce the victim to cough or sneeze, thereby broadcasting the bugs toward prospective new hosts. Similarly the cholera bacterium induces a massive diarrhea that spreads bacteria into the water supplies of potential new victims. For modification of a host's behavior, though, nothing matches the rabies virus, which not only gets into the saliva of an infected dog but drives the dog into a frenzy of biting and thereby infects many new victims.

Thus, from our viewpoint, genital sores, diarrhea, and coughing are "symptoms" of disease. From a bug's viewpoint, they're clever evolutionary strategies to broadcast the bug. That's why it's in the bug's interests to make us "sick." But what does it gain by killing us? That seems self-defeating, since a microbe that kills its host kills itself.

Though you may well think it's of little consolation, our death is really just an unintended by-product of host symptoms that promote the efficient transmission of microbes. Yes, an untreated cholera patient may eventually die from producing diarrheal fluid at a rate of several gallons a day. While the patient lasts, though, the cholera bacterium profits from being massively disseminated into the water supplies of its next victims. As long as each victim thereby infects, on average, more than one new victim, the bacteria will spread, even though the first host happens to die.

So much for the dispassionate examination of the bug's interests. Now let's get back to considering our own selfish interests: to stay alive and healthy, best done by killing the damned bugs. One common response to infection is to develop a fever. Again, we consider fever a "symptom" of disease, as if it developed inevitably without serving any function. But regulation of body temperature is under our genetic control, and a fever doesn't just happen by accident. Because some microbes are more sensitive to heat than our own bodies are, by raising our body temperature we in effect try to bake the bugs to death before we get baked ourselves.

Another common response is to mobilize our immune system. White blood cells and other cells actively seek out and kill foreign microbes. The specific antibodies we gradually build up against a particular microbe make us less likely to get reinfected once we are cured. As we all know there are some illnesses, such as flu and the common cold, to which our resistance is only temporary; we can eventually contract the illness again. Against other illnesses, though—including measles, mumps, rubella, pertussis, and the now-defeated menace of smallpox—antibodies stimulated by one infection confer lifelong immunity. That's the principle behind vaccination—to stimulate our antibody production without our having to go through the actual experience of the disease.

Alas, some clever bugs don't just cave in to our immune defenses. Some have learned to trick us by changing their antigens, those molecular pieces of the microbe that our antibodies recognize. The constant evolution or recycling of new strains of flu, with differing antigens, explains why the flu you got two years ago didn't protect you against the different strain that arrived this year. Sleeping sickness is an even more slippery customer in its ability to change its antigens rapidly.

We and our pathogens are now locked in an escalating evolutionary contest, with the death of one contestant the price of defeat, and with natural selection playing the role of umpire.

Among the slipperiest of all is the virus that causes AIDS, which evolves new antigens even as it sits within an individual patient, until it eventually overwhelms the immune system.

Our slowest defensive response is through natural selection, which changes the relative frequency with which a gene appears from generation to generation. For almost any disease some people prove to be genetically more resistant than others. In an epidemic, those people with genes for resistance to that particular microbe are more likely to survive than are people lacking such genes. As a result, over the course of history human populations repeatedly exposed to a particular pathogen tend to be made up of individuals with genes that resist the appropriate microbe just because unfortunate individuals without those genes were less likely to survive to pass their genes on to their children.

Fat consolation, you may be thinking. This evolutionary response is not one that does the genetically susceptible dying individual any good. It does mean, though, that a human population as a whole becomes better protected.

In short, many bugs have had to evolve tricks to let them spread among potential victims. We've evolved counter-tricks, to which the bugs have responded by evolving counter-counter-tricks. We and our pathogens are now locked in an escalating evolutionary contest, with the death of one contestant the price of defeat, and with natural selection playing the role of umpire.

The form that this deadly contest takes varies with the pathogens: for some it is like a guerrilla war, while for others it is a blitzkrieg. With certain diseases, like malaria or hook-worm, there's a more or less steady trickle of new cases in an affected area, and they will appear in any month of any year. Epidemic diseases, though, are different: they produce no cases for a long time, then a whole wave of cases, then no more cases again for a while.

Among such epidemic diseases, influenza is the most familiar to Americans, this year having been a particularly bad one for us (but a great year for the influenza virus). Cholera epidemics come at longer intervals, the 1991 Peruvian epidemic being the first one to reach the New World during the twentieth century. Frightening as today's influenza and cholera epidemics are, though, they pale beside the far more terrifying epidemics of the past, before the rise of modern medicine. The greatest single epidemic in human history was the influenza wave that killed 21 million people at the end of the First World War. The black death, or bubonic plague, killed one-quarter of Europe's population between 1346 and 1352, with death tolls up to 70 percent in some cities.

The infectious diseases that visit us as epidemics share several characteristics. First, they spread quickly and efficiently from an infected person to nearby healthy people, with the result that the whole population gets exposed within a short time. Second, they're "acute" illnesses: within a short time, you either die or recover completely. Third, the fortunate ones of us who do recover develop antibodies that leave us immune against a recurrence of the disease for a long time, possibly our entire lives. Finally, these diseases tend to be restricted to humans; the bugs causing them tend not to live in the soil or in other animals. All four of these characteristics apply to what Americans think of as the once more-familiar acute epidemic diseases of childhood, including measles, rubella, mumps, pertussis, and smallpox.

It is easy to understand why the

combination of those four characteristics tends to make a disease run in epidemics. The rapid spread of microbes and the rapid course of symptoms mean that everybody in a local human population is soon infected, and thereafter either dead or else recovered and immune. No one is left alive who could still be infected. But since the microbe can't survive except in the bodies of living people, the disease dies out until a new crop of babies reaches the susceptible age—and until an infectious person arrives from the outside to start a new epidemic.

A classic illustration of the process is given by the history of measles on the isolated Faeroe Islands in the North Atlantic. A severe epidemic of the disease reached the Faeroes in 1781, then died out, leaving the islands measles-free until an infected carpenter arrived on a ship from Denmark in 1846. Within three months almost the whole Faeroes population—7,782 people—had gotten measles and then either died or recovered, leaving the measles virus to disappear once again until the next epidemic. Studies show that measles is likely to die out in any human population numbering less than half a million people. Only in larger populations can measles shift from one local area to another, thereby persisting until enough babies have been born in the originally infected area to permit the disease's return.

Rubella in Australia provides a similar example, on a much larger scale. As of 1917 Australia's population was still only 5 million, with most people living in scattered rural areas. The sea voyage to Britain took two months, and land transport within Australia itself was slow. In effect, Australia didn't even consist of a population of 5 million, but of hundreds of much smaller populations. As a result, rubella hit Australia only as occasional epidemics, when an infected person happened to arrive from overseas and stayed in a densely populated area. By 1938, though, the city of Sydney alone had a population of over one million, and people moved frequently and quickly by air between London, Sydney, and other Australian cities. Around then, rubella

for the first time was able to establish itself permanently in Australia.

What's true for rubella in Australia is true for most familiar acute infectious diseases throughout the world. To sustain themselves, they need a human population that is sufficiently numerous and densely packed that a new crop of susceptible children is available for infection by the time the disease would otherwise be waning. Hence measles and other such diseases are also known as "crowd diseases."

Crowd diseases could not sustain themselves in small bands of hunter-gatherers and slash-and-burn farmers. As tragic recent experience with Amazonian Indians and Pacific Islanders confirms, almost an entire tribelet may be wiped out by an epidemic brought by an outside visitor, because no one in the tribelet has any antibodies against the microbe. In addition, measles and some other "childhood" diseases are more likely to kill infected adults than children, and all adults in the tribelet are susceptible. Having killed most of the tribelet, the epidemic then disappears. The small population size explains why tribelets can't sustain epidemics introduced from the outside; at the same time it explains why they could never evolve epidemic diseases of their own to give back to the visitors.

That's not to say that small human populations are free from all infectious diseases. Some of their infections are caused by microbes capable of maintaining themselves in animals or in soil, so the disease remains constantly available to infect people. For example, the yellow fever virus is carried by African wild monkeys and is constantly available to infect rural human populations of Africa. It was also available to be carried to New World monkeys and people by the transatlantic slave trade.

Other infections of small human populations are chronic diseases, such as leprosy and yaws, that may take a very long time to kill a victim. The victim thus remains alive as a reservoir of microbes to infect other members of

the tribelet. Finally, small human populations are susceptible to nonfatal infections against which we don't develop immunity, with the result that the same person can become reinfected after recovering. That's the case with hookworm and many other parasites.

All these types of diseases, characteristic of small, isolated populations, must be the oldest diseases of humanity. They were the ones that we could evolve and sustain through the early millions of years of our evolutionary history, when the total human population was tiny and fragmented. They are also shared with, or are similar to the diseases of, our closest wild relatives, the African great apes. In contrast, the evolution of our crowd diseases could only have occurred with the buildup of large, dense human populations, first made possible by the rise of agriculture about 10,000 years ago, then by the rise of cities several thousand years ago. Indeed, the first attested dates for many familiar infectious diseases are surprisingly recent: around 1600 B.C. for smallpox (as deduced from pockmarks on an Egyptian mummy), 400 B.C. for mumps, 1840 for polio, and 1959 for AIDS.

Agriculture sustains much higher human population densities than does hunting and gathering—on average, 10 to 100 times higher. In addition, hunter-gatherers frequently shift camp, leaving behind their piles of feces with their accumulated microbes and worm larvae. But farmers are sedentary and live amid their own sewage, providing microbes with a quick path from one person's body into another person's drinking water. Farmers also become surrounded by disease-transmitting rodents attracted by stored food.

Some human populations make it even easier for their own bacteria and worms to infect new victims, by intentionally gathering their feces and urine and spreading it as fertilizer on the fields where people work. Irrigation agriculture and fish farming provide ideal living conditions for the snails carrying schistosomes, and for other flukes that burrow through our skin as we wade through the feces-laden water.

If the rise of farming was a boon for our microbes, the rise of cities was a veritable bonanza, as still more densely packed human populations festered under even worse sanitation conditions. (Not until the beginning of the twentieth century did urban populations finally become self-sustaining; until then, constant immigration of healthy peasants from the countryside was necessary to make good the constant deaths of city dwellers from crowd diseases.) Another bonanza was the development of world trade routes, which by late Roman times effectively joined the populations of Europe, Asia, and North Africa into one giant breeding ground for microbes. That's when smallpox finally reached Rome as the "plague of Antonius," which killed millions of Roman citizens between A.D. 165 and 180.

Similarly, bubonic plague first appeared in Europe as the plague of Justinian (A.D. 542–543). But plague didn't begin to hit Europe with full force, as the black death epidemics, until 1346, when new overland trading with China provided rapid transit for flea-infested furs from plague-ridden areas of Central Asia. Today our jet planes have made even the longest intercontinental flights briefer than the duration of any human infectious disease. That's how an Aerolíneas Argentinas airplane, stopping in Lima, Peru, earlier this year, managed to deliver dozens of cholera-infected people the same day to my city of Los Angeles, over 3,000 miles away. The explosive increase in world travel by Americans, and in immigration to the United States, is turning us into another melting pot—this time of microbes that we previously dismissed as just causing exotic diseases in far-off countries.

When the human population became sufficiently large and concentrated, we reached the stage in our history when we could at last sustain crowd diseases confined to our species. But that presents a paradox: such diseases could never have existed before. Instead they had to evolve as new diseases. Where did those new diseases come from?

The explosive increase in world travel by Americans, and in immigration to the United States, is turning us into another melting pot— this time of microbes that we'd dismissed as causing disease in far-off countries.

Evidence emerges from studies of the disease-causing microbes themselves. In many cases molecular biologists have identified the microbe's closest relative. Those relatives also prove to be agents of infectious crowd diseases—but ones confined to various species of domestic animals and pets! Among animals too, epidemic diseases require dense populations, and they're mainly confined to social animals that provide the necessary large populations. Hence when we domesticated social animals such as cows and pigs, they were already afflicted by epidemic diseases just waiting to be transferred to us.

For example, the measles virus is most closely related to the virus causing rinderpest, a nasty epidemic disease of cattle and many wild cud-chewing mammals. Rinderpest doesn't affect humans. Measles, in turn, doesn't affect cattle. The close similarity of the measles and rinderpest viruses suggests that the rinderpest virus transferred from cattle to humans, then became the measles virus by changing its properties to adapt to us. That transfer isn't surprising, considering how closely many peasant farmers live and sleep next to cows and their accompanying feces, urine, breath, sores, and blood. Our intimacy with cattle has been going on for the 8,000 years since we domesticated them—ample time for the rinderpest virus to discover us nearby. Other familiar infectious diseases can similarly be traced back to diseases of our animal friends.

Given our proximity to the animals we love, we must constantly be getting bombarded by animal microbes. Those invaders get winnowed by natural selection, and only a few succeed in establishing themselves as human diseases. A quick survey of current diseases lets us trace four stages in the evolution of a specialized human disease from an animal precursor.

In the first stage, we pick up animal-borne microbes that are still at an early stage in their evolution into specialized human pathogens. They don't get transmitted directly from one person to another, and even their transfer from animals to us remains uncommon. There are dozens of diseases like this that we get directly from pets and domestic animals. They include cat scratch fever from cats, leptospirosis from dogs, psittacosis from chickens and parrots, and brucellosis from cattle. We're similarly susceptible to picking up diseases from wild animals, such as the tularemia that hunters occasionally get from skinning wild rabbits.

In the second stage, a former animal pathogen evolves to the point where it does get transmitted directly between people and causes epidemics. However, the epidemic dies out for several reasons—being cured by modern medicine, stopping when everybody has been infected and died, or stopping when everybody has been infected and become immune. For example, a previously unknown disease termed *o'nyong-nyong* fever appeared in East Africa in 1959 and infected several million Africans. It probably arose from a virus of monkeys and was transmitted to humans by mosquitoes. The fact that patients recovered quickly and became immune to further attack helped cause the new disease to die out quickly.

The annals of medicine are full of diseases that sound like no known disease today but that once caused terrifying epidemics before disappearing as mysteriously as they had come. Who alive today remembers the "English sweating sickness" that swept and terrified Europe between 1485 and 1578, or the "Picardy sweats" of eighteenth- and nineteenth-century France?

A third stage in the evolution of our

major diseases is represented by former animal pathogens that establish themselves in humans and that do not die out; until they do, the question of whether they will become major killers of humanity remains up for grabs. The future is still very uncertain for Lassa fever, first observed in 1969 in Nigeria and caused by a virus probably derived from rodents. Better established is Lyme disease, caused by a spirochete that we get from the bite of a tick. Although the first known human cases in the United States appeared only as recently as 1962, Lyme disease is already reaching epidemic proportions in the Northeast, on the West Coast, and in the upper Midwest. The future of AIDS, derived from monkey viruses, is even more secure, from the virus's perspective.

The final stage of this evolution is represented by the major, long-established epidemic diseases confined to humans. These diseases must have been the evolutionary survivors of far more pathogens that tried to make the jump to us from animals—and mostly failed.

Diseases represent evolution in progress, as microbes adapt by natural selection to new hosts. Compared with cows' bodies, though, our bodies offer different immune defenses and different chemistry. In that new environment, a microbe must evolve new ways to live and propagate itself.

The best-studied example of microbes evolving these new ways involves myxomatosis, which hit Australian rabbits in 1950. The myxoma virus, native to a wild species of Brazilian rabbit, was known to cause a lethal epidemic in European domestic rabbits, which are a different species. The virus was intentionally introduced to Australia in the hopes of ridding the continent of its plague of European rabbits, foolishly introduced in the nineteenth century. In the first year, myxoma produced a gratifying (to Australian farmers) 99.8 percent mortality in infected rabbits. Fortunately for the rabbits and unfortunately for the farmers, the death rate then dropped in the second year to 90 percent and eventually to 25 percent, frustrating hopes of eradicating rabbits completely from Australia. The prob-

lem was that the myxoma virus evolved to serve its own interests, which differed from the farmers' interests and those of the rabbits. The virus changed to kill fewer rabbits and to permit lethally infected ones to live longer before dying. The result was bad for Australian farmers but good for the virus: a less lethal myxoma virus spreads baby viruses to more rabbits than did the original, highly virulent myxoma.

For a similar example in humans, consider the surprising evolution of syphilis. Today we associate syphilis with genital sores and a very slowly developing disease, leading to the death of untreated victims only after many years. However, when syphilis was first definitely recorded in Europe in 1495, its pustules often covered the body from the head to the knees, caused flesh to fall off people's faces, and led to death within a few months. By 1546 syphilis had evolved into the disease with the symptoms known to us today. Apparently, just as with myxomatosis, those syphilis spirochetes evolved to keep their victims alive longer in order to transmit their spirochete offspring into more victims.

How, then, does all this explain the outcome of 1492—that Europeans conquered and depopulated the New World, instead of Native Americans conquering and depopulating Europe?

Part of the answer, of course, goes back to the invaders' technological advantages. European guns and steel swords were more effective weapons than Native American stone axes and wooden clubs. Only Europeans had ships capable of crossing the ocean and horses that could provide a decisive advantage in battle. But that's not the whole answer. Far more Native Americans died in bed than on the battlefield—the victims of germs, not of guns and swords. Those germs undermined Indian resistance by killing most Indians and their leaders and by demoralizing the survivors.

The role of disease in the Spanish conquests of the Aztec and Inca empires is especially well documented. In

1519 Cortés landed on the coast of Mexico with 600 Spaniards to conquer the fiercely militaristic Aztec Empire, which at the time had a population of many millions. That Cortés reached the Aztec capital of Tenochtitlán, escaped with the loss of "only" two-thirds of his force, and managed to fight his way back to the coast demonstrates both Spanish military advantages and the initial naïveté of the Aztecs. But when Cortés's next onslaught came, in 1521, the Aztecs were no longer naive; they fought street by street with the utmost tenacity.

What gave the Spaniards a decisive advantage this time was smallpox, which reached Mexico in 1520 with the arrival of one infected slave from Spanish Cuba. The resulting epidemic proceeded to kill nearly half the Aztecs. The survivors were demoralized by the mysterious illness that killed Indians and spared Spaniards, as if advertising the Spaniards' invincibility. By 1618 Mexico's initial population of 20 million had plummeted to about 1.6 million.

Pizarro had similarly grim luck when he landed on the coast of Peru in 1531 with about 200 men to conquer the Inca Empire. Fortunately for Pizarro, and unfortunately for the Incas, smallpox had arrived overland around 1524, killing much of the Inca population, including both Emperor Huayna Capac and his son and designated successor, Ninan Cuyoche. Because of the vacant throne, two other sons of Huayna Capac, Atahuallpa and Huáscar, became embroiled in a civil war that Pizarro exploited to conquer the divided Incas.

In the century or two following Columbus's arrival in the New World, the Indian population declined by about 95 percent. The main killers were European germs, to which the Indians had never been exposed.

7. SOCIOCULTURAL CHANGE: THE IMPACT OF THE WEST

When we in the United States think of the most populous New World societies existing in 1492, only the Aztecs and Incas come to mind. We forget that North America also supported populous Indian societies in the Mississippi Valley. Sadly, these societies too would disappear. But in this case conquistadores contributed nothing directly to the societies' destruction; the conquistadores' germs, spreading in advance, did everything. When De Soto marched through the Southeast in 1540, he came across Indian towns abandoned two years previously because nearly all the inhabitants had died in epidemics. However, he was still able to see some of the densely populated towns lining the lower Mississippi. By a century and a half later, though, when French settlers returned to the lower Mississippi, almost all those towns had vanished. Their relics are the great mound sites of the Mississippi Valley. Only recently have we come to realize that the mound-building societies were still largely intact when Columbus arrived, and that they collapsed between 1492 and the systematic European exploration of the Mississippi.

When I was a child in school, we were taught that North America had originally been occupied by about one million Indians. That low number helped justify the white conquest of what could then be viewed as an almost empty continent. However, archeological excavations and descriptions left by the first European explorers on our coasts now suggest an initial number of around 20 million. In the century or two following Columbus's arrival in the New World, the Indian population is estimated to have declined by about 95 percent.

The main killers were European germs, to which the Indians had never been exposed and against which they therefore had neither immunologic nor genetic resistance. Smallpox, measles, influenza, and typhus competed for top rank among the killers. As if those were not enough, pertussis, plague, tuberculosis, diphtheria, mumps, malaria, and yellow fever came close behind. In countless cases Europeans were

actually there to witness the decimation that occurred when the germs arrived. For example, in 1837 the Mandan Indian tribe, with one of the most elaborate cultures in the Great Plains, contracted smallpox thanks to a steamboat traveling up the Missouri River from St. Louis. The population of one Mandan village crashed from 2,000 to less than 40 within a few weeks.

The one-sided exchange of lethal germs between the Old and New worlds is among the most striking and consequence-laden facts of recent history. Whereas over a dozen major infectious diseases of Old World origins became established in the New World, not a single major killer reached Europe from the Americas. The sole possible exception is syphilis, whose area of origin still remains controversial.

That one-sidedness is more striking with the knowledge that large, dense human populations are a prerequisite for the evolution of crowd diseases. If recent reappraisals of the pre-Columbian New World population are correct, that population was not far below the contemporaneous population of Eurasia. Some New World cities, like Tenochtitlán, were among the world's most populous cities at the time. Yet Tenochtitlán didn't have awful germs waiting in store for the Spaniards. Why not?

One possible factor is that the rise of dense human populations began somewhat later in the New World than in the Old. Another is that the three most populous American centers—the Andes, Mexico, and the Mississippi Valley—were never connected by regular fast trade into one gigantic breeding ground for microbes, in the way that Europe, North Africa, India, and China became connected in late Roman times.

The main reason becomes clear, however, if we ask a simple question: From what microbes could any crowd diseases of the Americas have evolved? We've seen that Eurasian crowd diseases evolved from diseases of domesticated herd animals. Significantly, there were many such animals in Eurasia. But there were only five animals that became domesticated in the Americas: the turkey in Mexico and parts of

North America, the guinea pig and llama/alpaca (probably derived from the same original wild species) in the Andes, the Muscovy duck in tropical South America, and the dog throughout the Americas.

That extreme paucity of New World domestic animals reflects the paucity of wild starting material. About 80 percent of the big wild mammals of the Americas became extinct at the end of the last ice age, around 11,000 years ago, at approximately the same time that the first well-attested wave of Indian hunters spread over the Americas. Among the species that disappeared were ones that would have yielded useful domesticates, such as American horses and camels. Debate still rages as to whether those extinctions were due to climate changes or to the impact of Indian hunters on prey that had never seen humans. Whatever the reason, the extinctions removed most of the basis for Native American animal domestication—and for crowd diseases.

The few domesticates that remained were not likely sources of such diseases. Muscovy ducks and turkeys don't live in enormous flocks, and they're not naturally endearing species (like young lambs) with which we have much physical contact. Guinea pigs may have contributed a trypanosome infection like Chagas' disease or leishmaniasis to our catalog of woes, but that's uncertain. Initially the most surprising absence is of any human disease derived from llamas (or alpacas), which are tempting to consider as the Andean equivalent of Eurasian livestock. However, llamas had three strikes against them as a source of human pathogens: their wild relatives don't occur in big herds as do wild sheep, goats, and pigs; their total numbers were never remotely as large as the Eurasian populations of domestic livestock, since llamas never spread beyond the Andes; and llamas aren't as cuddly as piglets and lambs and aren't kept in such close association with people. (You may not think of piglets as cuddly, but human mothers in the New Guinea highlands often nurse them, and they frequently live right in the huts of peasant farmers.)

The importance of animal-derived diseases for human history extends far beyond the Americas. Eurasian germs played a key role in decimating native peoples in many other parts of the world as well, including the Pacific islands, Australia, and southern Africa. Racist Europeans used to attribute those conquests to their supposedly better brains. But no evidence for such better brains has been forthcoming. Instead, the conquests were made possible by Europeans nastier germs, and by the technological advances and denser populations that Europeans ultimately acquired by means of their domesticated plants and animals.

So on this 500th anniversary of Columbus's discovery, let's try to regain our sense of perspective about his hotly debated achievements. There's no doubt that Columbus was a great visionary, seaman, and leader. There's also no doubt that he and his successors often behaved as bestial murderers. But those facts alone don't fully explain why it took so few European immigrants to initially conquer and ultimately supplant so much of the native population of the Americas. Without the germs Europeans brought with them—germs that were derived from their animals—such conquests might have been impossible.

Pastoralism and the Demise of Communal Property in Tanzania

Susan Charnley

Susan Charnley is an anthropologist who currently holds a Ciriacy-Wantrup Post-doctoral Fellowship in Natural Resource Economics at the Energy and Resources Group, University of California, Berkeley. She is writing a book about pastoralism, property rights and ecological change on the Usangu Plains, Tanzania. E-mail: charnley@sonoma.edu

The Usangu Plains in southwestern Tanzania are the homelands of the Sangu peoples (of Bantu origins), who maintained a thriving pastoral economy until recently. Today, very few Sangu own livestock and most have become rice cultivators. In 1990 I went to Usangu to study this transformation out of pastoralism. I was told, "we are not Sangu anymore, we are just Tanzanians now." What had caused the Sangu to lose their livestock herds, and along with them, their sense of ethnic identity? Moreover, what was responsible for the growing signs of ecological deterioration and resource scarcity on Usangu's rangelands?

The Usangu Plains are a microcosm of what is occurring in many parts of pastoral Africa, where the demise of communal property systems and the loss of pastoral land are causing rangeland degradation, pastoral impoverishment and dramatic changes in the pastoral way of life. Historically, most African pastoral societies held rangelands under systems of communal property. These systems promoted the sustainable use of rangelands by controlling resource access, regulating resource use by community members and providing secure tenure rights, thus encouraging long-term conservation practices. Communal property also facilitated pastoral mobility over large geographic areas, enabling livestock to track seasonal and annual variations in water and forage availability.

Over the last few decades, many African pastoral property systems have been transformed. In some areas, communal grazing lands have undergone privatization. Elsewhere, pastoral land has been alienated to become State property, from which pastoralists are excluded. Other communal property systems have been converted to open access situations, in which resource access is uncontrolled and resource use is unregulated. These changes have had negative ecological and social consequences in many pastoral areas. The Usangu Plains provide one example of what happens when communal property systems break down.

The Demise of Communal Property on the Usangu Plains

The semi-arid Usangu Plains of southwestern Tanzania cover an area of approximately 15,500 sq. km. (Fig. 1). The northern half of the Plains is largely uninhabited due to inhospitable ecological conditions. Pastoral and agricultural activities are concentrated in the southern half of the Plains. There, vast grasslands, numerous watercourses (many perennial) and dry season swamps make the Plains favorable for livestock herding. Low and erratic rainfall patterns mean that rain-fed cultivation is a risky endeavor. However, the flat Plains with their fertile soils and many rivers are well suited to irrigation.

Between the mid-1800s and the mid-1900s, the Sangu people were rich in cattle, sheep and goats. While they were primarily pastoral in their economic orientation, they also practiced some rain-fed cultivation. The Sangu held Usangu's rangelands under a system of communal property. Rights to use resources were based on residence there, which in turn depended upon ethnically identifying as Sangu. Non-Sangu Africans could be denied the right to settle on the Plains by the Sangu Chief and thereby excluded from gaining resource access. Resource use was controlled by local headmen and the Chief.

Following independence in 1961, political and economic policies implemented by the Tanzanian government undermined Sangu systems of resource control. First, the offices of chief, subchief and headman were abolished, and along with them, the legitimacy of Sangu authority figures. New State political institutions were created. However, their role in natural resource management was nebulous and no effective regulatory bodies replaced pre-existing ones. Second, new government policies emphasized the national identity of Tanzanian citizens, as opposed to individual ethnic identities. Ethnicity could no longer be used to prevent someone from settling in a specific geographic

     From *Cultural Survival Quarterly*, Volume 20, Issue 1, Spring 1996, pp. 41-44. © 1996 by Cultural Survival, Inc.

area and using resources there. This made it easier for people to migrate and harder to exclude outsiders. Third, State policies favored agricultural (as opposed to pastoral) development. The Usangu Plains became a target area for irrigation development, which has since taken priority there, irrespective of the needs and rights of pastoralists. Fourth, the Land Acquisition Act of 1967 made it possible for the President of Tanzania to acquire any land within the country for a "public purpose." This act facilitated State land alienation. What were the consequences of these policies on the Usangu Plains?

Over the last thirty years, some 55,000 hectares of land in Usangu have been alienated as State property, including areas that were historically important for grazing. The Tanzanian State has established three large, mechanized, irrigated rice farms on this land (one is currently inoperable), and one ranch that produces commercial beef cattle. Rice is produced as a cash crop and is marketed in Tanzania's urban areas. An additional 7,000 hectares have been earmarked by the State for future alienation to establish new irrigation schemes.

Extensive areas of additional pasture have been converted to small-scale irrigated rice production, mainly by immigrant farmers from surrounding highland regions who have settled in Usangu over the last four decades. These farmers faced land scarcity at home and move to Usangu to take advantage of cash cropping opportunities opened by irrigation development. Approximately 25 different ethnic groups of farmers currently reside there and maintain exclusive claims to the land they have developed for agriculture.

Usangu's remaining rangelands have become open access. Pastoralists who were socially and ecologically marginalized in other parts of Tanzania have migrated and settled in Usangu, causing the regional livestock herd to more than double in size since the 1950s. Six different ethnic groups of livestock herders currently share Usangu's rangelands. In 1990, Sangu cattle comprised only 12% of the regional cattle population. Pastoral immigration into the region continues, with no way to control it or to limit resource access there. Herders belonging to each ethnic group follow their own cultural practices of resource use and management. Unfortunately, the practices of one group often disrupt and undermine those of another group, and herders don't wish to follow the practices of other ethnic groups. There is no comprehensive, regional resource management framework.

Finally, the government is currently reviewing a proposal to establish a game reserve in the single most important dry season grazing area that remains on the Plains. The bulk of Usangu's livestock herd (which includes roughly half a million cattle and 100,000 sheep and goats) grazes in this wetland area, known as Utengule Swamp, from July to December each year. Should the game reserve be created, these animals would be excluded from the swamp, and the pastoral economy of the Plains would collapse.

Pastoralists on the Usangu Plains lack secure land rights. Pastoral land in Usangu continues to be converted to other uses, while herd numbers grow due to immigration. Intense grazing pressure on remaining grasslands is causing severe bush encroachment there, rendering them less productive for grazing. Herders currently experience resource scarcity, particularly during the dry season, and perceive Usangu's rangelands as being degraded. Livestock diseases have become rampant in the region. Animals that are malnourished are particularly vulnerable to disease, and livestock mortality rates are high. Resource scarcity and resource competition are currently causing ethnic conflict in the region.

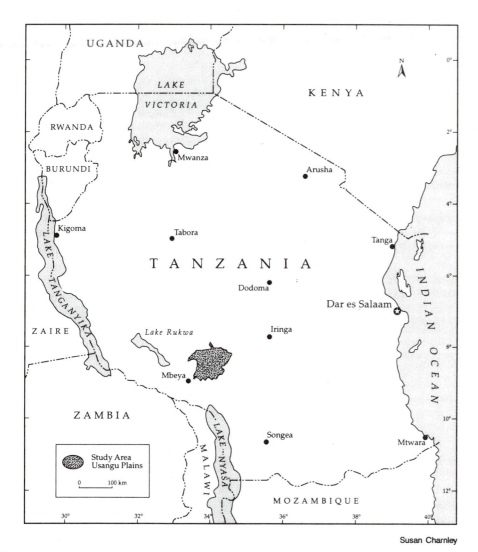

Susan Charnley

Figure 1. The Usangu Plains, Tanzania.

Some pastoral migrants in Usangu have attempted to move elsewhere, but have found that there is nowhere left to go. Others have begun to cultivate part-time in order to supplement their household incomes and conserve their herds. The Sangu have been virtually pushed out of pastoralism by widespread herd loss. They have been unable to adapt to the new social and ecological conditions under which herding now takes place on the Usangu Plains.

The Sangu have chosen irrigated rice cultivation as an economic alternative. However, irrigated agriculture is now highly competitive on the Usangu Plains. The supply of irrigation water is limited, the demand for it is high, and social institutions regulating its use are lacking. State-sponsored irrigation projects have priority access to river water in several locations, and elsewhere immigrant farmers have settled upstream of the Sangu. Thus, in years of low rainfall (two to three years out of five), there are downstream shortages of irrigation water, and the Sangu suffer crop failure. Rain-fed subsistence crops also fail in years of low rainfall. With no livestock on which to rely when crops fail, the Sangu frequently suffer economic hardship. Even in good years, they do not earn enough profits from rice to reinvest in livestock and rebuild herds. Yet, to the Sangu, livestock constitute wealth. Without cattle, they are poor.

The Sangu sense of ethnic identity revolved around the pastoral way of life and the ability to maintain political control over the Usangu Plains. Now, the Sangu feel powerless to control immigration, to prevent land alienation by the State, to control resource use on the Usangu Plains and to confront environmental problems there. In 1990, the Sangu comprised only 27 percent of Usangu's population. The Sangu have lost control over their homelands, lost their livestock herds, abandoned the pastoral way of life and are losing their sense of ethnic identity which was bound up in all of these things. They are becoming less Sangu and more Tanzanian.

Re-establishing Communal Property on the Usangu Plains

The demise of communal property and insecure pastoral land rights are the major underlying causes of rangeland degradation and pastoral resource scarcity on the Usangu Plains. The impoverishment of the Sangu people and loss of Sangu identity are both consequences of these problems. Similar processes are taking place in other parts of pastoral Africa. What can be done? Most of Usangu's pastoralists believe that if Usangu's remaining rangelands were protected from further alienation and encroachment, and a system of communal property were re-established there, rangeland degradation could be curbed, and the current livestock population could be supported.

The question of how to give Tanzanian pastoralists secure land rights and statutory control over pastoral resources in places such as the Usangu Plains is currently drawing the attention of several government institutions, NGOs and donor organizations in Tanzania. As Daniel Ndagala, Chairman of the Pastoral Network of Tanzania observed, it will be necessary to reconcile pastoral notions of "territory" with government notions of "land." In Tanzania, pastoralists view territory as being fluid. Geographic boundaries that delineate territories shift as ecological conditions fluctuate. Rainfall, water availability, forage quantity and quality, and disease conditions change constantly, and pastoral movements through territories are a response to these changes. Thus, boundaries as well as tenure rights expand and contract, depending upon environmental and social parameters. In contrast, the Tanzanian government maintains a more rigid concept of land. According to this view, land should be parceled into well defined, fixed geographic units. Specific tenure regimes and land use activities should be assigned to these bounded units.

The Tanzanian government has proposed two solutions to the problem of land rights for pastoralists. The first, which is currently being pursued, is to encourage pastoralists to settle in villages, to identify and demarcate village boundaries and to give villages legal land titles. Once village lands are secured, land use plans are drawn up that specify where agricultural versus grazing activities should take place. Although village councils (representative bodies) currently make land and resource use decisions regarding village lands, this power could be transferred to village assemblies (all adults residing in the village). With secure title to village lands, formally designated grazing areas and a voice in local land and resource use decisions, pastoralists should be in a better position. Despite these advantages, this approach has been criticized for limiting pastoral mobility and subdividing customary grazing lands.

The second solution is proposed by Tanzania's Range Development and Management Act (still in draft). This act calls for establishing "range development areas" in Tanzania's arid and semiarid zones. Each area would have a corresponding range development commission responsible for controlling settlement and natural resource use. Range development areas would be managed as communal property, and corporate groups of herders could form ranching organizations there. While this approach may protect pastoral land and encourage communal property, doubts remain as to how the commissions would operate, and ranching associations have a dubious history in Tanzania.

The best way forward will vary from place to place and from group to group. Nevertheless, it will be important to establish clear procedures for giving pastoral groups legal title to specified grazing areas. Of equal importance will be providing for institutional frameworks that will allow them to debate resource-related problems and devise communal property solutions to those problems from within. In the Usangu case, the situation is further complicated by the ethnic and cultural diversity of the current pastoral population, most of whom lack customary claims to resources in the region.

The best strategy for the Usangu Plains might be one that combines specific elements of the two approaches described above. An extensive geographic area in the central Plains, encompassing the wet and dry season pastures currently used by herders, could be demarcated and protected for exclusive pastoral use, analogous to a "range development area." This area would span the boundaries of several villages. Access rights could be associated with residence in one of these villages, with village assemblies regulating settlement there on the basis of natural resource availability. Village boundary demarcation and titling might help provide a legal foundation for regulating settlement and rights of resource entitlement in Usangu. Resource use and management decisions pertaining to the grazing commons could be made by an organization of pastoralists from these villages, having representatives from each ethnic group. Alternatively, these decisions could be made collectively by all pastoralists belonging to the village assemblies with appointed mediators.

Conclusion

The original "tragedy of the commons" argument made by Garrett Hardin in 1968 was based on the example of a grazing commons. Subsequent studies of African pastoralism have shown that communal property systems do not cause rangeland degradation in Africa; rather, they promote rangeland conservation. Communal property systems are not inherently ecologically destructive. Nevertheless, these systems have been under attack by African States, foreign donors, African elites and agriculturists. It is not the presence, but the demise of communal property systems that is an important cause of rangeland degradation, as the Usangu case study demonstrates. A first step, then, in promoting sustainable development in pastoral regions of Africa is to address issues of property rights. Ideally, pastoral lands should be protected from further encroachment and alienation. Systems of communal property should be re-established there, allowing pastoral peoples to regain local control over resources. Otherwise, African rangelands will become more vulnerable to degradation; African pastoralists will become increasingly marginalized and impoverished; and the decline of cultural diversity will continue.

Acknowledgments

I would like to thank Gail Charnley, William Durham and Louise Fortmann for their helpful comments on earlier versions of this paper.

References

Charnley, Susan. In Press. Pastoralism and Property Rights: The Evolution of Communal Property on the Usangu Plains, Tanzania. *Journal of African Economic History*.

____. 1994. Cattle, Commons, and Culture: The Political Ecology of Environmental Change on a Tanzanian Rangeland. Unpublished Doctoral Dissertation, Stanford University.

Hardin, Garrett. 1968. The Tragedy of the Commons. *Science* 162:1243–1248.

Homewood, Katherine. 1995. Development, Demarcation and Ecological Outcomes in Maasailand. *Africa* 65(3):331–350.

Lane, Charles and Richard Moorehead. 1994. Who Should Own the Range? New Thinking on Pastoral Resource Tenure in Drylands Africa. *Pastoral Land Tenure Series No. 3*. London: International Institute for Environment and Development.

URT (The United Republic of Tanzania). 1994. Report of the Presidential Commission of Inquiry into Land Matters. Volume 1: Land Policy and Land Tenure Structure. Dar es Salaam: The Ministry of Lands, Housing and Urban Development, Government of the United Republic of Tanzania.

Paavahu and Paanaqawu

The Wellsprings of Life and the Slurry of Death

A very long time ago there was nothing but water. In the east, Hurúing Wuhti, the deity of all hard substances, lived in the ocean. . . . The Sun also existed at that time. . . . By and by these two deities caused some dry land to appear in the midst of the water; the waters receding eastward and westward.
("Origin Myth," recorded by H. R. Voth, 1905)

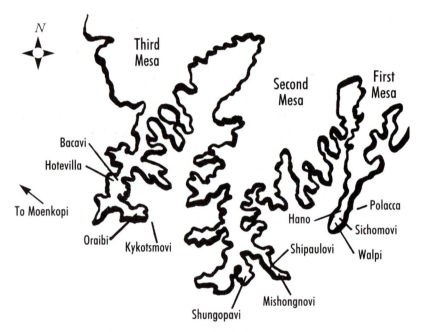

Hopi Mesas and their Villages

Modified from Page and Page, 1982.

Peter Whiteley

Peter Whiteley has conducted ethnographic research at Hopi since 1980. He has served as consultant and expert witness to the Hopi Tribe in Federal litigation since 1988, and recently as field consultant to BBC Television for a film on Hopi culture and the water issue. He has published two books on Hopi social history, Deliberate Acts: Changing Hopi Culture through the Oraibi Split *(University of Arizona Press, 1988), and* Bacavi: Journey to Reed Springs *(Northland Press, 1988);* Hopi Topoi, *a collection of essays, is forthcoming with Smithsonian Institution Press. He chairs the anthropology department at Sarah Lawrence College.*

Paavahu

Paahu *n. (pl. paavahu): spring, water*

So identical are they in Hopi thought that the very word for (natural) water and spring is the same: a reflection of experience in this semi-arid environment. No rivers or streams flow near the Hopi villages, except for the Moenkopi wash (the name, an index of its social importance, means "continuously flowing water place") that runs past the westernmost settlement of the same name. Springs are the prototypical water sources. They emerge from talus slopes on the sides of the sandstone mesas where the vil-

Spring-irrigated, terraced gardens on a Third Mesa slope below Hotevilla, tended by the women of Hotevilla.

lages are located, and have done so for a long time. Continuous Puebloan occupation of this area dates back 1500 years, and Oraibi, the oldest continuously inhabited village in North America, has been dated to at least 1150 C.E.

It is hard to imagine anything more sacred, as substance or symbol, than water in Hopi religious thought and practice. To be sure, some elements may appear more prominent: corn, the staff of life, which is ubiquitous in Hopi religious imagery; rattlesnakes from the spectacular Snake Dance; or masked performances by Kachina spirits. But intrinsic to these, and underlying much other symbolism in the panoply of Hopi ritual, is the concern with water. Springs, water and rain are focal themes in ritual costumes, kiva iconography, mythological narratives, personal names and many songs that call the cloud chiefs from the varicolored directions to bear their fruc-

tifying essence back into the cycle of human, animal and vegetal life.

That essence (as clouds, rain and other water forms) manifests the spirits of the dead. When people die, in part, they become clouds; songs call to the clouds as ascendant relatives. Arriving clouds are returning ancestors, their rain both communion with and blessing of the living. The waters of the earth (where Kachina spirits live) are, then, transubstantiated human life. Further, Paalölöqangw, the water serpent deity, lives in the springs. Paalölöqangw is appealed to in the Snake and Flute ceremonies and is portrayed in religious puppetry during winter night dances. The Flute ceremony is specifically devoted to the consecration and regeneration of major springs. The Lenmongwi (head of the Flute society), in an archetypal gesture, dives to the bottom of a particularly sacred spring to plant prayersticks for Paalölöqangw. At the winter

solstice ceremonies, feathered prayersticks are placed over major springs around every Hopi village as both protection and supplication.

Among sources of water there is a quasi-magnetic relationship: the Pacific Ocean, the Colorado River, rain, underground aquifers, springs and living plants are mutually attractive—"contagious" in the anthropological sense: "The land is a living organ, it breathes . . . the Hopis say that it is the underground water that sucks in, that breathes the rain" (Vernon Masayesva). Paatuwaqatsi (literally "the ocean") is simultaneously a central philosophical principle denoting the universally sustaining water of life. To attract the world's powers of moisture, springs are major foci of ritual attention. They have individual names—Kwaavaho, Saalako, Talakwavi, Paatuwi, Kookyangwva and many more—which occur frequently in ritual narrative and song. Spring water properly placed

213

Photo courtesy of the U.S. Dept. of the Interior, Indian Arts & Crafts Board, William and Leslie Van Ness Denman Collection

"Leenangw" (The Flute Ceremony) by Hopi artist, Fred Kabotie, ca. 1954.

in one's field, mud from spring bottoms as body-plaster in Kachina costumes and painted tadpoles or dragonflies on Kachina 'friends' (a term Hopis prefer to 'masks') all sympathetically entice the rain. Springs themselves, like maize in fields, were originally "planted" in the earth by deities or gifted individuals. Pilgrimages to reconsecrate and draw in regenerative power from especially significant springs at distant points are common in the religious calendar. Villages may be named for springs, such as the mother village, Shungopavi, "sand-grass spring place." Some clans have exceptional responsibilities to springs, such as Patki, the Divided Water clan.

In short, springs are key in Hopi social life, cultural values and the conceptualization of the landscape—all of which form the grounds of deeper religious thought and action. This is not entirely unpredictable for an agricultural society in a riverless environment with eight inches of precipitation annually. The prolific complexity of Hopi ritual attends to springs, specifically and in general, as sources of blessing and vehicles of prayer.

Paanaqawu
(literally, "fatal lack of water")

The springs, however, are drying up, and with them the essential force of Hopi religious life and culture itself. Flows have been progressively declining over the last three decades. Numer-

ous springs and seeps have ceased to produce enough water to sustain crops planted below them. The Moenkopi wash does not "continuously flow" any more, and the only major Hopi farming area that depends on irrigation water is in serious jeopardy. This year it was down to a trickle by late May; in the recent past Moenkopi children plunged into swimming holes long into the summer. Even the trickle was supplied only by two upstream tributaries; from the mainstream itself, all the water was channeled into impoundment ponds by Peabody Coal Company.

Peabody, which operates twenty-seven mines in the U.S., is now part of the British multinational, Hanson Industries. Peabody's total operating profit in 1994 was $230 million on coal sales of $1.8 billion. Hanson's total sales, including its chemical and tobacco interests, was $18 billion, and its total after-tax profit was $1.7 billion. This is no small enterprise. Peabody's Black Mesa-Kayenta Mine is the only mine in the country which transports its coal by slurry. The stripmined coal is crushed, mixed with drinking-quality water and then flushed by pipeline to the Mohave Generating Station in Laughlin, Nevada. The cities of Las Vegas and Phoenix—electric oases in the desert—buy some of the power, but most of it goes to the electric toothbrushes, garage door openers, outsize TV sets and other necessities of life in southern California.

Most of the slurry water comes directly from the 'Navajo,' or N-aquifer, located 1,000–3,000 feet within the geologic formation of Black Mesa (an upthrust plate of the Colorado Plateau) that tilts southwestward and ends up in the spring-studded, finger-like promontories that are the Hopi mesas. Peabody uses ca. 3,700 acre-feet (about 1.2 billion gallons) of water per year for the slurry, which is ten times as much as the annual water consumption of the entire Hopi community (ca. 9,000 people).

The pumping, Peabody has claimed, has no effect on the Hopi springs. Those springs, it maintains, are not fed by the N-aquifer but by the overlying 'Dakota' or D-aquifer, and by snowmelt. Hopis do not believe Peabody's position. However, an escalating series of letters from Hopi individuals and officials (both traditional leaders and Tribal Council chairs), petitions signed by several hundred Hopis, protests in public hearings, dissenting interpretations by independent geologists and repeated refusal by the Tribal Council to sanction the Department of the Interior's renewal of the mining lease have fallen on deaf ears. Flat rebuttals to Hopi protests continue to be retailed by Peabody and Hanson representatives. A personal invitation to direct dialogue (extended to Lord Hanson, Chairman of Hanson plc, in June 1994 by Tribal Chairman Ferrell Secakuku) has gone ignored. In April 1994, W. Howard Carson, President of Peabody Western Coal Company, voiced the company's party line: "Changes in the flows from their springs may be the result of drought conditions in the region, and perhaps from the increased pumpage from Hopi community wells located near these springs.... Peabody Western's pumping from wells that are 2,500–3,000 feet deep does not affect these springs" (*Los Angeles Times* 1994).

Even prior to this statement, however, top U.S. Geological Survey hydrologists concluded that Peabody's analysis was based on a wholly inadequate model. Among other shortcomings: "[T]he model is not sufficient to answer the concerns of the Hopi regarding adverse local, short-term impacts on wetlands, riparian wildlife habitat, and spring flow at individual springs" (Nichols 1993). Recent figures (U.S.G.S. 1995) suggest that declines in water level of area wells (ranging from 30 feet to 97 feet from 1965 to 1993) are up to two-thirds caused by the mine's pumping. Peabody's claim—that throughout the 35-year life of the mine it would use one tenth of one percent of N-aquifer water, which would naturally recharge itself—is seriously questioned by the Hopi Tribe. The Tribe's consulting geologists recently charted a recharge rate at 85% less than Peabody's estimate. (It has been suggested that Peabody is trying to suppress public release of these discrepant figures since—if verified—the company would be contractually required, according to the

terms of the lease, to post a bond for aquifer restoration.)

It seems evident, too, that depletion of the N-aquifer has had serious impacts on the D-aquifer, and on the springs themselves; the Moenkopi wash is directly affected since it is supplied by N-aquifer seepage. U.S.G.S. computer simulations predict total drying of some major Hopi wells within the next twenty-five years. Upstream Navajo communities are also significantly affected by the drying and by deteriorating water quality; Forest Lake has been particularly hard hit. In recent documents, Peabody has finally acknowledged that it takes water not only from the N-aquifer but also from other aquifers present, including the D-aquifer. This has come as no surprise to Hopis. But as Nat Nutongla, head of the Hopi Water Resources Department, states, "The elders regard all water as sacred. It doesn't matter whether the springs are supplied directly by the D-aquifer or the N-aquifer

or whatever; they represent *all* sources of water."

Peabody's position, that declines in Hopi springs derive from increased domestic and municipal consumption (reflecting population growth—principally Navajo—and water development by the Navajo and Hopi Tribes), is not entirely untrue. Tuba City wells and significant increase in local population since the 1960's directly impinge on Moenkopi area springs. Hopi use of domestic water has definitely expanded since newer villages adopted indoor plumbing over the last thirty years. But these changes, Hopis argue, are all the more reason not to waste the reserves of N-aquifer water. A serious, compromising quandary is that 80% of the Hopi Tribe's annual operating revenues are supplied by coal royalties and water lease fees from Peabody. The Hopi Tribal Council (or "Tribe")—a creation of the Indian Reorganization Act of 1934—is formally supported by about half the villages, though even anti-Council traditionalists

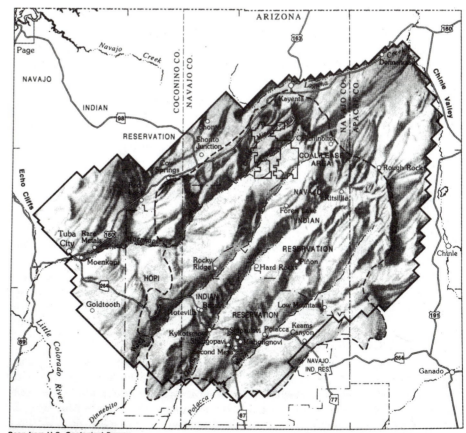

Base from U.S. Geological Survey
digital data, 1:100,000, 1980

Modified from Brown and Eychaner (1988)

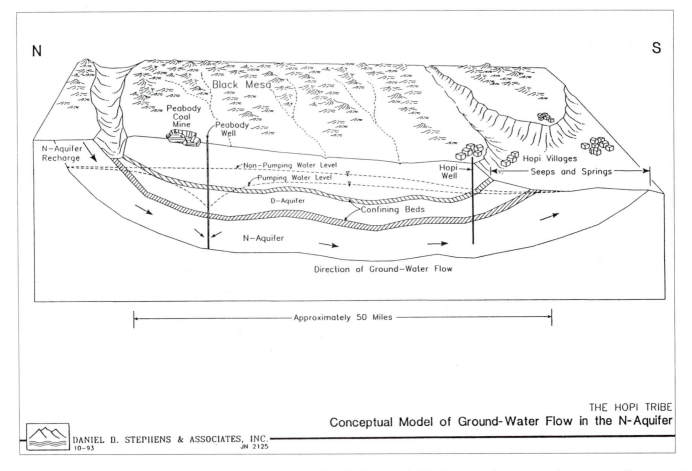

N

S

Black Mesa

Peabody
Coal
Mine

Peabody
Well

N–Aquifer
Recharge

Non-Pumping Water Level
Pumping Water Level

Hopi Villages
Seeps and Springs

Hopi
Well

D–Aquifer

Confining Beds

N–Aquifer

Direction of Ground-Water Flow

Approximately 50 Miles

THE HOPI TRIBE
Conceptual Model of Ground-Water Flow in the N-Aquifer

DANIEL B. STEPHENS & ASSOCIATES, INC.
10–93   JN 2125

rely on numerous benefits it administers. Many people feel they were duped by the Council's attorneys when the original leases were signed in the 1960's (there are independent indications of backroom deals), and that some Tribal leaders were coopted by Peabody. But this is scarcely a factional issue. Hopis directly involved with the Council, including the last two Chairmen (Ferrell Secakuku and Vernon Masayesva), have strongly opposed renewal of the coal leases in lieu of an alternative means of transporting the coal. Hopis of all factions—from traditionalist *Kikmongwis* (village chiefs) to modernist technocrats—have been unanimous and clear in their opposition to the use of pristine ground water to transport coal and in their disbelief in Peabody's denials that the pumping affects the springs.

The Tribal Council favors economic development and does not oppose the mine as such (which some traditionalists do). Part of the allure of the mine in the first place was the promise of Hopi employment. But Hopis now say Peabody

has aligned itself with the Navajo Nation and ignores Hopi interests, a position borne out in employment figures. Of up to 900 employed "Native Americans"— a useful elision in Peabody's public pronouncements—fewer than twenty are Hopis. The great majority are Navajos, represented by the United Mine Workers Union which enjoys a special relationship with the Navajo Labor Relations Board. The original leases guaranteed 50% of local employment to Hopis. And Peabody's overall attitude seems to be flagrant disdain for Hopi concerns. In Howard Carson's words, "We wouldn't [stop pumping] just to get the Hopi off our backs, because it could create another nightmare. These things snowball" (*Gallup Independent* 1993).

Several alternatives to the slurrying of aquifer water have been proposed, and progress has been made on one: another pipeline from Lake Powell which would provide domestic water for Hopis and Navajos and industrial uses for Peabody. But Peabody, ever mindful of the bottom line, is evidently using

delaying tactics, suspending negotiations and playing off the Tribes against each other (despite support for the project by Interior Secretary, Bruce Babbitt). Like most other negotiations involving Hopis and Navajos, this pipeline proposal is subject to the cumulative politics of the land disputes, and the Navajo Nation has sought concessions from the Hopi that it has been unable to gain otherwise. Such disputes affect Hopi religious freedom in other ways, including the gathering of fledgling eagles and pilgrimages to some springs. A major sacred spring, Kiisiwu, is on land partitioned to the Navajo Nation by Congress in 1974. This spring, associated with principal Kachina ceremonies, is visited by ritual-society pilgrims, especially during Powamuy (the "Bean Dance") and Niman (the "Home Dance"). Formerly, local Navajos maintained a respectful distance, but younger generations are impressed less by the religious purpose and more by secular conflict. Recently, there have been physical assaults. If Kiisiwu dries up it

24271/13, "New Year's Dance," no date, watercolor opaque by Fred Kabotie (Hopi), School of American Research Collections in the Museum of New Mexico.

may solve some temporal problems between Hopis and Navajos, but at what spiritual cost?

Meanwhile, the Hopis are deeply anxious about all spring declines for both obvious reasons and deeper metaphysical ones. Hopi moral philosophy, following a covenant entered into with the deity, Maasaw, upon emergence into the present world, charges people to take care of the earth and all its resources. Indeed, this is a significant measure of whether one is worthy of the name "Hopi" (which carries specific ethical implications). If Hopis break the covenant, cataclysm of cosmic proportions threatens. During the early 1980's when I began ethnographic research at Third Mesa, Tsakwani'yma, an older Spider clan man, would sometimes talk about prophecies he had heard from his uncle, Lomayestiwa (a "Hostile" leader at the 1906 Oraibi split). He returned to one,

repeatedly: A time would come when Paalölöqangw, the water serpent deity, would turn over and lash his tail deep within the waters of the earth, and all land-life would tumble back down to the bottom of the ocean. "Can you interpret it?" he would challenge. "It means earthquake. But it's also symbolic of the life we are leading today: koyaanisqatsi, a life of chaos." Then in 1987 and 1988, shortly after he passed on, there were two earthquakes on Black Mesa (a rarity), which the Arizona Earthquake Information Center connects to the removal of massive quantities of coal and water. The perception of some elders, that this is the result of having their souls literally sold out from under them (in the link between ground water and spirits of the dead), causes profound sadness and a sense of intractable religious desecration.

In addition to long-term Hopi interests, the continued pumping of more than a billion gallons of potable water every year for a coal slurry appears incredibly shortsighted from the perspective of regional geopolitics. The coming century will undoubtedly see ever more serious problems of water supply for major conurbations in the West. In this light, Hopi religious concerns with springs become metaphorical of larger issues of global development and natural resource management. But while typically attuned to such universal implications, Hopis in the immediate term are concerned with basic physical, cultural and spiritual survival. If the springs are to be saved (and along with them continued Hopi cultural and religious existence), Hanson's relentless drive toward short-term profits, at the expense of stakeholder concerns, needs a dramatic makeover in line with trends toward local-global balance pursued by more progressive multinationals. In the meantime, the pumps siphon the essence of life from the water-roots of Black Mesa and the Hopi springs are withering on the vine.

References

Clemmer, Richard O. 1978. Black Mesa and the Hopi. *Native Americans and Energy Development.* Joseph Jorgenson, ed. Cambridge: Anthropology Resource Center. (Very useful for earlier phases of Hopi resistance to the mine.)

_____. 1984. The Effects of the Energy Economy on Pueblo Peoples. *Native Americans and Energy Development,* 2. Joseph Jorgenson, ed. Boston: Anthropology Resource Center and the Seventh Generation Fund.

Gallup Independent. 12-20-1993. Coal mining may threaten Hopi water, culture. Gallup, NM.

Guerrero, Mirianna. 1992. American Indian Water Rights: The Blood of Life in Native North America. In *The State of Native America: Genocide, Colonization, and Resistance.* M. Annette Jaimes, ed. Boston: South End Press. (Includes useful bibliographic references to Native American water issues and conflicts more generally.)

Los Angeles Times. 4-30-1994. Coal Mining and Hopi Water. Letter to the Editor, by W. Howard Carson, President, Peabody Western Coal Company.

Nichols, William D. (Western Region Ground Water Specialist, U.S.G.S.) 10-28-1993. Letter to William M. Alley, Chief, Office of Ground Water, Water Resources Division, U.S.G.S.

U.S. Dept. of the Interior. 1990. Proposed Permit Application, Black Mesa-Kayenta Mine, Navajo and Hopi Indian Reservations, Arizona, 2 vols. *Final Environmental Impact Statement OSM-EIS-25.* Denver: Office of Surface Mining Reclamation and Enforcement. (Vol 2, "Comments and Responses," includes the full text of numerous Hopi letters, petitions, and oral testimony.)

U.S. Geological Survey. 1995. Results of Ground-Water, Surface-Water, and Water-Quality Monitoring, Black Mesa Area, Northeastern Arizona 1992–93. *Water Resources Investigations Report 95-4156.* Tucson: U.S.G.S.

Acknowledgments

Nat Nutongla and the Hopi Water Resources Department gave indispensable help and comments, and were most generous with sources. Vernon Masayesva provided especially trenchant feedback, both on Hopi concepts and hydrological matters. My thanks also to Jerry Brody for help in locating Fred Kabotie's Niman painting. I remain solely responsible for the content.

A Pacific Haze:
Alcohol and Drugs in Oceania

Mac Marshall

University of Iowa

All over the world people eat, drink, smoke, or blow substances up their noses in the perennial quest to alter and expand human consciousness. Most of these substances come from psychoactive plants native to different regions—coca, tobacco, and peyote, in the New World; khat, coffee, and marijuana in North Africa and the Middle East; betel and opium in Asia. Some people use hallucinogens from mushrooms or tree bark; others consume more exotic drugs. Produced by fermentation, brewing, or distillation of a remarkable variety of raw materials—ranging from fruits and grains to milk and honey—traditional alcoholic beverages were found almost everywhere before the Age of Exploration.

As European explorers trekked and sailed about the globe between 1500 and 1900, they carried many of these traditional drugs back to their homelands. Different exotic drugs became popular at different times in Europe as the explorers shared their experiences. In this manner, tea, tobacco, coffee, marijuana, and opium gained avid followers in European countries. Today, this worldwide process of drug diffusion continues at a rapid pace, with changes in attitudes toward different drugs and the introduction of new laws governing their use varying accordingly.

Oceanic peoples were no exception to the widespread quest to expand the human mind. From ancient times they used drugs to defuse tense interpersonal or intergroup relations, relax socially, and commune with the spirit world. Betel and kava were far and away the most common traditional drugs used in the Pacific Islands. The geographical distribution of these two drugs was uneven across the islands, and, in a few places (for example, Chuuk [Truk]), no drugs were used at all before the arrival of foreigners. Kava and betel were not only differentially distributed geographically, but they were also differently distributed socially. Every society had rules governing who might take them (and under what circumstances) that limited their consumption, often only to adult men.

In the four-and-a-half centuries since foreign exploration of the Pacific world began, the islanders have been introduced to several new drugs, most notably alcoholic beverages, tobacco, and marijuana. This chapter discusses substance use in the contemporary Pacific Islands by examining the history and patterns of use of the five major drugs found in the islands today: alcohol, betel, kava, marijuana, and tobacco. To the extent that reliable information exists, such recently introduced drugs as cocaine and heroin are also discussed. The primary concern of the chapter is with the negative social, economic, and health consequences that result from consumption of alcohol, tobacco, and marijuana in the contemporary Pacific Islands.

BETEL AND KAVA

"Betel" is a convenient linguistic gloss for a preparation consisting of at least three distinct substances, two of which are pharmacologically active: the nut of the *Areca catechu* palm, the leaves, stems, or catkins of the *Piper betle* vine, and slaked lime from ground seashells or coral. These substances usually are combined into a quid and chewed. In some societies, people swallow the resultant profuse saliva, while in others they spit out the blood red juice. Kava is drunk as a water-based infusion made from the pounded, grated, or chewed root of a shrub, *Piper methysticum.* Whereas betel ingredients can easily be carried on the person and quickly prepared, kava makings are not as portable, and its preparation calls for a more involved procedure. Betel is often chewed individually with little or no ceremony; kava is usually drunk communally, and frequently accompanied by elaborate ceremonial procedures.

Betel chewing appears to have originated long ago in Island Southeast Asia and to have spread into the islands of the Western Pacific from there. While betel use is widespread in Melanesia (including the New Guinea Highlands where it has recently been introduced), it is absent from the Polynesian Triangle, and it is found only on the westernmost Micronesian islands of Palau, Yap, and the Marianas (Marshall 1987a).

In most parts of the Pacific Islands where betel is chewed, its use occupies a social position akin to coffee or tea drinking in Western societies. For example, Iamo (1987) writes that betel is chewed to stimulate social activity, suppress boredom, enhance work, and increase personal enjoyment among the Keakalo people of the south coast of Papua New Guinea. Similarly, Lepowsky (1982) comments that for the people of Vanatinai Island in Papua New Guinea, shared betel symbolizes friendly and peaceful social relations. Iamo notes that betel consumption "is rampant among children, young people, and adults" in Keakalo; that is, it has few social constraints on its use, except in times of scarcity (1987:146). Similarly, "Vanatinai people chew betel many times a day," and they also begin chewing betel early in childhood: "By the age of eight to ten, boys and girls chew whenever they can find the ingredients" (Lepowsky 1982:335).

In those parts of Papua New Guinea where the betel ingredients can be produced in abundance, such as Keakalo and Vanatinai, they figure importantly as items of exchange or for sale as "exports" to surrounding peoples. The enterprising Biwat of East Sepik Province are remarkable in this regard. They trade *Areca* nut, *Piper betle,* and locally grown tobacco with other peoples in the vicinity, carry these products by canoe to the regional market town of Angoram (98 miles away), and occasionally even charter a small airplane to sell as far away as Mount Hagen in the Western Highlands Province (Watson 1987).

Traditionally, kava was drunk only in Oceania, the world region to which the plant appears native. Kava drinking occurred throughout the high islands of Polynesia (except Easter Island, New Zealand, and Rapa), on the two easternmost high islands of Micronesia (Pohnpei and Kosrae), and in various parts of Melanesia, particularly Fiji, Vanuatu, and New Guinea proper. Kava and betel were often in complementary distribution, although there were some societies where both were routinely consumed.

Whereas betel is chewed by males and females, old and young, kava is different. In most Pacific Islands societies, at least traditionally, kava drinking was restricted to men, and often to "fully adult" or high-status men. Although its consumption was thus restricted, young, uninitiated or untitled men, or young women, usually prepared it. These distinctions were notably marked in the elaborate kava ceremonies of Fiji, Tonga, and Samoa. Wherever it was used, however, kava played important parts in pre-Christian religion, political deliberations, ethnomedical systems, and general quiet social interaction among a community's adult men.

On the island of Tanna, Vanuatu, for example, Lindstrom (1987) argues that getting drunk on and exchanging kava links man to man, separates man from woman, establishes a contextual interpersonal equality among men, and determines and maintains relations of inequality between men and women. Kava is drunk every evening on Tanna at a special kava-drinking ground, separated from the village, and from which women and girls are excluded. Lindstrom argues that kava (which is grown by women) is both itself an important exchange item and symbolically represents male appropriation and control over women and their productive and reproductive capacities. Tannese men fear that women intoxicated on kava would become "crazed" and usurp men's control over them, become sexually wanton, and cease to cook. Lindstrom concludes, "Gender asymmetry in Tannese drunken practice maintains and reproduces social relations of production and exchange" (1987:116).

Among the Gebusi of Papua New Guinea's Western Province, the men of a longhouse community force their male visitors to drink several bowls of kava in rapid succession, usually to the point of nausea. This is done to prevent the chief antagonists at ritual fights or funeral feasts "from disputing or taking retaliatory action against their hosts during a particularly tense moment in the proceedings" (Knauft 1987:85). Forced smoking of home-grown tobacco is used in an analogous manner "to forestall escalation of hostilities" among a people for whom homicide tied to sorcery accusations is a leading cause of male mortality. As on Tanna, Gebusi women never drink kava. Both peoples link kava to sexuality: Lindstrom (1987:112–113) describes a Tannese-origin myth of kava that he calls "kava as dildo"; Knauft (1987:85–88) notes that kava often serves as a metaphor for semen in jokes about heterosexual relations or the ritual homosexuality practiced by the Gebusi.

As is typically the case in human affairs, these long-known and highly valued drug substances were deeply rooted in cultural traditions and patterns of social interaction. Pacific Islands peoples had developed culturally controlled ways of using betel and kava that usually precluded abuse.[1] Users also were unlikely to develop problems because of the rela-

tively benign physiological effects of these two substances and because neither drug by itself seems to produce serious harmful disease states when consumed in a traditional manner.

Kava drinking leads to a variety of physical effects, perhaps the most pronounced of which are analgesia, muscle relaxation, and a sense of quiet well-being. In addition to its ceremonial and recreational uses, kava is a common drug in Oceanic ethnomedicine, and kava extracts also are employed in Western biomedicine. Of the various drugs discovered by human beings around the world, kava seems to be one of the least problematic. Its physiological effects induce a state of peaceful contemplation and euphoria, with the mental faculties left clear, and it produces no serious pathology unless taken (as by some Australian Aborigines since 1980) at doses far in excess of those consumed by Pacific Islanders. The most prominent effects of prolonged heavy kava consumption among Oceanic peoples are a dry scaly skin, bloodshot eyes, possible constipation and intestinal obstruction, and occasional weight loss (Lemert 1967). Even excessive kava use does not produce withdrawal symptoms, and all of the above conditions are reversible if drinking is discontinued.

The situation with betel is somewhat more complex. The main physical effect obtained by betel chewers is central nervous system stimulation and arousal producing a sense of general well-being (Burton-Bradley 1980). Arecoline, the primary active ingredient in betel, also stimulates various glands, leading to profuse sweating and salivation, among other things. Beginners typically experience such unpleasant symptoms as nausea, diarrhea, and dizziness, and prolonged use leads to physiological addiction. There is some preliminary experimental evidence that arecoline enhances memory and learning, and it is being explored as a possible medicine for patients suffering from Alzheimer's disease (Gilbert 1986).

Considerable controversy surrounds the health risks of betel chewing, particularly as regards its possible role in the development of oral cancer (MacLennan et al. 1985). This debate has been confounded by the fact that many betel chewers in Southeast and South Asia (where most of the clinical data have been collected) add other ingredients to the betel chew, most commonly, and notably, tobacco. A summary of the epidemiological evidence available to date leads to the conclusion that chewing betel using traditional ingredients without the addition of tobacco probably does not carry any significant risk for oral cancer (Gupta et al. 1982).[2] Occasionally, a betel chewer develops what Burton-Bradley (1966) calls "betel nut psychosis," following a period of abstinence and in response to a heavy dose of the drug. This acute reversible toxic psychosis is characterized by delusions and hallucinations in predisposed individuals, but it must be emphasized that its occurrence is rare. There is thus no conclusive evidence that regular betel chewing without the addition of tobacco results in physical or mental health problems for most people. Like kava, betel appears to produce a relatively harmless "high."

As usually taken in Oceania, not only do kava and betel consumption pose few—if any—health risks, but neither drug leads to intoxicated behavior that is socially disruptive (indeed, quite the contrary). The plants from which these substances are derived are locally grown and quite readily available, and the processes for making and taking these two traditional drugs do not require commercial manufacture. In the past twenty years, some cash marketing of both drugs has developed, but this is primarily by smallholders or local concerns, and neither substance is handled by multinational corporations. Thus, kava and betel do not have negative social and economic consequences for the Pacific Islands societies where they are used.

ALCOHOLIC BEVERAGES

Pacific Islanders, like most North American Indians, had no alcoholic beverages until Europeans brought them early in the contact period. Initially, most islanders found alcohol distasteful and spat it out, but eventually they acquired a fondness for what sometimes was called "white man's kava." During

"Driving Under the Influence" Accident, Weno Island, Chuuk, Federated States of Micronesia (1985). (Photo by M. Marshall)

the late eighteenth and first half of the nineteenth century, whalers, beachcombers, missionaries, and traders arrived in the islands in growing numbers. Many of them were drinkers and provided models of drunken behavior for the islanders to copy. Some of them established saloons in the port towns, and alcohol was widely used as an item of trade with the islanders. By at least the 1840s, missionaries to the islands, reflecting temperance politics in the United States and Great Britain, began to speak out forcefully against "the evils of drink" (Marshall and Marshall 1976).

As the European and American powers of the day consolidated colonial control over Oceania in the nineteenth century, they passed laws prohibiting islanders from consuming beverage alcohol. While such laws usually had strong missionary backing, they were also intended to maintain order, protect colonists from the possible "drunken depredations of savages," and serve what were deemed to be the islanders' own best interests. Despite prohibition, production of home brews continued in some areas, theft provided an occasional source of liquor, and the drinking of methylated spirits offered a potentially deadly alcohol alternative in some parts of the Pacific (Marshall 1988:579–582).

Colonially imposed prohibition laws remained in place until the 1950s and 1960s, when they were set aside one after another in the era of decolonization. Since then, the establishment of new Pacific nations has fostered a maze of legal regulations surrounding alcohol use, and it has also led to the encouragement of alcohol production and marketing. In many different parts of the Pacific Islands, problems have accompanied the relaxation of controls and the expansion of availability.

It is generally true around the world that more men drink alcoholic beverages than women, and that men drink greater quantities than women, but these gender differences are particularly pronounced in most of Oceania. In many of the islands, there are strong social pressures against women drinking, reinforced by church teachings, that effectively keep most women from even tasting alcoholic beverages. With a few exceptions, it is usually only Westernized women in the towns who drink on any sort of a regular basis. Boys below age fourteen or fifteen seldom, if ever, drink, but by the time they are in their late teens or early twenties, nearly all of them partake of alcohol. So much is this the case that in Chuuk (Truk) drinking

Wall Painting (by Robert Suine), Kuglame Taverne, Simbu Province, Papua New Guinea (1980). (Photo by M. Marshall)

and drunkenness is called "young men's work" (Marshall 1987b).

These gender differences have resulted in profoundly different attitudes toward alcohol by men and women that sometimes have resulted in outspoken social opposition by women to men's drinking and its attendant social problems (see Marshall and Marshall 1990). Weekend binge drinking by groups of young men—especially in towns—frequently leads to social disruption and confrontations that have been labeled "weekend warfare" in one Micronesian society (Marshall 1979).

For many Pacific Islanders, alcoholic beverages have come to symbolize "the good life" and active participation in a modern, sophisticated lifestyle. Beer is usually the beverage of choice in Oceania, and, in some places, it has been incorporated into ceremonial exchanges surrounding such events as bride price payments, weddings, and funerals. In the Papua New Guinea Highlands' Chuave area, beer is treated as an item of wealth and "has assumed a cen-

tral role in inter- and intraclan prestations" (Warry 1982:84). Cartons of beer have been endowed with a number of social and symbolic qualities in common with pork, the most highly esteemed traditional valuable. For example, the success of a ceremony is judged, increasingly, by the amount of beer, as well as pork, available for display and distribution; beer in cartons has a known value and the twenty-four bottles are easily divisible; like pigs, the stacked cartons of beer (sometimes as many as 240!) are appropriate items for display; alcohol is a social facilitator in these sometimes tense feast situations; beer—like pork and other foodstuffs—is consumable; and, like pork, beer is used at feasts both as a tool to create relationships and as a weapon to slight rivals (Warry 1982).

The chief problems associated with alcohol use in Oceania are social ones, although it is difficult to divorce these from the interrelated public health and economic costs. Among the more prominent and widespread social problems are domestic strife, particularly wife beating; community fighting and disruption, often with attendant trauma and occasional fatalities; crime, and drunk-driving accidents.

In the post–World War II era, these alcohol-related problems have been a continuing concern of community-based and government agencies in Pacific Islands countries. For example, a seminar was held in 1977 on "Alcohol Problems with the Young People of Fiji" (Fiji National Youth Council 1977), and, in 1986, Catholic youth in the Highlands of Papua New Guinea rallied to oppose alcohol abuse (The Times of Papua New Guinea 1986a). Other examples of community-based concerns are church women's groups who championed a legal prohibition against alcohol on Weno, Chuuk (Moen Island, Truk) (Marshall and Marshall 1990), and an ecumenical Christian training center in Papua New Guinea (the Melanesian Institute) that has given voice to village peoples' concerns over abuse of alcohol for many years. Within a decade after it became legal for Papua New Guineans to drink, the government felt it necessary to sponsor an official Commission of Inquiry in 1971 to assess the widely perceived prob-

lems that had ensued. Less than ten years later, another investigation of alcohol use and abuse under national government auspices was launched in Papua New Guinea through its Institute for Applied Social and Economic Research (IASER). Such government commissions and groups of concerned citizens usually produce recommendations for action; however, serious and effective alcohol control policies are rarely forthcoming.

Although they have received less attention in the literature, primarily because of the absence of adequate hospital records and autopsy reports for Pacific Islands countries, the physical and mental illnesses linked to either prolonged heavy ethanol intake or binge drinking appear to be considerable. Among these are alcoholic cirrhosis, cancers of the upper respiratory and upper digestive tracts, death from ethanol overdose, alcoholic psychoses, and suicide while under the influence of alcohol.

In recent years, researchers have focused on non-insulin-dependent diabetes mellitus (NIDDM), which has increased in urbanized and migrant Pacific Islands populations (for example, Baker et al. 1986; King et al. 1984). With changes from traditional diets to "modern" diets of refined foods and higher intakes of fats, sugar, sodium, and alcoholic beverages, some Micronesian and Polynesian populations have shown what is thought to be a hereditary susceptibility to NIDDM, which apparently is only expressed with a change from the traditional rural lifestyle. Urban and migrant islanders typically engage in less physical activity and have higher levels of obesity than their rural nonmigrant counterparts. Given that individuals with diabetes are more vulnerable to the hypoglycemic effects of alcohol because alcohol interferes with hepatic gluconeogenesis (Franz 1983:149; see also Madsen 1974:52–53), heavy drinking that may produce complications for diabetics poses an added health risk.

TOBACCO

Although the Spanish and Portuguese introduced tobacco into the East Indies from the New World in the late sixteenth and early seventeenth centuries, and although this new drug spread rather quickly to the island of New Guinea via traditional trade routes, *Nicotiana tabacum* did not reach most Pacific Islands until the nineteenth century. It became a basic item of trade and even served as a kind of currency during the heyday of European exploration and colonization of Oceania. The first German plantations on the north coast of New Guinea near Madang were tobacco plantations, and the crop continues to be grown commercially in Fiji and Papua New Guinea. In the 1800s, pipe and homemade cigar smoking were quite popular; today manufactured cigarettes dominate the market in most parts of the Pacific Islands. The prevalence of tobacco smoking by both men and women in Pacific Islands populations is much higher than in the developed countries of Australia, New Zealand, and the United States, and higher than in most developing nations elsewhere in the world (Marshall 1991). In some isolated rural parts of Oceania, nearly everyone in a community smokes—including children as young as eight or ten years of age.

With the decline in tobacco use in the developed nations of the West, the multinational corporations that control global production and marketing of this drug have shifted their emphasis to the huge and rapidly growing market in the Third World. Developing countries offer few restrictions to tobacco companies: most such countries have no maximum tar and nicotine levels, no laws restricting sales to minors, no advertising limits, no required health warnings, and no general public awareness of the serious health risks associated with smoking (Stebbins 1990). As a result, tobacco consumption has grown steadily in Third World countries, leading public health experts to predict and document the beginning of a major epidemic of diseases known to be linked to chronic tobacco use. During the 1980s, numerous studies have been published by health care professionals and other concerned individuals noting these alarming trends and calling for action. Studies documenting these problems exist for Africa, Latin America, and Asia, and researchers have

Cigarette advertisements on the outside of a store, Goroka, Eastern Highlands Province, Papua New Guinea (1980). (Photo by M. Marshall)

begun to chronicle the same sad story for Oceania (Marshall 1991).

As with the upsurge in alcohol use and its aggressive marketing by multinational corporations in Pacific Islands countries, so it is, too, with the production and sale of commercial tobacco products, particularly cigarettes. Almost any store one enters in Oceania today displays tobacco advertisements prominently inside and out, and has numerous tobacco products readily available for sale. Among the many ploys used to push their brands, the tobacco companies sponsor sweepstakes contests with large cash prizes which can be entered by writing one's name and address on an empty cigarette pack and dropping it into a special box for a drawing. Tobacco firms also routinely sponsor sporting events, with trophies and prizes in cash and in kind. In other promotions, those who present fifteen empty packs of the pertinent brands are given "free" T-shirts emblazoned with the cigarette brand name.

The association of tobacco smoking with serious cardiovascular and respiratory diseases—lung cancer, chronic bronchitis, and emphysema—is by now well known. These diseases are particularly linked to the smoking of flue-cured commercial cigarettes, which now have been readily available in Oceania for

about thirty years. As the Pacific Islanders who have smoked such cigarettes for many years develop health problems, more suffer from these smoking-related illnesses (Marshall 1991). One New Zealand study shows that those Maori women who smoke heavily during pregnancy produce infants of a lower average birth weight than those of Europeans or other Pacific Islanders in New Zealand (Hay and Foster 1981). Another study shows Maori women to have a lung cancer rate that is among the world's highest (Stanhope and Prior 1982).

As yet, there have been few efforts to gain control over the smoking epidemic in Pacific Islands countries. In one, the Fiji Medical Association announced a campaign to ban cigarette advertising following a directive from the Fiji Ministry of Health to stop smoking in all patient areas in government hospitals (*Pacific Islands Monthly* 1986). But the most encouraging program has been mounted in Papua New Guinea. In the early 1980s, an antismoking council was established there by members of the medical profession (Smith 1983), and, following several years of public debate, Parliament passed the Tobacco Products (Health Control) Act in November 1987. This law mandates various controls on tobacco advertising, requires health warning labels on cigarette packs and cigarette advertisements, and provides the authority to declare various public places as nonsmoking areas. As of March 1990, these included all national and provincial government offices, the offices and buildings of all educational institutions (other than staff quarters), all hospitals, health centers, clinics and aid posts, cinemas and theatres, public motor vehicles (PMVs), and all domestic flights on scheduled airlines. While there are some enforcement problems, the Department of Health has mounted an aggressive antismoking campaign (tied to the anti-betel-chewing campaign), and this is likely to have a positive impact over the next few years.

Despite the encouraging signs in Papua New Guinea, public-health-oriented antismoking campaigns have met with relatively small success to date in the face of the large sums of money devoted to advertising by the tobacco multinationals. Much more effort is needed in community and public health education if this preventable epidemic is to be brought under control in Oceania.

MARIJUANA

Unlike the use of alcohol, betel, kava, and tobacco, marijuana smoking is uniformly illegal in Oceania. Nonetheless, the plant is now grown quite widely in the islands and has a substantial number of devotees. In part because its cultivation and use is against the law, fewer data are available on marijuana smoking than on the other four common Pacific drugs.

Native to central Asia, marijuana diffused to Oceania much more recently than alcohol or tobacco. While it doubtless was present in such places as Hawaii and New Zealand well before World War II, in other island areas like Micronesia or the New Guinea highlands, it appears to have been introduced only during the 1960s and 1970s.

While considerable controversy surrounds the long-term health effects of marijuana smoking, certain things are by now well known and give cause for concern. Marijuana induces an increased cardiovascular work load, thus posing a potential threat to individuals with hy-

pertension and coronary atherosclerosis. Both of these health problems have been on the rise in Pacific Islands populations, especially in urban areas (Baker et al. 1986; Patrick et al. 1983; Salmond et al. 1985), and both can only be worsened by marijuana use.

Marijuana smoke is unfiltered and contains about 50 percent more cancer-causing hydrocarbons than tobacco smoke (Maugh 1982). Recent research has shown that "marijuana delivers more particulate matter to the smoker than tobacco cigarettes and with a net four-times greater burden on the respiratory system" (Addiction Research Foundation 1989:3). This same work revealed significant structural changes in the lungs of marijuana smokers, with a higher rate among those who also smoked tobacco. These changes are associated with chronic obstructive lung disease and with lung cancer. Another study has found significant short-term memory impairment in cannabis-dependent individuals that lingers for at least six weeks after use of the drug is stopped (Schwartz et al. 1989). As was discussed above for tobacco, the limited amount of research that has been done shows respiratory illnesses to be major serious diseases in Oceania. Clearly, smoking marijuana will simply raise the incidence of health problems that were already significant in the Pacific Islands even before marijuana gained popularity.

In the Pacific Islands, as in the United States, marijuana growing is attractive because it yields a higher cash return per unit of time per unit of land than other agricultural crops. Even though marijuana is grown as a cash crop and often sold by the "joint" the plant is easy to grow, requires little attention, and thrives in most island environments. As a result, most marijuana consumed in the Pacific Islands, like betel and kava, is locally grown and not imported by drug cartels or multinationals. Even so, marijuana grown in the islands is sometimes exported to larger and more lucrative markets (Nero 1985). This has become the subject of major police concern in Papua New Guinea, where there are some indications that organized crime may be involved in the purchase of marijuana grown in the

highlands to be sent overseas (for example, *Niugini Nius* 1990). It will be well nigh impossible to uproot marijuana from Oceania today, but much more could be done to educate islanders about the health risks associated with its use.

OTHER DRUGS

As of 1989, hard drugs such as cocaine and heroin have made little headway in Pacific Islands communities. The most dramatic example of a place where such penetration has begun is Palau, where heroin first showed up in the early 1970s (Nero 1985:20–23). By 1985, cocaine was being used in Palau as well, and, by then, a number of Palauan heroin addicts had been sent to Honolulu for detoxification and treatment (Polloi 1985).

Although the Palauan case is somewhat unusual for the Pacific Islands at present, there are increased reports of hard drugs being shipped *through* the islands from Asia for metropolitan markets in Australia, New Zealand, and North America. Clearly, given the ease of air travel and relatively lax security and customs checks, more hard drugs will appear in the islands in the coming years.

CONCLUSIONS

Oceania's traditional drugs—betel and kava—create few if any social problems and pose minimal health risks to users. Moreover, these drugs are locally produced, and even when they are sold in the market the profits remain in islanders' hands and enrich the local economy. From an economic perspective, the cropping and selling of marijuana in most of the Pacific Islands operates in much the same way: small growers cultivate the plant for their own use or to sell in local markets. The major differences between marijuana and betel and kava are that marijuana is illegal and that smoking marijuana poses significant health risks. Oceania's other two major drug substances are produced and distributed in a very different manner and pose much more serious social and public health problems.

Over the past decade, an accumulation of studies has shown that alcoholic

Last Chance for First Peoples

Can gene banks preserve the past?

Stephen Mills

Levi Yanomami squatted beneath the grassy fringe of the *moloca* (great thatched lodge), where an assembly of the world's tribal leaders sat patiently. The setting was the Kari-Oca Indian village an hour outside Rio de Janeiro, at the first-ever World Conference of Indigenous Peoples, where native peoples hoped to encourage world leaders to save the natural world from environmental disaster.

Levi was about to perform a little voodoo and answer tribal prayers, if only the chieftains would listen—and heed their own call for help in the face of cultural extinction. Clad only in red running shorts (for decorum's sake), flip-flops, and an arm band of shocking pink parrot feathers, Levi cut a discordant figure. But the best was yet to come—verging on the miraculous.

Levi entered the hut and began to sing in guttural chants, stretching his stocky frame to appear gaunt as he paced up and down in stilted egret-like steps while beating his chest. His chants changed to choking fits and bodily contortions. Abruptly he left the circle to consult his companion, Davi Kopenawa Yanomami, a soothsayer who would interpret Levi's spiritual visions, tell him not to be afraid, and to continue the ritual. For more than half an hour, Levi wailed, stomped, and writhed, occasionally returning to Davi for comfort and advice.

Levi's physical incantations reached near hysteria, then subsided suddenly. As he wandered off mumbling, the entire hut and its occupants rose slowly as if on a cushion of air and hovered two feet off the ground—for this observer, anyway.

"We can speak for the earth because we have treated it well."

No kidding. Oh yeah, you say, what was I on? Air, it seemed. Eerie, uncanny, and downright spooky. This had to be some trick of the mind, but I could have sworn. . . . Stumbling as I tried to step two feet down onto the ground only confounded my disbelief.

Tribal leaders emerged, exchanging knowing looks while Western observers appeared dazed and confused, still in a trance. Some remained in denial, unable to accept their own metaphysical encounter. But many others wanted to believe, and everyone's story was different. "It was as if I turned into an exotic bird and flew off into the forest," remarked one colleague, while others spoke of leaving their bodies, as in astral travel. The general consensus was that this was definitely a "happening."

But what exactly *had* happened, and just what was the message to the rest of the world? In essence, the tribal leaders' message was simply that only spiritual reverence for the earth would save it— and to fail would be fatal. As Kari-Oca organizer Marcus Terena remarked,

"We can speak for the earth because we have treated it well."

Several thousand miles away north of the equator, an American university professor sat and also contemplated the collective fate of indigenous peoples threatened with cultural extinction. Luigi Cavalli-Sforza, a professor of genetics at Stanford University, is well aware that native peoples will be the first domino to fall in efforts to exploit the world's last remaining natural resources. "I am one of a group of scientists," he explains, "who have elected, on the initial suggestion of a smaller group of scientists, including myself, to collect a sample of the world population for a coordinated genetic study with modern means of analysis." Cavalli-Sforza is also chair of the international executive committee of the Human Genome Diversity project, which plans to study genetic samples from around the world including samples from indigenous peoples.

But scientific research is not enough. Professor David Maybury-Lewis, founder and president of Cultural Survival which fights for indigenous rights worldwide, expresses his concern that some scientists may overlook the need for more strident measures in regards to protecting indigenous peoples than the cataloging of their DNA. "If you're fearful of their dying out, you would have some kind of responsibility to do something for them as well. Just doing science and saying this is what I do, and what happens to them is none of my business, is quite unacceptable," he says.

Professor Cavalli-Sforza defends the value of his research, while acknowledging the obvious problem that genetic research cannot resolve what is essentially an economic problem. "I don't believe that a particular indigenous people could be damaged by our studies. There are examples where some people have been studied genetically, and it has been very good for them." But he says, "There are many other ethnic groups, indigenous or not, that need economic support or at least protection from abuse."

The struggle for cultural survival begs many questions: Who are indigenous peoples, what are their problems, who are the players in their survival or demise, and what are the viable alternatives to their extinction?

The answers may come from many places, including political, economic, and scientific quarters which heretofore have been thought to be inimical to indigenous interests. In politics, changing attitudes in the United Nations, and positive signs from the Clinton administration have raised hopes for new support on indigenous issues. Science and technology, traditionally feared by indigenous groups because it identified and exploited their resources at their expense, have found new ways to preserve and harness rainforests' resources which may be the key to the forests' and their people's future survival. And indigenous peoples themselves have seized the initiative and begun to fight back through legal channels and protests which have attracted international attention and support.

The world's approximately 500 million indigenous people, sometimes called "first peoples," are found throughout the world, from Australian Aborigines and African tribesmen to Native American and Amazon Indians. Conversely, and perversely, they are also described as the "Fourth World," firmly lodged at the bottom of the global socio-economic pecking order.

Summing up their plight, veteran campaigner for indigenous peoples' rights, Jason Clay, remarked: "What we're talking about here is a quiver of arrows between them and cultural extinction—they have nothing else with

From Huti tribesmen in Africa to Asmat tribes in Brazil, indigenous peoples are fighting to save their cultural identity, while scientists hope to preserve genetic evidence that will help uncover the history of migration.

which to deal with the problem." Similarly, Julian Burger, a U.N. coordinator responsible for indigenous peoples, explains that "indigenous cultures are threatened by forms of contemporary development when they are removed from their lands. However," he points out, "they are not victims. They are organizing in order to defend their interests."

Despite this bleak assessment, there are signs of significant change. In the political arena, the United Nations, heretofore intractable on the issue of sovereign rights for indigenous peoples, designated 1993 as the U.N. Year of the World's Indigenous People. It has been a critical window of opportunity for the cause, providing a world platform for debate, raising money for community projects, and drawing up a universal Declaration of Indigenous Rights. Rigoberta Menchú, the Guatemalan Quiché Indian and 1993 Nobel Peace Prize winner for her crusade against the brutal repression of her people, was named goodwill ambassador for the U.N. indigenous year, and has successfully launched a Decade of Indigenous People, which began in 1994, to extend and expand the program.

Considerable hope has also been generated by President Clinton's pledge to address the needs of impoverished Native American Indians, with speculation that he will support the indigenous cause internationally.

Indigenous peoples themselves have now also actively joined the fight to defend their rights and resources through protests and the courts, aided by media campaigns by private organizations like Cultural Survival and the Body Shop. Both of these organizations also help them economically by creating markets for sustainable products they harvest from their wild homelands.

Meanwhile, back in the lab, the tribal gene bank will allow scientists to study the origins of vanishing tribes long after they are gone. It is part of a much larger international project by the London-based Human Genome Organization (HUGO) to map all the human genes. When all the information is in, the tribal gene bank will be used to help draw up mankind's entire family tree, revealing how humanity colonized the planet over the past 100,000 years.

The project has already identified as many as 600 groups of interest. This number will probably be reduced to about 100 distinct or pure ethnic groups including the Marsh Arabs in southern Iraq, believed to be descended from the ancient Sumerians and currently threatened by Saddam Hussein's plan to eliminate his Shi'ite political foes; Stone Age Amazonian Yanomamo Indians and highland Papua New Guineans, both threatened by invasion of their lands; and African pygmies and bushmen and the Ainu peoples of Japan, all threatened by assimilation.

In his genetic study of tribes to plot the migration of man across the planet over millennia, Cavalli-Sforza has already had considerable success as a pioneer of "gene geography" since he first began gene mapping 40 years ago. His earlier research supports archaeological evidence that mankind first emerged from Africa 100,000 years ago and demonstrates that intensive farming practices which began in the Fertile Crescent led to a population and cultural explosion that triggered migration across Europe. The establishment of communities and cities effectively froze genetic drift, making it possible to track movement through genetic similarities. For example, the timing of the diffusion of farming showed that the spread was slow and regular, taking some 4,000 years to cover the approximately 4,000 kilometers from the Fertile Crescent to the remotest area north of Britain a rate of 1 kilometer a year.

Perhaps the most compelling and widely cited argument for safeguarding indigenous environments (and hence their human inhabitants) is the environments' unequalled abundance and diversity of medicinal plants. The case has again been made by various researchers who say that many indigenous lands, especially rainforests, may hold the key to treating pernicious ailments like AIDS, cancer, and heart disease. Genetic scientists argue that preserving precious indigenous knowledge to unlock the secrets of potential

plant species is an essential element in the equation.

Although 1.4 million plant species have been cataloged, there may be as many as 100 million different species, of which up to 80 percent are found in rainforests. One estimate further claims that about 80 percent of the world's population rely on plant-derived medicines for health products.

Recent discoveries of cancer-fighting extracts from plants as diverse as broccoli and the yew tree have sparked a scramble to find other miracle cures. As a result, chemical prospecting, biodiversity, and ethnobotany are among the new mantras in pharmaceutical boardrooms in the race to capitalize on biotech products. In the United States alone, 25 percent of all prescription drugs are plant-derived, and the biotech industry, currently worth $2 billion a year, is expected to soar to $50 billion by the year 2000. Businesses are beginning to realize that preserving the rainforest is an investment in that future.

Scientists have recently discovered that rainforests are actually more profitable left standing for their medicinal uses than cut down for lumber, farming, ranching, or new settlements. For instance, in a recent study, Dr. Michael Balick, director of the Institute of Economic Botany at the New York Botanical Garden, studied small plots of native forest which yielded herbal remedies worth $1,346 per acre, based on sustainable yields. In contrast, clearing rainforests for agriculture is worth only $137 per acre in Brazil and $117 per acre in Guatemala.

According to Dr. Balick, "It seems clear now that the decision whether to cut a forest or preserve it revolves around the question of how much money a farmer can make, how effectively he or she can feed the family. One of our jobs is to find economically viable alternatives to deforestation."

Scientists have also demonstrated the flaw in the argument that old growth forests can simply be replanted. Studies clearly show that understory flowering plants of replanted secondary forests are only one-third as abundant and only one-half as diverse as in original

old-growth forests, and may take as long as 1,000 years to fully recover.

Through his work for the National Cancer Institute, Dr. Balick is involved in a $1.2 million, five-year partnership with colleagues from many countries, including Belize, working directly with traditional healers to evaluate, promote, and preserve natural medicines. If any successful medicines are developed, royalties will be paid to the indigenous communities. A similar effort to preserve and prospect for medicinal plants in the forests of Costa Rica has been sponsored by Merck & Company, the world's largest drug maker, which has invested $1 million in the project and also promised royalties for any successful drugs developed.

Dr. Balick also points out that the value of plants is intrinsically tied to indigenous peoples' knowledge of which plants are useful and how to prepare them. But he warned that much of that precious knowledge is being lost forever as forest-dwellers increasingly come into contact with the outside world.

"I work with the Maya, for example, in Central America," Balick said, "who were thought to have crossed the Bering Strait 25,000 years ago. By my calculations, that's given them at least 200 generations of trial and error experimentation to become familiar their environment. And most of this is being lost in this generation.

"The great tragedy," he continues, "is that we are on the cusp of identifying hundreds if not thousands of useful plants for medicine, food, and fiber, and the forest is being converted at unprecedented rates. It's a false economic analysis that leads to the conclusion that land is more valuable cut than forest left standing. It's terribly sad to see 300-year-old trees being cut down, and then the fires that follow. You see devastation of both plant and animal life, and you know that devastation to humans is not far behind."

The level of suffering for native peoples was all too apparent at the Kari-Oca indigenous conference in Brazil. Between colorful spectacles—of Xingú Indians daubed in bright body paint and blowing bamboo pipes, Karaja Indians donning exquisite feather

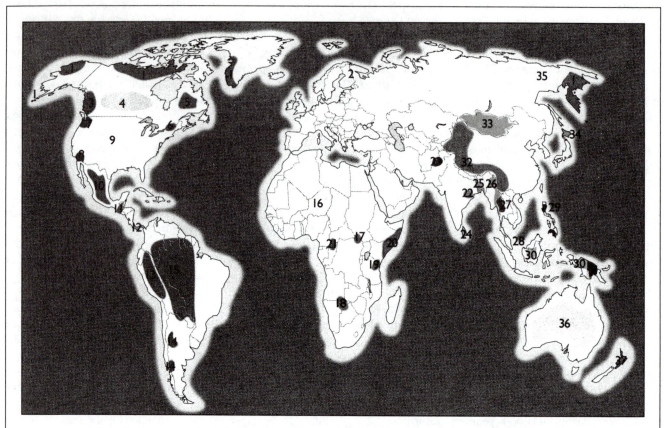

MAP OF INDIGENOUS PEOPLES

1. Arctic: Inuit (Eskimo) in Alaska, Canada, Greenland, and the former USSR; Aleut in Alaska
2. Europe: Saami in Norway, Sweden, Finland, and the former USSR
3. Pacific Coast: Haida, Tlingit, Kwakiutl, Bella Coola, Tsimshian, Nootka
4. Central Canada: Cree, Meti, Chipewyan, Blackfoot, Dene
5. Eastern Canada: Innu, Cree, including James Bay Cree
6. Canada/United States border: Micmac; the Six Nation Confederacy, or Haudenosaunee, comprising Mohawk, Oneida, Onondaga, Cayuga, Seneca, Tuscarora
7. Northwestern United States: Nez Perce
8. Southwestern United States: Navajo, Uti, Dine, Pueblo, including Hopi, Keres, Zuni
9. Plains States: Crow, Cheyenne, Arapaho, Pawnee, Comanche, Oglala Sioux, Shoshone
10. Mexico: Mayan descendants—Lacandon, Yucatec; Aztec descendants—Huichol, Tarahumara, Nahua, Zapotec; also refugees
11. Guatemala, Belize: Maya, including Chol, Chuj, Kekchi, Quiche; Nicaragua: Miskito, Sumu, Rama; El Salvador, Honduras: Lenca, Pipile
12. Panama: Kuna, Guaymi
13. Highland Peru, Bolivia, Ecuador, Colombian Highlands: Quechua, Aymara
14. Argentina, Chile: Mapuche
15. Amazon Basin—Brazil: Tukano, Xavante, Yanomami, Parakana, Kreen-Akrore, Nambikwara, Kayapo, Makuxi, Waimiri-Atroari; Amazon Basin—Ecuador, Bolivia, Peru, Colombia, Venezuela: Amarakaeri, Amuesha, Aguaruna, Matsigenka, Yagua, Shipibo, Tukano, Panare, Sanema, Secoya, Shuar, Quichua, Guajiro, Yanesha, Waorani, Ufaina; Paraguay: Ache, Ayoreo, Guarani, Toba-Maskoy; Guyana, French Guiana, Surinam: Arawak, Lakono, Kalinja, Wayana, Akawaio
16. Sahara, Sahel: Tuareg, Fulani
17. Southern Sudan: Dinka, Nuer, Shilluk
18. Angola, Botswana, Namibia: San (Bushmen)
19. Kenya, Tanzania: Maasai
20. Ethiopia: Oromo, Somali, Tigrayan, Eritrean
21. Zaire, Cameroon, Central African Republic, Congo: Mbuti, Efe, Lese
22. India: Naga, Santal, Gond, Kameng, Lohit, Dandami
23. Afghanistan, Pakistan: Pathan
24. Sri Lanka: Vedda
25. Bangladesh: Chittagong Hill Tract Peoples, including Chakma, Marma, Tripura
26. Myanmar (Burma): Karen, Kachin, Shan, Chin
27. Thailand: Karen, Hmong, Lisu
28. Malaysia: Penan, Kayan, Iban
29. Philippines: Kalinga, Ifugao, Hanunoo, Bontoc, Bangsa Moro
30. Indonesia—Kalimantan: Dayak; Lembata: Kedang; West Papua (Irian Jaya): West Papuan, including Asmat, Dani
31. Papua New Guinea: Mae-Enga, Dani, Tsembaga
32. China: Tibetan, Uighur
33. Mongolia: Mongolian
34. Japan: Ainu
35. The former USSR: Yuit, Kazakh, Saami, Chukchi, Nemet
Oceania
36. Australia: Aborigines
37. New Zealand: Maoris
Pacific Islands: Kanak, Hawaiian, Tahitian, Chamorro

head-dresses for photo sessions, and plaintive song rituals by Japanese Ainu and Norwegian Sammi peoples—native spokesmen sat grouped in circles and testified about the systematic destruction of their people and their environment.

Mimmie Degawan spoke of the "Total War Policy" by the Philippine government to eliminate resistance to hydroelectric and logging projects on ancestral lands. "If the government takes away our land, we will starve and cease to exist as a people," she said. "So we have to resist—to resist is to exist. They not only walk through the land and kill people, but also drop bombs on entire communities."

Sinjbout Jackman recounted how the new civilian government in Bangladesh has pursued a policy of genocide against the Juma hill people. In one recent massacre, soldiers herded 1,200 villagers into their homes and burned them alive. Murder, torture, and rape remain daily terrors for the Juma. Jackman said, "My people have been compelled to leave their own villages and forced to live in cluster villages like in Vietnam and Peru. They are effectively enslaved, working for the military camps and the forest service. The government doesn't want us, they want our land."

Charles Uwiragiye of the African Batwa pygmy tribe in Rwanda, the world's fastest growing country, related how population explosion had triggered an invasion of his tribal lands. "We are the first people, the indigenous people, but two other tribes came in and took everything," he said. "We have problems of being removed from our lands, and other people replacing us. My people were thrown away, just like you throw away rubbish."

The desperation was summed up by Kanhok Kayapo of the northern Brazilian Kayapo tribe. "We need help to stop the white man from cutting down our forest and killing our people. The white man says Indians don't work, don't plant, and sends his machines to plant for himself. But the Indian does work, with the plow, and plants many things. He asks why the Indian wants to live in the forest, but he doesn't

want to live in the forest. He just wants to take it away from us." His brother, Tutopombo Kayapo added, "Who is going to help us? Will any government help us? I don't think so. I have asked before, and nothing happened, so I'm asking again. You say you don't want the forest to be burned away. So send us money to help my people, to buy medicine so they don't die. We will use it to keep the woods safe."

Threaded through these countless stories of invasion, slaughter, and displacement is the stark realization that the laws of nations were never designed to protect their rights. Worse still, many governments do not even recognize the existence of these tribes as a legitimate group of peoples.

Closer to home, in the United States, there is considerable concern about the fate of Native American Indians. The Oglala Sioux Indians in South Dakota, descendants of those who suffered the horrific defeat at Wounded Knee, are among the poorest citizens in America. According to the government's own Census Bureau statistics, 63.8 percent live below the poverty line, compared with the national average of 15.1 percent; and death rates from suicide, alcoholism, infant mortality, diabetes, and homicide are some of the highest in the country. Among Native Americans' many concerns are disputes over sovereign rights, land rights, gambling casinos on reservations, and efforts to entice reservations to accept toxic and nuclear waste.

Robert Leavitt, the former education and public policy director at Cultural Survival, a Boston-based organization supporting indigenous rights worldwide, is nonetheless optimistic about changes to come. "Clinton made some effort during his election campaign to reach out to Native American Indians," Leavitt noted. "He has since followed through in terms of further consultation with Native American leaders and in terms of making several appointments. Al Gore is at least knowledgeable and understanding of native affairs, and when they organized the Oregon Forest Summit, they asked Native Americans to participate. Hillary Clinton has talked about the deplorable

state of health care on reservations. Ada Deer, the incoming head of the Bureau of Indian Affairs, is very well-respected and is a Native American Indian, which is not usually the case. Carol Browner, the head of the Environmental Protection Agency, is concerned about the government and companies targeting reservations for toxic and nuclear-waste dumping. Bruce Babbitt, Secretary of the Interior, has worked with Native Americans in Arizona. So on the Native American Indian side, we're more optimistic, and there should be some steps forward."

The current education and public policy director at Cultural Survival, Marchell Weshaw, is similarly encouraged. "I'm indigenous myself, so I see the whole indigenous rights issue on a personal level as well as a professional one. I do see conditions improving. The indigenous peoples—as communities and as nations—are coming together to make a stand. The positive aspect is that they're doing it for themselves. I also think that public awareness has grown steadily within the last five years, riding piggyback on the environmental movement."

On the other hand, Leavitt notes that there had been much less support from the Clinton administration for global indigenous rights, and a signal lack of financial commitment. "There's a real unwillingness to accept the idea of group rights on an international level—that groups, peoples, collectively have sovereign rights over land, natural resources, and governance," he says.

The United States has rejected an appeal to fund the U.N. Year of the World's Indigenous People. A State Department official said the United States was in substantial arrears to the United Nations already and owed millions more for peacekeeping activities, adding, "That's not to say the year isn't important. It's a matter of having to make choices. We have obligations that we legally need to meet before we can go about making grants that are purely voluntary."

Despite the lack of U.S. support, the U.N. program on indigenous issues, coupled with private projects, remains the best hope of future gains for native peoples. A U.N. voluntary fund has already raised over $300,000 with donations from other developed nations.

Six community projects recommended for approval include two democracy and indigenous-rights programs in Bolivia and the Philippines; a chicken and rabbit farm for Mapuche Indian women in Chile; a reforestation project in Guatemala; a community bakery in Ecuador; and a community center in Belize. The news of the grant for the community center in Belize provoked Garifuna peoples' representative, Felix Miranda, to observe, "This is good news. The community center will allow us to open a museum of artifacts together with books and displays about our history, and provide a cultural focus for the community."

Similar projects worldwide by private groups have also provided economic alternatives to environmental destruction for indigenous peoples. Among the best-known proponents of this philosophy is the London-based Body Shop. Through its Fair Trade project, the Body Shop has several co-op agreements with native peoples who produce sustainable products like nut oil in Brazil, Nepalese paper, New Mexico's organic blue-corn oil, Mexican cactus body scrubs, Bangladeshi baskets, and Siberian birchwood combs. Body Shop spokesman Mark Johnston said the company seeks to "make consumerism a moral act. I remember going back to Nepal and being flabbergasted at how well the project had helped the community put all its kids through school and buy smokeless ovens, because smoke-related respiratory ailments are a problem in that part of Asia. It was the same with the Nanhu women in Mexico, who in the absence of their men—forced to find work elsewhere—were able to feed, clothe, and house their children. It's as basic as that, and very rewarding."

Cultural Survival Enterprises trades in sustainable products like Brazil nuts for Rainforest Crunch, Zambian organic honey and beeswax, Minnesotan wild rice, and Amazon rainforest cookies, with plans for many new product lines. Since its 1989 launch, product sales have totaled $2.5 million, and a 5 percent price premium has yielded another $250,000 which is plowed back into participating communities. The program has attracted another $600,000 from foundations, governments, and businesses to start new projects. Former program director, Jason Clay, said, "People have to take responsibility for their consumption, and ultimately they can force corporations to market sustainable products they want to buy."

As executive director of Rights and Resources, a private Washington, DC, agency which defines and defends native resources, Clay plans to develop an early-warning database system to identify and prevent potential disasters for indigenous peoples before they happen. "I think we need to start looking at root causes," Clay said. "Humanitarian assistance after the fact, when people are in real jeopardy, is fundamentally wrong. We need to be able to see more accurately what forces contribute to persecution, ethnocide, and genocide, so that when those indicators appear, we can target attention on those areas to actually prevent those killings from occurring."

For those involved in the struggle, the strategy for the future is clear: Consolidate the United Nations' lead to defend indigenous rights at both the grassroots and international levels; harness science and technology to identify, protect, and safely utilize indigenous resources; economically empower native peoples to finance legal campaigns for their sovereign and resource rights; encourage alternative land use through consumer demand for sustainable products; and build public support for indigenous issues through education and media campaigns.

Many problems remain, from ethnic cleansing in the Balkans which threatens to discredit indigenous calls for autonomy, to the Asian block's refusal to address serious human-rights abuses against native peoples, to the resource plunder of Siberia in Russia's desperate search for foreign investment.

Despite many hopeful signs, Clay conceded, "It's still going to be a thousand points of fight—not light. For those of us who have been doing this work for the last 20 years, the work in 1995 will be just as hard as the work in 1994, but the work has to go on."

"If over the next 10 years, we as a world don't do something, it will be too late for many cultures," Robert Leavitt said. "But we do have a wonderful opportunity to build a much stronger movement for indigenous peoples. What we have to do is institutionalize the gains. The real challenge for Cultural Survival—and other organizations involved—and indigenous peoples themselves, is to cement our gains, strengthen indigenous participation in the United Nations and Native American participation n the U.S. government, and take advantage of popular culture and concern, so that the movement goes from being flavor of the month to flavor of the decade, and beyond."

From Hammocks to Health

A weavers' society of Amerindian women in Guyana is preserving a traditional craft, and spinning a network of programs in farming, nutrition, and sanitation.

Mary Ann Simpkins

Mary Ann Simpkins is the author of Travel Bug Canada *and coauthor of* Ottawa Stories. *She lives in Ottawa with her Guyanese husband.*

Hanging in London's British Museum is a hammock described as "the finest example of Amerindian craft produced in this century." An intricate, meticulously crafted weave with elaborate side fringes, the hammock is unique because of its width: it could hardly be crafted on a standard loom. Produced just in the last few years by native weavers in the Rupununi, the largest of Guyana's ten regions, the hammock has also been the catalyst for widespread improvements within Guyanese society.

Approximately fifteen thousand Amerindians live in small villages scattered throughout the Rupununi savannas. Covering approximately five thousand square miles, this area of grasslands, swamps, and forested mountains borders Brazil and Suriname. The lack of a good road between the Rupununi and Guyana's population centers on the coast, the high cost of air transportation, and the absence of telephone service isolate the region. Even within the area, some villages are completely cut off from others during the five-month rainy season.

Fields of bones testify to the tribal warfare that plagued this region as late as 1910. Intermarriage between members of the three main tribes now occurs, but generally the Wai Wai stick to the most southeast region of the Rupununi, while the north and central regions are home to the Wapishana and Macushi.

In the 1980s, as Guyana's economy deteriorated, life became harder for these Amerindians, and many began migrating across the Tacutú River to Brazil

---

Many Amerindians still reside in one- or two-room thatched roof mud huts and exist on hunting, fishing, and subsistence farming. Their small plots of land are usually located in the better soil at the base of the mountains, a walk from their villages of five to fifteen miles.

In the 1980s, as Guyana experienced an economic downturn, life became even harder for these Amerindians, who relied on flown-in supplies, and many began migrating across the Tacutú River to Brazil. Within two hours of Lethem, the largest town in the Rupununi, having a population of two thousand, and the government administration center, are two bustling Brazilian towns, Boa Vista and Bom Fim, which lure Amerindians as young as twelve years old to cross the river for jobs as maids and farmers.

In contrast, international aid workers have been pouring into the Rupununi. Among them was VSO (Voluntary Service Organization) volunteer Matthew Squire, who came from England in 1990 to teach woodworking to young people. But finding only boys participated, he looked around for skills to teach the girls. Hammock weaving was a tradition among the Amerindians, but machine-made hammocks could be brought so cheaply from Brazil that the skill was gradually dying out. Only a few still practiced the weaving of their ancestors. Seeking help to organize a hammock-making course for the girls, Squire contacted two experienced weavers.

In 1991 these weavers, along with several other Amerindian women, formed the Rupununi Weavers Society (RWS). The goal was to pass along the skills of this ages-old tradition, thereby generating income for the most disadvantaged Amerindians—women who were either elderly, handicapped, widowed, or single mothers. Vanda Radzik, a member of Red Thread, a Guyanese women's organization assisting RWS in networking and fundraising, says, "A very important part of transferring this old technology to a new generation was cultural affirmation." The program was also a way to combat outward migration and the resulting social destabilization in the four villages targeted.

Squire provided the technical assistance and, to insure the authenticity of the techniques and designs, he consulted books on Amerindian art and crafts, studying the different weaves of the Wapishana and Macushi. The Wapishana use an intricate double-weave technique, while the Macushi people produce single-weave bar hammocks, so called because of the bar woven in the design. Since the Wapishana hammock is more solidly woven (weighing about fifteen pounds), it was felt this design would more likely find a market in developed countries.

Some immediate problems had to be resolved before production could begin. Cotton farming had sharply declined during the previous decade: The fiber was nearly impossible to find. An application to the United Nations Partners in Development Program (UNDP) awarded RWS with US$4,497 to purchase cotton and encourage cotton farming.

Only a few women had weaving frames: Many were very old and falling apart. Squires designed a new, better loom, which his woodworking students constructed. Spindles were made from turtle shells.

More serious was the problem that many women had no time to spend spinning or weaving. Looking after children and daily food preparation filled their days. However, through social program contributions, each woman received two and a half pounds of flour per working day, freeing them from the laborious process of making farinha flour from cassava, their principal food preparation task.

Other contributions included food as well as sewing machines, exercise books, and money for trucking goods into the interior. The unpaved road between Georgetown and Lethem takes a minimum of two days and nights of hard driving in the dry season. Trips of three weeks or longer are not uncommon during the rainy season.

RWS insured the cooperation of the village's governing body, the *touchaus* (captains) and councillors. Clothes, bowls, and other goods, for instance, are distributed in the presence of the *touchau* and two councillors. "By having them participate, we show respect to their village authority and, at the same time, keep them up-to-date on the development within their community," says Shirley Melville, current RWS chairperson.

For each hammock, one woman weaves the main body, another prepares the elaborate fringes, and yet another makes the skaline—the attachment for the rope stringing up the hammock. The selling price is between US$300 and $500 each. From this, the weaver of the body receives the equivalent of about US$97, while the fringes and skaline work pays roughly US$55. Making a hammock can take between one week and three months, about five hundred hours of work, and since earnings are based on the amount of time they put in, the women also develop bookkeeping skills. After deducting payments to the workers and the high freight charges, the little money remaining goes back to RWS.

The weavers have chosen not to receive money for their work, voting instead to be paid in food, clothing, cooking utensils, and other practical goods. "When we asked why they didn't want money, they said the men would take the money from them," states Father Antony Metcalfe, a Jesuit priest in the Rupununi and, along with another priest and minister, a RWS trustee. The work has made a big difference to Emalane Baretto. "We Amerindians have a hard life," she says, "but the

Shirley Melville, RWS chairperson, *left,* proudly shows off a finished hammock, while two weavers work together on a hammock's fringe, *above.* Impressed with the women's success, some men and teenage boys have become weavers and spinners.

weavers' group is really helping us ordinary women."

In December 1993, RWS unveiled its handmade hammocks at a weaving demonstration, exhibition, and sale, which it hosted at Georgetown's top hotel, the Forte Crest Pegasus. However, the lack of infrastructure in the country has hindered sales. "Marketing of anything is a problem for Guyana," advises Radzik. Compounding the difficulty is the high sale price. To fill the gap, give the weavers work, and consumers a more accessibly priced, handmade Amerindian product, RWS now weaves purses, eyeglass cases, and other cotton goods, which are carried in Georgetown craft shops at prices starting from US$11.

About ten weavers work on looms that nearly fill the principal room in their homes. Seeing the benefits to the women spurred some teenage boys and men into becoming weavers and spinners, while the predominantly male *touchaus* and councillors help grade the cotton and encourage cotton farming. In the first year, less than three pounds of cotton was collected. The most recent crop yielded more than two hundred pounds, both white and brown. No dyes are used; the hammocks are made of only two natural colors.

Fresh from its weaving success, RWS has expanded far beyond its original intentions, developing programs in farming, nutrition, and health and sanitation. Peanuts are being planted along with cotton, and to develop better agricultural practices and increase food production, the UNDP funded the building of a bond, or storage area, and the purchase of farm implements.

With the Amerindian diet consisting predominantly of cassava, yams, and beef, workshops on food and nutrition were developed to introduce greens into the diet, and a cookbook, prepared by Lethem resident Elaine Foo, gives recipes using local ingredients to prepare properly balanced meals. Many Amerindians in the four villages targeted for this food and nutrition program have set up small kitchen gardens adjacent to their homes.

In conjunction with Red Thread and with US$10,000 from UNICEF, RWS ran a health and sanitation program in three communities. Workshops and demonstrations mainly focused on the causes of the major health problems in the region—diarrhea, cholera, and malaria. Over one hundred outhouses have now been built and, since the region lacks a pure water supply, instruction has been given on how to treat water. Now 159 washstands have replaced the water buckets that used to be left sitting on the floor: For some, a bucket, let alone one with a cover, was beyond their means. And, after the health program dealt with the importance of dental care, participants began asking for toothbrushes and toothpaste.

The RWS raised the status of women by bringing them into the decision-making process, a great breakthrough in this traditional, male-dominated society

The RWS raised the status of women by bringing them into the decision-making process, a great breakthrough in this traditionally male-dominated society. Now, in its most recent endeavor, RWS is focusing on the men themselves. With the help of machinery and woodworking tools funded by the German government, the group has ventured into bridge building and has won contracts to build two wooden bridges. Their bids were lower than the bid from a private contractor, yet after covering such overhead expenses as fuel for chain saws, generator, and transport to pick up the men,

©MARY ANN SIMPKINS (3)

The Rupununi Weaver's Museum building, *above left,* which is scheduled to double in size this year because of increasing demand for training programs, displays modern-day products woven by RWS members, such as this purse, *left,* as well as traditional portrayals of Amerindian life long ago (see next page).

each worker earned more than double what a private contractor pays a laborer. "It is a better bridge than one built by an engineer. It's neater and the shoring to keep the bank from collapsing underneath is much better," says Father Metcalfe. The authorities must agree with his evaluation because they have already asked RWS to bid on another contract.

The strength of RWS is now physically visible just outside of Lethem. The five-acre compound houses a central storage facility, a workshop for carpentry and other projects, a building for training and for accommodating trainees, and another housing a small administration office and museum. There, murals of Amerindian life of long ago surround the displays, products made by RWS, and artifacts contributed by different villages, items such as a blow pipe, rubberlike figures sculpted from

the balata tree, and numerous ax heads discovered in the Rupununi savannas. An increased emphasis on training will result in doubling the size of the museum building in 1996. At the same time, RWS intends to expand its reach to sixteen villages in the Rupununi.

Today, the RWS is run by a working body of thirty volunteers and an eight-member elected executive, all coming from different villages and representing separate resources, including health, business, and agriculture. This diversity enables RWS to run many of its own workshops, rather than importing speakers and technical experts from outside the region. This network system for encouraging and assisting self-reliance has had a marked effect on its beneficiaries, its 350 members. "They are much more lively, much more happy," says Father Metcalfe. "They are still hesitant to as-

sert themselves, but they have a certain feeling of independence, which they never had before, and of course with the men being brought in on the agricultural and wood-cutting side, things are beginning to hum."

The RWS has become such an important force within the Rupununi that the UNDP has asked the group to be the umbrella organization for overseeing its own projects in the region. Through the remarkable achievement of the RWS, the men and women of the Rupununi have been able to use their time-honored techniques in hammock weaving as a means not only of preserving their cultural heritage but also of promoting their renewable resources and improving the quality of life for themselves and other Amerindian peoples of southwestern Guyana.

Index

Credits/Acknowledgments

Cover design by Charles Vitelli

1. Anthropological Perspectives
Facing overview—United Nations photo #111,042.

2. Culture and Communication
Facing overview—United Nations photo by Doranne Jacobson.

3. The Organization of Society and Culture
Facing overview—United Nations photo. 74-76—Photo courtesy of Kenneth Good.

4. Other Families, Other Ways
Facing overview—United Nations photo. 106—Photo courtesy of Enid Schildkrout. 115—United Nations photo by Ian Steele.

5. Gender and Status
Facing overview—United Nations photo by Ian Steele.

6. Religion, Belief, and Ritual
Facing overview—United Nations photo by P. Teuscher.

7. Sociocultural Change: The Impact of the West
Facing overview—© Sally Weiner Grotta—Stock Market. 232—*Omni* photos by Malcolm Kirk. 234—*Omni* map by Steven Stankiewicz. 238-240—Photos courtesy of Mary Ann Simpkins.

ANNUAL EDITIONS ARTICLE REVIEW FORM

■ NAME: _____ DATE: _____

■ TITLE AND NUMBER OF ARTICLE: _____

■ BRIEFLY STATE THE MAIN IDEA OF THIS ARTICLE: _____

_____

■ LIST THREE IMPORTANT FACTS THAT THE AUTHOR USES TO SUPPORT THE MAIN IDEA:

_____

_____

_____

_____

■ WHAT INFORMATION OR IDEAS DISCUSSED IN THIS ARTICLE ARE ALSO DISCUSSED IN YOUR TEXTBOOK OR OTHER READINGS THAT YOU HAVE DONE? LIST THE TEXTBOOK CHAPTERS AND PAGE NUMBERS:

_____

_____

_____

_____

_____

■ LIST ANY EXAMPLES OF BIAS OR FAULTY REASONING THAT YOU FOUND IN THE ARTICLE:

_____

_____

_____

_____

■ LIST ANY NEW TERMS/CONCEPTS THAT WERE DISCUSSED IN THE ARTICLE, AND WRITE A SHORT DEFINITION:

_____

_____

_____

_____

*Your instructor may require you to use this ANNUAL EDITIONS Article Review Form in any number of ways: for articles that are assigned, for extra credit, as a tool to assist in developing assigned papers, or simply for your own reference. Even if it is not required, we encourage you to photocopy and use this page; you will find that reflecting on the articles will greatly enhance the information from your text.

We Want Your Advice

ANNUAL EDITIONS revisions depend on two major opinion sources: one is our Advisory Board, listed in the front of this volume, which works with us in scanning the thousands of articles published in the public press each year; the other is you—the person actually using the book. Please help us and the users of the next edition by completing the prepaid article rating form on this page and returning it to us. Thank you for your help!

ANNUAL EDITIONS: ANTHROPOLOGY 97/98
Article Rating Form

Here is an opportunity for you to have direct input into the next revision of this volume. We would like you to rate each of the 44 articles listed below, using the following scale:

1. **Excellent: should definitely be retained**
2. **Above average: should probably be retained**
3. **Below average: should probably be deleted**
4. **Poor: should definitely be deleted**

Your ratings will play a vital part in the next revision. So please mail this prepaid form to us just as soon as you complete it.
Thanks for your help!

Rating	Article	Rating	Article
	1. Doing Fieldwork among the Yąnomamö		22. Who Needs Love! In Japan, Many Couples Don't
	2. Doctor, Lawyer, Indian Chief		23. Society and Sex Roles
	3. Eating Christmas in the Kalahari		24. Yellow Woman and a Beauty of the Spirit
	4. A Cross-Cultural Experience: A Chinese Anthropologist in the United States		25. Status, Property, and the Value on Virginity
	5. Cultural Relativism and Universal Rights		26. Bundu Trap
	6. Language, Appearance, and Reality: Doublespeak in 1984		27. The War against Women
	7. Why Don't You Say What You Mean?		28. The Initiation of a Maasai Warrior
	8. Empire of Uniformity		29. The Little Emperors
	9. Shakespeare in the Bush		30. Psychotherapy in Africa
	10. Understanding Eskimo Science		31. The Mbuti Pygmies: Change and Adaptation
	11. Hunting, Gathering, and the Molimo		32. The Secrets of Haiti's Living Dead
	12. Why Women Change		33. Rituals of Death
	13. The Yąnomami Keep on Trekking		34. Body Ritual among the Nacirema
	14. Keepers of the Oaks		35. Superstition and Ritual in American Baseball
	15. Too Many Bananas, Not Enough Pineapples, and No Watermelon at All: Three Object Lessons in Living with Reciprocity		36. Heart of Darkness, Heart of Light
			37. Why Can't People Feed Themselves?
	16. From Shells to Money		38. The Arrow of Disease
	17. Life without Chiefs		39. Pastoralism and the Demise of Communal Property in Tanzania
	18. When Brothers Share a Wife		40. Paavahu and Paanaqawu: The Wellsprings of Life and the Slurry of Death
	19. Young Traders of Northern Nigeria		41. A Pacific Haze: Alcohol and Drugs in Oceania
	20. Death without Weeping		42. Growing Up as a Fore
	21. Arranging a Marriage in India		43. Last Chance for First Peoples
			44. From Hammocks to Health

(Continued on next page)

ABOUT YOU

Name _____ Date _____

Are you a teacher? ❏ Or a student? ❏

Your school name _____

Department _____

Address _____

City _____ State _____ Zip _____

School telephone # _____

YOUR COMMENTS ARE IMPORTANT TO US !

Please fill in the following information:

For which course did you use this book? _____

Did you use a text with this *ANNUAL EDITION*? ❏ yes ❏ no

What was the title of the text? _____

What are your general reactions to the *Annual Editions* concept?

Have you read any particular articles recently that you think should be included in the next edition?

Are there any articles you feel should be replaced in the next edition? Why?

Are there other areas that you feel would utilize an *ANNUAL EDITION?*

May we contact you for editorial input?

May we quote you from above?

ANNUAL EDITIONS: ANTHROPOLOGY 97/98

BUSINESS REPLY MAIL

First Class   Permit No. 84   Guilford, CT

Postage will be paid by addressee

**Dushkin Publishing Group/
Brown & Benchmark Publishers**
Sluice Dock
Guilford, Connecticut 06437

No Postage
Necessary
if Mailed
in the
United States